lonely planet

Vancouver & Victoria

"All you've got to do is decide to go
and the hardest part is over.

So go!"

TONY WHEELER, COFOUNDER – LONELY PLANET

JOHN LEE, BRENDAN SAINSBURY

Contents

Plan Your Trip 4

Explore Vancouver & Victoria 46

Understand Vancouver 229

Survival Guide 243

Vancouver Maps 264

COVID-19

We have re-checked every business in this book before publication to ensure that it is still open after the COVID-19 outbreak. However, the economic and social impacts of COVID-19 will continue to be felt long after the outbreak has been contained, and many businesses, services and events referenced in this guide may experience ongoing restrictions. Some businesses may be temporarily closed, have changed their opening hours and services, or require bookings; some unfortunately could have closed permanently. We suggest you check with venues before visiting for the latest information.

(left) **Vancouver Harbour** Catch water and city views from here.

(right) **Grouse Mountain p182** The so-called 'Peak of Vancouver.'

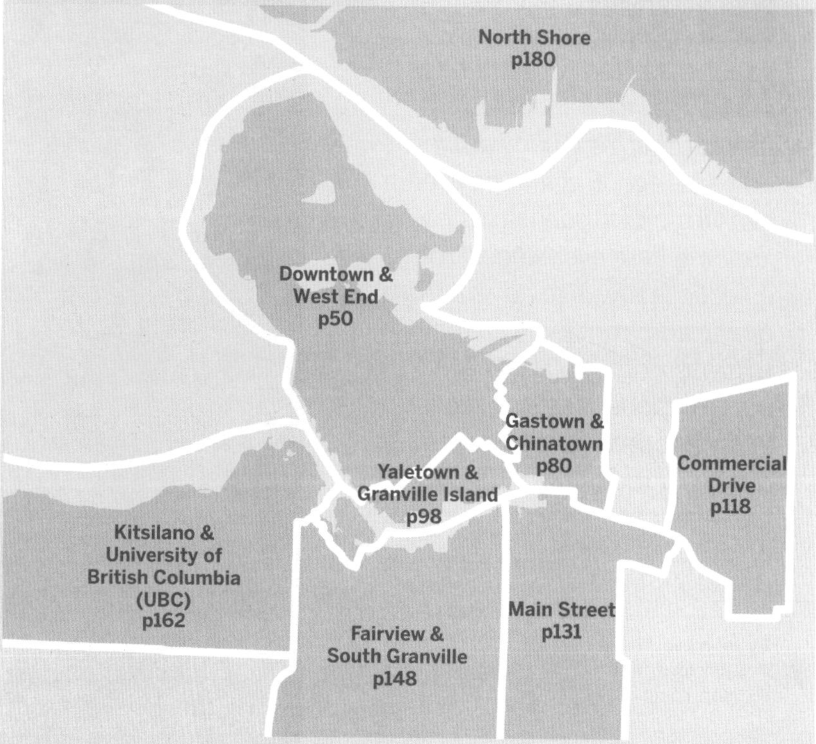

Right: Lynn Canyon Suspension Bridge (p183)

WELCOME TO

Vancouver & Victoria

Mirrored towers reflecting nearby snow-capped peaks. City beaches dotted with laid-back locals. I fell for Vancouver's natural charms when I arrived 25 years ago. But it's the ever-evolving urban scene that has kept me here ever since. From eclectic festivals to adventurous dining and from indie shopping to grassroots arts, I've never run out of experiences to discover in my adopted home – and I don't just mean the intriguing craft-beer scene (although, personally, that really helps).

By John Lee, Writer
@johnleewriter
For more about our writers, see p288

Vancouver's Top Experiences

1 GRAND OUTDOORS

Nature is always calling your name in Vancouver. From immersive city parks and deeply tranquil woodland hikes to mesmerizing oceanside promenades that skirt busy urban beaches, it couldn't be easier to hit the great outdoors here. Follow the locals and you'll soon be communing with British Columbia's spectacular temperate rainforest – and likely spotting a curious raccoon or a beady-eyed bald eagle along the way.

LAUGHINGMANGO/GETTY IMAGES ©

Walk the Seawall

Vancouver's favorite outdoor hangout, 400 hectare Stanley Park is striped with tree-shaded trails and inviting picnic spots. But its 8.8km seawall perimeter route – shared by bikers, skaters and walkers – is a life-affirming combination of forest views, mountain vistas and shimmering ocean panoramas. p52

LISSANDRA MELO/SHUTTERSTOCK ©

IRRA/SHUTTERSTOCK ©

MARTIN PATOCKA/SHUTTERSTOCK ©

Hit the Beach

A languid summer afternoon at Kitsilano Beach is the ideal way to wind down and forget all about your phone. You'll meet chatty locals, watch sailboats bobbing in the ocean and glimpse swathes of golden sunlight reflected on the distant downtown towers. p166

Take a Hike

A great launchpad for outdoor adventures throughout the wider region, Vancouver is also home to plenty of its own escape-from-it-all nature hikes. Sidestep the crowds by heading to Pacific Spirit Regional Park where towering Douglas firs, dense ferns and twittering birdlife await. p168

2 SUSHI, SEAFOOD & MORE

Combining a taste-tripping menu of global culinary influences with a deep commitment to regional ingredients, Vancouver is a lip-smacking lure for adventurous foodies. From the best Asian dining outside Asia to boat-fresh seafood and just-picked Fraser Valley farm produce, there are plenty of reasons to loosen your belt and discover a smorgasbord of utterly memorable dishes here.

Eat the Neighborhoods

Gastown and Chinatown are jam-packed with deliciously diverse dine-out options, from authentic dim-sum restaurants to hip ramen spots and from old-school diners to artsy cafes. You'll also find great indie coffeeshops and craft beer bars here. p80

TOTORORO/GETTY IMAGES ©

NONG AMORY/SHUTTERSTOCK ©

RONNIECHUA/GETTY IMAGES ©

Peruse the Public Market

A revitalized former industrial enclave, Granville Island is studded with theaters and galleries. But its cavernous Public Market is the tastiest lure for food fans, complete with stands selling everything from piquant cheeses to fresh-caught fish and from choice charcuterie to near-legendary donuts. p100

Dive into Richmond

Craving Canada's most authentic Asian dining? A SkyTrain hop from downtown Vancouver, Richmond has more than 800 restaurants – most of them deeply focused on regional dishes from China, Japan, Korea and beyond. Don't miss the summer-long Richmond Night Market (pictured left) where dozens of food stands congregate.

3 REMARKABLE HISTORY

There are lots of evocative and informative reminders of the past in Vancouver, so long as you know where to look. From a carefully preserved Victorian-era mansion to a guided walking tour that brings to life the city's salacious yesteryear underbelly, the past is accessible around almost every corner here. Keep your eyes peeled in neighborhoods such as Gastown and Chinatown (pictured bottom right) where some of the city's oldest buildings still remain.

Step into the Past

A charming reminder of the life and times of a middle-class Victorian-era family, rooms inside the West End's Roedde House Museum have been carefully recreated with period antiques. p61

MICHELE FALZONE/GETTY IMAGES ©

Gritty Backstory

Vancouver started on the muddy streets and in the dodgy saloons of Gastown. A Forbidden Vancouver walking tour exposes the grubby characters and sordid tales that launched the modern-day city. p248

Bask in the Neon

The Museum of Vancouver is crammed with exhibits illuminating the region's colorful backstory. But its darkened room of vintage neon signs from old Vancouver businesses is a highlight. p166

4 WALKABLE NEIGHBORHOODS

A compact city that's easy to explore on foot – the transit system is also user-friendly when you need to venture further – Vancouver visitors should spend at least part of their time hoofing it here. Several stroll-worthy districts radiate from the downtown core and are well worth a few hours of laid-back exploring. There are also plenty of cafes and coffeeshops to hit when refuelling is required.

Heritage Architecture

Explore vintage architecture on a summertime Architectural Institute of British Columbia walking tour. Tours of six Vancouver neighborhoods are typically available. p248

Exercise your Appetite

A one-time warehouse district, Yaletown was reinvented a few years back. It's now a walk-worthy enclave of inviting restaurants, chic stores and even a gallery or two. p98

Wander the West End

There's a wealth of well-maintained 1950s apartment buildings in this neighborhood plus a surfeit of stores and restaurants on Davie Street and Denman Street. p61

5 AMAZING GARDENS

Vancouver's greatest green spaces aren't just forested parks; there's also a sparkling array of carefully cultivated gardens to discover. From ornamental flowerbeds to undercover tropical plants to turtle-bobbling ponds, the city serves-up a winding vine of horticultural attractions. Need more? Stroll neighborhoods such as Kitsilano and Shaughnessy to spot a wealth of praise-worthy private gardens.

ANNHFHUNG/GETTY IMAGES ©

VIVIANWW2000/SHUTTERSTOCK ©

Veer to VanDusen

The city's leading horticultural attraction, the paths of VanDusen Botanical Garden (pictured top left) weave between several themed areas. The guided tours are highly recommended. p150

A Tropical Paradise

Your don't have to give up on gardens if its raining; instead seek shelter at Bloedel Conservatory. The climate-controlled dome's verdant foliage is also home to some highly colorful birds. p150

Find Inner Peace

A tranquility break from Chinatown, Dr Sun Yat-Sen Classical Chinese Garden (pictured above) is a white-walled oasis encircling a mirror-calm pond. Turtles occasionally ripple the water here. p83

6 BIG VIEWS

TAYLOR MCCOLL/SHUTTERSTOCK ©

KLARKA0608/SHUTTERSTOCK ©

CHRISTINE NANJI/GETTY IMAGES ©

Vancouver's jewel-like natural setting is arguably its greatest asset. There are several top locations in and around the city where you can slow down, breathe deeply and drink in some eye-opening West Coast views. From lofty mountaintop promontories to shimmering glass tower cityscapes to tree-framed shorelines with pyrotechnic sunsets, adjust your camera to panorama mode and start gazing.

Snap the Glass Towers

The hilltop peak at Queen Elizabeth Park is famous for its ever-changing views of downtown Vancouver (pictured above left) framed by the grand crags of the snowcapped North Shore Mountains. p150

Climb that Mountain

On sunny days, the summit of North Vancouver's Grouse Mountain offers dramatic views of the city, glinting in the ocean far below. p182

Find Beach Bliss

For Vancouver's best sunset, hit Stanley Park's Third Beach Pictured below left). Perch on a log alongside the locals for a golden evening view striped with countless colors. You won't want to leave. p58

What's New

Many Vancouverites refocused on their hometown during the pandemic. Nature took center stage, with outdoor pursuits such as park visits, forest walks and birding surging in popularity. Other trends have also taken off recently, from plant-based dining to street-art murals and more.

Plant-Based Restaurants

Amazing vegan and vegetarian dining has risen faster than a (dairy-free) soufflé here. Even die-hard carnivores savour the options at many of the city's brilliant meat-free restaurants. Comfort food specialists such as MeeT (p86) are serving-up satisfying umami-forward bowls and burgers, while the fancy Chef's Menu tasting plate feast is a must at Acorn (p136).

Urban Birding

The pandemic reacquainted many Vancouverites with local nature – and birding especially has surged in popularity. Feather fans of all ages now hang out in Stanley Park (p52), Queen Elizabeth Park (p150) and shoreline Vanier Park (p166), among others. Keep your camera handy in the city for hummingbirds, bald eagles, northern flickers and many more. And don't miss the new bcbirdtrail.ca website, complete with regional routes and spotting tips.

e-Bike Tours

Cycle City Tours (p248) has been guiding pedal-ready Vancouver visitors on bike explorations here for years. But if you're not quite up to cycling for three hours – or you just want to give these newish gizmos a spin – hop on an electric bike instead. The city highlights tour takes you through Gastown, Chinatown, Stanley Park and more.

Patio Dining

Few Vancouver restaurants used to offer outdoor dining due to regular rainy weather and rigid city bylaws. But COVID-19 changed all that; rules have been relaxed and plenty of restaurants have added covered, heated patios to facilitate socially distanced dining. Among Vancouver's best

LOCAL KNOWLEDGE

WHAT'S HAPPENING IN VANCOUVER

John Lee, Lonely Planet writer

While Vancouver has weathered COVID-19 relatively well, the long-term effects on the city remain to be seen. Attractions, bars and stores have often struggled to keep up with safety orders. But restaurants (with their razor thin margins) were hit even harder, and the number of closures has been enormous. It's not all doom and gloom, though. Many new eateries have recently opened. And there's a growing sense among locals that the future will be brighter. There's also a feeling that some things have changed for the better. Many Vancouverites have discovered a new love for the city's natural side, and a large number have taken the time to reexamine their lives. Working from home has become the new normal for many. And many of those who were languishing in unfulfilling jobs have realized they've had enough. Beyond the pandemic, some ongoing themes of Vancouver life remain, with rising real estate prices and homelessness continuing to keep newspaper headline writers busy.

patio dining hot spots are Vij's (p153), Havana (p125) and Keefer Bar (p93).

Bookstore Renaissance

Online and big box retailers failed to finish off all the independent bookshops in Vancouver. In fact, recent years have seen a strengthening of many beloved stores and even the opening of several new ones. Stalwarts like Pulpfiction (p144) have gone from strength-to-strength, while newer editions such as Paper Hound (p76) and Massy Books (p95) have become bestsellers as well.

Mural Crawling

Back-alley street art has always been here. But when the Vancouver Mural Festival (p134) launched a while back, it kickstarted a citywide movement that brought this underground scene firmly into the mainstream. Summer visitors can watch artists at work during the festival, but wandering the streets at any time of year delivers an alfresco gallery of kaleidoscopically colorful creations. Start your crawl at the Main Street and Broadway intersection.

Sour Beer Surge

Arguably Canada's craft beer capital, Vancouver's surfeit of walk-in microbreweries has spilled across the city like a puddle of frothy ale in recent years. But while ultrahoppy IPAs were once the one-note approach among local beermakers, the scene has recently matured into a far wider array of specialties. Never tried sour beers? You'll find some excellent and accessible options at Brassneck (p138).

Single-Use Waste Solutions

From January 2022, Vancouver has banned plastic shopping bags, foam takeout food containers and plastic straws, in most instances. City bylaws also mean that single-use cups will attract an additional charge of 25c each. Keep these rules in mind and plan ahead on your next day out in the city.

Indy Thrifting

A rag pile of cool vintage clothing stores has popped up here in recent years, coalescing into a popular scene for belt-tightening locals and savvy visitors alike. There's an inviting array of options to poke around on Main Street and Commercial Drive, with must-see shops and markets including Mintage (p129), Eastside Flea (p95) and Front & Company (p143).

North Vancouver Rising

A SeaBus hop across Burrard Inlet from downtown, North Vancouver used to be all about the Lonsdale Quay Public Market. Now, North Van is surging and there's more to do around Lonsdale Avenue. A gallery, ice rink and museum have opened, former shipyard sheds have been renovated for festivals and events, and new restaurants have arrived. Even the venerable market is being spruced up for the future.

LISTEN, WATCH & FOLLOW

www.lonelyplanet.com/canada/vancouver/articles

Miss 604 (Miss604.com) Popular blog covering local happenings.

Daily Hive Vancouver (www.dailyhive.com/vancouver) News, events and openings.

Stir (www.createastir.ca) Charting Vancouver's arts and culture scene.

Scout Magazine (www.scoutmagazine.ca) Hip dining and culture site.

FAST FACTS

Food trend: Vegan comfort food

Official city bird Anna's hummingbird

Number of visitors 8 million/year

Pop 631,500

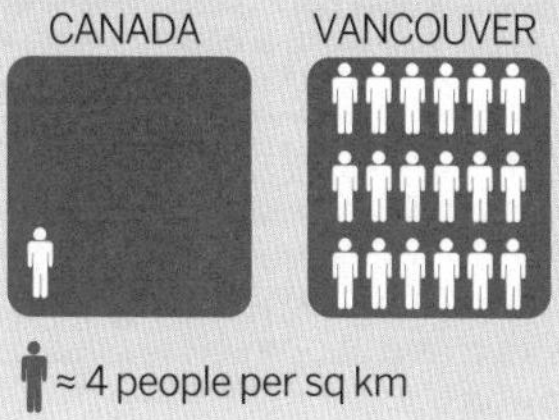

Need to Know

For more information, see Survival Guide (p243)

Currency
Canadian dollar ($)

Language
English

Visas
Not required for visitors from the US and many other countries for stays of up to 180 days. Required by those from more than 130 other countries.

Money
ATMs are widely available. Credit cards are accepted at all accommodations and most businesses.

Cell Phones
Local SIM cards may be used with some international phones. Consult your service provider for roaming charges.

Time
Pacific Time (GMT/UTC minus eight hours)

Tourist Information
Tourism Vancouver Visitor Centre (Map p266; ☎604-683-2000; www.tourismvancouver.com; 200 Burrard St, Downtown; ⊙9am-5pm; Ⓢ Waterfront) provides free maps, accommodations bookings and brochures on the city and beyond.

Daily Costs

Budget: Less than $100
- Dorm bed: $50
- Food-court meal: $10; pizza slice: $3
- Happy-hour beer special: $6
- All-day transit pass: $10.25

Midrange: $100–$300
- Double room in a standard hotel: $200
- Dinner for two in a neighborhood restaurant: $40 (excl drinks)
- Craft beer for two: $15
- Museum entry: $15–$25

Top End: More than $300
- Four-star hotel room: from $350
- Fine-dining meal for two: $100
- Cocktails for two: $25
- Taxi trips around the city: $5 and up

Advance Planning

Three months before Book summer-season hotel stays and sought-after tickets for hot shows, festivals and live performances.

One month before Book car rental and reserve a table at a top restaurant or two. Buy tickets for Vancouver Canucks and Vancouver Whitecaps games.

One week before Check the *Georgia Straight*'s online listings (www.straight.com) to see what local events are coming up.

Useful Websites

Miss 604 (www.miss604.com) Vancouver's favorite blogger.

Scout Magazine (www.scoutmagazine.ca) Hip food and bar scene zine.

Inside Vancouver (www.insidevancouver.ca) What to do in and around the city.

Daily Hive (www.dailyhive.com/vancouver) Online magazine showcasing local news and happenings.

Tourism Vancouver (www.tourismvancouver.com) Official tourism site.

Lonely Planet (www.lonelyplanet.com/vancouver) Destination information, hotel reviews, traveler forums and more.

WHEN TO GO

December to March for skiing. Summer crowds roll in from June to September. Spring and Fall for great weather and reduced hotel rates.

Vancouver, BC

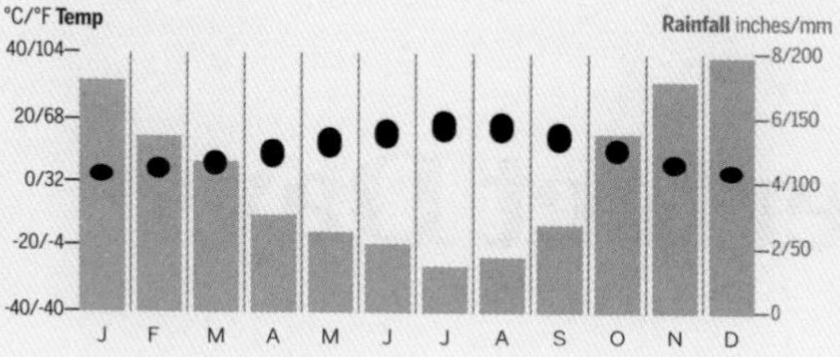

Arriving in Vancouver

Vancouver International Airport Situated 13km south of the city in Richmond. Canada Line trains to downtown typically take around 25 minutes and cost $8 to $10.75, depending on the time of day. Alternatively, taxis cost up to $45.

Pacific Central Station Most trains and long-distance buses arrive from across Canada and the US at this station on the southern edge of Chinatown. Across the street is the Main St-Science World SkyTrain station. From there it's just five minutes to downtown ($3).

BC Ferries Services from Vancouver Island and the Gulf Islands arrive at Tsawwassen, one hour south of Vancouver, or Horseshoe Bay, 30 minutes from downtown in West Vancouver. Both are accessible by regular transit bus services.

For much more on **arrival** see p244

Getting Around

Transit in Vancouver is cheap, extensive and generally efficient.

- **Bus** Extensive network in central areas with frequent services on many routes.
- **Train** SkyTrain system is fast but limited to only a few routes. Especially good for trips from the city center.
- **SeaBus** A popular transit ferry linking downtown Vancouver and North Vancouver.

For much more on **getting around** see p246

Sleeping

Metro Vancouver is home to more than 23,000 hotel, B&B and hostel rooms, the majority around the downtown core. Airbnb also operates here, although a regulatory crackdown has recently reduced their number. Book far ahead for summer, unless you fancy sleeping rough in Stanley Park. Rates peak in July and August, but there are good spring and fall deals here (alongside increased rainy days).

Useful Websites

- **Tourism Vancouver** (www.tourismvancouver.com) Wide range of accommodations listings and package deals.
- **Hello BC** (www.hellobc.com) Destination British Columbia (BC) accommodations service.
- **Accredited BC Accommodations Association** (www.accreditedaccommodations.ca) Wide range of B&Bs in Vancouver and beyond.
- **Lonely Planet** (www.lonelyplanet.com/canada/vancouver/hotels) Recommendations and bookings.

For much more on **sleeping** see p203

Perfect Days

Day One

Gastown (p82)

Start your wander around old town Gastown in **Maple Tree Square**. Admire the **'Gassy Jack'** statue of John Deighton and reflect on the fact that Vancouver might not be around today if it wasn't for the pub he built here. Since it's a little too early for a drink, peruse the cool shops along Water St, including **Herschel Supply** and **John Fluevog Shoes**.

Lunch Ever-popular Tacofino (p85) is one of the city's finest taco joints.

Chinatown (p82)

Your lunch spot is just a a few steps from Chinatown, another top historic 'hood. Spend some time winding around the kaleidoscopically hued streets. Don't miss the **Chinatown Millennium Gate** on Pender and the aromatic grocery and apothecary stores on Keefer St. Use your magnifying glass to sleuth out the **Vancouver Police Museum** before ending your afternoon at the delightfully tranquil **Dr Sun Yat-Sen Classical Chinese Garden**.

Dinner Combine old and new at the retro-feel Chinatown BBQ (p88).

Main Street (p131)

Hop on bus 3 and head south on Main St. Within a few minutes, you'll be at **Brassneck**, Vancouver's favorite microbrewery. Drink deeply, and don't miss the Passive Aggressive pale ale.

Day Two

Main Street (p131)

Have a lazy late start then get moving with a hearty breakfast at **Fable Diner**. Next, explore the many shops radiating around the Main St and Broadway intersection, including vintage-fave **Mintage Mall** and arts and craft purveyors **Bird on a Wire**. Then hop on bus 3 southwards to the 18th Ave intersection.

Lunch Join the locals for Vietnamese specialties at Anh & Chi (p136).

Main Street (p131)

Across the street, snap a few shots of the **Main Street Poodle** statue then wander southwards on Main. Check out Vancouver's best indie stores, from vinyl-loving **Neptoon Records** to the delightfully quirky **Regional Assembly of Text** stationery store. Back on the bus, backtrack north to the intersection with Broadway and transfer to the 99B Line express, heading east; you'll be at Commercial Dr in 10 minutes.

Dinner Head to Tangent Cafe (p120) for curry bowls and craft beer.

Commercial Drive (p118)

Spend the evening bar- (or coffeehouse-) hopping along the Drive. Whatever you do, don't miss **Storm Crow Tavern**, Vancouver's original nerd pub; release your inner Vulcan at the bar.

RAFAL MICHAL GADOMSKI/SHUTTERSTOCK ©

Rose Garden at UBC

Day Three

Stanley Park (p58)

Get here before the crowds to stroll the **seawall**, photograph the **totem poles** and nip into the **Vancouver Aquarium** to commune with the aquatic critters. Consider exploring the park by bike if you have time. You'll find some beady-eyed blue herons hanging out at **Lost Lagoon** – duck into the **Stanley Park Nature House** to find out more about them.

Lunch Visit Prospect Point Bar & Grill (p68) for fish, chips and forest views.

West End (p61)

Fully explore the tree-lined West End neighborhood just outside the park, including Davie and Denman Sts. Save time for **English Bay Beach** and, a few blocks away, **Roedde House Museum**. There are also plenty of coffee and shopping spots to lure your attention.

Dinner Dive into some Indian street-food dishes at Mumbai Local (p69).

West End (p61)

Davie St is the center of Vancouver's gay nightlife scene, and the area has plenty of cool options for folks of all persuasions to hang with the locals. Consider a sunset-viewing cocktail at **Sylvia's Bar & Lounge** in the neighborhood's ivy-covered heritage hotel.

Day Four

University of British Columbia (UBC; p165)

Start your day at the biggest university in British Columbia (BC), exploring a surprising wealth of attractions. The **Museum of Anthropology** and **Beaty Biodiversity Museum** are must-sees, while the green-thumbed should also check out the **UBC Botanical Garden** and the **Nitobe Memorial Garden**. Stick around and explore the waterfront campus: it's dotted with intriguing public artworks.

Lunch Dine with the students at ever-welcoming Koerner's Pub (p173).

Kitsilano (p166)

Hop on bus 4 from UBC and you'll soon be on boutique-lined 4th Ave. You'll find plenty of cool independent shops and places to eat here. Don't miss **Silk Road Tea**, **Zulu Records** and the travel-themed store, **Wanderlust**. Add coffee at **49th Parallel Coffee** or an ice cream at **Rain or Shine**.

Dinner Tuck into vegetarian comfort food at local legend Naam (p171).

Granville Island (p103)

Continue on to Granville Island for drinks at **Granville Island Brewing Taproom** before catching a raucous improv show at **Vancouver Theatre sports League** (just remember: if you sit in the front, they'll likely pick on you).

Month By Month

TOP EVENTS

Vancouver International Film Festival, September

Vancouver International Jazz Festival, June

Bard on the Beach, June–September

Pacific National Exhibition, August

Eastside Culture Crawl, November

January

Vancouver's quietest month is usually cold, gray and dank weather-wise, with occasional sparkling blue skies to keep the locals from getting too miserable. Aside from the January 1 hangover cure, most happenings are indoors.

Polar Bear Swim

This chilly New Year's Day affair has been taking place annually in English Bay since 1920. At around 2:30pm more than a thousand people charge into the ocean…and most usually leap out shivering a few seconds later.

Dine Out Vancouver

From around mid-January, restaurants across the city offer two weeks of great-value *prix-fixe* tasting menus for $15, $25, $35 or $45. Book ahead via the event's website (www.dineout vancouver.com) – top spots always sell out.

PuSh Festival

A three-week season of innovative theater, music, opera and dance from around the world, or around the corner. Adventurous performance-art fans will love this unusual showcase (p37), staged at venues across the city from mid-January.

February

There are good off-peak hotel deals to be had here (except around Valentine's Day) and the weather may be warming a little – but don't count on it.

Chinese New Year

This multiday celebration (www.cbavancouver.ca) in and around Chinatown can take place in January or February, but it always includes plenty of color, dancing and great food. Highlights are the Dragon Parade and firecrackers.

Vancouver International Wine Festival

The perfect way to warm yourself up in winter, the city's longest-running booze fest (https://vanwine fest.ca) showcases the tasty libations of different domestic and international regions every year.

March

Spring is beginning to bud around the city, which also means the rain is starting to kick in. Bring a waterproof jacket and complain about the relentless deluges, and you'll fit right in.

Vancouver International Dance Festival

Local, national and international hoofers come together for this calf-stretching spree of performances. The International Dance Festival (www.vidf.ca) showcases the city's credentials as a major dance capital.

April

Dry spells become longer as the month progresses. Expect to see the city's blossom trees in full and fragrant glory, along with an attendant chorus of selfie-snappers.

Vancouver Cherry Blossom Festival

A multi-week celebration of the city's flowering cherry trees. Expect special events, guided walks and lots of opportunities to deplete your camera battery. Check the website (www.vcbf.ca) for happenings and a live map of local viewing sites.

Sun Run

One of North America's largest street races, the Sun Run (www.vancouversunrun.com) lures 50,000 runners, speed walkers and wheezing wannabes for a spirited jaunt around the city in the fourth week of April.

May

The rain is intermittently forgotten as the promise of summer arrives. Several farmers markets start up for the season while pale-legged shorts-wearers start gearing up for the arrival of some real sun.

Victoria Day Parade

The provincial capital city plays host to a colorful street fiesta on the third Monday of May, complete with dancers and marching bands. It usually starts on the corner of Douglas and Finlayson Sts and runs down Douglas St, luring thousands of smiling locals.

Vancouver Craft Beer Week

Reflecting a frothy surge in regional microbrewing, this ever-expanding late-May booze fest (https://vancouvercraftbeerweek.com) runs from pairing dinners to tasting events. Expect to rub shoulders with brewmeisters from Phillips to Four Winds plus some from the US; now's your chance to conduct an international taste test.

Vancouver International Children's Festival

Bristling with kid-friendly storytelling, performances and activities at venues around Granville Island, late-May's multiday Children's Festival (p25) is highly popular. Expect to be charmed by face painters and balloon twisters while your ice-cream-smeared kids run riot.

Richmond Night Market

Hop on SkyTrain's Canada Line to Richmond's Bridgeport Station and you'll be a short walk from the weekend Night Market (www.richmondnightmarket.com), a steam-shrouded cornucopia of adventurous Asian street food that kicks off in May (and runs till October).

June

The summer good times roll as all Vancouverites shed some layers for the next three months. Neighborhood street parties also kick off and it's time to crank up the barbecue.

Bard on the Beach

Shakespeare performed the way it should be: in tents with the North Shore mountains peaking peacefully behind the stage. The four-play roster from Bard on the Beach (p173) runs from June to September. Book ahead.

Dragon Boat Festival

An epic weekend splashathon around mid-June, the colorful Dragon Boat Festival (https://concorddragonboatfestival.ca) churns the normally placid waters of False Creek. Around 100,000 landlubbers turn up to cheer on close to 200 teams and partake of a mini-festival of music, theater and food.

Car Free Vancouver Day

An increasingly popular annual event, Car Free Day Vancouver (p121) is held in a number of different city neighborhoods in June and July. Expect closed-off streets to be surrendered to live music, market stalls, quirky performers and food stands.

Vancouver International Jazz Festival

Vancouver's Jazz Fest (p241) is a huge multiday music party from late June that combines superstar performances (Oscar Peterson and Diana Krall in the past) with smile-triggering free outdoor shows around the city.

July

The city is in full-on beach-bumming mode, with the very idea of rain a distant memory (except when there's an occasional cracking thunder storm). Dress light and head outside for most of this month.

Canada Day Celebrations

Canada Place is the main Vancouver location for Canada Day celebrations marking the country's July 1 birthday. From 10am onwards expect food, live music, impromptu renditions of 'O Canada' and (eventually) fireworks. Granville Island also hosts smaller but equally proud celebrations.

Vancouver Folk Music Festival

Kitsilano's Jericho Beach is the venue for the sunny, weekend-long Folk Music Festival (p241), featuring alfresco shows from folk to world music and beyond. Don your sunblock and join the 30,000-odd hippies and hipsters at one of Vancouver's most enduring music events.

Celebration of Light

One of North America's largest fireworks competitions, the Celebration of Light (p63) takes place in English Bay over three nights in late July and early August. Competing countries (different ones every year) put on their most spectacular displays.

(Top) Vancouver International Jazz Festival (p21)
(Bottom) Pride Week (p44) celebrations

August

It's the peak of summer, which means locals are in full sun-kissed patio mode and a tasty menu of local-grown fruit – from peaches to cherries – hits the city.

Pride Week

A multiday kaleidoscope of LGBT+ shows, parties and concerts culminating in Western Canada's largest pride parade (http://www.vancouverpride.ca). Typically the first Sunday of August, this saucy West End mardi gras draws up to 500,000 people with its disco-beat floats and gyrating, scantily clad locals.

Pacific National Exhibition

From the third week of August onwards, this country fair (p124) has evolved into a three-week community party of live music, family-friendly performances (check out the Superdogs) and artery-clogging food stands. Don't forget the fairground, with its historic wooden roller coaster.

Vancouver Mural Festival

Transforming alfresco walls in and around the Main St area into eye-popping canvases, this street-art celebration (p134) includes guided walks and live demonstrations.

September

Summer is waning but there are usually still plenty of golden sunny days to go before the leaves start turning. The blue-skied end of the month especially is many Vancouverites' favorite time of year.

Vancouver Fringe Festival

One of the city's biggest arts events, the Fringe (p110) features a lively 11-day roster of wacky theatrics from the second week of September, drawing thousands to large, small and unconventional Granville Island venues. Expect short plays and comedy revues, with tickets typically around the $12–15 mark.

Vancouver International Film Festival

This giant, highly popular film festival (p37) celebrates smaller, art-house movies and international hidden gems. Its 17-day roster from late September covers hundreds of screenings of local, national and international films, and features gala events and industry schmoozes. Book ahead.

October

It's time to scamper back inside as the rain returns and locals rediscover their waterproof jackets for the rest of the year. Some sunny days remain though, illuminating the fading fall foliage.

Vancouver Writers Fest

A six-day, late-October literary event, the Writers Fest (p242) offers Granville Island readings, workshops and forums with dozens of local and international scribblers. Past guests have included Margaret Atwood and Salman Rushdie.

November

Time to wrap up if you want to partake of the events around the city this month. Scarves and umbrellas are often a good idea in November.

Eastside Culture Crawl

Hundreds of local artists in Vancouver's Eastside open their private or shared studios to visitors at this excellent four-day showcase (p91) in mid-November. Expect to come across a wild and wacky array of works, from found art installations to woodblock prints of marauding crows.

Bright Nights in Stanley Park

With Christmas coming, this month-long event sees a swath of the park covered in fairy lights and Yuletide dioramas. There's also a Christmas-themed train ride. Visit www.vancouver.ca/parks/events/brightnights for information.

December

Santa Claus Parade

Rivaling the Pride Parade for spectator numbers, this giant Christmas procession (p25) in the first week of December is a family favorite. Expect youth orchestras, carol-singing floats and, right at the end, the great man himself. And, yes, he's the real one.

With Kids

Vancouver is stuffed with attractions for children, including interactive science centers, animal encounters and outdoor activities to tire them out. Several festivals are especially kid-tastic, while transport experiences, including SeaBus and SkyTrain, are highlights for many.

ADDA83/SHUTTERSTOCK ©

Science World by architect Bruno Freschi (p133)

Animal Encounters

Grouse Mountain (p182) is home to resident grizzly bears in their own enclosure; there are also summertime bird-of-prey displays.

Maplewood Farm (p182) is ideal for younger kids who can't wait to hang out with the goats and chickens.

Vancouver Aquarium (p51) offers otters, iridescent jellyfish and dolphins to view, plus trainer encounters if your kids are keen on behind-the-scenes tours.

Bloedel Conservatory (p152) provides a delightful way to commune with hundreds of exotic birds; ask nicely and staff might let your child feed several at once from a bowl.

Science & Nature

Science World (p133), packed with hands-on activities, has mastered the art of teaching kids through an abundance of fun. Its outdoor area is the city's favorite summertime hangout for children, especially under-10s.

HR MacMillan Space Centre (p166) is perfect for astronomically minded children, with plenty of push-button games and activities.

Capilano Suspension Bridge Park (p182) offers a great way to learn about the local outdoors. After inching over the canyon on the (deliberately) wobbly wooden bridge, take some short trails through the forest to learn about the towering trees and local critters.

Stanley Park Nature House (p61) gives kids the opportunity to quiz friendly volunteers about the park's flora and fauna and partake of wildlife tours, especially in summer.

Outdoor Action

Second Beach Pool (p79) in Stanley Park is one of the city's best summertime hangouts for kids who love to swim. This side of the park also has a popular playground, as does the Lumberman's Arch area, where you'll find an outdoor water park as well.

Granville Island Water Park (p115) is even bigger and not far from the ever-popular Kids Market (p103).

Kitsilano Beach (p166) is ideal if your children want to play on the sand; it's very popular with families.

Festivals & Events

Vancouver International Children's Festival (www.childrensfestival.ca; Granville Island; ⏲late May; 👪; 🚌50) is packed with entertainers and face-painting shenanigans.

Pacific National Exhibition (p124) is crammed with shows, activities and fairground rides for kids of all ages. Don't miss the piglet races.

Car Free Day Vancouver (p121) takes over several main thoroughfares around the city and has lots of family-friendly activities.

The Santa Claus Parade (www.vancouversantaclausparade.com; W Georgia St, Downtown; admission free; ⏲early Dec; 👪; S Burrard) FREE is Vancouver's best chance to see the big man himself, plus attendant floats, bands and music.

History Huggers

BC Sports Hall of Fame & Museum (p102) traces the region's sporting past via kid-friendly displays and activities.

Kidsbooks (p175), Vancouver's biggest family bookstore, has tomes on everything – history included.

NEED TO KNOW

Accommodations Children can usually stay with parents at hotels for no extra charge. Some hostels have family rooms. Hotels can recommend trusted babysitting services.

Equipment Strollers, booster seats and toys can be rented from Wee Travel (www.weetravel.ca).

Resources For local tips, resources and family-focused events, visit www.kidsvancouver.com.

Academie Duello (p79) offers kid-friendly swordplay lessons – plus hugely popular Knight Camps.

Transport Fun

Kids of a certain age really enjoy getting around Vancouver. Taking the seat at the front of a SkyTrain is all about pretending to be the driver, while the front window seats on a SeaBus jaunt to North Vancouver are almost as coveted. Taking a bathtub-sized ferry around False Creek is also fun, and hopping aboard the chugging Stanley Park Train (p54) is a must.

Vancouver Aquarium (p53)

Like a Local

It often seems that Vancouverites combine an outdoorsy sensibility with an almost bacchanalian love for artisan booze and fusion food-truck dining. Luckily for visitors, that means you're never far from uncovering an intriguing scene or two; just follow the locals and plunge right in.

MAJAPHOTO/SHUTTERSTOCK ©

Kitsilano Farmers Market (p175)

Great Outdoors

Visitors craving fresh air head en masse to shoreline Stanley Park, but you're more likely to run into Lycra-clad Vancouverites biking the Arbutus Greenway (p166) or hiking the super-steep Grouse Grind (p182) in North Vancouver.

Tasting Lounges

Vancouver's history can be divided into pre- and post-craft beer eras – everyone likes to forget that factory-made lager was the norm here until recently. These days, locals crowd the city's quirky microbrewery tasting lounges as if they've always been here. Looking for a crawl-worthy 'hood? Try East Vancouver (p126).

Indie Shopping

Robson St is lined with chain stores. But if you want to browse some cool independent boutiques with the locals, check out Main St, particularly south of the 18th Ave intersection. Top spot? Regional Assembly of Text (p142).

Farmers Markets

Locals avoid jam-packed Granville Island Public Market in summer. Instead, they fill their cloth shopping bags with BC fruit, veggies and baked treats at the city's pop-up markets. Kitsilano Farmers Market (p175) is one of the biggest and best.

NEED TO KNOW

- **Compass Cards** Transit-using Vancouverites typically deploy stored-value Compass Cards to get around. Buy one for $6 at SkyTrain station vending machines, load it up and you're good to go.
- **Mobi** Vancouver's public bike-share scheme (p246) has docking stations around the city; there's also an extensive network of dedicated bike lanes to use them on.

For Free

There is a full array sights and activities to enjoy in Vancouver without opening your wallet. Follow the locals and check city blogs and you'll soon be perusing art shows, noodling around parks and taking in a gratis tour or two.

SONGQUAN DENG/SHUTTERSTOCK ©

Sun Yat-Sen Park (p83)

Free Attractions

From nature to local history, there are several fee-free places to visit here.

Engine 374 Pavilion (p102) in Yaletown preserves the locomotive that pulled the first transcontinental passenger train into Vancouver.

Stanley Park Nature House (p61) gives a fascinating introduction to the region's flora and fauna.

Sun-Yat Sen Park, the adjoining freebie alternative to the Dr Sun Yat-Sen Classical Chinese Garden (p83), has many of the same visual attributes.

Lynn Canyon Park (p183) is the access point to a smaller alternative to tt

Discounts Galore

From cheap nights to free tours, reduce your costs with these tips.

Vancouver Art Gallery (p55) entry is by donation on Tuesday evenings from 5pm to 9pm.

Museum of Anthropology (p164) entry is $10 on Thursday evenings from 5pm to 9pm.

Tickets Tonight (☎604-684-2787; www.ticketstonight.ca) sells tickets for day-of-performance theater shows at half price.

Vancouver Tour Guys (p248) offers gratuity-only (budget for $5 to $10) walking tours.

Need to Know

Websites Bored in Vancouver (www.boredinvancouver.com) has many suggestions for free events and activities around the city.

Discount Cards If you're planning to visit many places, a City Passport (www.citypassports.com; $30) can be a good idea.

Happy Hour Many Vancouver bars and restaurants offer happy-hour deals. Typically from 3pm to 6pm (often weekdays only), these include discounted drinks and appetizers.

Under the Radar Vancouver

Frequently cited as one of the world's best cities, Vancouver receives more than eight million visitors per year. While summertime crowds at popular attractions like Capilano Suspension Bridge and Granville Island Public Market are common, there are ways to sidestep the masses and discover authentic, under-the-radar experiences.

DEYMOSHR/SHUTTERSTOCK ©

Vancouver Public Library (p60)

Lesser-Explored Neighborhoods

First-time Vancouver visitors typically congregate on the cobbled streets of Gastown and Chinatown or crowd the scenic seawall trail around Stanley Park. But there's much more to the city than these areas. Join the locals exploring the independent stores and cafes on Main Street (p49) or hit the shops and restaurants of 4th Avenue in Kitsilano (p175). Both are easy to reach via transit bus from downtown Vancouver. From Kitsilano, add a visit to the nearby University of British Columbia (UBC) campus. This shoreline uni is home to a full menu of cultural attractions that are rarely crowded – don't miss the Museum of Anthropology (p164) and the Beaty Biodiversity Museum (p167).

Underrated Attractions

Culture fans can bypass the often-busy Vancouver Art Gallery by checking out Yaletown's Contemporary Art Gallery (p60) and North Vancouver's shoreline Polygon Gallery (p182). History buffs should not miss the West End's Roedde House Museum (p61), the edge-of-Chinatown Vancouver Police Museum (p82) or Yaletown's free-entry Engine 374 Pavilion (p102), home to the first transcontinental passenger that trundled into Vancouver in 1887. Need more hidden gem history? Back on the UBC campus, head downstairs at the main library building to discover the little-known Chung Collection (p168), a gratis-entry museum lined with fascinating Chinese pioneer exhibits and colorful displays of vintage Canadian Pacific Railway memorabilia.

Tranquil Nature

It's not hard to veer off the beaten path and find some calming spots to commune with nature here. Definitely don't miss Stanley Park, but rather than exclusively adhering to the busy seawall, dive into its woodland interior on some of the park's quieter tree-lined routes (expect to spot raccoons, wrens and chittering Douglas squirrels). Across the city, the trails of gigantic Pacific Spirit Regional Park (p168) are also rarely crowded. And for a quick breather during a downtown visit, head to the Vancouver Public Library (p60) where a 'secret' ninth-floor rooftop garden awaits.

Crowd-Free Dining

Peak season dining often requires advance planning in bustling restaurant districts such as Gastown, Yaletown and Granville Island. But eating off the beaten path means noshing with the locals and not having to wait too long for a table. Consider the multitudinous mid-priced international eateries on Denman Street; the independent bars and restaurants on Main Street; and the kaleidoscopic menu of cafes, restaurants and coffeehouses lining both sides of Commercial Drive. Food trucks are also a feature of the city but they can be hard to find unless you know where they usually are – the square on the north side of the Vancouver Art Gallery (p55) typically has a few. Keep in mind that many restaurants and bars offer happy hour dining; off-peak deals that combine value-priced specials and the chance to snag an easy table in joints that are usually crowded at other times.

Escape the City

It's easy to forget that Vancouver is the metro hub of an expansive wider community that's studded with other towns and cities. Public transit makes accessing many of these easy, providing accessible day-out options for urban explorers. Asian food fan? Richmond is a 20-minute Canada Line SkyTrain hop from downtown and it's the home of hundreds of highly authentic Asian restaurants. Beer nut? Port Moody is also on the SkyTrain system and, just steps from Moody Centre Station, there are several top microbreweries situated just a few storefronts apart. Need more? Transit routes also connect Vancouver to Burnaby, Langley, North Vancouver and beyond, while a day trip to Bowen Island includes a sigh-triggering BC Ferries journey – shimmering ocean and mountain views included – plus tranquil nature hikes and hilltop coastal views.

Night-Out Alternatives

Arthouse-loving Vancouver film fans eschew the city's big box movie theaters in favor of downtown's Cinematheque (p74) and Vancity Theatre (p74). Movies are also part of the mix at the Rio Theatre (p127), near the Commercial Drive SkyTrain Station. Alongside cult and indie flicks, there are also live shows and sportscasts here. Beer-loving bar fans also tend to sidestep Vancouver's noisier watering holes and head to the city's frothy surfeit of microbrewery tasting lounges. Like little neighborhood bars, these friendly joints include under-the-radar gems such as Off the Rail (p126), Bomber Brewing (p126) and Callister Brewing (p126), each located just a short stroll apart in East Vancouver. And if ping-pong is your night-out desire, Back and Forth Bar (p92) has tables, beer specials and a laid-back vibe.

Ramen dish

Dining Out

Vancouver has an eye-popping array of generally good-value dine-out options: authentic Asian restaurants, finger-licking brunch spots, fresh-catch seafood joints and a locally sourced farm-to-table scene are all on the menu here. You don't have to be a local to indulge: just follow your taste buds and dinner will become the most talked-about highlight of your Vancouver visit.

Seafood

One reason Vancouver has great sushi is the top-table seafood available right off the boat. Given the length of British Columbia's coastline, it's no surprise restaurants (whether Asian, Mexican, West Coast or French) find plenty of menu space for salmon, halibut, spot prawns and more. If you're a seafood fan, you'll be in your element; even fish and chips are typically excellent. Start your aquatic odyssey at Granville Island, where the Public Market has seafood vendors and Fisherman's Wharf is just along the seawall.

Farm to Table

After decades of favoring imported ingredients, Vancouver now fully embraces regional food and farm products. Restaurants can't wait to tell you about the Fraser Valley duck and foraged morels they've just discovered. Seasonal is key, and you'll see lots of local specials on menus; ask your server for insights. Most restaurants have also taken their BC love affair to the drinks list: Okanagan wines have been a staple here for years but BC craft beer and artisan liquor are also relished by thirsty locavores.

Asian Smorgasbord

Vancouver (and the adjoining city of Richmond) is home to the best Asian dining scene outside Asia. From great sushi and ramen spots to lip-smacking hot pot and *banh mi* sandwich joints, you're spoilt for choice here. Adventurous foodies should combine award-winning restaurants with smaller mom and pop places, not to mention food trucks and summertime night markets, for the full experience.

Street-Food-a-Palooza

A late starter to North America's street-food movement, Vancouver now has one of Canada's tastiest scenes. The downtown core often has the highest concentration of trucks, with everything from Korean sliders to salmon tacos to barbecued brisket sandwiches. Check out what's on the street during your visit at www.streetfoodapp.com/vancouver.

International Dining

Vancouver's ethnic cuisine scene doesn't begin and end with Asia. In a city built on immigration, the menu here is a United Nations of dining options, from excellent Spanish and Greek restaurants to highly popular Mexican joints. Follow the locals: they'll often lead you to unassuming family-run places. Not sure what to go for? Many restaurants have great-value happy-hour dining deals, typically on weekday afternoons.

Farmers Markets

A tasty cornucopia of regional produce hits Vancouver's farmers markets from June to October. And they're a great way to stuff your face and meet the locals at the same time. Seasonal treats to look out for include lush peaches, juicy cherries and sweet blueberries, while home-baked treats and arts and crafts are frequent accompaniments. Check locations and dates for many of these markets at www.eatlocal.org.

Veggie Hot Spot

Vancouver's vegan and vegetarian dining scene has entered a taste-tripping golden age in recent years. A full menu of delicious new places to eat has suddenly popped up and many are luring traditional carnivores with their hearty comfort-food dishes (think burgers and brunches). Keen to adopt a more plant-based diet? This is the city to kick things off in.

NEED TO KNOW

Price Ranges

The following price ranges refer to a main course.

$ less than $15

$$ $15–$25

$$$ more than $25

Opening Hours

- Restaurants generally open from 11:30am for lunch and serve dinner from 5pm to 10pm (or later).
- Breakfast is typically from 7am to 10am; later on weekends, when many places also serve brunch.
- Some restaurants close on Mondays in Vancouver, so check ahead before you head out.

Reservations

- Not every restaurant accepts reservations but call ahead for higher-end places. Many restos seat without bookings, especially for early dinners (from 5pm to 6pm). Note that Vancouver's restaurant dress code is generally relaxed; you'll spot jeans and fleeces at almost every dining level here.

Taxes & Tipping

- GST (Goods & Services Tax) of 5% is added to restaurant bills for food.
- Alcohol attracts GST plus 10% PST (Provincial Sales Tax).
- Tipping is standard; typically it's 15% of the bill, although 18% is becoming common. Some restos add a tip automatically for large groups: check your bill carefully.

Happy Hour

- Many Vancouver bars and restaurants have happy-hour pricing. For restaurants, this typically means appetizer specials every afternoon (sometimes excluding weekends), often between 3pm and 6pm. It's a great way to sample a few dishes without blowing your vacation budget.

Rangoli (p155), cafe-like satellite of Cambie Street's landmark Vij's (p153)

Eating by Neighborhood

➡ **Downtown & West End** (p50) Food trucks and a full range of restaurants; many international midrange options in West End.

➡ **Gastown & Chinatown** (p80) Innovative independent places to eat in Gastown; authentic Asian dining in Chinatown.

➡ **Yaletown & Granville Island** (p98) High-end restos in Yaletown; some good Granville Island seafood spots.

➡ **Commercial Drive** (p118) Brilliant neighborhood dining, with excellent patios.

➡ **Main Street** (p131) Quirky indie restaurants and neighborhood hangouts.

➡ **Fairview & South Granville** (p149) Fine dining and friendly neighborhood haunts.

➡ **Kitsilano & University of British Columbia (UBC)** (p162) Fine dining at midrange prices in Kits; cafes and local mini-chains at UBC.

Lonely Planet's Top Choices

Vij's (p153) The city's favorite Indian restaurant.

St Lawrence Restaurant (p87) French Québec dining in a Montréal-style bistro setting.

Anh & Chi (p136) Sparkling modern Vietnamese restaurant.

Forage (p69) Showcasing farm-to-table West Coast dining.

Acorn (p136) The city's best vegetarian restaurant.

Caffè La Tana (p120) 1950s-style Italian charmer serving delicious fresh-made pasta.

Best by Budget

$

Baghdad Cafe (p64) Heaping chicken, lamb and rice dishes; loved by local students.

Bestie (p88) Bratwursts and fries in a quirky Chinatown setting.

Poke Guy (p64) Downtown favorite; fresh and generously portioned bowls.

Hawkers Delight (p134) Heaping Malaysian street-food dishes.

DD Mau (p103) Crispy Vietnamese *banh mi* sandwiches.

$$

Forage (p69) Farm-to-table specialists with tempting West Coast dishes.

Greek Gastown (p86) Perfectly executed modern Greek dining.

Dock Lunch (p136) Homestyle dining among the Main St locals.

Salmon n' Bannock (p151) First Nations restaurant with traditionally inspired dishes.

Campagnolo (p89) Warm and welcoming homestyle Italian dining.

$$$

St Lawrence Restaurant (p87) Québecois French cuisine at one of Vancouver's best dine-out spots.

Vij's (p153) Sleek but ever-welcoming contemporary Indian restaurant.

Chambar (p67) Belgian-influenced West Coast menu in a warm, candlelit setting.

Bishop's (p171) West Coast seasonal dining at its finest.

Best Asian Dining

Anh & Chi (p136) Contemporary Vietnamese restaurant loved by hungry locals.

Heritage Asian Eatery (p152) Well-priced top-notch rice bowls and more.

Bao Bei (p90) Supercool modern Chinese dining.

Phnom Penh (p89) Taste-tripping Cambodian and Vietnamese dining.

Hawkers Delight (p134) Predominantly Malaysian street-food dishes.

Toshi Sushi (p135) Super-fresh sushi with a warm welcome.

Best Vegetarian

Acorn (p136) The city's best veggie restaurant; book ahead.

MeeT in Gastown (p86) Vegan comfort dishes in a chatty backstreet setting.

Vegan Cave (p85) Gastown favorite serving amazing plant-based pizzas.

Naam (p171) Kitsilano vegetarian legend, open 24 hours.

Best Breakfast

Paul's Omelettery (p153) Breakfast-specializing neighborhood haunt.

Templeton (p65) Diner joint with heaping breakfasts.

Jam Cafe (p66) Tempting breakfast and brunch dishes.

Dutch Wooden Shoe Cafe (p152) Old-school breakfast pancake dining.

Tangent Cafe (p120) Commercial Dr's neighborhood breakfast hangout.

Sophie's Cosmic Cafe (p171) Satisfying breakfasts in a kitsch-covered diner.

Best Ice Cream

Earnest Ice Cream (p135) Heritage-building setting for top-notch artisan ice cream.

Rain or Shine (p152) Purple-and-yellow-hued favorite with tons of great flavors.

Uno Gelato (p169) Luring Kitsilano locals and more with delicious treats.

Elephant Garden Creamery (p121) Clever but ever-delicious Asian fusion flavors.

La Casa Gelato (p122) Italian ice creamery with hundreds of tempting choices.

Best Food Blogs

Vancouver Foodster (www.vancouverfoodster.com)

Scout Magazine (www.scoutmagazine.ca)

Sherman's Food Adventures (www.shermansfoodadventures.com)

Food Gays (www.foodgays.com)

Van Foodies (www.vanfoodies.com)

LONELY PLANET/GETTY IMAGES ©

Irish Heather Pub (p91)

Bar Open

Vancouverites spend a lot of time drinking. And while British Columbia (BC) has a tasty wine sector and is undergoing an artisanal distilling surge, it's the regional craft-beer scene that keeps many quaffers merry. For a night out with locally made libations as your side dish, join savvy city drinkers in the bars of Gastown, Main St and beyond.

Craft Beer

BC is Canada's craft-beer capital, with around 200 beer producers dotted throughout the province, including dozens in Vancouver. You can plan an easy stroll (or stumble) around an inviting cluster of microbrewery tasting rooms on and around Main St. A little further out, and radiating from the northern end of Commercial Dr, you'll discover another easy-to-explore area sometimes called 'Yeast Vancouver.' You'll also find bars around the city falling over themselves to showcase intriguing regional brews; ask your server what's local and/or seasonal and be sure to look out for favorite BC producers such as Four Winds, Powell Street, Strange Fellows and Twin Sails. For more information on the city's beery happenings, visit www.camra vancouver.ca.

Wine & Liquor

It's not just beer that's raised the bar in Vancouver. The city's drinking scene has improved immeasurably from the not-too-distant days when a lame Manhattan was the height of local sophistication. Grape-based quaffing kicked off the revolution with a flight of established wine bars giving curious oenophiles plenty of ways to slake their thirsts. The cocktail scene took longer to grow but it now combines quirky nightspots with sleek high-end options. Adding to the scene, distinctive craft distilleries have also popped up around the region; look out for intriguing BC options at many city bars. And don't forget that Vancouver's happy-hour rules mean you can afford to be adventurous and discover something new.

Clubbing

While downtown's Granville Strip draws the barely clad booties of mainstream clubbers, there are other, less limelight-hogging areas catering to just about every peccadillo. Cover charges run from $5 to $20 ('the ladies' often get in free before 11pm) and dress codes are frequently smart-casual – ripped jeans and sportswear will not endear you to the bouncers who are just looking for people to send home. Bring ID: most clubs accept over-19s but some want you to be over 25.

Alternative Night Out Ideas

Pick up a copy of the free *Georgia Straight* weekly, the city's best listings newspaper, for additional night-out ideas. If you're stuck, consider the quarterly FUSE party night (p75) at the Vancouver Art Gallery; the pinball room at grungy Pub 340 (p93); Grandview Lanes bowling (p129) on Commercial Dr; playing board games at Storm Crow Alehouse (p157); the ping-pong tables at Back and Forth Bar (p92); or the delightful letter-writing club at the Regional Assembly of Text (p142).

NEED TO KNOW

Opening Hours

Pubs and bars serving lunch open before midday, with swankier operations waiting until 5pm. Most bars close sometime between 11pm and 2am, although some stay open to 4am. Nightclubs usually open at 9pm (although they don't really get going until 11pm) and most close at 3am or 4am.

How Much?

- It's $5 to $8 for a large glass of beer here, but always ask about daily specials.
- A glass of wine costs anything over $7, cocktails up to $20.
- Your bill will include 10% Provincial Sales Tax (PST).
- Entry to clubs is $5 to $20, with weekends being particularly expensive.

Tipping

Table servers expect $1 per drink, or 15% to 18% when you're buying a round. Even if you order and pick up your beverage at the bar, consider dropping your change in the prominently placed tips glass.

Drinking & Nightlife by Neighborhood

- **Downtown & West End** (p70) Granville Strip is lined with party-hard clubs and bars, while the West End's Davie St is gay nightlife central.
- **Gastown & Chinatown** (p90) Craft-beer taverns as well as indie bars and clubs.
- **Yaletown & Granville Island** (p109) Yaletown has some slick bars and a huge brewpub, while Granville Island is fine for pre-theater drinks.
- **Commercial Drive** (p125) Neighborhood pubs and old-school coffee bars abound; plus try the nearby 'Yeast Van' microbreweries.
- **Main Street** (p138) Where in-the-know hipsters drink at some of the city's best indie bars and microbrew tasting rooms.

Lonely Planet's Top Choices

Brassneck Brewery (p138) Vancouver's favorite microbrewery tasting room.

Grapes & Soda (p158) Local hot spot with a great wine list.

Storm Crow Alehouse (p157) Large nerd pub with board games and sci-fi props on the walls.

Key Party (p139) Tiny bar hidden behind a 'fake' accountancy office storefront.

Alibi Room (p90) Superb BC and beyond craft-beer selection wrapped in a friendly tavern vibe.

Shameful Tiki Room (p139) Evocative, cavelike cocktail haunt.

Best Microbreweries

Brassneck Brewery (p138) Wood-lined tasting room with ever-changing beer line-up.

Powell Brewery (p126) Popular producer with lively tasting room.

Parallel 49 Brewing Company (p126) Busy tasting room with its own 'indoor food truck.'

Off the Rail (p126) Upstairs tasting bar with a wide array of smooth libations.

R&B Brewing (p140) Comfy rec room vibe with well-priced beer.

Andina Brewing Company (p126) Cool brewery with a South American flavor.

Best Beer Bars

Alibi Room (p90) Vancouver's fave craft-beer tavern, with around 50 mostly BC drafts.

Whip (p139) Laid-back neighborhood pub with good BC beer selection.

St Augustine's (p127) Sports-bar vibe with dozens of rare-for-Vancouver craft drafts.

Railway Stage & Beer Cafe (p71) Upstairs watering hole with a good array of BC taps.

Sing Sing Beer Bar (p140) White-walled Main St hangout with some tasty BC drafts.

Brewhall (p141) Cavernous beer hall with own-made brews and much more.

Best Cocktail Joints

Shameful Tiki Room (p139) Windowless tiki-themed cave with strong concoctions.

Diamond (p90) Alluring upstairs room with perfect classic cocktails.

Prohibition (p71) Subterranean downtown joint with sparkling cocktail selection.

Liberty Distillery (p109) Granville Island craft producer with a cool saloon-look bar.

Keefer Bar (p93) Chinatown's fave lounge with great drinks and a cool-ass vibe.

Best Happy Hours

Liberty Distillery (p109) 3pm to 6pm Monday to Thursday.

Uva Wine & Cocktail Bar (p71) 2pm to 5pm daily.

Cascade Room (p140) 4pm to 6pm daily.

Keefer Bar (p93) 5pm to 7pm Sunday to Friday.

Sing Sing Beer Bar (p140) 3pm to 6pm daily.

Best Patios

Galley Patio & Grill (p173) Neighborhood haunt with great English Bay views.

Six Acres (p90) Small patio in the shadow of Gastown's Gassy Jack statue.

Narrow Lounge (p139) Tiny 'secret garden' back area with intimate party vibe.

Storm Crow Alehouse (p157) Large outdoor seating area at this popular 'nerd pub.'

Parallel 49 Brewing Company (p126) Large patio for supping flights of housemade beer.

Best for Live Music

Guilt & Co (p90) Subterranean bar with regular shows.

Railway Stage & Beer Cafe (p71) A small stage plus a great craft beer selection.

Uva Wine & Cocktail Bar (p71) Check ahead for live jazz nights.

Pat's Pub (p95) Old-school bar with live jazz shows.

Best for Food

Devil's Elbow Ale & Smoke House (p71) Carnivorous menu and top brews from BC's Howe Sound Brewing.

Irish Heather (p91) Great place for sausage and mash with a pint of Guinness.

Cascade Room (p140) The Sunday roast is a local legend.

Alibi Room (p90) Hearty elevated comfort food and an excellent beer list.

Whip (p139) An enticing menu with plenty of gastropub flair.

Showtime

You'll never run out of options if you're looking for a good time here. Vancouver is packed with activities from high- to lowbrow, perfect for those craving a play one night, a hockey game the next, and a rocking poetry slam to follow. Ask the locals for tips and they'll likely point out grassroots happenings you never knew existed.

Film

While some independent movie theaters have closed in recent years, there are still plenty of places to catch blockbusters as well as a couple of downtown art-house cinemas for those who like subtitles rather than car chases: check out www.cinemaclock.com to see what's on while you're here. Visiting cinephiles will also be thrilled at the huge range of movie festivals. Consider the highly popular **Vancouver International Film Festival** (www.viff.org; ⏲late Sep) in late September, as well as smaller film fests such as May's **DOXA Documentary Film Festival** (www.doxafestival.ca) and November's **Vancouver Asian Film Festival** (www.vaff.org).

Theater

Vancouver has a long history of treading the boards. The Arts Club Theatre Company (p240) is the city's leading troupe, with three stages dotted around Vancouver. Expect challenging shows and visiting companies at the Cultch (p128) and Firehall Arts Centre (p93). Depending on the time of your visit, catch January's **PuSh Festival** (www.pushfestival.ca; tickets from $10; ⏲mid-Jan), September's Vancouver Fringe Festival (p110) or the summer-long Bard on the Beach (p173), where Shakespeare plays are performed in tents against a mountain backdrop.

Live Music

Superstar acts appear at sports stadiums and city theaters (and with the big venue comes a big ticket price), while smaller indie bands crowd mid-sized venues and tiny, broom-closet spaces around town. Local independent record stores will give you the lowdown on Vancouver acts to catch; many also sell tickets to shows. The scene here is not all about brooding indie bands: Vancouver has wide musical tastes and, with some digging, you'll find jazz, folk, classical and opera performances, often with festivals to match.

Dance

Vancouver is a major center for Canadian dance, offering an esoteric array of classical ballet and edgy contemporary fare. The city is home to more than 30 professional companies as well as many internationally recognized choreographers. To touch base with the region's hotfoot crowd, pirouette over to downtown's Dance Centre (p75). Also, plan your visit to coincide with July's **Dancing on the Edge festival** (www.dancingontheedge.org).

Entertainment by Neighborhood

- **Downtown & West End** (p74) Home to top entertainment venues, from theaters to cinemas.
- **Gastown & Chinatown** (p93) Location of several under-the-radar venues.
- **Yaletown & Granville Island** (p110) The island is a hotbed of theaters and festivals.
- **Commercial Drive** (p127) Location of several locally loved performance spaces.
- **Main Street** (p141) Home of some cool indie venues.

NEED TO KNOW

Costs

➡ Theater tickets typically start at $30.

➡ Cinema tickets start at $12, with matinees and Tuesday shows often cheaper.

➡ Live music shows are free or cheap in pubs and bars; from $30 in other live venues (plus fees).

Buying Tickets

➡ See www.ticketmaster.ca for live shows and events around Vancouver.

➡ See www.ticketstonight.ca for shows as well as half-price deals available on the day.

What's On?

➡ Pick up Thursday's freebie *Georgia Straight* (www.straight.com) for what's on in the week ahead.

➡ Head online to Live Van (www.livevan.com) for up-to-the-minute local gig listings.

Lonely Planet's Top Choices

Commodore Ballroom (p74) Vancouver's fave band venue.

Arts Club Theatre Company (p240) Leading theatrical troupe, with three city venues.

Bard on the Beach (p173) Shakespeare plays in waterfront Vanier Park tents.

Pacific Cinematheque (p74) Friendly and eclectic art-house cinema.

Guilt & Co (p90) Intimate subterranean live music spot.

Best Cinemas

Cinematheque (p74) Long-established art-house cinema.

Vancity Theatre (p74) Slick downtown art-house cinema.

Rio Theatre (p127) Indie venue with lively late-night Friday and Saturday screenings.

Cineplex Odeon International Village Cinemas (p95) Vancouver's favorite mainstream cinema venue.

Cineplex Park Theatre (p159) Single screen with new movies and live theater broadcasts.

Best Alternative Film Fests

DOXA Documentary Film Festival (www.doxafestival.ca)

Vancouver Asian Film Festival (www.vaff.org)

Vancouver International Mountain Film Festival (www.vimff.org)

Vancouver Latin American Film Festival (www.vlaff.org)

Vancouver Queer Film Festival (www.queerfilmfestival.ca)

Best Live Theaters

Stanley Theatre (p158) Historic Arts Club theater venue with great end-of-season musicals.

Cultch (p128) Heritage building converted into an excellent theater complex.

Firehall Arts Centre (p93) Cool fringe venue with an eclectic roster.

Malkin Bowl (p75) Outdoor Stanley Park stage where summer musicals are performed.

BMO Theatre Centre (p141) The Arts Club's studio theater, cleverly reconfigured for each show.

Best Comedy Nights

Vancouver Theatresports (p111) Improv comedy troupe in a Granville Island theater.

Yuk Yuk's Comedy Club (p159) Traditional comedy venue with local and visiting stand-ups.

Rio Theatre (p127) Multidiscipline independent venue with regular live comedy including Story Story Lie.

Kino (p159) Fun Cambie Village venue with weekly stand-up and open-mic nights.

Best Alternative Nights Out

Vancouver Poetry Slam (p128) Commercial Drive fixture with a chance to perform your epic.

Celluloid Social Club (p142) Regular event where local movie-makers screen and discuss their work.

Kino (p159) Flamenco performances several nights a week on a small stage.

Jericho Folk Club (p175) Long-running folkie night out.

DELPIXART/GETTY IMAGES ©

Treasure Hunt

Vancouver's retail scene has developed dramatically in recent years. Hit Robson St's mainstream chains, then discover the hip, independent shops of Gastown, Main St and Commercial Dr. Granville Island is stuffed with artsy stores and studios, while South Granville and Kitsilano's 4th Ave serve up a wide range of tempting boutiques.

Independent Fashion

Vancouver has all the usual clothing chain suspects, but it also has a bulging shopping bag of independent stores with well-curated collections from local and international designers. Get off the beaten path to Main St and Commercial Dr for quirky vintage and artsy fashions. Or peruse the main drags of Gastown, South Granville and Kitsilano's 4th Ave for one-of-a-kind boutique gems. Keep your eyes peeled for pop-up shops and check the pages of *Vancouver* magazine and the *Georgia Straight* for retail happenings such as Gastown's 'shop hops' – seasonal evenings of late openings with a partylike vibe. Before you arrive, see Vancouver fashion blogs www.aliciafashionista.com and www.tovogueorbust.com for the local lowdown.

Arts & Crafts

The city's arts scene dovetails invitingly with its retail sector. There are dozens of intriguing private galleries, showcasing everything from contemporary Canadian art to authentic First Nations carvings and jewelry. There are also opportunities to buy art from local indie galleries and from the many artisan studios on Granville Island. In addition, there

NEED TO KNOW

Opening Hours

Typical downtown retail hours are from 10am to 5pm or 6pm Monday to Saturday, and from noon to 5pm Sunday. Some stores and malls stay open later on Fridays and Saturdays, especially during the Christmas season.

Consumer Taxes

The price on most items in shops does not include tax, which is added when you head to the cash register to pay. Typically, you will pay 5% GST as well as 7% PST.

are dozens of arts and crafts fairs throughout the year – they're a great way to meet local producers and creative Vancouverites. Check local listings publications or www.gotcraft.com for upcoming events.

Souvenirs

For decades, visitors to Vancouver have been returning home with suitcases full of maple-sugar cookies and vacuum-packed smoked salmon. You can still pick up these items, typically in the large souvenir stores lining the north side of Gastown's Water St. But it doesn't have to be this way. Consider consigning your Gastown-clock fridge magnet to the garbage and aiming for authentic First Nations art or silver jewelry; a book on Vancouver's eye-popping history (*Sensational Vancouver* by Eve Lazarus, for example); some delightful locally made pottery from Granville Island; or a quirky Vancouver-designed T-shirt from the fashion stores on Main St.

Shop the Museums

The city's museums and galleries offer some unexpected buying opportunities. You don't have to see an exhibition to visit these shops, and keep in mind that you're helping to fund the institutions you're buying from. Perhaps the best of the bunch is the Museum of Anthropology (p164) shop with its fantastic array of First Nations and international indigenous artworks, ranging from elegant silver jewelry to fascinating masks. Kitsilano's Museum of Vancouver (p166) has recently expanded its shop and now offers retro-cool T-shirts plus First Nations–themed souvenirs. Back downtown, the Vancouver Art Gallery (p55) stocks clever contemporary knickknacks and large art books to decorate your coffee table. And if you need to buy something cool for a kid back home, hit the Science World (p133) gift shop for all manner of intriguing educational goodies.

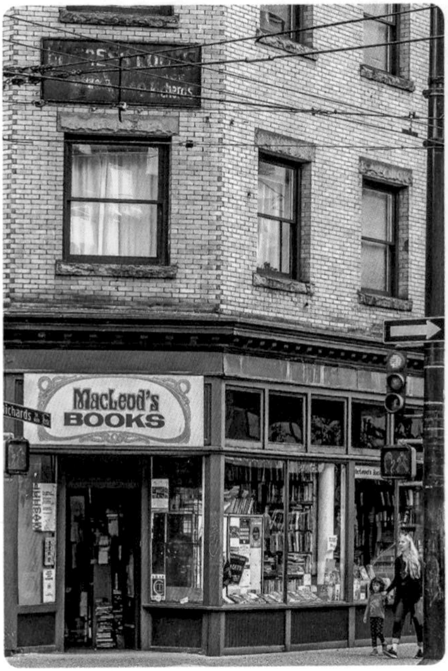

MacLeod's Books (p76)

Shopping by Neighborhood

- **Downtown & West End** (p76) Mainstream fashion boutiques on Robson St and in Pacific Centre mall.
- **Gastown & Chinatown** (p95) Independent fashion and vintage shops.
- **Yaletown & Granville Island** (p111) Swish boutiques in Yaletown; artisan studios on the island.
- **Commercial Drive** (p129) Vintage stores and hippy-esque shops.
- **Main Street** (p142) Indie shopping from records stores to cool boutiques, especially south of 18th Ave.
- **Fairview & South Granville** (p159) Independent stores on Cambie St; galleries and boutiques on South Granville.
- **Kitsilano & University of British Columbia (UBC)** (p175) Hit Kitsilano's West 4th Ave for boutiques and outdoor clothing stores.

Lonely Planet's Top Choices

Regional Assembly of Text (p142) Brilliantly creative stationery store with a little gallery nook.

Pacific Arts Market (p159) Friendly gallery space showcasing dozens of regional creatives.

Mountain Equipment Co-op (p142) Outdoor-gear and clothing megastore.

Red Cat Records (p142) Main St music store legend.

Eastside Flea (p95) Regular weekend-long indoor market with artisan and vintage wear focus.

Karameller Candy Shop (p111) Cool Swedish sweetie store in Yaletown.

Best Bookshops

Paper Hound (p76) Perfectly curated, mostly used, downtown bookstore.

Massy Books (p95) Tome-lined Chinatown shop with secret bookcase nook.

KidsBooks (p175) Giant, child-focused bookstore.

Macleod's Books (p76) Local legend crammed with teetering stacks of used books.

Pulpfiction Books (p144) Vancouver's favorite multi-branch used-book store.

Lucky's Books & Comics (p144) Esoteric hidden gem with loyal Main St following.

Best Record Shops

Red Cat Records (p142) Cool array of vinyl and CDs.

Neptoon Records (p143) Classic vinyl-focused store, perfect for browsing.

Noize to Go (p95) Vinyl-hugging hot spot on the edge of Chinatown.

Zulu Records (p176) Giant selection in a *High Fidelity*–like setting.

Audiopile (p130) Well-priced new and used recordings, especially in the bargain racks.

Best Vintage Stores

Mintage Mall (p143) Upstairs shared vendor space in Mount Pleasant.

Eastside Flea (p95) Vintage clothes and crafts at this regular event.

Front & Company (p143) Lined with ironically cool used (plus new) clothing.

Wildlife Thrift Store (p76) Gigantic downtown shop with well-priced used clothing racks.

Best for Indie Designer Wear

Smoking Lily (p143) Cool clothes for the pale-and-interesting set.

Woo To See You (p112) Cleverly curated array of independent designer clothing from around the world.

John Fluevog Shoes (p95) Funky footwear, designed in Vancouver.

Gravity Pope (p176) Side-by-side fashion and footwear stores in Kitsilano.

Herschel Supply (p96) Vancouver-grown bags and accessories legend.

Best for Arts & Crafts

Pacific Arts Market (p159) Upstairs gallery lined with the works of dozens of artists and artisans.

Hill's Native Art (p144) First Nations creations from British Columbia (BC) and beyond.

Bird on a Wire Creations (p143) Irresistible selection of artisan-made goodies.

Granville Island Broom Company (p112) Handmade traditional brooms and more.

Urban Source (p143) Create your own masterpiece via this beloved craft store.

Best for Outdoor Gear

Mountain Equipment Co-op (p142) Western Canada's favorite outdoor-gear department store.

Arc'teryx (p177) Top-quality outerwear, made in BC.

Sports Junkies (p145) Great used gear and equipment.

Wanderlust (p176) Guidebooks plus a huge range of luggage and accessories.

Active Vancouver

Vancouver's variety of outdoorsy activities is a huge hook: you can ski in the morning and hit the beach in the afternoon; hike or bike scenic forests; paddleboard along the coastline; or kayak to your heart's content – and it will be content, with grand mountain views as your backdrop. There's also a full menu of spectator sports to catch here.

Running

For heart-pounding runs (or even just an arm-swinging walk), the 8.8km Stanley Park Seawall (p52) is Vancouver's top circuit. It's mostly flat, apart from some uphill sections where you might want to hang onto a passing bike. The University of British Columbia (UBC) is another popular running destination, with tree-lined trails throughout Pacific Spirit Regional Park. The Arbutus Greenway (p166) linear park is also an enticing option.

Hiking

Hiking is popular on local trails, including the infamous Grouse Grind (p182). Lighthouse Park and Whytecliff Park are also scenic North Shore gems. If you're heading into the mountains, be prepared for ever-changing conditions – the weather can alter suddenly and a sunny day in the city might not mean similar conditions in the mountains. For more information on local trails, see www.vancouvertrails.com.

Cycling & Mountain Biking

Vancouver is a cycle-friendly city with designated urban routes and a public bike-share scheme. For maps and resources, visit www.vancouver.ca/cycling. There's also a very active mountain-biking community on the North Shore; start your research via www.nsmba.ca and consider the forested runs at Mt Seymour (p188), including the 10km Seymour Valley Trailway.

Skiing & Snowboarding

You'll find excellent alpine skiing and snowboarding areas as well as cross-country skiing trails less than 30 minutes from downtown – it's where you'll find most locals when the powder arrives. The season typically runs from late November to early April, and the main ski areas are Grouse Mountain (p188), Cypress Mountain (p188) and Mt Seymour (p188).

On the Water

It's hard to beat the joy of a sunset kayak around the coastline here. But hitting the water isn't only about paddling: there are also plenty of opportunities to surf, kiteboard and stand-up paddleboard. Why not join the locals at the Jericho Sailing Centre to find out what's available? And when you want to head under the briny, there are several operators that can hook you up in and around the city.

Activities by Neighborhood

- **Downtown & West End** (p78) Adjoined by Stanley Park, Canada's favorite urban green space.
- **Kitsilano & University of British Columbia (UBC)** (p177) Kits is the center of local watersports, along with beloved local beaches.
- **North Shore** (p188) A magnet for skiers and snowboarders in winter plus hikers and mountain-bikers in summer.

Lonely Planet's Top Choices

Stanley Park Seawall (p52) Breathtakingly scenic walking, jogging and cycling trail.

Grouse Grind (p182) Steep rite-of-passage hiking trail.

Arbutus Greenway (p166) Walk, jog or bike the city's new linear park, from Kitsilano to the Fraser River.

Cypress Mountain (p188) Local-favorite ski and snowboard area.

Mt Seymour (p188) Ideal mountain-biking terrain.

Best Hikes

Grouse Grind (p182) 'Mother Nature's Stairmaster' is a steep climb to an attraction-packed lofty peak.

Stanley Park (p58) Swap the busy Seawall for the park's surfeit of tranquil interior trails.

Mt Seymour (p183) A verdant, sometimes-steep climb with dramatic mountain and city vistas.

Lighthouse Park (p184) Transit-accessible North Shore trail through the forest to a craggy, picnic-friendly oceanfront.

Lynn Canyon Park (p183) Many great rainforest walks available, including the signature Baden Powell Trail.

Best for Biking

Mobi (p246) Citywide public bike-share scheme.

Cycle City Tours (p248) Guided bike rides around Vancouver; rentals also available.

Reckless Bike Stores (p115) Popular bike-renting business, offering cruisers, mountain bikes and more.

Spokes Bicycle Rentals (p79) Kit out the family with various rental bikes; perfect for exploring nearby Stanley Park.

Stanley Park Seawall (p52) The city's favorite bike trail is 8.8km of forest and ocean delights.

Pacific Spirit Regional Park (p168) Tree-shaded trails in a nature-hugging 763-hectare park.

Best for Skiing

Grouse Mountain (p188) Popular and busy, especially for night skiing.

Cypress Mountain (p188) Former Olympic venue; great for snowboarding.

Mt Seymour (p188) Laid-back and quieter; popular with families.

Best Spectator Sports

Vancouver Canucks (p75) City's fave NHL hockey passion.

Vancouver Whitecaps (p111) The city's Major League Soccer team.

BC Lions (p111) Canadian Football League team, playing at BC Place.

Vancouver Canadians (p158) Minor league fun at a nostalgic old-school stadium.

NEED TO KNOW

Websites

Vancouver Parks & Recreation (www.vancouver.ca/parks) Comprehensive listings and information on city facilities and green spaces.

Bike Hub (www.bikehub.ca) Connect with the city's urban biking community.

Let's Go Biking (www.letsgobiking.net) Suggested bike routes around the region.

Outdoor Vancouver (www.outdoorvancouver.ca) Information on the local outdoorsy scene, including events and trail guides.

Buying Tickets

Vancouver Canucks (www.nhl.com/canucks) hockey tickets are the hardest to snag; book ahead via the team's website. It's easier – and cheaper to catch Whitecaps soccer matches or BC Lions Canadian football games, plus minor league Vancouver Canadians baseball. See individual team websites or Ticketmaster (www.ticketmaster.ca) for single tickets.

LGBTIQ+

Vancouver's LGBTIQ+ scene is part of the city's culture rather than a subsection of it. The legalization of same-sex marriage here makes it a popular spot for those who want to tie the knot in scenic style. But if you just want to kick back and have a good time, this is also Canada's top gay-tastic party city.

West End

The West End's Davie St is the traditional center of Vancouver's LGBTIQ+ scene. Sometimes called the Gay Village, this is Canada's largest 'gayborhood' and it's marked by hand-holding locals, pink-painted bus shelters and rainbow-striped street crossings. There's a full menu of scene-specific pubs and bars, and it's a warm and welcoming district for everyone, LGBTIQ+ or straight. Find the perfect spot sitting at a street-side cafe pretending to check your phone while actually checking out the passing talent; you can expect to make friends pretty quickly here. Commercial Dr is also a traditional center of the lesbian scene. Vancouver is highly gay-friendly, so you can expect events and happenings all around the city.

Nightlife

You're unlikely to run out of places to hang with the locals in Vancouver's lively LGBTIQ+ scene. Davie St, in particular, is home to a full bar crawl of diverse watering holes, from pubby haunts to slick lounge bars. You'll also find places to shake your thang on the dance floor here. But it's not all about the West End; look out for gay-friendly nights at clubs and bars around the city.

Pride Week

➡ Showing how far the scene has progressed since the days when Vancouver's gay community was forced to stay in the closet, **Pride Week** (www.vancouverpride.ca; West End; ⏲Aug) is now Canada's biggest annual LGBTIQ+ celebration. Staged around the first week of August, the centerpiece is the parade – a huge street fiesta of disco-pumping floats, drum-beating marching bands and gyrating, barely clad locals dancing through the streets as if they've been waiting all year for the opportunity. The parade is only the most visual evidence of Pride Week; this is also the time to dive into galas, drag contests, all-night parties and a popular queer film fest. Book your area hotel far in advance, since this is a highly popular event for visitors. During the same week, East Vancouver's annual **Dyke March** (www.vancouverdykemarch.com) concludes with a festival and beer garden in Grandview Park on Commercial Dr.

LGBTIQ+ by Neighborhood

➡ **Downtown & West End** (p50) West End's Davie St is Vancouver's gay scene central.

➡ **Commercial Drive** (p118) Traditional center of Vancouver's lesbian community.

Lonely Planet's Top Choices

Pride Week Canada's best pride celebration, with a rocking street parade.

Fountainhead Pub (p73) Laid-back, beer-friendly gay community pub.

1181 (p73) Smooth lounge bar; great spot to see and be seen.

Little Sister's Book & Art Emporium (p77) Long-time 'gayborhood' legend, stocking books and beyond.

Best Gay Bars

Fountainhead Pub (p73) Popular community pub with a lively patio.

Pumpjack Pub (p74) Sometimes raucous spot, great for making new friends.

1181 (p73) Smooth lounge bar with slick clientele.

Best Places to Watch the Pride Parade

Delany's Coffee House (p73) Denman St coffee shop with street-side tables.

Fountainhead Pub (p73) From the patio, wolf-whistling the passing locals.

Pumpjack Pub (p74) Watch the show through the open windows.

Vancouver Pride Society Float Catch it all from the back of a float!

Best Places to Recover After a Night Out

Little Sister's Book & Art Emporium (p77) Calm down and catch up on your reading.

Sylvia's Bar & Lounge (p72) Sip a hair-of-the-dog cocktail and watch the sunset.

Stanley Park Seawall (p52) Blow away the cobwebs with a jog, bike or hangover-busting walk.

NEED TO KNOW

➡ Check the online directory of the Gay & Lesbian Business Association of BC (www.loudbusiness.com) for all manner of local businesses, from dentists to spas and hotels.

➡ For local events and the inside track on the community, check www.gayvan.com and www.davievillagepost.ca.

➡ Head to www.superdyke.com for insights on the local lesbian scene.

➡ For support and resources of all kinds, Qmunity (www.qmunity.ca) provides discussion groups, a health clinic and advice for LGBTIQ+ locals and visitors.

➡ Contact Vancouver Pride Society (www.vancouverpride.ca) for the latest info on the Pride festival.

➡ For a fascinating introduction to the city's LGBTIQ+ history, check out the Really Gay History Tour hosted by **Forbidden Vancouver** (p248).

EINSTEIN BARATHYRAJ/SHUTTERSTOCK ©

Pride Week participant

Explore Vancouver & Victoria

VANCOUVER'S TOP EXPERIENCES

Neighborhoods at a Glance

❶ Downtown & West End p50

Vancouver's bustling heart occupies an ocean-fringed peninsula that divides into three: the grid-pattern city center of glass towers fanning from the intersection of Granville and West Georgia Sts; the West End's well-maintained residential side streets; and Stanley Park, Canada's finest urban green space.

❷ Gastown & Chinatown p80

Rapidly transforming in recent years, historic Gastown's brick-paved streets now house cool independent bars, boutiques and restaurants. Almost as old, sprawling Chinatown has recently begun gentrifying at an even faster rate – hence the new condo blocks and hipster coffee shops. These fascinating adjoining areas invite plenty of on-foot exploration.

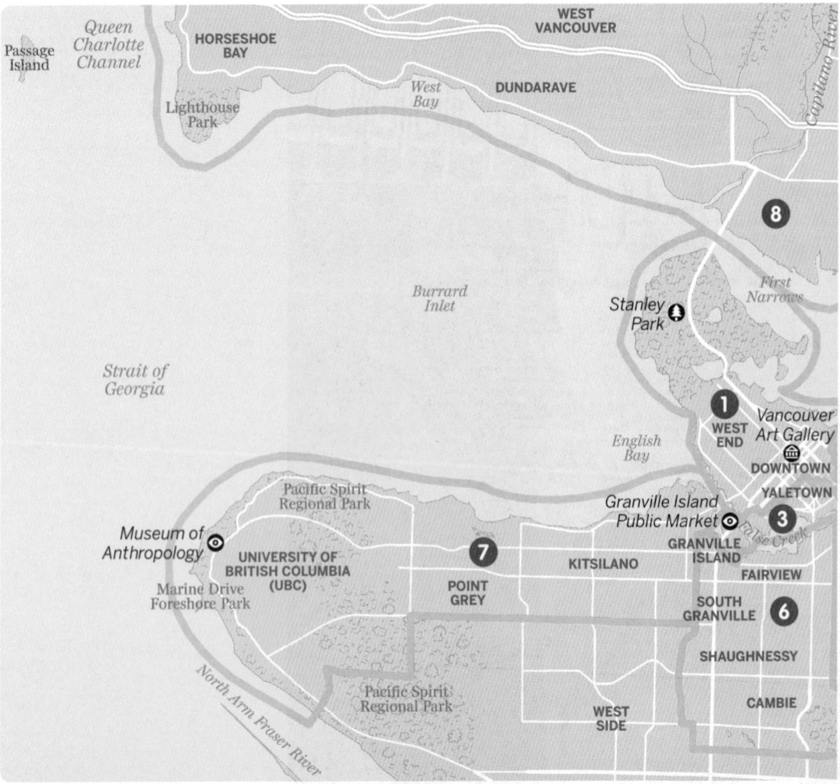

❸ Yaletown & Granville Island p98

A former rail yard on the edge of downtown, Yaletown is now lined with chic restaurants and posh boutiques. Across False Creek, Granville Island was an industrial hub for decades before being transformed in the 1970s into a haven of theaters, artisan studios and Western Canada's best public market.

❹ Commercial Drive p118

One of Vancouver's liveliest and most eclectic neighborhoods for a half-day stroll, the Drive is studded with quirky stores and coffee shops, each with their own distinctive, ever-welcoming character. A great dining strip, it's also near Vancouver's (and perhaps Canada's) tastiest microbrewery district.

❺ Main Street p131

The skinny-jeaned heart of Vancouver's hipster scene houses many of its best independent cafes, shops and restaurants. A great area to meet locals away from the city center, the area is developing rapidly. And that includes the Olympic Village, a waterfront neighborhood on False Creek that's continuing to add new ways to eat, drink and be merry.

❻ Fairview & South Granville p148

Combining the boutiques and restaurants of well-to-do South Granville with Fairview's busy Broadway thoroughfare and the cozy Cambie Village area, there's something for everyone here. It's also a great spot to meet the locals where they live, shop and socialize. Green-thumbed visitors will also find some top-notch park and garden attractions.

❼ Kitsilano & University of British Columbia (UBC) p162

Vancouver's West Side includes two major highlights: Kitsilano, with its beaches, heritage homes and browsable 4th Ave shopping and dining district; and the verdant UBC campus with its museums, galleries and garden attractions.

❽ North Shore p180

A scenic SeaBus hop from downtown Vancouver delivers you to a popular public market plus transit bus links to North Vancouver, West Vancouver and some of the region's most popular outdoor attractions, including major ski areas. Save time for North Van's landmark new art gallery (plus soon-to-open new museum), helping to transform a once-gritty shipyard district.

Downtown & West End

Neighborhood Top Five

❶ **Stanley Park Seawall** (p52) Strolling or cycling the winding perimeter pathway for incredible views of the forest-fringed ocean.

❷ **Marine Building** (p57) Spotting the multiple ocean- and transport-themed motifs on the exterior of this art-deco skyscraper masterpiece, then ducking inside to peruse the grand marble lobby.

❸ **Roedde House Museum** (p61) Nosing around the antique-lined rooms of this handsome, middle-class heritage home, an evocative reminder of well-to-do yesteryear Vancouver.

❹ **Vegan Pudding & Co** (p64) Hunting down this tiny hole-in-the-wall counter and trying to choose between matcha, chocolate and black sesame varieties.

❺ **Vancouver Public Library** (p60) Hitting the 9th-floor elevator button and heading up to a lofty public garden, complete with cityscape views.

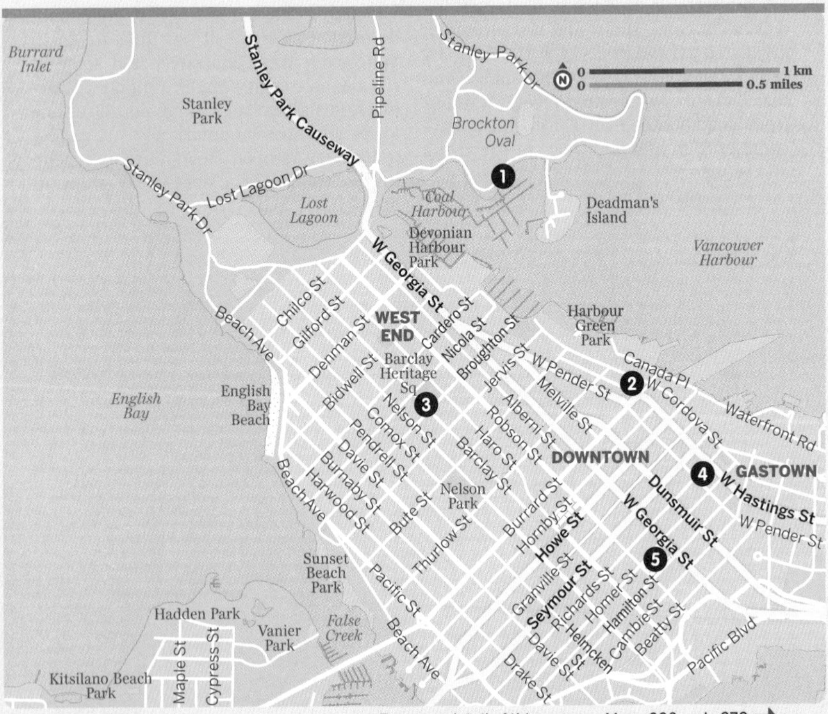

For more detail of this area see Map p266 and p270

Explore Downtown & West End

Radiating from the intersection of Granville and Georgia Sts, the downtown core is easily walkable. But start your exploration a few blocks north at waterfront Canada Place, heading slightly uphill along Burrard or Granville Sts. You'll pass plenty of stores and cafes before reaching Robson St, downtown's main shopping drag. Browse the boutiques here before arriving at the Robson and Denman intersection. Check out the West End's midrange restaurants, side-street heritage homes and friendly 'gayborhood' vibe. From either end of Denman, you can stroll into Stanley Park. Hitting the seawall here is highly recommended. It takes several hours to loop the park via this 8.8km pathway or you can just dip your toes in: walk the seawall from Georgia St to the totem poles and back or wander around Lost Lagoon where you'll almost certainly see raccoons, herons and sunbathing turtles.

Local Life

➡ **Bookshops** The intersection of Richards and W Pender Sts is home to several browse-tastic used bookstores, including old-school Macleod's Books (p76) and nearby young pup, Paper Hound (p76).

➡ **Restaurants** Join locals at the well-priced West End eateries on Denman and Davie Sts, including Japanese, Spanish and Indian options.

➡ **Galleries** Entry is by donation on Tuesday evenings at Vancouver Art Gallery (p55), and free on the first Friday of the month at the Bill Reid Gallery of Northwest Coast Art (p57).

Getting There & Away

➡ **Walk** Downtown's grid-system streets are highly walkable. It takes 30 minutes to reach Stanley Park from Vancouver City Centre station.

➡ **Train** SkyTrain's Expo Line and Canada Line both run through downtown. The lines come together (via a short indoor walk) at Waterfront Station.

➡ **Bus** Bus 5 runs along Robson and Denman Sts, bus 6 along Davie St, bus 10 along Granville St and bus 19 into Stanley Park.

➡ **Car** There are car parks and parking meters throughout downtown. The West End has metered parking; Stanley Park has pay-and-display parking.

Lonely Planet's Top Tip

Downtown has to two art-house cinemas. **Vancity Theatre** (p74), home of the **Vancouver International Film Festival** (p37), runs a full roster of movies year-round. The **Cinematheque** (p74) is equally popular; don't miss August's film noir season.

Best Places to Eat

➡ Forage (p69)

➡ Poke Guy (p64)

➡ Mumbai Local (p69)

For reviews, see p63. ➡

Best Places to Drink

➡ Railway Stage & Beer Cafe (p71)

➡ Uva Wine & Cocktail Bar (p71)

➡ Devil's Elbow Ale & Smoke House (p71)

➡ Prohibition (p71)

➡ Sylvia's Bar & Lounge (p72)

For reviews, see p70. ➡

Best Places to Shop

➡ Paper Hound (p76)

➡ Mink Chocolates (p76)

➡ Hunter & Hare (p76)

➡ Golden Age Collectables (p76)

➡ West End Farmers Market (p77)

For reviews, see p76. ➡

MICHAEL MCGIMPSEY/ALAMY STOCK PHOTO ©

TOP EXPERIENCE

CYCLE THE SEAWALL AT STANLEY PARK

One of North America's largest urban green spaces, Stanley Park is revered for its dramatic forest-and-mountain oceanfront views. But there's more to this 400-hectare woodland than looks. The park is studded with nature-hugging trails, family-friendly attractions, sunset-loving beaches and tasty places to eat. There's also the occasional unexpected sight to search for (besides the raccoons that call the place home).

DON'T MISS

- Seawall
- Lost Lagoon
- Stanley Park Nature House
- Stanley Park Train
- Third Beach

PRACTICALITIES

- Map p287, B2
- www.vancouver.ca/parks
- West End
- P, family-friendly
- bus 19

Seawall

Built in stages between 1917 and 1980, the park's 8.8km **seawall** (Map p287; Stanley Park; bus 19) trail is Vancouver's favorite outdoor hangout. Encircling the park, it offers spectacular waterfront vistas on one side and dense forest on the other. You can walk the whole thing in roughly three hours or rent a bike to cover the route far faster. Keep in mind: cyclists and in-line skaters must travel counterclockwise on the seawall, so there's no going back once you start your trundle (unless you walk). Also consider following the 25km of trails that crisscross the park's interior, including Siwash Rock Trail, Rawlings Trail and the popular Beaver Lake Trail (some routes are for pedestrians only). The Beaver Lake route is especially recommended; a family of beavers resides there and you'll likely spot them swimming around their large den.

The seawall also delivers you to some of the park's top highlights. You'll pass alongside the stately **HMCS Discovery** (Map p287; 1200 Stanley Park Dr, Deadman's Island) naval station and a twee **cricket pavilion** (Map p287; Brockton Oval) that looks like an interloper from Victorian England. About 1.5km from the W Georgia St entrance, you'll come to the ever-popular **totem poles** (Map p287; Brockton Point). Remnants of an abandoned 1930s plan to create a First Nations 'theme village,' the bright-painted poles were joined by some exquisitely carved Coast Salish welcome arches a few years back. For the full First Nations story, consider a fascinating guided park walk with Talaysay Tours (p248).

Once you've taken photos of the totems, continue on to the nearby **Nine O'Clock Gun** (Map p287; Seawall), which fires at 9pm nightly, and **Lumberman's Arch** (Map p287), which is a good spot to see Alaska cruise ships sliding past. From here, you can cut into the park to the popular **Vancouver Aquarium** (Map p287; ☎604-659-3400; www.vanaqua.org; 845 Avison Way, adult/child $38/21; ⏰9:30am-6pm Jul & Aug, 10am-5pm Sep-Jun; 👪) or continue around the seawall; it gets wilder and more scenic as you pass under the Lions Gate Bridge and face down the Pacific Ocean.

Natural Attractions

If you're keen to spot critters in their natural habitats, Stanley Park is studded with appeal for wildlife fans. A few steps from the park's W Georgia St entrance lies **Lost Lagoon** (Map p287), which was originally part of Coal Harbour. After a causeway was built in 1916, the new body of water was renamed, transforming itself into a freshwater lake a few years later. Today it's a bird-beloved nature sanctuary – keep your eyes peeled for blue herons – and its perimeter pathway is a favored stroll for wildlife nuts; expect to see a raccoon or two here. Plunging deeper into the park's more secluded trails, you'll also likely spot wrens, hummingbirds and chittering little Douglas squirrels. And while they mostly give humans a wide berth, you might also come across a coyote or two; treat them with respect and give them a wide berth as well. For an introduction to the area's flora and fauna, start at the Stanley Park Nature House (p61). You'll find friendly volunteers and exhibits on wildlife, history and ecology – ask about their well-priced guided walks.

Beaches & Views

If it's sandy beaches you're after, the park has several alluring options. **Second Beach** is a family-friendly area on the park's western side, with a grassy playground, an ice-cream-serving concession and a huge outdoor swimming pool (p79). It's also close to **Ceperley Meadows**, where **Fresh Air Cinema** (www.freshaircinema.ca; 👪) FREE offers popular free outdoor movie screenings in summer. But for a little more tranquility, try **Third Beach**. A sandy expanse with plenty of logs to sit against, this is a favored summer-evening destination for Vancouverites. The sky often comes alive with pyrotechnic color, while chilled-out locals munch through their picnics.

THE HOLLOW TREE

In its early tourist destination days, a giant western red cedar was Stanley Park's number one attraction. Although dead, the tree's bottom section had a massive hollowed-out area, inside which visitors would pose for photos, sometime in their cars. The fragile structure still remains, while artist Douglas Coupland has celebrated it with a latter-day golden replica. Take the Canada Line to Marine Drive Station in South Vancouver and you'll see this public artwork just across the street.

The only person to be legally buried in Stanley Park is writer Pauline Johnson. A champion of First Nations culture, her book on Coast Salish legends was a bestseller. When she died in 1913, thousands of locals lined the streets to mark her passing. Her memorial is a few steps from the seawall's Siwash Rock landmark.

There's a plethora of additional vistas in the park, but perhaps the most popular is at **Prospect Point.** One of Vancouver's best lookouts, this lofty spot is located at the park's northern tip. In summer you'll be jostling for elbow room with tour parties; heading down the steep stairs to the viewing platform usually shakes them off. Also look out for scavenging raccoons here (don't pet them). The area's recently revitalized Prospect Point Bar & Grill (p70) offers refreshments – aim for a deck table.

Statue Spotting

Stanley Park is studded with statues, all of which come to life at night (okay, just kidding). On your leisurely amble around the tree-lined idyll, look out for the following and award yourself 10 points for each one you find. If you locate them all, reward yourself with a pint at Stanley's Bar & Grill (p73). If you're on the seawall, it shouldn't be hard to spot *Girl in a Wetsuit*, a 1972 bronze by Elek Imredy that sits in the water. But how about the Robbie Burns statue unveiled by British prime minister Ramsay MacDonald in 1928 or the dramatic bronze of Canadian sprint legend Harry Jerome, who held six world records and won a bronze at the 1964 Summer Olympics? Here's a clue for the next one: it's near Malkin Bowl (p75). Marking the first official visit to Canada by a US president, this elegant statue is actually a memorial: after visiting in 1923, Warren Harding died a week later in San Francisco.

For Kids

It doesn't take much to plan an entire day with children here. As well as the aquarium and the Nature House, there are a couple of additional must-dos for under-10s. Beeline to the large **waterpark** (Map p287; Seawall; ⏲mid-Jun–Sep; 👪) FREE overlooking the waterfront near Lumberman's Arch; there's also a playground here. Dry the kids off with a trundle on the **Stanley Park Train** (Map p287; ☎604-257-8531; Pipeline Rd; adult/child $6.80/3.40; ⏲10am-5pm Jun-Sep, plus Easter, Halloween & Christmas; 👪); just a short stroll from the aquarium, this popular replica of the first passenger train that rolled into Vancouver in 1887 is a firm family favorite. The ride assumes several additional incarnations during the year: at Halloween, it's dressed up for ghost fans; and from late November it becomes a Christmas-decorated theme ride that's the city's most popular family-friendly Yuletide activity.

Don't forget to sample some ice creams at the counter alongside Prospect Point Bar & Grill (p70). And if it's still light when you're leaving the park, visit the man behind the fun day you've just had. Take the ramp running parallel with the seawall near the W Georgia St entrance and you'll find an almost-hidden **statue of Lord Stanley** (Map p287) with his arms outstretched, nestled in the trees. On his plinth are the words he used at the park's 1889 dedication ceremony: 'To the use and enjoyment of people of all colors, creeds and customs for all time.' It's a sentiment that still resonates loudly here today.

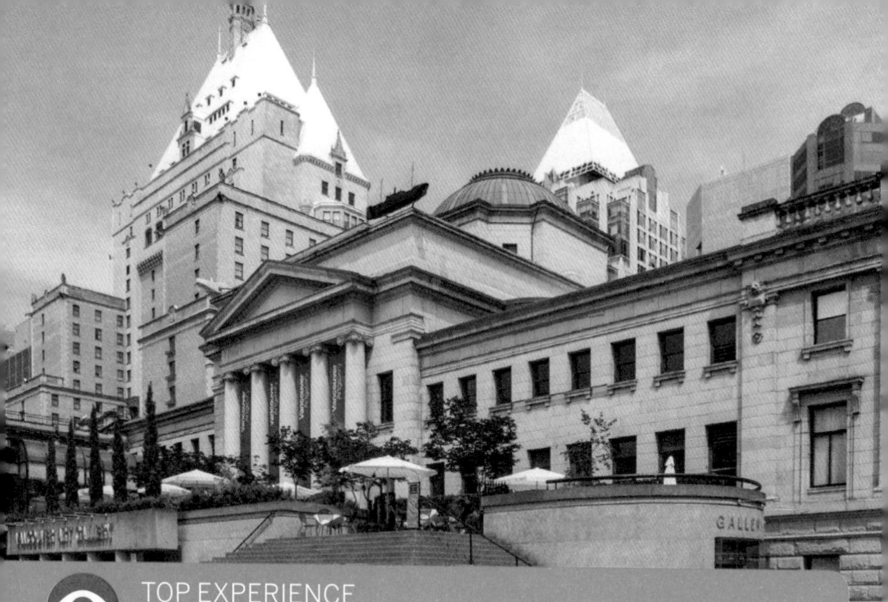

DEYMOSHR/SHUTTERSTOCK ©

TOP EXPERIENCE
EXPERIENCE NEW ART AT THE VAG

Residing in a heritage courthouse building but inching towards opening a fancy new venue any year now, the Vancouver Art Gallery (VAG) is the region's most important art gallery. Transformed in recent decades, it's also a vital part of the city's cultural scene. Contemporary exhibitions – often showcasing the Vancouver School of renowned photoconceptualists – are combined with blockbuster traveling shows from around the world.

VAG 101

Before you arrive at the VAG, check online for details of the latest exhibitions; the biggest shows of the year are typically in summer and it's often a good idea to arrive early or late in the day to avoid the crush, especially at the beginning or end of an exhibition's run. But the VAG isn't just about blockbusters. If you have time, explore this landmark gallery's other offerings. Start on the top floor, where British Columbia's most famous painter is often showcased. Emily Carr (1871–1945) is celebrated for her swirling, nature-inspired paintings of regional landscapes and First Nations culture. Watercolors were her main approach, and the gallery has a large collection of her works.

The city's more recent contribution to art is conceptual and postconceptual photography – usually referred to jointly as photoconceptualism. As you work your way around the gallery, you'll likely spot more than a few examples of works in this genre by the Vancouver School, a group of local artists from the 1980s onwards who have achieved national and international recognition. These include Roy Arden, Rodney Graham, Stan Douglas and – the most famous of the bunch – Jeff Wall. The best way to learn about these artists and others on display at the gallery is to take a free guided tour: these are usually held throughout the day on Thursdays, Saturdays and Sundays (especially in summer).

DON'T MISS

- Gallery tours
- FUSE
- Emily Carr paintings
- Gallery cafe
- Gallery shop

PRACTICALITIES

- Map p266, E3
- 604-662-4700
- www.vanartgallery.bc.ca
- 750 Hornby St, Downtown
- adult/child $24/6.50
- 10am-5pm Wed-Mon, to 9pm Tue
- 5

PLAZA NAMING RIGHTS

Almost $10 million was spent refurbishing the handsome plaza on the north side of the art gallery, which reopened to great fanfare in 2017. Along with new paving, seating and lighting, the city's main alfresco gathering place also gained a new First Nations name. The plaza's official moniker now incorporates the languages of the Musqueam, Squamish and Tsleil-Waututh. Don't worry about pronunciation; the City has created a handy YouTube video to show you how to say it.

With its columns and Trafalgar Sq–style lions, the grand 1907 VAG building was originally the Provincial Law Court. It was designed by Francis Rattenbury, who created many colonial-era British Columbia buildings, plus the yesteryear home in Vancouver's West End that's now Roedde House Museum (p61). His most famous constructions are in provincial capital Victoria, where his Parliament Buildings and Empress Hotel still loom over the Inner Harbour.

Join the Locals

The gallery isn't just a place to geek out over cool art. In fact, locals treat it as an important part of their social calendar. Every few months, the VAG stages regular FUSE (p75) socials, which transform the domed heritage venue into a popular evening event with DJs, bars, performances and gallery tours. Vancouverites dress up and treat the event as one of the highlights of the city's art scene. You'll likely see some of the same crowd at the gallery's regular roster of lectures and art talks. There are also family FUSE events where arty kids can have some fun, usually with plenty of interactive shenanigans.

The gallery's on-site, upper-level cafe is also one of downtown's most popular hangouts. Boasting the largest patio in the area, it's the perfect spot to drink in the downtown vibe, even if you're not visiting an exhibition. On your way out, hit the gallery shop; it's crammed with artsy trinkets, from Mondrian coasters to feline-themed nail clippers, and has some great art books.

Offsite

Three blocks from the VAG on W Georgia St – in the shadow of the Shangri-La Hotel – **Offsite** (Map p270; www.vanartgallery.bc.ca; 11 W Georgia St, West End; S Burrard) FREE is the gallery's somewhat incongruous but always thought-provoking outdoor installation space. The works are changed twice-yearly and they often inspire passersby to whip out their camera phones. Past installations have varied wildly but have included gigantic photo portraits of Chinese children, scale models of old cannery buildings and undulating earthquake debris. Take an easy detour to this street-side installation, and get ready to take some photos.

New Gallery

The VAG has been complaining about the limitations of its heritage building venue for many years and plans have now been announced for a new and far larger purpose-built art museum a few blocks away at the corner of W Georgia St and Cambie St. The dramatic plans resemble a towering array of wooden blocks piled on top of each other in what will certainly be one of the city's most striking contemporary structures. Although it may be several years before a new gallery opens, a feverish fundraising drive has been under way for some time and the construction project is expected to break ground any year now. Check the VAG's website for the latest updates. And also mull the future of the existing gallery building, which may become a new museum or cultural venue for the city.

SIGHTS

You can easily spend a whole day exploring the attractions and natural sights of Stanley Park. But the downtown core and the West End have their own appeal, including art galleries, historic buildings and bustling main streets that are the city's de facto promenades.

Downtown

VANCOUVER ART GALLERY — GALLERY

See p55.

★MARINE BUILDING — HISTORIC BUILDING

Map p266 (355 Burrard St, S Burrard) Vancouver's most romantic old-school tower block, and also its best art-deco building, the elegant 22-story Marine Building is a tribute to the city's maritime past. Check out its elaborate exterior of seahorses, lobsters and streamlined steamships, then nip into the lobby, which is like a walk-through artwork. Stained-glass panels and a polished floor inlaid with signs of the zodiac await.

Also check out the inlaid-wood interiors of the brass-doored elevators. The Marine Building was the tallest building in the British Empire when it was completed in 1930 and it's said to have bankrupted its original owners. It now houses offices.

BILL REID GALLERY OF NORTHWEST COAST ART — GALLERY

Map p266 (☎604-682-3455; www.billreidgallery.ca; 639 Hornby St, adult/youth/child $13/6/free; ⊙10am-5pm May-Sep, 11am-5pm Wed-Sun Oct-Apr; S Burrard) Showcasing detailed carvings, paintings, jewelry and more from Canada's most revered Haida artists and others around the region, this open-plan gallery occupies a handsome bi-level hall. Bookended by a totem pole at one end and a ceiling-mounted copper-lined canoe at the other, explore the cabinets of intricate creations and the stories behind them, including some breathtaking gold artifacts. On the mezzanine level, you'll come face-to-face with an 8.5m-long bronze of intertwined magical creatures, complete with impressively long tongues.

Reid, who died in 1998, is one of Canada's most celebrated artists; his work is on the back of the country's $20 bill. Guided tours and artist workshops are regularly scheduled here; check the website for upcoming tour times. And if you're traveling on a budget, keep in mind that admission is free on the first Friday of every month between 2pm and 5pm.

CHRIST CHURCH CATHEDRAL — CATHEDRAL

Map p266 (☎604-682-3848; www.thecathedral.ca; 690 Burrard St, ⊙10am-4pm Mon-Fri; S Burrard) FREE Completed in 1895 and designated as a cathedral in 1929, the city's most attractive Gothic-style church is nestled incongruously alongside looming glass towers. When services aren't being held, casual visitors are warmly welcomed: check out the dramatic hammerbeam wooden ceiling plus the slender glass-encased bell tower that was recently added to the exterior. The cathedral is also home to a wide range of cultural events, including regular choir and chamber music recitals and the occasional Shakespeare reading.

Peruse the kaleidoscopic array of stained-glass windows here, including a swirling contemporary creation on the cathedral's W Georgia St side.

CANADA PLACE — LANDMARK

Map p266 (☎604-665-9000; www.canadaplace.ca; 999 Canada Place Way, P 👪; S Waterfront) FREE Vancouver's version of the Sydney Opera House – judging by the number of postcards it appears on – this iconic landmark is shaped like sails jutting into the sky over the harbor. Both a cruise-ship terminal and a convention center, it's also a stroll-worthy pier, providing photogenic views of the busy floatplane action and looming North Shore mountains. Here for Canada Day on July 1? This is the center of the city's festivities, with displays, live music and a finale fireworks display.

Inside and outside the building there are permanent reminders of Canada's history and culture, from totem poles (inside) to the Canadian Trail (outside), a walking route illuminating the nation's 13 provinces and territories. Check out the pedestrian tunnel connecting the building to Waterfront Centre; it's lined with large-format photos of yesteryear Vancouver.

FLYOVER CANADA — THEATER

Map p266 (☎604-620-8455; www.flyovercanada.com; 999 Canada Pl, adult/child $33/23; ⊙10am-9pm, reduced hours in winter; 👪; S Waterfront) A breathtaking movie-screen simulator ride that makes you feel as if you're swooping across the entire country, waggling your legs

Stanley Park

A HALF-DAY TOUR

It's easy to be overwhelmed by Stanley Park, one of North America's largest urban green spaces. But there are ways to explore this spectacular waterfront swathe – from its top sites to hidden gems – without popping any blisters.

From the Georgia St entrance, trace the seawall around the shoreline to Brockton Point's ❶ **totem poles**. An early arrival means getting some snaps of these brightly painted carvings without fighting crowds.

From here, continue along the seawall. You'll pass a squat, striped lighthouse before reaching the Lumberman's Arch area. Duck under the road bridge and plunge into the park's tree-lined heart. Just ahead is ❷ **Vancouver Aquarium**, the park's most popular attraction.

Next up, follow the path to the ❸ **Stanley Park Train**. If you have kids in tow, take them for a trundle on this replica of the locomotive that pulled the first transcontinental passenger train into Vancouver.

From here, follow Pipeline Rd to the Tudoresque pavilion a few minutes away. In front is the ❹ **Malkin Bowl**, a hidden outdoor theater. Poke around the nearby manicured gardens, then continue southwards to Lost Lagoon. Follow the shoreline clockwise to ❺ **Stanley Park Nature House**, where you can learn about the park's flora and fauna.

Continue to the lagoon's western tip, then head to the ocean front ahead. Now on the park's rugged western side, follow the seawall northbound to ❻ **Third Beach**. Find a log perch and prepare for Vancouver's best sunset.

TOP TIPS

- When cycling the seawall, keep in mind that wheeled traffic is one-way only.
- The park is home to raccoons. Take pictures, but don't feed them.
- There are restaurants in the park if you're peckish.
- The meadow near Lumberman's Arch is a top picnic spot.

STUART DEE/GETTY IMAGES ©

Third Beach
Second Beach gets the crowds but Third Beach is where the savvy locals head. This is the perfect spot to drink in a sunset panorama over the lapping Pacific Ocean shoreline.

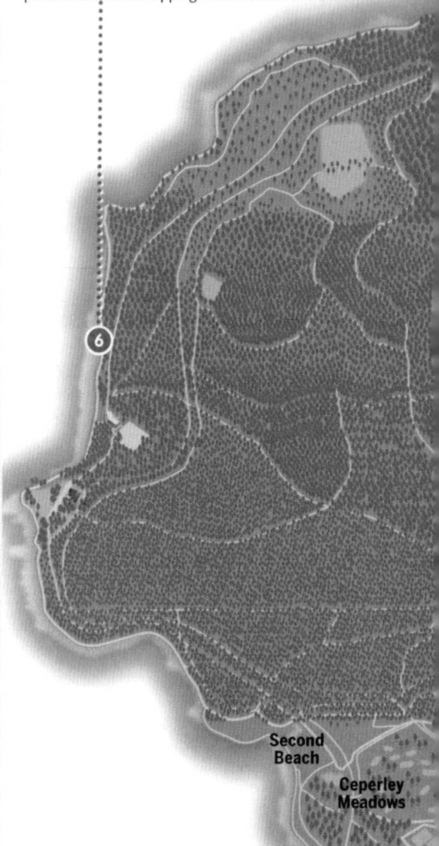

MARC STULKEN/SHUTTERSTOCK ©

Stanley Park Nature House
The freshwater Lost Lagoon was created when the Stanley Park Causeway was built. Its shoreline Nature House illuminates the park's plant and animal life and runs guided walks.

ASIF ISLAM/SHUTTERSTOCK ©

RAINER PLENDL/SHUTTERSTOCK ©

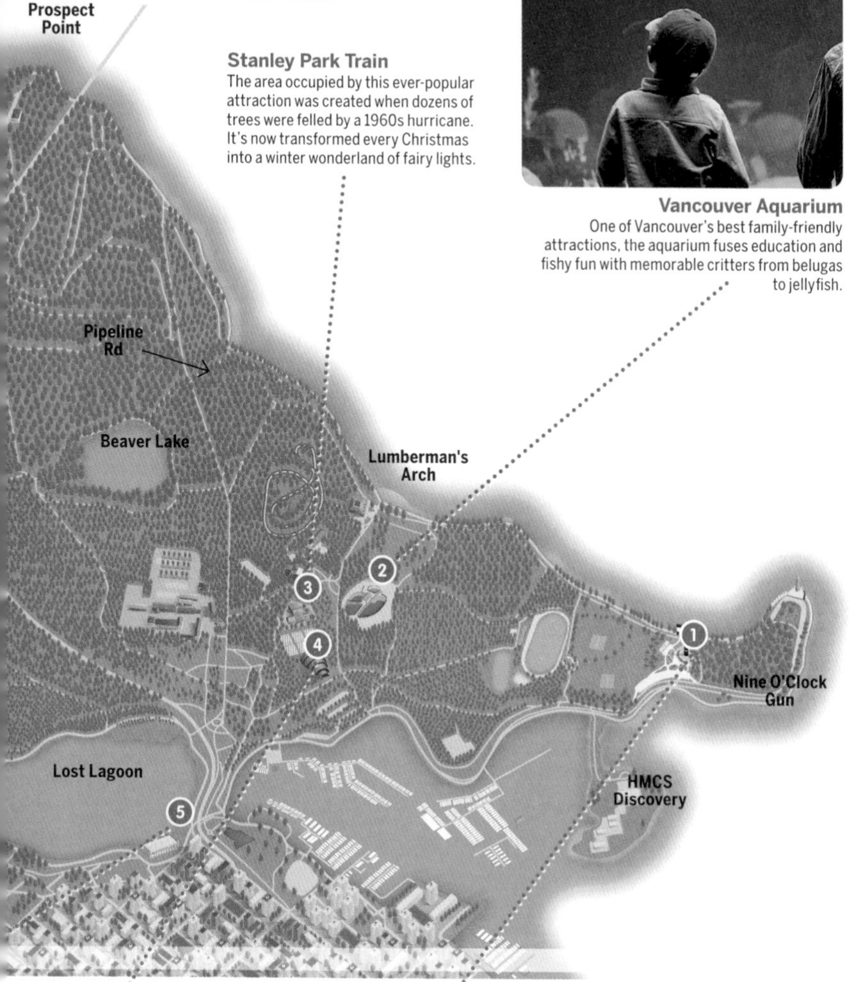

Stanley Park Train

The area occupied by this ever-popular attraction was created when dozens of trees were felled by a 1960s hurricane. It's now transformed every Christmas into a winter wonderland of fairy lights.

Vancouver Aquarium

One of Vancouver's best family-friendly attractions, the aquarium fuses education and fishy fun with memorable critters from belugas to jellyfish.

Malkin Bowl

Built by Vancouver mayor WH Malkin, this alfresco theater replaced an original bandstand. At the back of the seating area, you'll find a memorial statue to US president WG Harding.

Totem Poles

First Nations residents were still living here when Stanley Park was designated in 1888, but these poles were installed much later. The current poles are replicas of 1920s originals, carved in the 1980s.

LONELY PLANET/GETTY IMAGES ©

LOCAL KNOWLEDGE

HIDDEN ARTWORK

Enter the lobby of the **RBC Royal Bank** (Map p270; ☎604-665-6991; www.rbcroyalbank.com; 1025 W Georgia St, Downtown; ⊙9am-5pm Mon-Fri; SBurrard) at the corner of W Georgia and Burrard Sts, and head up in the escalator that's directly in front of you. At the top you'll find one of the largest First Nations artworks in Western Canada. Measuring 30m long and 2.5m high, the nine carved and painted red cedar panels of the spectacular 'Ksan Mural dramatically cover an entire wall of the building. It took five carvers three months to create in 1972, and it tells the story of Weget (or Man-Raven) and his often mischievous exploits. Well worth a look, the artwork seems a world away from the bustling streets outside. Continue your art crawl at the nearby Vancouver Art Gallery's Offsite (p56) location, a public art installation next to the Shangri-La Hotel (p209) that's changed twice a year and is well worth a selfie or two.

over grand landscapes and city landmarks from coast to coast. En route, your seat will lurch, your head will be sprayed and you'll likely have a big smile on your face. And once the short ride is over, you'll want to do it all again.

Book your tickets via the company's website for a 15% price reduction. And if you're here during the Christmas season, there's a special festive version of the ride.

JACK POOLE PLAZA — PLAZA

Map p266 (1085 Canada Pl, SWaterfront) Recalling Vancouver's 2010 Olympic Winter Games, this handsome waterfront public space is the permanent home of the tripod-like Olympic Cauldron. The flame is lit for special occasions (you can pay to have it switched on if you like). The plaza offers great views of the mountain-backed Burrard Inlet, and you can follow the shoreline walking trail around the Convention Centre West Building for public artworks and historic plaques.

CONTEMPORARY ART GALLERY — GALLERY

Map p266 (CAG; ☎604-681-2700; www.contemporaryartgallery.ca; 555 Nelson St; ⊙noon-6pm Tue-Sun; 🚌10) FREE A flexible three-room space, often with a different show in each, this smart, white-walled gallery exhibits striking, sometimes complex works in a wide range of media. Check ahead for talks, events and regular show openings, and save time for a visit to its tiny bookshop nook, lined with a cleverly curated array of volumes, art journals and framed prints.

The CAG has never been a snooty gallery space and it's also been working hard in recent years to broaden its appeal, including a recent collaboration to cover local buses in dramatic wrap-around art.

VANCOUVER PUBLIC LIBRARY — LIBRARY

Map p266 (☎604-331-3603; www.vpl.ca; 350 W Georgia St, Downtown; ⊙10am-9pm Mon-Thu, to 6pm Fri & Sat, 11am-6pm Sun; P 👪; SStadium-Chinatown) This dramatic Colosseum-like building must be a temple to the great god of libraries. If not, it's certainly one of the world's most magnificent book-lending facilities. Designed by Moshe Safdie and opened in 1995, its collections (including lendable musical instruments) are arranged over several floors. Head straight up to floor nine for the **Rooftop Garden**, a lofty, tree-lined outdoor plaza lined with tables and chairs: it's perfect for a view-hugging coffee break.

There's free wi-fi, and computer terminals if you don't have your own device. The library also hosts a lively roster of gratis book readings and events. Save time for the library shop; it's crammed with cool bookish gifts.

OR GALLERY — GALLERY

Map p266 (☎604-683-7395; www.orgallery.org; 555 Hamilton St; ⊙noon-5pm Tue-Sat; SStadium-Chinatown) FREE A small, contemporary, artist-run gallery with a loyal in-the-know following; check out the ever-changing, often abstract shows here, from photography to multimedia and beyond. There are regular talks to deepen your understanding of the exhibits; the website lists upcoming events. And don't miss the word-based public art installations on the exterior of the heritage hotel building the gallery occupies.

There's also an intriguing array of cool art books for sale here, many of them produced directly by artists; check ahead for book launches.

ROGERS ARENA STADIUM

Map p266 (☎604-899-7400; www.rogersarena.ca; 800 Griffiths Way; tours adult/child $18/12; ⏲tours 10:30am, 12:15pm & 2pm Wed-Sat, noon, 1:30pm & 3pm Sun; P; S Stadium-Chinatown) This large multipurpose stadium hosts the National Hockey League's Vancouver Canucks. On game nights, when the 20,000-capacity venue heaves with fervent fans, you'll enjoy the atmosphere even if the rules are a mystery. It's also home to a large Canucks team shop and is a favored arena for money-spinning stadium rock acts. Behind-the-scenes one-hour tours take you into the hospitality suites and the nosebleed press box up in the rafters, and are popular with visiting sports fans.

If you're coming for a game, special game-day tours are also available ($25 per person); these include the chance to catch 30 minutes of team practice before you take the stadium tour.

VANCOUVER LOOKOUT VIEWPOINT

Map p266 (☎604-689-0421; www.vancouverlookout.com; 555 W Hastings St; adult/child $18.25/9.50; ⏲8:30am-10:30pm Jun-Sep, 9am-9pm Oct-May; P; S Waterfront) Expect your lurching stomach to make a bid for freedom as the glass elevator whisks you 169m to the apex of this needle-like viewing tower in just 40 seconds. Once up top, there's not much to do but check out the awesome 360-degree vistas of city, sea and mountains unfurling around you. For context, peruse the historic photo panels that show just how much the downtown core has changed over the years.

Tickets are valid all day; return for a soaring sunset view of the city to get your money's worth. There's also a small discount if you buy from the website in advance. If you want to save even more, drop by on Urban Grind days in March when $5 gives you the chance to walk up the 633 steps from the ground floor to the Lookout. If you're still alive when you reach the top, you'll get a free beer.

PENDULUM GALLERY GALLERY

Map p266 (☎604-250-9682; www.pendulumgallery.bc.ca; 885 W Georgia St, HSBC Bldg; ⏲9am-6pm Mon-Wed, to 9pm Thu & Fri, to 5pm Sat; S Burrard) FREE A creative use for a cavernous bank building atrium, this gallery offers a varied roster of temporary exhibitions. It's mostly contemporary art and can range from striking paintings to challenging photographs and quirky arts and crafts. The space also houses one permanent exhibit: a gargantuan 27m-long buffed aluminum pendulum that will be swinging over your head throughout your visit.

⊙ West End

STANLEY PARK PARK

See p52.

★**ROEDDE HOUSE MUSEUM** MUSEUM

Map p270 (☎604-684-7040; www.roeddehouse.org; 1415 Barclay St; $5, Sun $8; ⏲1-4pm Tue-Fri & Sun; 🚌5) For a glimpse of what the West End looked like before the apartment blocks, visit this handsome 1893 Queen Anne–style mansion, now a lovingly preserved museum. Designed by infamous architect Francis Rattenbury, the yesteryear, antique-studded rooms have a lived-in feel while its guided tour (included with admission) tells you all about its middle-class Roedde family residents. Look out for the cylinder record player, 250-year-old grandfather clock and the taxidermied deer heads that were hunted in Stanley Park in 1906.

Consider visiting on Sunday when your $8 ticket includes cookies and tea served in vintage china teacups. This is also one of Vancouver's most evocative live music venues, staging regular jazz or classical concerts (tickets $15) in its downstairs rooms. The home is in **Barclay Heritage Square**, a one-block site containing nine historic West End houses dating from 1890 to 1908.

STANLEY PARK NATURE HOUSE NATURE RESERVE

Map p287 (☎604-257-8544; www.stanleyparkecology.ca; north end of Alberni St, Lost Lagoon, Stanley Park; ⏲10am-5pm Tue-Sun Jul & Aug, 10am-4pm Sat & Sun Sep-Jun; 👪; 🚌19) FREE Illuminating the breathtaking array of flora and fauna just steps from the busy streets of the West End, this charming nature center is a great introduction to Stanley Park's wild side. The chatty volunteers will tell you all you need to know about the area's critters, from coyotes to Douglas squirrels and from blue herons to black-capped chickadees. Guided nature walks are also offered or you can wander the park's trails on your own armed with your new-found wildlife expertise.

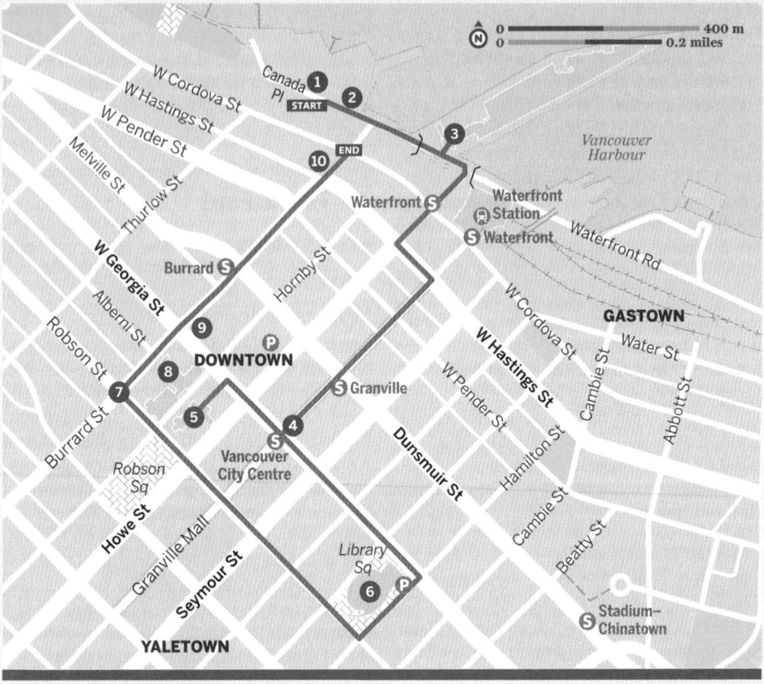

Neighborhood Walk Downtown Grand Tour

START OLYMPIC CAULDRON
END MARINE BUILDING
LENGTH 3KM; ONE HOUR

Start at the 1 **Olympic Cauldron**, a shiny reminder of the 2010 Winter Games, then continue southeast to the adjacent 2 **Convention Centre West Building**. Peruse the outdoor artworks around its perimeter, then head to next door's landmark 3 **Canada Place** (p57). Watch the floatplanes diving onto the water from its outer promenade.

Next, head southwest along Howe St, turn left onto W Hastings St and then right onto bustling Granville St. Follow this uphill thoroughfare past coffee shops, clothing stores and the sprawling Pacific Centre shopping mall.

Get your bearings at the busy 4 **Granville & W Georgia** intersection, then nip across one block to the 5 **Vancouver Art Gallery** (p55). The plaza on its north side is a food truck magnet.

From here, stroll southeast a couple of blocks to the Colosseum-like 6 **Vancouver Public Library** (p60). Pop inside, hit the elevators to level 9 and you'll reach the lofty Rooftop Garden with its amazing cityscape views.

Head northwest from here along Robson St, the city's mainstream shopping strip. Browse to your credit card's content, but also check out the restaurants for dinner options.

Take a breather at the intersection of 7 **Robson & Burrard streets**, then turn right along Burrard with the mountains ahead of you. Duck into the grand 8 **Fairmont Hotel Vancouver** (p207), then return to Burrard and continue downhill to 9 **Christ Church Cathedral** (p57). You'll soon be back at Canada Place. But before that, visit the 10 **Marine Building** (p57), an art-deco skyscraper masterpiece.

The guided walks are great value, priced from $7 per person, and you can check the website to see what's on the calendar during your visit. Booking ahead is recommended in summer.

A-MAZE-ING LAUGHTER STATUE

Map p270 (Morton Park, cnr Davie St & Denman Sts; 6) Created by Yue Minjun, one of Vancouver's most-photographed public artworks is just a few steps from English Bay Beach. Expect to see groups of smiling visitors snapping shots of the 14 oversized bronzes, each of them looking like they're about to explode with overabundant giggles.

ENGLISH BAY BEACH BEACH

Map p270 (cnr Denman St & Beach Ave; 5) Wandering south on Denman St, you'll spot a clutch of palm trees ahead announcing one of Canada's best urban beaches where a summertime party atmosphere has locals catching rays and panoramic ocean views... or just ogling the volleyballers prancing around on the sand.

Be sure to snap a few photos of the beach's towering *inukshuk* (Inuit sculpture), south of the main area, or just continue along the seawall into neighboring Stanley Park (p58). The beach is a popular (but crowded) spot to catch the annual **Celebration of Light** (www.hondacelebrationoflight.com; English Bay; late Jul; ; 6) fireworks festival, and it's also where the city's wildly popular **Polar Bear Swim** takes place on January 1.

COAL HARBOUR SEAWALL WATERFRONT

Map p270 (Canada Pl to Stanley Park; S Waterfront) An idyllic 2km waterfront stroll from Canada Place to Stanley Park, this is a perfect way to spend a sunny afternoon. En route you'll pass the landmark convention center, the sparkling Olympic Cauldron and intriguing historic panels. Take a break at the grassy nook of Harbour Green Park as well as the *Light Shed* artwork, a replica of one of the many marine sheds that once lined this area.

Look out for the cozy houseboats in the marina near the Westin Bayshore hotel, where Howard Hughes holed up for three months in 1972. Continue a few more minutes and you'll be on the fringes of Stanley Park (p58), where the seawall continues right around the park.

ROBSON STREET AREA

Map p266 (604-669-8132; www.robsonstreet.ca; Robson St, Downtown; 5) Locals, tourists and recent immigrants – count the number of accents you catch as you stroll here – throng the shops and restaurants of Robson St, Vancouver's de facto urban promenade. While most shops are of the ubiquitous chain-store variety, the strip is worth a wander for its urban vibe, especially on summer evenings when buskers and street cartoonists set up shop.

It's also worth heading to the Stanley Park (p58) end of the strip, where you'll find a modern 'mini-Asia' of *izakayas* (Japanese neighborhood pubs) and noodle bars populated by homesick Japanese and Korean students. Turn the corner to your left on to Denman St to discover a United Nations of cheap-and-cheerful dining. Tired of walking? Bus 5 runs the length of Robson as well.

EATING

Vancouver's downtown and West End areas offer a jam-packed menu of dining options, from sushi joints to busy brunch spots and from sandwich bars to top-end fine dining. And while Stanley Park is a short stroll or an easy bus hop to many nearby options, it also has its own eateries if you're looking to sate your appetite without straying too far from the seawall.

Downtown

★**CHANCHO TORTILLERIA** MEXICAN $

Map p266 (604-428-8494; www.chancho.ca; 1206 Seymour St; mains $8-12; 11:30am-7pm Mon-Sat, to 5:30pm Sun; ; 10) Look for the pig-and-pineapple sign outside this authentic Mexican hole-in-the-wall, which has painted walls, plastic garden chairs and a super-friendly welcome. It's the food that'll keep you smiling, though; order meat or vegetarian fillings by weight, all served with beans, salsa, pickled red cabbage and house-made tortillas.

Avoid the lunchtime rush if you can, and be sure to try a blood-red hibiscus beverage. Pinto-bean soup is a good alternative on chilly days.

WORTH A DETOUR

BELLA GELATERIA

You'd be forgiven for feeling skeptical about just how good North American gelato can be. After all, this isn't Italy. But that's before you've found the time to step into downtown's little Bella Gelateria. Dive into the dozens of ever-changing flavors and you'll likely find eye-rollingly amazing treats such as Thai coconut and salted caramel.

★VEGAN PUDDING & CO — DESSERTS $

Map p266 (778-379-0545; www.veganpuddingco.com; 422 Richards St; dessert $3-5; 11am-7pm Mon-Sat; ; 14) There's a cult-like following in Vancouver for this hole-in-the-wall counter serving utterly delicious custard-style puddings made from kabocha squash, coconut milk and flavors including strawberry, chocolate and matcha green tea. It's a silky-smooth revelation to those who think dairy is the only way. All ingredients are organic and you'll also find these puddings at green grocery stores around the city.

You are well advised to buy more than one pot since you'll want to start the next one as soon as you've finished the first.

BAGHDAD CAFE — MIDDLE EASTERN $

Map p266 (604-428-2525; www.facebook.com/baghdadcafevancouver; 548 Seymour St; mains $7-12; 9am-10pm Mon-Sat; Granville) A slender, fancy-free spot serving hearty, good-value Iraqi dishes to in-the-know diners. Expect friendly service, platters of chicken and lamb with rice and fresh-chopped salad, plus line-ups at lunchtime as local students and office workers flock in. Iraqi tea is often on the menu and if you can't find a seat, nearby Cathedral Square has lots of alfresco perches.

FINCH'S — CAFE $

Map p266 (604-899-4040; www.finchteahouse.com; 353 W Pender St; mains $6-12; 9am-5pm Mon-Fri, 11am-4pm Sat; ; 4) For a coveted seat at one of the dinged old tables, arrive off-peak at this sunny, super-friendly corner cafe, which combines creaky wooden floors and a junk-shop bric-a-brac aesthetic. Join hipsters and office workers who've been calling this their local for years and who come mainly for the freshly prepared baguette sandwiches (pear, blue Brie, prosciutto and roasted walnuts recommended).

POKE GUY — HAWAIIAN $

Map p266 (778-379-8455; www.thepokeguy.ca; 420 Richards St; mains $9-14; 11am-7pm Mon-Fri, 11:30am-6pm Sat; ; 14) Trip down the steps (not literally) to this busy spot and you'll find one of the city's favorite *poke* destinations. Expect friendly service, heaped bowls of fresh, quality ingredients and a choice of set options (salmon belly *lomi lomi* recommended) or build-your-own bowls, all available in two sizes. Good value: you'll feel fully fortified for your downtown on-foot exploration.

Aside from the ahi, albacore and sockeye options, there's also a popular tofu bowl for vegetarians here.

TRACTOR — CAFE $

Map p266 (604-343-1195; www.tractorfoods.com; 335 Burrard St, Marine Bldg; 7am-9:30pm Mon-Fri, from 8am Sat & Sun; ; Waterfront) At this healthy fast-food cafeteria, step up to the counter and choose a protein (chicken, ahi tuna or tofu, for example) as well as two sides to add to your rice or power greens bowl. Soups, stews, salads and toasted sandwiches are also available but make sure you add a house-made lemonade – there's usually a tempting flavor or two.

HERITAGE ASIAN EATERY — ASIAN $

Map p270 (778-737-1108; www.eatheritage.ca; 1108 W Pender St; mains $12-18; 11am-8pm; ; Burrard) A contemporary hole-in-the-wall favored by local office workers (avoid the lunchtime peak, if you can), this friendly fusion joint specializes in hearty rice bowls (duck or pork belly recommended) made with top-notch ingredients. Add a side of spicy chicken wings if you're starving and pick up a warm egg custard bun to go on your way out the door.

CARTEMS DONUTERIE — DESSERTS $

Map p266 (778-708-0996; www.cartems.com; 534 W Pender St; doughnuts from $3.25; 7am-8pm Mon-Thu, to 10pm Fri, 10am-10pm Sat, 10am-6pm Sun; ; 14) Vancouver's coolest doughnut emporium offers a raft of fresh-made fusion treats with irresistible flavors including Earl Grey, salted caramel and the truly spectacular smoked maple walnut, all served with a large dollop of smiley service. Pick up a large red box of take-out doughnuts for the road – essential for staving off sugar-related starvation and making new friends on the bus.

Still hungry? There are Kitsilano and Main St branches as well.

DIRTY APRON DELICATESSEN CAFE $

Map p266 (604-879-8588; www.dirtyapron.com/delicatessen; 540 Beatty St; mains $9-12; 8:30am-5:30pm Mon-Fri, to 5pm Sat; Stadium-Chinatown) Avoid the cult of Jam (p66), the lineup-heavy brunchery along the street, and slip into this friendly cafe with its gourmet soups and baguette sandwiches, coffee bar bakery treats and tempting breakfast menu (served until 11am weekdays and 2pm weekends). Start your day with avocado toast or a salmon-topped biscuit then peruse the for-sale shelves of artisan sauces and condiments.

JAPADOG JAPANESE $

Map p266 (604-569-1158; www.japadog.com; 530 Robson St; mains $6-12; 6:30am-10pm Mon-Fri, 7:30am-11pm Sat, 7:30am-9pm Sun; 10) You'll have spotted the lunchtime line-ups at the Japadog hotdog stands around town, but this was their first storefront, opening back in 2010. The ever-*genki* Japanese expats serve up a menu of lip-smacking wonder wieners – think turkey smokies with miso sauce and crunchy shrimp tempura dogs – but there are also irresistible fries (try the butter and *shoyu* version).

The menu has recently branched out into breakfast and there's also a fun dessert to dive into: a deep-fried bun filled with ice cream. The tiny tables are usually taken here, but the take-out window does a roaring trade.

WAKWAK BURGER BURGERS $

Map p266 (778-998-0285; www.facebook.com/wakwakburgerdesu; 511 Granville St; burgers $3-5; 11am-7pm Mon & Wed-Fri, noon-6pm Sat; Waterfront) Downtown's best cheap and cheerful burger option, this popular Japanese-fusion food truck offers a great-value $2.99 staple. Made with hand-formed patties, it's far superior to the usual fast-food joints. There are also several slightly pricier alternatives, including a finger-licking teriyaki cheeseburger. Add fries and a drink for $3.70, then snag a nearby bench and beware the hungry-looking gulls.

BELLA GELATERIA ICE CREAM $

Map p266 (604-569-1010; www.bellagelateria.com; 1001 W Cordova St; cone from $6.75; 11am-10pm Mon-Thu, to 11pm Fri, 10:30am-11pm Sat, 10:30am-10pm Sun; Waterfront) An ownership change has not diminished the slavering appeal of this queue-magnet gelato spot, especially since inventive flavors such as black sesame, salted caramel and matcha green tea await. Seats are at a premium, so pick up your cone to-go and head around the corner to the red metal benches on Burrard St; they're perfect for sunny-day gelato-scoffing basking.

FIELD & SOCIAL CAFE $$

Map p266 (778-379-6500; www.fieldandsocial.com; 415 Dunsmuir St; mains $13-15; 11am-7pm Mon-Thu, to 3pm Fri, 10:30am-3pm Sat; Stadium-Chinatown) A plant-diet-loving cafe with a menu of 10 or so top-notch, fresh-tossed salads made with seasonal, regional ingredients. This is a great place to salve your conscience over all those Tim Hortons doughnuts you've been eating. Order at the end of the L-shaped counter – we recommend the delicious Rustic Orzo bowl – and find a communal table spot to dive in.

TEMPLETON DINER $$

Map p266 (604-685-4612; www.thetempleton.ca; 1087 Granville St; mains $8-18; 8:30am-10pm Sun-Thu, to 11pm Fri & Sat; 10) A chrome-and-vinyl 1950s-look diner with a twist, Templeton serves plus-sized organic burgers, addictive fries, vegetarian quesadillas (plus vegan options) and the best hangover cure in town – the 'Big Ass Breakfast.' Play the mini jukeboxes on the tables and add a local R&B craft beer to your meal. Avoid weekend peak times or you'll be queuing for ages.

LOCAL KNOWLEDGE

You can't throw a Tim Hortons doughnut in the city center without hitting a restaurant. While there are plenty of midrange options and a smattering of celebrity-fave high-end locations radiating from Robson St, there are also some rewarding ethnic eateries and quirky backstreet joints hidden slightly off the beaten path.

FOOD TRUCK FRENZY

Keen to emulate the legendary street-food scenes of Portland and Austin, Vancouver jumped on the kitchen-equipped bandwagon a few years back. On fine-weather days, there are typically dozens of vendors dotted around the city, serving everything from halibut tacos to Korean sliders, pulled-pork sandwiches to French crepes. Prices are typically $10 to $14 per main.

While there are a number of experimental fusion trucks, several have quickly risen to the top; look out for local favorites Tacofino, Chickpea, Le Tigre, Mom's Grilled Cheese and Vij's Railway Express. Locating the trucks can sometimes be challenging; there are usually a couple outside the Vancouver City Centre Canada Line station and on busy stretches of downtown arteries such as Georgia, Robson and around the Vancouver Art Gallery perimeter. Also look out for the trucks at local festivals, city farmers markets and outside some microbreweries (you're allowed to eat your truck takeout inside the brewery tasting rooms).

For up-to-the-minute listings, hours and locations, the handy www.streetfoodapp.com/vancouver website tells you exactly where to go. But if you're keen to loosen your belt and sample as many options as you can in one belly-busting afternoon, hop on the SkyTrain to New Westminster in late July or early August. That's when the one-day, free-entry **Columbia StrEAT Food Truck Fest** invites more than 100 trucks to strut their kitchen-busting stuff alongside several live music stages. See www.downtownnewwest.ca for details.

JAM CAFE — BREAKFAST $$

Map p266 (☎778-379-1992; www.jamcafes.com; 556 Beatty St; mains $9-17; ⊙8am-3pm; 📶✍; Ⓢ Stadium-Chinatown) The Vancouver outpost of Victoria's wildly popular breakfast and brunch superstar lures the city's longest line-ups, especially on weekends. Reservations are not accepted so you're well advised to dine off-peak and during the week. You'll find a white-walled room studded with Canadian knickknacks and a huge array of satisfying options, from chicken and biscuits to red-velvet pancakes.

CAFE MEDINA — BISTRO $$

Map p266 (☎604-879-3114; www.medinacafe.com; 780 Richards St; mains $9-19; ⊙8am-3pm Mon-Fri, from 9am Sat & Sun; 📶; Ⓢ Vancouver City Centre) At this lively, wood-floored breakfast-brunch-lunch favorite, finding a table can be tricky. But it's worth the wait if you're a waffle fan: the light and fluffy treats come with gourmet toppings including raspberry caramel and chocolate lavender. Alternatively, go the savory route: excellent paella and cassoulet dishes are available, while the Wolves Breakfast will fill you up for days.

It's never too early for a breakfast libation, of course; the full drinks menu here includes a daily 9am-to-11am happy hour with beer, cocktail and mimosa specials.

TWISTED FORK BISTRO — BREAKFAST $$

Map p266 (☎604-568-0749; www.forkandfriends.ca; 1147 Granville St; mains $17.50; ⊙8:30am-4pm; 📶; 🚌10) Granville Strip's best brunch, this narrow, art-lined bistro feels as if it should be somewhere else. But even clubbers need to eat well sometimes. The menu is a well-curated array of classic and adventurous choices, which means selecting from endlessly tempting options. Go the eggs Benny route, with pulled pork or smoked salmon (or both).

If you were out late the night before, there are five hair-of-the-dog cocktail options to salve your aching head. Try them all if you're really struggling.

GYOZA BAR — JAPANESE $$

Map p266 (☎604-336-5563; www.gyozabar.ca; 622 W Pender St; mains $9-18; ⊙11:30am-9pm Mon & Tue, to 10pm Wed-Fri, noon-10pm Sat, noon-9pm Sun; 📶; 🚌14) A long, brick-lined room with a chatty vibe and a menu packed with Japanese comfort dishes, there's much more than gyoza on the table here. Start with an order of those soft, crispy-edged parcels (classic pork recommended) then dive into a brothy bowl of ramen noodles. Looking for a weekend brunch alternative? Their pulled pork bao benny is delicious.

CHAMBAR EUROPEAN $$$

Map p266 (☎604-879-7119; www.chambar.com; 568 Beatty St; mains $28-36; ⏰8am-11pm; P; S Stadium-Chinatown) This giant, brick-lined cave is a juggernaut of Vancouver's dining scene, serving an ever-changing all-day menu of sophisticated Belgian-esque dishes from morning waffles to excellent *moules frites* to a lip-smacking dinnertime lamb shank with figs and couscous. An impressive wine and cocktail list (try a blue-fig martini) is coupled with a great Belgian beer menu dripping with *tripels* and *lambics*.

LE CROCODILE FRENCH $$$

Map p270 (☎604-669-4298; www.lecrocodilerestaurant.com; 909 Burrard St; mains $22-46; ⏰11:30am-2:30pm Mon-Fri & 5:30-10pm Mon-Sat; 🚌2) Behind half-curtained windows in a somewhat unassuming building that looks more like a cast-off from a shopping mall, this excellent Parisian-style dining room is right up there with the city's top-end best. Instead of focusing on experimental shenanigans that only please the chefs, it's perfected a menu of classic French dishes, each prepared with consummate cooking skill and served by perfect, snob-free wait staff.

Try the sumptuous slow-roasted rack of lamb, washed down with a smashing bottle of red from the mother country.

HAWKSWORTH NORTHWESTERN US $$$

Map p266 (☎604-673-7000; www.hawksworthrestaurant.com; 801 W Georgia St; mains $38-58; ⏰7am-11pm; P 📶; S Vancouver City Centre) The fine-dining anchor of the top-end Rosewood Hotel Georgia (p207) is a see-and-be-seen spot for swank dates and business meetings. Created by and named after one of Vancouver's top chefs, David Hawksworth. Its menu is a fusion of contemporary West Coast approaches with clever international influences, hence dishes such as ling cod with orange lassi. There's also a *prix fixe* lunch ($28). Reservations are recommended for dinner.

West End

LITTLE JUKE CHICKEN $

Map p270 (☎604-336-5853; www.jukefriedchicken.com; 1074 Davie St; mains $6-16; ⏰11am-10:30pm Sun & Tue-Thu, to 11:30pm Fri & Sat; 📶; 🚌6) The tiny West End satellite of a popular Chinatown southern fried chicken joint, expect a finger-licking array of tender, deliciously coated pieces (from two to 10 pieces) or, better yet, go for a hearty bowl of chicken fries or the bulging Big Boy sandwich. There's a good selection of local craft beer drafts. Planning on dining in? Make sure to arrive during off-peak hours to ensure a table.

KINTARO RAMEN NOODLE RAMEN $

Map p270 (☎604-682-7568; 788 Denman St; mains $6-10; ⏰11:30am-11pm; 🚌5) One of Vancouver's oldest noodle shops, fancy-free Kintaro feels just like it could be a bustling ramen spot in a Tokyo backstreet. Arriving off-peak is a good idea to avoid queues and ensure you can snag a counter seat to watch all of the steam-shrouded action. Miso ramen is recommended; a brimming bowl of sprouts, bamboo shoots and thick slices of barbecued pork all served up in a tasty broth. When you're done, walk off your noodle belly in Stanley Park.

Keep in mind that there are lots of other, newer noodle joints in this area; if you can't stand queuing, it's just a short walk to the next one.

TACOFINO OASIS MEXICAN $

Map p270 (☎604-428-8453; www.tacofino.com; 1050 W Pender St; mains $10-16; ⏰11am-7pm Mon-Thu, to 3:30pm Fri; 📶; S Burrard) Brilliantly funky but fiendishly well hidden in an office-district back alley, this small satellite of BC's homegrown taco purveyor is well worth hunting down. Snag a tiny pink table and peruse a well-curated array of burritos (pork belly is highly recommended) and 'not burritos' (as the menu states) including tacos and nachos. Local workers flock here in their numbers at lunchtime; happy hour from 3pm.

GREENHORN CAFE CAFE $

Map p270 (☎604-428-2912; www.greenhorncafe.com; 994 Nicola St; mains $7-13; ⏰7am-6pm Mon-Fri, 8am-5pm Sat & Sun; 📶; 🚌5) Named after three novice pioneers who once bought some land in this area, this well-hidden cafe is a popular local bolt-hole. Residents from nearby apartments gather here to chat over coffee in the woodsy front area or head upstairs for sit-down breakfasts and light lunches (wild mushroom baguette recommended). It's often busy during weekend

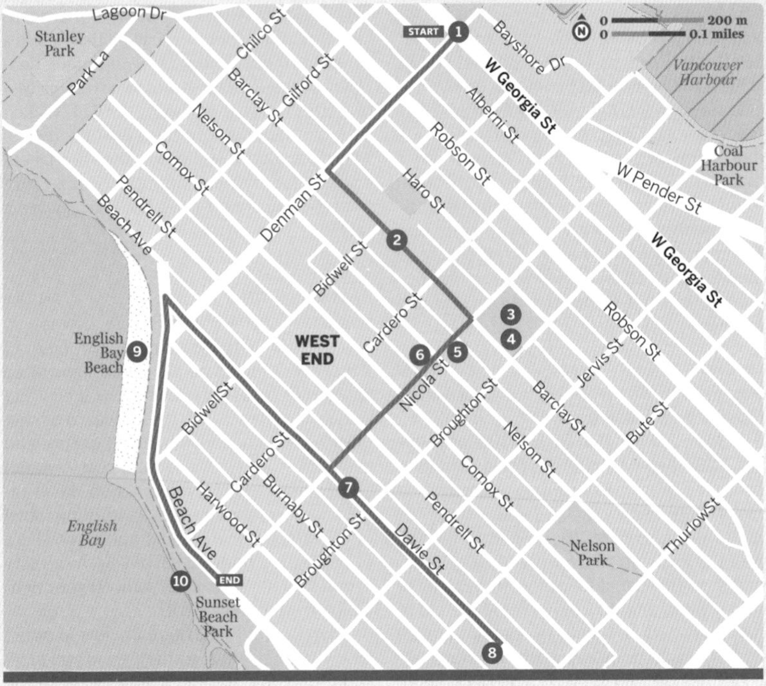

Neighborhood Walk
West End 'Hood & Heritage Stroll

START CORNER OF W GEORGIA & DENMAN STS
END SUNSET BEACH
LENGTH 2KM; ONE HOUR

This urban walk takes you through one of Vancouver's most attractive residential areas, combining clapboard houses with vintage apartment buildings.

Start at the corner of 1 **W Georgia and Denman streets** and head south along Denman. You'll pass dozens of restaurants – choose one for dinner – plus plenty of enticing shops.

Turn left on 2 **Barclay Street** and stroll the residential heart of Vancouver's vibrant LGBTIQ+ community. There are some lovely old apartment buildings and heritage homes here. Recent years have also seen barred owls colonizing the area. It's a great neighborhood for photos, especially if the trees are in their finest fall colors.

Continue to the historic houses at 3 **Barclay Heritage Square**, an evocative reminder of yesteryear Vancouver. Visit the best of the bunch: antique-lined 4 **Roedde House Museum** (p61).

From here, head southwest along Nicola St, ducking into 5 **Greenhorn Cafe** (p67) for coffee. You'll soon reach the 1907-built 6 **Firehall No 6**. Still in use, it looks like a museum. There's often a shiny fire truck basking outside.

Continue to 7 **Davie Street**, a teeming cafe-lined area and the social hub of Vancouver's LGBTIQ+ community. It has many bars and clubs. If it's time to eat, turn left along Davie to 8 **Mumbai Local** (p69), where Indian street food awaits.

After eating, backtrack northwest along Davie to 9 **English Bay Beach** (p63), snapping photos of the public artwork of chuckling bronze figures, then turning left along Beach Ave. It overlooks 10 **Sunset Beach Park**. Sit on a grassy bank and watch the scene or catch a mini-ferry to Granville Island just across the water.

brunchtimes, when eggs Benny dishes lure the ravenously hungry.

GUU WITH GARLIC
JAPANESE $

Map p270 (☎604-685-8678; www.guu-izakaya.com; 1698 Robson St; mains $8-16; ⏲11:30am-2:30pm & 5:30pm-12:30am Mon-Sat, 11:30am-2:30pm & 5:30pm to midnight Sun; 🚌5) One of Vancouver's best *izakayas*, this welcoming, wood-lined joint is a cultural immersion. Rice and noodle bowls are available but it's best to experiment with some Japanese bar tapas, including *okonomiyaki* pancakes and deep-fried *takoyaki* octopus balls. Reservations are only accepted for groups of three or more, so it's best to arrive early for a seat.

BREKA BAKERY & CAFE
BAKERY $

Map p270 (☎604-620-8200; www.breka.ca; 818 Bute St; sandwiches $7-9; ⏲24hr; 📶; 🚌5) One of Vancouver's few 24/7 eateries, this local bakery mini-chain has rapidly expanded across the city in recent years; this location is ideal if you need a break from Robson St shopping. There's a gigantic array of value-priced fill-you-up baked goodies, from scones to doughnuts to chocolate babka cakes, as well as sandwiches and breakfast bagels.

Alongside the indoor and patio seats, there's also a collection of public seats and benches on the closed-off street outside. If you're in self-catering accommodation, this is a good place to pick up a loaf or two of fresh bread.

★FORAGE
CANADIAN $$

Map p270 (☎604-661-1400; www.foragevancouver.com; 1300 Robson St; mains $16-35; ⏲6:30-10am & 5-11pm Mon-Fri, 7am-2pm & 5-11pm Sat & Sun; 📶; 🚌5) 🍃 A popular farm-to-table eatery, this sustainability-focused restaurant is the perfect way to sample regional flavors. Brunch has become a firm local favorite (halibut eggs benny recommended), and for dinner there's everything from bison steaks to slow-cooked salmon. Add a flight of British Columbia (BC) craft beers, with top choices from the likes of Four Winds, Strange Fellows and more. Reservations recommended.

If you're dining alone, the U-shaped central bar is ideal – and it's a good spot to slowly explore some BC wines and ciders as well.

MUMBAI LOCAL
INDIAN $$

Map p270 (☎604-423-3281; www.mumbailocal.ca; 1148 Davie St; mains $15-25; ⏲11am-10pm; 📶🌶; 🚌5) Seated alongside a striking Mumbai-themed mural, dive into some street-food snacks and dishes inspired by the homestyle cuisine of this bustling Indian city. We loved the *chaat* sampler made up of crunchy savory treats plus the chickpea and potato patties in a bun, but make sure you don't miss the *dabba* combo of condiments, stew, dal, bread and rice served in a multilayer tiffin tin.

There are lots of vegetarian choices here and, whatever you order, be sure to add some cardamom tea (or a BC craft beer) to the mix.

ESPANA
SPANISH $$

Map p270 (☎604-558-4040; www.espanarestaurant.ca; 1118 Denman St; plates $6-13; ⏲5-11pm Sun-Thu, to 1am Fri & Sat; 🚌5) Reservations aren't taken but it's worth queuing to get into one of Vancouver's most popular Spanish tapas joints. The seats (at small tables and at the long bar) are crammed close and evenings are like a candlelit cave of food-related chatter. The crispy squid and the cod and anchovy-stuffed olives are delish, while the fried chickpeas dish is a revelation.

There's a weekday happy hour here from 4pm-to-6pm. And, booze-wise, there's a small but authentic sherry list plus a good array of Spanish wines – why not go down the bubbly cava route and toast your lovely meal?

SURA KOREAN CUISINE
KOREAN $$

Map p270 (☎604-687-7872; www.surakoreancuisine.com; 1518 Robson St; mains $10-20; ⏲11am-3:30pm & 5-10pm; 🅿; 🚌5) From the 1400-block of Robson St onwards, you'll find a smorgasbord of authentic Korean and Japanese eateries. A cut above its ESL-student-luring siblings, slick Sura offers awesome Korean comfort dishes in a cozy, bistro-like setting. Try the spicy beef soup, *kimchi* pancakes and excellent *dolsot bibimbap*: beef, veggies and a still-cooking egg in a hot stone bowl.

The set-course lunches ($15 or $20; two-person minimum order) are a great deal if you want to try as many flavors as possible; each comes with lots of little plates to dip into. Reservations not accepted.

RIOTOUS BEHAVIOR

When the 2010 Winter Olympics were staged in Vancouver, locals were surprised and delighted that the jam-packed nighttime streets never spilled over into trouble. So, when the Vancouver Canucks hockey team entered a play-off run in 2011, few were concerned that things might turn ugly – despite the distant memory of hockey riots here during a similar play-off run back in 1994.

On the night of June 15, 2011, however, just after the Canucks lost to the Boston Bruins, the downtown core rapidly descended into chaos. Hundreds of booze-fueled 'fans,' most of whom had been watching the game at an outdoor live-screening site, began rampaging through the city, smashing store windows, setting fire to police cars and looting dozens of shops, including the Bay and London Drugs. The police seemed unable to quell the rioters and control of the city center was lost for several hours. The region watched the unfolding events on its TV screens in horror.

The next day, after the violence had subsided, a different group of locals turned out on the streets. Armed with brooms and buckets, and rallied by a social media call-to-action that asked Vancouverites to show what the city was really all about, hundreds arrived to help with the massive cleanup. Interviewed on TV, many expressed their anger at what had happened the night before, as well as their determination to help the recovery efforts.

As for the rioters, many were outed and eventually charged by the police after posting photos of themselves on social media during the evening's flame-licked iniquity.

PROSPECT POINT BAR & GRILL — CANADIAN $$

Map p287 (☎604-669-2737; www.prospectpoint.com; 5601 Stanley Park Dr, Stanley Park; mains $16-24; ⏰9am-7pm, reduced hours off-season; 🚌19) A sparkling renovation has transformed this historic wood-beamed cafe into a full-service bistro and bar serving elevated comfort food from burgers to *poke* bowls to panko-crusted fish and chips. You'll also find BC craft beers: perfect for toasting your luck at finding one of the city's best patios, a tree-framed treasure overlooking the grand Lions Gate Bridge.

TIMBER — PUB FOOD $$

Map p270 (☎604-661-2166; www.timbervancouver.com; 1300 Robson St; mains $12-19; ⏰noon-midnight Tue-Thu, to 1am Fri, 11am-1am Sat, 11am-midnight Sun; 🚌5) The startled stuffed beaver by the door (the googly eyes don't help) shouldn't put you off this fun resto-pub, combining a great BC-focused beer menu with a tongue-in-cheek array of calorific Canadian comfort grub. Dive into bison burgers, house-made potato chips and deep-fried cheese curds alongside a tempting array of local-made ales, BC wines and smooth Canadian whiskies.

The beer list often includes choice quaffs from Persephone, Dageraad and Off the Rail; a $15, four-sample tasting flight is available. Happy hour is 3pm to 6pm daily; look out for deals on beer, wine and snacks. Reservations not accepted.

DAVIE DOSA COMPANY — INDIAN $$

Map p270 (☎604-669-5899; www.daviedosacompany.com; 1235 Davie St; mains $9-17; ⏰11am-11pm; 🌶; 🚌6) Specializing in perfectly prepared South Indian dosas – huge, satisfyingly crisp rice-and-lentil crêpes crammed with fillings such as butter chicken or delicious curried cauliflower – this charming candlelit joint is a Davie St magnet. Authentic dishes fill the menu, but be sure to include some *idly*, a fluffy bread-style starter served with spicy chutneys.

Vegetarians are well served, and there's a tempting selection of desserts to tuck into.

DRINKING & NIGHTLIFE

The Granville Strip between Robson St and Granville Bridge is lined with mainstream bars where partying, heavy boozing and occasional street brawling (especially on weekends) are the main attraction. A short walk away, you'll find more discerning options in the West End's neighborhood pubs and bars, including several LGBTIQ+-friendly haunts along Davie St. Even better, head to the superior nightlife of Gastown or Main St.

Downtown

★MARIO'S COFFEE EXPRESS COFFEE

Map p266 (☎604-608-2804; www.facebook.com/marioscoffeeexpress; 595 Howe St; ⏰6:30am-4pm Mon-Fri; Ⓢ Burrard) A java-lover's favorite that only downtown office workers seem to know about. You'll wake up and smell the coffee long before you make it through the door here. The rich aromatic brews served up by the eponymous Mario himself are just the kind of ambrosia that makes Starbucks aficionados weep. You might even forgive the wonderfully cheesy 1980s Italian pop percolating through the shop.

Hidden in plain view, this is arguably downtown's best coffee spot.

PROHIBITION BAR

Map p266 (☎604-673-7089; www.rosewoodhotels.com/vancouver; 801 W Georgia St; ⏰7pm-1am Thu, 5pm-3am Fri & Sat; Ⓢ Vancouver City Centre) A sleek subterranean bar with a chic 1920s look and a serious commitment to great cocktails; push through the speakeasy-feel dungeon doors on the Howe St sidewalk and descend into decadent reverie. There's live music from Thursday to Saturday, plus late-night DJ action on Friday and Saturday (arrive before 8:30pm to avoid the cover charge).

The premium-priced cocktails cover classics and contemporary libations, while there's also a huge array of top-notch wines and spirits to treat yourself to. This is a place to dress up and pretend that the food menu's truffle fries are your usual approach to snacking.

RAILWAY STAGE & BEER CAFE BAR

Map p266 (☎604-564-1430; www.facebook.com/RailwaySBC; 579 Dunsmuir St; ⏰4pm-2am Sun-Thu, 11am-3am Fri & Sat; 📶; Ⓢ Granville) The near-legendary former Railway Club has been resurrected as a slightly more scrubbed-up version of its belovedly grungy original incarnation. There are still regular live performances, especially on weekends, while the expanded draft beer menu covers an ever-changing array of locally brewed beers; Hoyne Dark Matter is particularly recommended. A range of sandwiches and salad bowls keep the serving hatch busy and the communal long tables full.

A welcoming spot that still has a loyal following, it can get loud here. Drop by on weekday afternoons if you're keen for a quieter chat and happy-hour specials.

UVA WINE & COCKTAIL BAR LOUNGE

Map p266 (☎604-632-9560; www.uvavancouver.com; 900 Seymour St; ⏰2pm-2am; 📶; 🚌10) This sexy nook fuses a heritage mosaic floor with a dash of mod class. Despite the cool appearances, there's a snob-free approach that encourages taste-tripping through an extensive by-the-glass wine menu and some dangerously delicious cocktails – we love the Diplomat. Food is part of the mix (including shareable small plates) and there's a daily 2pm to 5pm happy hour.

DEVIL'S ELBOW ALE & SMOKE HOUSE PUB

Map p266 (☎604-559-0611; www.devilselbowalehouse.com; 562 Beatty St; ⏰11:30am-midnight Mon-Thu, to 1am Fri, 10am-1am Sat, 11:30am-midnight Sun; Ⓢ Stadium-Chinatown) This cavelike brick-and-art-lined pub has the feel of a well kept local secret. It's the type of place where you can go to combine comfort grub of the deep-fried pickles and Texas beef brisket variety with frothy beers from a top BC microbrewery – it's owned by the team behind Howe Sound Brewing. Great drafts include Hopraiser IPA and Rail Ale Nut Brown. Can't decide? Simply order a tasting flight and dive right in.

If you're feeling brave, make sure to try the Wooly Bugger Barley Wine, which puts hairs on the chests of everyone in the area, whether or not they're drinking it. The weekday $15 beer-included lunch deal is recommended, but there's also an extensive happy hour menu (2pm to 5pm Sunday to Thursday) with a tempting array of $5 beers and great food deals.

ONE UNDER SPORTS BAR

Map p266 (☎604-559-4653; www.oneunder.ca; 476 Granville St; ⏰noon-midnight Mon-Thu, to 2am Fri & Sat, 10am-midnight Sun; Ⓢ Waterfront) Vancouver's virtual golf club, this subterranean golf-themed bar is home to six big-screen simulation bays where (from $50 per hour) you can swing a club at your choice of dozens of courses around the world. Add a few rounds of drinks and some bar grub (pizzas recommended) and you've got the makings of a unique night out. On Sundays and Mondays, the simulators are half price.

You pay per bay rather than per person, so this is a good deal for small groups. Book ahead for the time you really want; you can reserve via the website up to three weeks in advance. And you don't have to play to hit the bar here; this is also a popular spot to catch TV sports with like-minded quaffers.

NEMESIS COFFEE COFFEE

Map p266 (www.nemesis.coffee; 302 W Hastings St; 8am-6pm Mon-Fri, 9am-5pm Sat & Sun; ; 14) A sleek, Scandinavian-look cafe with a serious commitment to great java – aim for a little wooden side-booth and you'll soon be hanging out with cooler-than-you students from the nearby schools. The coffee, including top-grade espresso varieties, is served in glasses and there's an array of brunch and lunch dishes from scotch eggs to avocado toast. Don't miss the house-baked cookies.

It's in an interesting location: just across the brick-paved street from Victory Square's towering cenotaph and kitty-corner to the handsome, often-photographed heritage Dominion Building.

ROXY CLUB

Map p266 (604-331-7999; www.roxyvan.com; 932 Granville St; 8pm-3am; 10) A raucous old-school nightclub that still has plenty of fans – including lots of partying youngsters who seem to be discovering it for the first time – this brazen old-timer is downtown's least pretentious dance space. Expect to be shaking your booty next to near-teenage funsters, kid-escaping soccer moms and UBC students letting loose.

If you really want to dive into the Granville Strip club scene, this is where to do it.

JOHNNIE FOX'S IRISH SNUG IRISH PUB

Map p266 (604-685-4946; www.johnniefox.ca; 1033 Granville St; 11:30am-1am Sun-Thu, to 2am Fri & Sat; 10) The glass front means you can peer through the windows before committing to this small Granville St Irish pub. You'll find a gaggle of beer-swilling fellas having a grand old time to a soundtrack of live or recorded Celtic tunes. A lively spot for a Guinness (especially on weekends), it has a menu of pub-grub classics (filled Yorkshire puddings recommended).

There's live music of the toe-tapping variety four nights a week here, and Sunday evening's $12 roast dinner is a good deal.

REPUBLICA COFFEE ROASTERS COFFEE

Map p266 (604-628-0485; www.republicaroasters.com; 321 W Pender St; 8am-5pm Mon-Fri, 10am-4pm Sat; ; 4) The first downtown Vancouver location for this long-time Fort Langley java roaster is a brick-lined little nook with friendly counter staff and none of the hipster edge of some local coffee shops. Snag a window perch and watch the Pender St action unfold as you sup a well-prepared fair-trade beverage and perhaps nibble on a chunky cookie or two.

West End

★SYLVIA'S BAR & LOUNGE BAR

Map p270 (604-681-9321; www.sylviahotel.com; 1154 Gilford St; 7am-11pm Sun-Thu, to midnight Fri & Sat; 5) Part of the permanently popular Sylvia Hotel (p208), this was Vancouver's first cocktail bar when it opened in the mid-1950s. Now a comfy, wood-lined neighborhood bar favored by in-the-know locals (they're the ones hogging the window seats as the sun sets over English Bay), it's a charming spot for an end-of-day wind down. There's live music on Wednesdays, Thursdays and Sundays.

There's a full dining menu here, including a 'late-riser breakfast' that's served until 4:30pm daily. And here's some scurrilous history for you: this is one of the bars Errol Flynn is reputed to have frequented during his booze-fueled final days, before dying in the city in 1959.

CARDERO'S MARINE PUB PUB

Map p270 (604-669-7666; www.vancouverdine.com; 1583 Coal Harbour Quay; 11:30am-midnight; 19) Nestled between Coal Harbour's bobbing boats, the restaurant here is fine but the little pub on the side is better. With cozy leather sofas, a wood-burning fireplace and great views of the marina, it has a decent menu of comfort food (we recommend the wok dishes and the fried oysters) plus good draft beers, including local favorite Stanley Park Brewing.

There's live music, typically of the guitar-wielding singer-songwriter variety, every night. And the weekday happy hour (3pm to 6pm) includes $5 beer and wine specials plus a tempting array of food deals from tuna sliders to chicken *karaage*.

CITIZEN OF THE CENTURY

Pioneer-era Vancouver was teeming with all sorts of characters, but while most of them have faded into history, some have only grown in stature over the intervening years.

Born in Trinidad in 1863, Joe Fortes arrived in Vancouver in 1885, when only a few hundred African American men were counted among the many thousands of people living in the fledgling townsite.

Risking his life and saving a mother and child during the area's 1886 Great Fire, he later settled around English Bay in the West End of the city. From here he became a casual but dedicated lifeguard, saving dozens of lives and teaching thousands of local children to swim over the course of his life as a Vancouverite.

The city made him its first official lifeguard in 1897, later presenting him with a gold watch for his devoted service in 1910. When he died in 1922, his funeral was one of the biggest the city had ever seen. Fortes' memory still lives on today: a city restaurant and a public library are named after him, Canada Post released a stamp depicting him in 2013, and the Vancouver Historical Society named him 'Citizen of the Century' during the city's 1986 centenary year.

1181 LGBTIQ+

Map p270 (www.facebook.com/1181Lounge; 1181 Davie St; ⏲7pm-3am; 🚌6) Currently in its third iteration, 1181 is an intimate Davie St 'gayborhood' mainstay, a loungey, two-room late-night hangout where flirty cocktails rule. Check ahead for events and happenings (the new schedule was still being firmed up on our visit) but expect a wide array of options from drag nights to improv comedy to DJ dance parties.

Living by it's motto of "It's all love here", this is one of the area's classiest LGBTIQ+ friendly bars.

FOUNTAINHEAD PUB GAY

Map p270 (☎604-687-2222; www.fthdpub.com; 1025 Davie St; ⏲11am-midnight Mon-Thu & Sun, to 2am Fri & Sat; 🚌6) The area's loudest and proudest gay neighborhood pub, this friendly joint is all about the patio, which spills out onto Davie St like an overturned wine glass. From here, you can take part in the ongoing summer-evening pastime of ogling passersby or retreat to a quieter spot inside for a few lagers or a naughty cocktail: anyone for a Crispy Crotch or a Slippery Nipple?

This is the perfect place to meet up before, during or after the city's annual Pride Parade.

DELANY'S COFFEE HOUSE COFFEE

Map p270 (☎604-662-3344; www.delanyscoffeehouse.com; 1105 Denman St, West End; ⏲6am-7pm Mon-Fri, from 6:30am Sat & Sun; 📶; 🚌5) A laid-back, wood-and-art-lined neighborhood coffee bar that's the java-hugging heart of the West End's LGBTIQ+ community, Delany's is a good perch from which to catch the annual Pride Parade, although you'll have to get here early if you want a front-row seat. The usual array of cookies and muffins will keep you fortified while you wait.

A good spot to pick up a take-out coffee for a stroll to nearby English Bay Beach (p63).

STANLEY'S BAR & GRILL BAR

Map p287 (☎604-602-3088; www.stanleysbargrill.com; 610 Pipeline Rd, Stanley Park; ⏲11am-5pm; 🚌19) Duck into this spot, nestled into one end of the handsome, century-old Stanley Park Pavilion. Snag a patio seat under the gigantic red parasols and grab a thist quenching beery respite from your exhausting day of park exploring. There's a full range of Stanley Park Brewing tipples plus some good pub grub; the fish and chips is especially recommended.

You don't have to leave the city to enjoy Canadian wildlife. While you're sitting here drinking among the trees, keep your eyes peeled for passing eagles and herons plus a Douglas squirrel or two. And if you're planning on heading for a show at Theatre Under the Stars (p74), this is a great spot to drink and dine beforehand; the theater is just steps away.

PUMPJACK PUB GAY

Map p270 (www.pumpjackpub.com; 1167 Davie St; ⏲1pm-2am; 🚌6) Glancing through the open window as you walk past on a summer night tells you all you need to know about this popular gay pub: it's a great place to meet leather-clad, often hairy locals ever-ready to make a new friend in town for a quick visit. Expect weekend queues as the local bears vie for a pickup. A long-time local favorite.

CELEBRITIES GAY

Map p270 (☎604-681-6180; www.celebritiesnightclub.com; 1022 Davie St; ⏲10pm-3am Tue, Fri & Sat; 🚌6) The city's favourite gay club has elevated its room to a new level of neon-lit cool in recent years. The club hosts a series of sparkling, sometimes sequined, event nights throughout the week, including a raucous Playhouse Saturday when everyone seems to hit the dance floor.

☆ ENTERTAINMENT

Studded with an eclectic mix of cinema, theater and live music options, Vancouver's downtown core has some great night-out entertainment possibilities, plus a couple of unexpected venues beyond the city center.

★THEATRE UNDER THE STARS PERFORMING ARTS

Map p287 (TUTS; ☎604-631-2877; www.tuts.ca; 610 Pipeline Rd, Malkin Bowl, Stanley Park; tickets from $30; ⏲Jul & Aug; 🚌19) The charming Malkin Bowl provides an atmospheric alfresco stage for the summertime TUTS season, usually featuring two interchanging Broadway musicals. It's hard to find a better place to catch a show, especially as the sun fades over the surrounding Stanley Park (p58) trees. The troupe's production values have massively increased in recent years, and these productions are slick, professional and energetic.

It's one of the best ways to spend a summer evening in Vancouver, and many locals have been coming here for decades. Food and drinks are available on-site and bringing a blanket to wrap around you as the night cools is an excellent idea. Cast your eyes skyward for the occasional bat or bald eagle as well.

★CINEMATHEQUE CINEMA

Map p266 (☎604-688-8202; www.thecinematheque.ca; 1131 Howe St, Downtown; tickets $12, double bills $16; 🚌10) This beloved cinema operates like an ongoing film festival with a daily-changing program of movies. A $3 annual membership is required – organize it at the door – before you can skulk in the dark with other chin-stroking movie buffs who probably named their children (or pets) after Fellini and Bergman.

The high point of the year for some is August's annual classic film noir season; check ahead for the dates.

★COMMODORE BALLROOM LIVE MUSIC

Map p266 (☎604-739-4550; www.commodoreballroom.com; 868 Granville St, Downtown; tickets from $30; 🚌10) Local bands know they've made it when they play Vancouver's best mid-sized venue, a restored art-deco ballroom that still has the city's bounciest dance floor – courtesy of tires placed under its floorboards. If you need a break from moshing, collapse at one of the tables lining the perimeter, catch your breath with a bottled brew and then plunge back in.

Check the calendar as soon as you book your Vancouver-bound flights; international acts often play here and it's a great space to see anyone. The historic Commodore has been entertaining locals since 1929 and everyone from Count Basie to the Dead Kennedys has played here over the years (although apparently they weren't on the same bill).

ORPHEUM THEATRE THEATER

Map p266 (☎604-665-3035; www.vancouvercivictheatres.com; 601 Smithe St, Downtown; tickets from $29; 🚌10) Opened in 1927, Vancouver's grandest old-school theater has a gorgeous and beautifully maintained baroque interior, making it the perfect place to catch a rousing show with the Vancouver Symphony Orchestra, who call this place home. There are frequent additional performers throughout the year; check ahead to see what's on during your stay. The theater is also a National Historic Site.

In summer, there are often free guided tours of this storied venue; call ahead to see if they're on during your visit.

VANCITY THEATRE CINEMA

Map p266 (☎604-683-3456; www.viff.org; 1181 Seymour St, Downtown; tickets $13, double bills $20; 🚌10) The state-of-the-art headquar-

VANCOUVER'S FAVORITE PUBLIC ARTWORK

Head towards the West End's English Bay Beach and you'll be stopped in your tracks by 14 very tall men (p63) – and the crowds of people snapping selfies with them. *A-maze-ing Laughter* by Yue Minjun comprises a gathering of oversized bronze figures permanently engaged in a hearty round of chuckling. It's impossible not to smile as you behold the spectacle but it's worth remembering that it's simply the most popular legacy from the **Vancouver Biennale** (www.vancouverbiennale.com), a festival that runs for two-year stretches in the city and brings large, sometimes challenging art installations to local streets. After the two-year run, some of these artworks remain as permanent fixtures. Check the Biennale's website for the latest line-up of works around the city.

ters of the Vancouver International Film Festival (p37) screens a wide array of movies throughout the year in the kind of auditorium that cinephiles dream of: generous legroom, wide armrests and great sight lines from each of its 175 seats. It's a place where you can watch a four-hour subtitled epic about paint drying and still feel comfortable.

Check the ever-changing schedule for shows and special events, and remember that a $2 annual membership is mandatory.

VOGUE THEATRE LIVE MUSIC

Map p266 (☎604-569-1144; www.voguetheatre.com; 918 Granville St, Downtown; 🚌10) A 1940s heritage venue – check out the retro art-deco figure perched on top of the streamlined exterior – the Vogue was bought and refurbished a few years back. Happily it hasn't changed much and it's a great old-school venue to see bands. It's an all-seater, which sometimes means tension between those who want to sit and those of the mosh-pit persuasion.

The roster here is eclectic but it's often a fave venue for visiting acts looking for a good-sized downtown venue.

VANCOUVER CANUCKS HOCKEY

Map p266 (☎604-899-7400; www.nhl.com/canucks; 800 Griffiths Way, Rogers Arena, Downtown; tickets from $47; ⏲Sep-Apr; Ⓢ Stadium-Chinatown) Recent years haven't been hugely successful for Vancouver's National Hockey League (NHL) team, which means it's sometimes easy to snag tickets to a game if you're simply visiting and want to see what 'ice hockey' (no one calls it that here) is all about. You'll hear 'go Canucks, go!' booming from the seats and in local bars on game nights.

There's a large merchandise shop at the stadium, which is open even when there are no games; it's a good spot to pick up cool souvenirs for sporting kids (and adults) back home.

DANCE CENTRE PERFORMING ARTS

Map p266 (☎604-606-6400; www.thedancecentre.ca; 677 Davie St, Downtown; tickets from $10; 🚌10) Vancouver's dance headquarters, this cleverly reinvented old bank building offers a kaleidoscopic array of activities that makes it one of Canada's foremost dance centers. Home to resident companies – Ballet BC is based here – it also hosts classes, workshops, performances and events throughout the year; check the website calendar to see what's coming up.

FUSE ARTS CENTER

Map p266 (☎604-662-4700; www.vanartgallery.bc.ca/fuse; 750 Hornby St, Vancouver Art Gallery, Downtown; $29; ⏲8pm-midnight; 🚌5) Cross-reference with the Vancouver Art Gallery's website (p55) before you arrive and you might find there's an upcoming FUSE event to add to your vacation itinerary. Staged every few months, the after-hours party of DJs, performances, curator tours and bars makes for a great way to rub shoulders (and chins) with the city's arty intellectuals.

MALKIN BOWL PERFORMING ARTS

Map p287 (www.malkinbowl.com; 610 Pipeline Rd, Stanley Park; 🚌19) Formerly just a summertime venue for musicals, this smashing Stanley Park (p58) stage has become an increasingly popular spot for alfresco live music. Elvis Costello, Franz Ferdinand and the Flaming Lips have had audiences jumping up to punch the air here, often while partaking of a homegrown BC cigarette or two.

Check the website to see what's coming up and book ahead.

SCOTIABANK THEATRE CINEMA

Map p266 (☎604-630-1407; www.cineplex.com; 900 Burrard St, Downtown; tickets adult/child $13/9; 🚌2) Downtown's shiny multiplex is big enough to have its own corporate sponsor and it's the most likely theater to be screening the latest must-see blockbuster. In contrast, it also shows occasional live broadcast performances from major cultural institutions such as London's National Theatre and New York's Metropolitan Opera. Drop by on Tuesdays for discounted admission.

SHOPPING

Centered on Robson St, you'll find all the usual chains and mainstream boutiques downtown. Nosing into the West End means discovering a wider range of independent stores and businesses.

★**PAPER HOUND** BOOKS

Map p266 (☎604-428-1344; www.paperhound.ca; 344 W Pender St, Downtown; ⊙10am-7pm Sun-Thu, to 8pm Fri & Sat; 🚌14) Proving the printed word is alive and kicking, this small but perfectly curated secondhand bookstore is a dog-eared favorite among locals. A perfect spot for browsing, you'll find tempting tomes (mostly used but some new) on everything from nature to poetry to chaos theory. Ask for recommendations; they really know their stuff here. Don't miss the bargain rack out front.

The store is in the heart of a downtown area historically known as Book Row. Once you're done here, check out the three or four other used-book stores that call this area home.

GOLDEN AGE COLLECTABLES BOOKS

Map p266 (☎604-683-2819; www.gacvan.com; 852 Granville St, Downtown; ⊙10am-9pm Mon-Sat, 11am-6pm Sun; 🚌10) If you're missing your regular dose of *Hulkverines* or you just want to blow your vacation budget on a highly detailed life-sized model of Conan the Barbarian, head straight to this Aladdin's cave of the comic-book world. While the clientele is unsurprisingly dominated by males, the staff is friendly and welcoming – especially to wide-eyed kids buying their first *Amazing Spider-Man*.

This is also the best place to be in the city on the annual Free Comic Book Day (first Saturday in May), when there's a party atmosphere and gratis goodies for all – whether or not you dress up as the latest *Doctor Who* regeneration (extra points if you come as a Dalek).

MINK CHOCOLATES FOOD

Map p266 (☎604-633-2451; www.minkchocolates.com; 863 W Hastings St, Downtown; ⊙7:30am-6pm Mon-Fri, 9:30am-5pm Sat & Sun; 📶; Ⓢ Waterfront) If chocolate is the main food group in your book, follow your candy-primed nose to this choccy shop and cafe in the downtown core. Select from the kaleidoscopic array of colorfully boxed ganache-filled bars, including top-seller Mermaid's Choice, then hit the drinks bar for the best velvety hot choc you've ever tasted. Then have another.

MACLEOD'S BOOKS BOOKS

Map p266 (☎604-681-7654; 455 W Pender St, Downtown; ⊙10am-6pm Mon-Sat, from 11am Sun; Ⓢ Granville) From its creaky floorboards to its scuzzy carpets and ever-teetering piles of books, this legendary locals' fave is a great place to peruse a cornucopia of used tomes. It's the ideal spot for a rainy-day browse through subjects from dance to the occult. Check the windows for posters of local readings and artsy happenings around the city.

A few steps in from the door, look out for the travel section. It's ideal for picking up a guidebook to 1983 Lisbon, just in case you're a time-traveler planning a trip.

WILDLIFE THRIFT STORE VINTAGE

Map p266 (☎604-682-0381; www.wildlifethriftstore.com; 1295 Granville St; ⊙10am-8pm; 🚌10) Downtown's biggest vintage store houses multiple racks of used clothing that invite a serious browse-a-thon. Alongside the well-priced yesteryear T-shirts and cool summer frocks that your mum used to wear, you'll find books, CDs and kitsch knickknacks, especially on the upstairs mezzanine level where a life-sized Elvis cut-out surveyed the proceedings from above on our visit.

Store proceeds are directed to several worthy causes, which means you can feel good about blowing your shopping budget here.

HUNTER & HARE VINTAGE

Map p266 (☎604-559-4273; www.hunterandhare.com; 334 W Pender St, Downtown; ⊙11am-7pm Mon-Sat, noon-5pm Sun; 🚌14) A lovely little store specializing in well-curated consignment clothing and accessories for women, this is the place to head to if you've left your summer frock at home by mistake. Smiley staff can point you in the right direction and prices are enticingly reasonable. It's not all used togs; there's also jewelry, greeting cards and beauty products from local artisan producers.

WEST END FARMERS MARKET — MARKET

Map p270 (☎604-879-3276; www.eatlocal.org; 1100 Comox St; ⏰9am-2pm Sat Jun–mid-Oct; 🚌6) Vancouver's best urban alfresco farmers market is in the heart of the West End, alongside **Nelson Park** (Map p270; 1030 Bute St; 🚌2). It runs during the warmest months of the year and it's a great way to meet locals. The strip of 30 or so stalls often includes baked treats, arts and crafts, and shiny piles of freshly picked, locally grown fruit and veg.

Look out for seasonal blueberries, cherries, apricots and peaches, and expect a busker or two as you wander around gorging on your purchases.

VANCOUVER CHRISTMAS MARKET — MARKET

Map p270 (☎778-200-0167; www.vancouverchristmasmarket.com; 1055 Canada Pl, Jack Poole Plaza, Downtown; adult/child $12/5; ⏰11:30am-9:30pm late Nov-24 Dec; 👪; Ⓢ Waterfront) This German-style Christmas market lures thousands of Yuletide-loving locals to its alfresco waterfront location every festive season. They come for stalls hawking arts and crafts (including lots of German Christmas ornaments) as well as hearty grub, from bratwursts to warm pretzels. Smile-triggering Christmas music and fortifying *glühwein* stoke the air of jollity, but don't miss a carousel ride as well.

KONBINIYA JAPAN CENTRE — FOOD

Map p270 (www.konbiniya.com; 1238 Robson St, West End; ⏰11am-midnight; 🚌5) Like walking into a Tokyo convenience store, the shelves here are crammed with brightly packaged Japanese goodies from Calbee potato chips to Pocky chocolate sticks. Pick up a can of Pocari Sweat and save time to peruse the wall of vending machines near the door; where else will you find the latest Peach John figure to add to your collection?

Expect to see lots of homesick language students looking for Melty Kiss candies. If your accommodations are self-catering, this is a good place to pick up cheap instant noodles and Glico curry mixes. Don't want to cook? Buy some *onigiri* triangular rice snacks or hit the crepe hatch on the store's exterior.

SIGNATURE BC LIQUOR STORE — ALCOHOL

Map p270 (☎604-660-4572; www.bcliquorstores.com; 768 Bute St, West End; ⏰9:30am-11pm Mon-Sat, to 9pm Sun; 🚌5) The 'Signature' in the name means this well-located shop – just off Robson St at Bute – is one of the larger-format BC government liquor stores. You'll find a big selection of pretty much anything you might want to imbibe, including a back wall of regional and international beers, and a large array of wines from around the world.

If you're a beer fan, make sure you peruse the BC craft beer selection. Many are available in (larger) single bottles, so you can sample a few without committing to a six-pack.

ROOTS — CLOTHING

Map p270 (☎604-629-1300; www.roots.com; 1001 Robson St, Downtown; ⏰10am-6pm Mon-Fri, to 7pm Sat, to 5pm Sun; 🚌5) Basically a maple-leaf-emblazoned version of the Gap, Roots designs athletic, plaid-accented streetwear that's unmistakably Canadian. Its retro-style jogging pants, hoodies and toques (if you don't know what a toque is, this is the place to find out) are ever-popular. There are additional outlets (usually in malls) throughout the city.

Check the sale rails for end-of-season deals. You might even pick up an ironic trappers hat for just a few bucks. If you're Australian, you'll know the name of this store has naughty connotations back home; which means it's a good place to buy a T-shirt souvenir emblazoned with the Roots legend.

LITTLE SISTER'S BOOK & ART EMPORIUM — BOOKS

Map p270 (☎604-669-1753; www.littlesisters.ca; 1238 Davie St, West End; ⏰9am-10pm Sun-Thu, to 11am Fri & Sat; 🚌6) Launched almost 40 years ago as one of the only LGBTIQ+ bookshops in Canada, Little Sister's is a bazaar of queer-positive tomes, plus magazines, clothing and toys of the adult type. If this is your first visit to Vancouver, it's a great place to network with the local LGBTIQ+ scene. Check the notice boards for events and announcements from the community.

HOLT RENFREW CLOTHING

Map p266 (☎604-681-3121; www.holtrenfrew.com; 737 Dunsmuir St, Downtown; ⊙10am-7pm Mon & Tue, to 9pm Wed-Sat, 11am-7pm Sun; Ⓢ Granville) High-end-label lovers flock here to peruse the artfully presented D&G, Armani and Issey Miyake togs and accoutrements arrayed over several brightly lit floors. Service is personal from well-dressed staffers, and there are awesome end-of-season sales. The recent arrival of slick US chain Nordstrom nearby has challenged its lofty position as Vancouver's swankiest clothing and accessories department store.

DOWNTOWN FARMERS MARKET MARKET

Map p266 (☎604-879-3276; www.eatlocal.org; 688 Hamilton, Queen Elizabeth Theatre Plaza, Downtown; ⊙3-7pm Thu Jun-Sep; Ⓢ Stadium-Chinatown) This farmers market has popped up outside the Queen Elizabeth Theatre in recent years and it's popular with office workers on their way home. The usual mix of baked treats and local fresh produce from cherries to blueberries makes its 25+ stands worth a look, and there's often live music and a few food trucks to keep things interesting.

VANCOUVER PEN SHOP STATIONERY

Map p266 (☎604-681-1612; www.facebook.com/vanpenshop; 512 W Hastings St, Downtown; ⊙9:30am-5:30pm Mon-Fri, 10am-5pm Sat; 🚌14) Two things about this store are pleasingly old-fashioned: staff greet you and ask how they can help, and the items they're selling harken to a bygone age when fine pens and penmanship were markers (no pun intended) of civilization. It's not all gold-nibbed fountain pens, though; there are writing tools for every budget, plus cool stationery and retro-look Vancouver prints.

LULULEMON ATHLETICA CLOTHING

Map p266 (☎604-681-3118; www.lululemon.com; 970 Robson St, Downtown; ⊙10am-9pm Mon-Sat, to 8pm Sun; 🚌5) Flagship downtown store of the Vancouver-based chain that made ass-hugging yoga wear a mainstream fashion, this is the shop for that archetypal West Coast look. Sporty tops and stretchy pants for women are the collection's backbone, but menswear is also in the mix. The range has recently expanded to include cycling and jogging gear.

BIRKS JEWELLERY

Map p266 (☎604-669-3333; www.maisonbirks.com; 698 W Hastings St, Downtown; ⊙10am-6pm Mon-Fri, to 5:30pm Sat, noon-5pm Sun; Ⓢ Waterfront) A Vancouver institution since 1879 – hence the landmark freestanding clock outside – Birks crafts exquisite heirloom jewelry and its signature line of timepieces. It's an upscale place, similar to Tiffany & Co in the US, and ideal for picking up that special something in a classy blue embossed box for a deserving someone back home.

PACIFIC CENTRE MALL

Map p266 (☎604-688-7235; www.pacificcentre.ca; cnr Howe & W Georgia Sts, Downtown; ⊙10am-7pm Mon & Tue, to 9pm Wed-Fri, to 8pm Sat, 11am-7pm Sun; Ⓢ Granville) If rain curtails your shopping activities, duck inside downtown Vancouver's main mall. You'll find all the usual chain and department store suspects, plus highlights such as Harry Rosen and Purdy's Chocolates. You can also check your email for free at the Apple Store. There's a large food court if you need a pit stop from all that retail therapy.

SPORTS & ACTIVITIES

★VANCOUVER FOODIE TOURS TOURS

(☎604-295-8844; www.foodietours.ca; tours from $65) A popular culinary-themed city stroll operator running three taste-tripping tours in Vancouver; choose between Best of Downtown, Gastronomic Gastown and Granville Island tours. Friendly red-coated guides lead you through belly-pleasing wanders with plenty to eat and drink; the trick is not to dine before you arrive.

★CYCLE CITY TOURS CYCLING

Map p266 (☎604-618-8626; www.cyclevancouver.com; 648 Hornby St, Downtown; tours from $65, bicycle rentals per hour/day $9.50/38; ⊙9am-6pm, reduced hours in winter; Ⓢ Burrard) Striped with bike lanes, Vancouver is a good city for two-wheeled exploring. But if you're not great at navigating, consider a guided tour with this popular operator. Their Grand Tour ($90) is a great city intro, while their Craft Beer Tour ($90) includes brunch and three breweries. Alternatively, go solo with a rental; there's a bike lane outside the store.

LOCAL KNOWLEDGE

URBAN BIRDING

You don't have to go far to spot some beady-eyed locals in this city. Birding has become a popular pastime for many Vancouverites and if you're keen to join in the feather-fancying fun, consider spending an hour or two in Stanley Park (p58), **Vanier Park**, **Pacific Spirit Park** or **Queen Elizabeth Park**. Many city streets are also lined with established trees that are home to a surprisingly diverse array of beak-tastic critters: on our West End exploration, we spotted hummingbirds, barred owls and northern flicker woodpeckers. Heading into adjoining Stanley Park, you might also see wrens, chickadees, downy woodpeckers, bald eagles, coots, ducks, cormorants and herons – which are also famous for nesting in a large and noisy heronry here every spring.

If you've ever fancied trying an electric bike, they offer that option on one of their guided tours. They also have a rentals-only store at 1344 Burrard St.

SECOND BEACH POOL — SWIMMING

Map p287 (☎604-257-8371; www.vancouverparks.ca; cnr N Lagoon Dr & Stanley Park Dr, Stanley Park; adult/child $6.10/3.05; ⏰10am-8pm Jun-Aug, reduced hours in low season; 👪; 🚌19) This smashing outdoor pool shimmers like a gem right beside the ocean shoreline. It has lanes for laps but you'll be weaving past children on most summer days; kids take over during school vacations, making it hard to get anywhere near the waterslide (we've tried). If you're traveling with under-10s, they'll love the chance to hang with local kids here.

Arrive early for a poolside towel spot. There's also a playground nearby and a concession stand if you really need ice creams.

ACADEMIE DUELLO — MARTIAL ARTS

Map p266 (☎604-568-9907; www.academieduello.com; 412 W Hastings St, Downtown; classes from $99; ⏰11am-8pm Mon-Fri, 10am-5pm Sat; 👪; 🚌14) The perfect way to unleash your inner knight, this popular downtown sword-play school offers thrilling classes and workshops for kids and adults, showing you how to wield everything from rapiers to longswords. If you're traveling with your children, see if there's a Knight Camp on the schedule; the five-day favorite is great fun and sells out every time it runs.

BEE'S KNEES EBIKE TOURS & RENTALS — CYCLING

Map p270 (☎604-262-8852; www.beeskneesrentals.com; 1315 Burrard St, West End; rentals from $25, tours from $59; ⏰9:30am-6pm; 🚌2) Keen to explore Vancouver by bike without sweating too much? The friendly folks here can rent you an e-bike for your own electric two-wheeled jaunt or take you around on one of their popular guided tours, covering urban landmarks and sparkling scenic views. And if you're here at a colder time of year, they also provide ski and snowshoe rentals.

SPOKES BICYCLE RENTALS — CYCLING

Map p270 (☎604-688-5141; www.spokesbicyclerentals.com; 1798 W Georgia St, West End; adult bicycle rental per hr/day from $8.57/34.28; ⏰8am-9pm, reduced hours in low season; 👪; 🚌5) On the corner of W Georgia and Denman Sts, this is the biggest of the bike shops servicing the Stanley Park cycling trade. It can kit you and your family out with all manner of bikes, from cruisers to tandems to kiddie one-speeds. Ask for tips on riding the Seawall; it extends far beyond Stanley Park.

Gastown & Chinatown

Neighborhood Top Five

❶ **Alibi Room** (p90) Tucking into the city's best array of regional craft beers while rubbing shoulders with the locals; small sampler glasses recommended.

❷ **Eastside Flea** (p95) Nosing around the artisan stalls, vintage-clothing stands and tasty food trucks at this regular hipster market.

❸ **Vancouver Police Museum & Archives** (p82) Discovering the city's murky, sometimes murderous past at this hidden-gem museum; summertime Sins of the City walking tours included.

❹ **St Lawrence Restaurant** (p87) Feasting on fine French-Canadian cuisine and feeling like you're hanging out in old-town Montréal.

❺ **Herschel Supply Co** (p96) Perusing the bags, packs and clothing at the large flagship store of this globally successful Vancouver company.

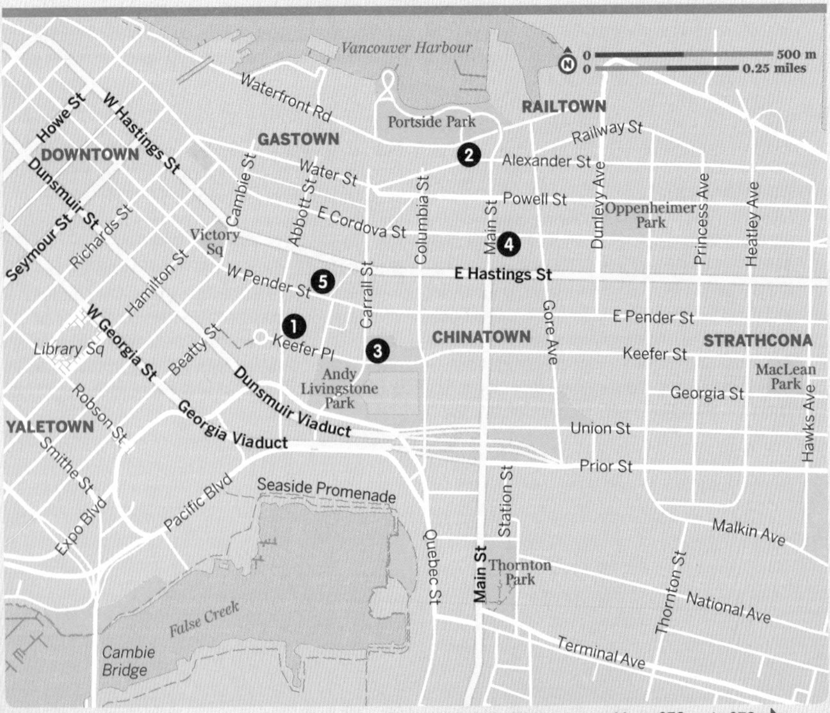

For more detail of this area see Map p272 and p273

Explore Gastown & Chinatown

Radiating from the jaunty Gassy Jack statue in brick-paved Maple Tree Sq, Gastown's main thoroughfares are Powell, Water, Carrall and Alexander Sts. You'll find plenty of shops and restaurants on Water St, while its adjoining side streets house a more recent wave of hip bars, stores and coffee shops. Wandering southeast from Maple Tree Sq, you'll enter the heart of the Downtown Eastside, where many of the city's poorest residents reside. Hastings St runs across Carrall and is this rougher area's main drag. A block across is Chinatown, denoted by its dragon-topped street lamps. Gastown and Chinatown are easily explored on foot and make for a fascinating urban wander, coupled with end-of-day refreshments in some of the city's best bars and restaurants.

Local Life

➡ **Bars** Sidestep downtown's Granville Strip drunks on a bar crawl of Gastown's top watering holes. You'll find hipster locals as well as more British Columbia (BC) craft beer than you can shake a merry stick at. Be sure to include the excellent Alibi Room (p90).

➡ **Shops** Gastown and Chinatown are studded with cool stores but a growing number of vintage shops have also popped up on area side streets in recent years; check out several on Columbia St between Pender and Hastings.

➡ **History** Vancouver's best heritage buildings line this area, from tile-topped apothecaries to handsome century-old stone edifices repurposed as cool bars and restaurants. Make sure you look higher than shop level for evocative glimpses of the past.

➡ **Market** Every hipster in Vancouver seems to flock to the festive-feeling Eastside Flea (p95). They come to browse the vintage and artisan stalls, nosh at the food trucks and sip a craft beer or two from the long bar.

Getting There & Away

➡ **Train** SkyTrain's Waterfront Station is at the western edge of Gastown, near the start of Water St. Stadium-Chinatown station is on the edge of Chinatown and a 10-minute stroll south of Gastown.

➡ **Bus** Bus 14 heads northwards from downtown's Granville St then along Hastings, which makes it handy for both Gastown and Chinatown. Buses 3, 4, 7 and 8 also service the area.

➡ **Car** There is metered parking throughout Gastown and Chinatown, with some nonmetered parking east of Main St.

Lonely Planet's Top Tip

Gastown and Chinatown are part of the Downtown Eastside, a neighborhood with many social challenges and a high proportion of residents with addiction or mental-health issues. But you're far more likely to be asked for 'spare change' in the city center, and muggings here are rare. Stay street smart and avoid the fetid back alleys and side streets (especially at night).

Best Places to Eat

➡ St Lawrence Restaurant (p87)
➡ Greek Gastown (p86)
➡ Campagnolo (p89)
➡ Nuba (p87)
➡ MeeT in Gastown (p86)

For reviews, see p85. ➡

Best Places to Drink

➡ Alibi Room (p90)
➡ Guilt & Co (p90)
➡ Back and Forth Bar (p92)
➡ Diamond (p90)

For reviews, see p80. ➡

Best Places to Shop

➡ Eastside Flea (p95)
➡ Massy Books (p95)
➡ Herschel Supply Co (p96)
➡ John Fluevog Shoes (p95)

For reviews, see p95. ➡

SIGHTS

Just wandering the historic, sometimes cobbled streets of Gastown and Chinatown on foot is the best way to spend a few hours in this part of the city. But there are also a couple of unique, must-see attractions worth stopping off at.

Gastown

GASSY JACK STATUE
MONUMENT

Map p272 (Maple Tree Sq; 4) It's amusing to think that Vancouver's favorite statue is a testament to the virtues of drink. At least that's one interpretation of the John 'Gassy Jack' Deighton bronze, perched atop a whiskey barrel here in Maple Tree Sq. Erected in 1970, it recalls the time when Deighton arrived here in 1867 and built a pub, triggering a ramshackle development that ultimately became Vancouver.

Rivaling the nearby Steam Clock for most-photographed Gastown landmark, the statue is roughly on the site of Deighton's first bar; he soon built a second, grander one nearby.

MAPLE TREE SQUARE
SQUARE

Map p272 (intersection of Alexander, Water, Powell & Carrall Sts; 4) The spot where the inaugural city-council meeting was held under a large maple tree drips with old-town charm. Snap a photo of the jaunty statue of Jack, plus the nearby **Byrnes Block**, the oldest Vancouver building still in its original location.

Stocked with historic buildings completed just after the 1886 Great Fire, Carrall St has a picturesque array of handsome heritage architecture. And a famous image from Vancouver's early days shows the first city council meeting being held here in a sagging tent, complete with a hand-painted 'city hall' sign.

STEAM CLOCK
LANDMARK

Map p272 (cnr Water & Cambie Sts; S Waterfront) Halfway along Water St, this oddly popular tourist magnet lures the cameras with its tooting steam whistle. Built in 1977, the clock's mechanism is actually driven by electricity; only the pipes on top are steam fueled (reveal that to the patiently waiting tourists and you might cause a riot). It sounds every 15 minutes, and marks each hour with little whistling symphonies.

Once you have taken the required photo, spend time exploring the rest of brick-cobbled Water St. One of Vancouver's most historic thoroughfares, its well-preserved heritage buildings contain shops, galleries and resto-bars. Be sure to cast your gaze above entrance level for cool architectural features, including statuary faces.

WOODWARD'S
NOTABLE BUILDING

Map p272 (149 W Hastings St; 14) The project that catalyzed latter-day Downtown Eastside redevelopment, this former iconic department store was a derelict shell after closing in the early 1990s. Successive plans to transform it failed until it was eventually recreated and reopened as the home of new shops and condos, a trigger for what many have labeled neighborhood gentrification. Check out the monumental 'Gastown Riot' photo montage inside.

The Woodward's W-shaped red neon sign that stood atop the building for decades was replaced with a reproduction when the new development was completed; the old one is preserved behind glass at ground level near the Cordova St entrance. If you get the angle right (which might mean lying on the sidewalk), you can snap an image of both signs at the same time.

DOMINION BUILDING
NOTABLE BUILDING

Map p272 (205 W Hastings St; 14) A handsome architectural vestige of yesteryear Vancouver, this copper-hued, French-style vintage skyscraper across from **Victory Square** is well worth a photo or two. Inside, it's now home to dozens of offices and a basement restaurant.

Chinatown

★VANCOUVER POLICE MUSEUM & ARCHIVES
MUSEUM

Map p272 (604-665-3346; www.vancouverpolicemuseum.ca; 240 E Cordova St; adult/child $12/8; 9am-5pm Tue-Sat; 3) Illuminating Vancouver's crime-and-vice-addled history, this quirky museum is situated in what was formerly the coroner's courtroom (spot the elaborate cross-hatched ceiling) and sprucing up exhibits including a spine-chilling gallery of real-life cases (weapons includ-

BEYOND THE STEAM CLOCK

Walking along Water Street, you'll likely bump into a gaggle of whispering visitors clustered around the Steam Clock (p82), a freestanding timepiece famous for its time-marking steam-whistle displays. But while locals tend to roll their eyes at this camera-luring pedestrian obstruction, there's no need to curtail your lens-swiveling ways once the whistling has stopped. Gastown is full of additional photo opportunities, so long as you know where to go. Start with the jaunty Gassy Jack Statue in Maple Tree Square; snap the area's historic buildings above storefront level (some with eerie statuary faces); look for cool architectural details at the Dominion Building and the **Flack Block** (Map p272; 163 W Hastings St, Gastown; 14); and try to get the perfect angle to snap the old and new neon 'W' signs at the renovated Woodward's Building. Need more? Adjoining Chinatown is stuffed with photo-worthy highlights as well.

ed). The star attraction is the old autopsy room, complete with preserved slivers of human tissue; bullet-damaged brain slices are among them. Add a Sins of the City (p95) area walking tour to learn all about Vancouver's salacious olden days; tours run April to October and include museum entry.

Aside from its walking tours, the museum hosts an inventive array of additional activities, including a speaker series, September to April movie screenings, and late-opening adult nights (bar service in the morgue included). Check the website events page for upcoming happenings.

★DR SUN YAT-SEN CLASSICAL CHINESE GARDEN & PARK GARDENS

Map p273 (604-662-3207; www.vancouverchinesegarden.com; 578 Carrall St; adult/child $14/10; 9:30am-7pm mid-Jun–Aug, 10am-6pm Sep & May–mid-Jun, 10am-4:30pm Oct-Apr; S Stadium-Chinatown) A tranquil break from bustling Chinatown, this intimate 'garden of ease' reflects Taoist principles of balance and harmony. Entry includes an optional 45-minute guided tour, in which you'll learn about the symbolism behind the placement of the gnarled pine trees, winding covered pathways and ancient limestone formations. Look out for the colorful carp and lazy turtles in the jade-colored water.

The adjacent **Dr Sun Yat-Sen Park** isn't quite as elaborate as its sister, but this free-entry spot is also a pleasant oasis with whispering grasses, a large fishpond and a small pagoda. Check the website for events including special exhibitions and summertime evening concerts.

CHINATOWN MILLENNIUM GATE LANDMARK

Map p273 (cnr W Pender & Taylor Sts; S Stadium-Chinatown) Inaugurated in 2002, Chinatown's towering entrance is the landmark most visitors look for. Stand well back, since the decoration is mostly on its lofty upper reaches, an elaborately painted section topped with a terra-cotta-tiled roof. The characters inscribed on its eastern front implore you to 'Remember the past and look forward to the future.'

The gate sits on the same site as a previous, temporary wooden one, built here for a royal visit in 1912. The lions on either side of the Millennium Gate originally had polished granite balls in their mouths, but they mysteriously disappeared soon after the gate was unveiled and have never been found.

JACK CHOW BUILDING NOTABLE BUILDING

Map p273 (www.jackchow.com; 8 W Pender St; S Stadium-Chinatown) This unusual spot was known for decades as the Sam Kee Building until Jack Chow Insurance changed the name and spruced it up. Listed in the *Guinness Book of World Records* as the planet's shallowest commercial building, the new approach includes a synchronized musical light show on the outside of the structure that catches the eye as you walk past.

It's interesting to note that this century-old building is only here as the result of a dispute. Chang Toy, the Sam Kee Co owner, bought land at this site in 1906, but in 1926 all but a 1.8m-wide strip was expropriated by the city to widen Pender St. Toy's revenge was to build anyway, and up sprang the unusual 'Slender on Pender' dwelling.

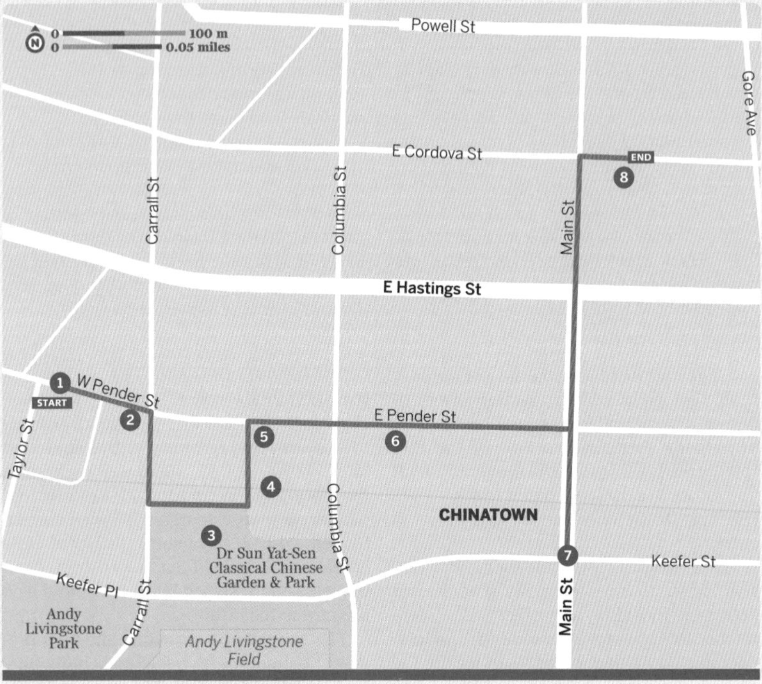

Neighborhood Walk
Chinatown Culture & History Crawl

START CHINATOWN MILLENNIUM GATE
END VANCOUVER POLICE MUSEUM
LENGTH 1.5KM; ONE HOUR

Stroll Canada's largest Chinatown and immerse yourself in culture and heritage. Start near the intersection of W Pender and Taylor Sts, where the giant 1 **Chinatown Millennium Gate** (p83) dominates proceedings. Walk east under the gate and you'll come to the quirky 2 **Jack Chow Building** (p83), reputedly the world's narrowest office block. Peer in the windows and spot the glass sidewalk panels, reminders of a subterranean public baths complex.

Turn right onto Carrall St. The entrance to the lovely 3 **Dr Sun Yat-Sen Classical Chinese Garden & Park** (p83) is on your left. Inside, check out tranquil pools, intriguing limestone formations, and gnarly pine and bonsai trees on a guided tour; you might also spot some live turtles. When you exit, walk north towards Pender St, noticing the 4 **bronze memorial** on the red tiles that commemorates the contribution of Chinese workers to building Canada's train system, and then the white-paneled 5 **alternative Chinatown gate** that was built for Expo '86.

Turn right onto Pender and stroll east for a couple of blocks. You'll pass antique Chinatown buildings – some of the city's oldest storefronts – plus several dragon-topped street lamps; you're now entering the heart of historic Chinatown. Look for 6 **Sai Woo** (p89) on your right; a dinner option for later. Continue along Pender to Main St. Explore the traditional Chinese stores on and around Main, especially one block south on 7 **Keefer Street**. Then, return to Main, turn right and walk a couple of blocks north to Cordova St.

Turn right on Cordova for the 8 **Vancouver Police Museum & Archives** (p82), where you can spend an hour exploring the city's past, from unsolved crimes to a yesteryear mortuary room.

EATING

Gastown's handsome heritage buildings are stuffed with innovative gourmet hangouts and convivial comfort-food haunts. Things change rapidly here, so keep your eyes peeled for new openings. In Chinatown, Pender and Keefer Sts (between Columbia St and Gore Ave) are your best bets for authentic Chinese dining, including some with contemporary fusion flourishes.

Gastown

VEGAN CAVE — VEGAN $

Map p273 (604-423-4211; www.facebook.com/vegancave; 415 Abbott St; mains $8-15; 11am-10pm Mon-Fri, noon-10pm Sat, noon-7:30pm Sun; ; 14) Specializing in delicious plant-based pizzas that easily hook carnivores as well, choose from a dozen-or-so topping varieties (Freaky Greeky, made with cashew feta, recommended) plus one of their four grain-free bases (go for yam-casava). You'll soon be rolling your eyes with pleasure and planning which one to order next. Super-friendly service, plus vegan cheesecake desserts are also on the menu.

BIRDS & THE BEETS — CAFE $

Map p272 (604-893-7832; www.birdsandbeets.ca; 55 Powell St; mains $6-11; 7am-6pm Mon-Fri, 9am-5pm Sat & Sun; ; 4) A friendly, local-favorite hangout with a small menu of delicious, made-to-order salads, sandwiches and breakfast items (try the avocado-and-poached-egg brioche sandwich). It's easy to spend an hour, especially if you have a sun-dappled window seat, at this slender, wood-floored charmer. Also a great spot to grab a pit-stop coffee or a fresh-baked $5 sourdough loaf.

In the evenings, from Wednesday to Saturday (6pm to 11pm), the Powell St side of the business transforms into a pop-up wine bar. Expect small-plate treatss and a wide array of natural wines from BC and beyond. For more information, visit www.juicebaryvr.com.

TACOFINO TACO BAR — MEXICAN $

Map p272 (604-899-7907; www.tacofino.com; 15 W Cordova St; tacos from $6; 11:30am-10pm Sun-Wed, 11:30am-midnight Thu-Sat; ; 14) Food-truck favorite Tacofino made an instant splash with this huge, handsome dining room (think stylish geometric-patterned floors, hive-like lampshades and a tiny back patio). The simple menu focuses on a handful of taco options plus nachos, soups and a selection of beer, agave and tequila flights. Fish tacos are the top seller, but we love the super-tender lamb *birria* version.

Drop by for happy hour, from 3pm to 6pm daily, when you can scoff two tacos for $10. And if you're hungry for takeout, there's a busy burrito counter at the front of the restaurant.

PUREBREAD — BAKERY $

Map p272 (604-563-8060; www.purebread.ca; 159 W Hastings St; baked items $3-6; 8:30am-6pm; ; 14) When Whistler's favorite bakery opened here, salivating Vancouverites began flocking in en masse. Expect to stand slack-jawed in front of the glass panels as you try to choose from a cornucopia of cakes, pastries and bars. Cake-wise, we love the coconut buttermilk loaf, but make sure you also pick up a crack bar or salted caramel bar to go (or preferably both).

And if you think power bars taste like the soles of old running shoes, sink your teeth into Purebread's velvet-soft go go bar, then walk it all off with a 50km stroll.

NELSON THE SEAGULL — CAFE $

Map p272 (604-681-5776; www.nelsontheseagull.com; 315 Carrall St; mains $6-11; 8am-4pm Mon-Fri, 9am-4pm Sat & Sun; ; 14) Gastown's hippest cafe, the mosaic-floored Seagull is also amazingly welcoming. Locals drop in to admire each other's MacBooks, lingering over flat-white coffees while indulging in the kind of wholesome treats that might be made by a gourmet grandma. Start the day with poached eggs on house-baked sourdough toast and return for the ploughman's lunch served on a board.

Grab a seat at the long table and you'll soon be in with the locals. Then peruse the walls for locally created artworks before taking a peek at the large open kitchen at the back; if you're here when the bread's being baked, you'll be in culinary heaven (takeout loaves are available).

MEAT & BREAD — SANDWICHES $

Map p272 (www.meatandbread.com; 370 Cambie St; mains $8-12; 11am-5pm Mon-Sat, 11am-4pm Sun; 14) Arrive early to sidestep the lunchtime line-ups at Vancouver's favorite sandwich mini-chain and you might snag a seat. If not, hang with the locals at the long

DOWNTOWN EASTSIDE: REGENERATION OR GENTRIFICATION

Radiating from the Main and Hastings Sts intersection, the Downtown Eastside was once Vancouver's primary business and shopping district. But by the 1970s the banks, flagship stores and neon-accented restaurants had closed or departed and the area had descended into a depressing ghetto of lives blighted by drugs and prostitution. The neighborhood that time forgot, though, has been on a rapid upward curve in recent years.

The catalyst for change was the massive Woodward's (p82) redevelopment that opened in 2010, transforming a former department store that had stood empty and crumbling for more than a decade with new shops and condo units. It triggered the restoration of dozens of other old buildings in the neighborhood, many of them ironically still here because developers had treated this area as a no-go zone for decades while tearing down buildings of similar age in other parts of the city. Now handsomely renovated, these include the copper-colored Dominion Building (p82) and the beautifully upgraded Flack Block (p83). Don't stay too long outside the monumental-looking **Carnegie Community Centre** (Map p273; 401 Main St, Chinatown; 9am-11pm; 3), though. The city's original public library is a lovely building – with stained-glass windows of Shakespeare, Spenser and Milton – but the milling crowds and barely concealed drug deals taking place outside can be overwhelming for some visitors.

Nostalgia fans should also keep their eyes peeled for heritage neon signs in this area, mostly along Hastings St. Look out for fine examples at the Ovaltine Cafe and Save on Meats.

Not surprisingly, while many have praised efforts to restore and renovate the Downtown Eastside's historic look, accusations of gentrification have been strongly voiced. As hipster bars and boutique shops continue to pop up in old buildings here, the locals who have called the area home for decades are being priced out. It remains to be seen whether a balance can be found that pleases everyone.

table, tucking into the daily-changing special or the ever-popular, nicely juicy porchetta sandwich. The finger-licking grilled cheese is also delicious, seriously challenging the hipsters trying to eat it without getting it on their beards.

Wash it all down with a craft beer or glass of wine, and expect to come back: this place has an almost cult-like following.

SAVE ON MEATS — DINER $

Map p272 (604-569-3568; www.saveonmeats.ca; 43 W Hastings St; mains $6-15; 11am-7pm Sun-Thu, 11am-11pm Fri & Sat; 14) A former old-school butcher shop that's been transformed into a popular hipster diner. Slide into a booth or hop on a swivel chair at the superlong counter and tuck into comfort dishes. They range from a good-value $6 all-day breakfast to the satisfying SOM burger, paired with a heaping tangle of 'haystack' fries. Add a BC-brewed Persephone beer to keep things lively.

If you really want to get in the groove, try a boozy 'adult milkshake.' There are several good vegetarian options on the menu, too; falafel burger recommended.

MEET IN GASTOWN — VEGAN $$

Map p272 (604-696-1111; www.meetonmain.com; 12 Water St; mains $10-16; 11am-11pm Sun-Thu, 11am-midnight Fri & Sat; Waterfront) Serving great vegan comfort dishes without the rabbit-food approach, this wildly popular spot can be clamorously busy at times. But it's worth the wait for a wide-ranging array of herbivore- and carnivore-pleasing dishes, from rice bowls and mac 'n' cheese (made from vegan cashew 'cheese') to hearty burgers and poutine-like fries slathered in nut-based miso gravy (our recommendation).

In a shaded courtyard area just off Water St (the city's tiny original jail once stood nearby), it also has a small patio for alfresco dining.

GREEK GASTOWN — GREEK $$

Map p272 (604-423-3360; www.thegreekbyanatoli.com; 221 Carrall St; mains $13-27; 11:30am-11pm Mon-Wed, 11:30am-midnight Thu & Fri, 2pm-midnight Sat, 2-11pm Sun; 4) A smartly hip update on traditional Greek tavernas, this exposed-brick, white-tabled eatery serves up delicious new takes on dishes such as moussaka and velvet-soft lamb. Start with a house-made dip taster served with piping-hot pita and don't forget to add a side of lemon potatoes. The dishes are deceptively rich and filling, and there's a full array of BC craft beers.

NUBA — MIDDLE EASTERN $$

Map p272 (☎604-688-1655; www.nuba.ca; 207 W Hastings St; mains $9-30; ⏰11:30am-10pm Mon-Fri, noon-10pm Sat, 5-10pm Sun; ☑; 🚌14) Tucked under the landmark Dominion Building, this Lebanese restaurant attracts budget noshers and cool hipsters in equal measure. If you're not sure what to go for, split some tasty, surprisingly filling meze dishes, including excellent hummus and falafel, or just dive straight into a shareable La Feast for two that covers all the bases (including the inevitable doggie-bag takeout).

There are plenty of vegetarian options here as well as a homey, fresh-made feel to the food. Consider taking a photo of the building on your way out; the copper-topped edifice is among the most iconic old buildings in the city and was once one of the tallest.

★ST LAWRENCE RESTAURANT — FRENCH $$$

Map p272 (☎604-620-3800; www.stlawrencerestaurant.com; 269 Powell St, Railtown; mains $34-44; ⏰5:30-10:30pm Tue-Sun; 🚌4) Resembling a handsome wood-floored bistro that's been teleported straight from Montréal, this sparkling, country-chic dining room is a Railtown superstar. The Québecois approach carries over onto a small menu of elevated, perfectly prepared old-school mains such as trout in brown-butter sauce and the utterly delicious duck-leg confit with sausage. French-Canadian special-occasion dining at its finest.

ASK FOR LUIGI — ITALIAN $$$

Map p272 (☎604-428-2544; www.askforluigi.com; 305 Alexander St, Railtown; mains $25-28; ⏰11:30am-2:30pm & 5:30-10:30pm Tue-Fri, 9:30am-2:30pm & 5:30-11pm Sat & Sun; ☑; 🚌4) Consider an off-peak weekday lunch if you don't want to wait too long for a table at this white-clapboard little charmer; reservations are not accepted. Inside, you'll find a checkerboard floor and teak-lined interior crammed with tables and delighted diners tucking into (and sharing) plates of elevated, from-scratch-made pasta; think pappardelle-and-duck ragu and don't miss the hearty Luigi's meatballs.

Despite the top-notch dishes, this Railtown hot spot never feels snobbish, especially during weekend-brunch service when the room is animated with lively local chatter. And while rabbit and octopus make frequent dinner-menu appearances, there are always a couple of enticing vegetarian options as well.

PIDGIN — ASIAN $$$

Map p272 (☎604-620-9400; www.pidginvancouver.com; 350 Carrall St; mains $21-38; ⏰5pm-midnight Sun-Thu, 5pm-1am Fri & Sat; 🚌14) Fusing an eclectic, inventive and ever-changing Asian and French approach with a contemporary, hipster lounge room filled with small tables and eye-opening artworks, the trick here is to order and share dishes such as foie gras rice bowls and duck breast with hoisin sauce. An enticing tasting menu ($65 per person) is also available if you're feeling adventurous.

Drop by for the daily 5pm-to-6pm happy hour and start your evening with a cool cocktail or two.

L'ABATTOIR — FRENCH $$$

Map p272 (☎604-568-1701; www.labattoir.ca; 217 Carrall St; mains $39-44; ⏰5:30-10pm daily & 10am-2pm brunch Sat & Sun; 🚌4) Gastown's best special-occasion restaurant, this candlelit, brick-lined spot makes an art of attending to every detail. Be careful not to fill up on starters of seared scallops and baked oysters before tucking into their eye-rollingly delicious French-influenced West Coast mains, ranging from honey-glazed duck to roasted lamb saddle. Don't forget cocktails; there's a serious commitment to top-notch libations here.

Reservations are recommended. There's also a popular and comparatively well-priced weekend brunch service if you want to start the day off in style.

Chinatown

★OVALTINE CAFE — DINER $

Map p272 (☎604-685-7021; www.facebook.com/ovaltinecafe; 251 E Hastings St; mains $7-10; ⏰6:30am-3pm Mon-Sat, 6:30am-2pm Sun; 🚌14) Like being inside Edward Hopper's *Nighthawks* diner painting, this time-capsule greasy spoon instantly transports you to the 1940s. Snag a booth alongside the hospital-green walls or, better yet, slide onto a tape-repaired spinning stool

JAPANTOWN

The Chinese weren't the only group to arrive from Asia in the early days of Vancouver. A couple of blocks east of Chinatown, Japantown was once home to many residences, shops and businesses that served the fledgling city's Japanese community. Centered on an area around Oppenheimer Park, this intriguing historic district is worth a wander if you're in the vicinity. You'll find some of the city's oldest small wooden homes, many of them reminders of a sometimes forgotten period in Vancouver's past.

at the long counter. Truck-stop coffee is de rigueur here, alongside burgers, sandwiches and fried breakfasts that haven't changed in decades.

It's a uniquely evocative reminder of yesteryear Vancouver (check out the near-legendary neon sign outside), so save time to peruse the art-deco flourishes on the cabinets. And if you're in the area and you simply want to check it out, drop by for an afternoon slice of apple pie and ice cream.

BESTIE — GERMAN $

Map p273 (604-620-1175; www.facebook.com/bestiewurst; 105 E Pender St; mains $4-11; 11:30am-10pm Sun-Thu, 11:30am-midnight Fri & Sat; ; 3) Like a food truck with a permanent home, this white-walled hole-in-the-wall specializes in Berlin-style currywursts – hearty sausages slathered in curry sauce, served with crunchy fries. It's popular with passing hipsters, so arrive off-peak for a chance to snag the little cubby-hole window table: the best in the house. Fresh-baked pretzels and a well-curated array of local craft beers only serve to enhance the whole experience.

The owners have also been making their own cider in recent years; ask for a sample and then add a large glass to your order.

SAY HEY CAFE — SANDWICHES $

Map p273 (604-564-4604; www.sayheycafe.ca; 156 E Pender St; sandwiches $10-13; 11am-4pm Mon-Sat; ; 3) This corridor-like hole-in-the-wall eatery fuses a friendly hipster vibe with a menu of seriously satisfying, lovingly constructed submarine sandwiches. On toasted, sesame-studded buns, the selection ranges from top-selling meatball and all-day breakfast hoagies to a juicily delicious mortadella-packed option. Vegetarians are well served by the ever-changing Anti-Hero sandwich, and there's an array of Asian soft drinks; Mister Brown canned coffee included.

Sides of soup, beans and salad are also served if you're feeling superhungry. Whatever sub you order – all are wrapped in butcher paper – it's best to eat it here while the toast is still warm.

PAZZO CHOW — ITALIAN $

Map p273 (604-563-1700; www.pazzochow.com; 620 Quebec St; mains $10-14; 8am-6pm Mon-Thu, 10am-6pm Sat; Stadium-Chinatown) When you're done with dumplings in Chinatown, hunt down this tiny, homestyle hole-in-the-wall, serving rustic pasta and focaccia sandwich specials (check the chalkboard) to a loyal band of mostly takeout customers.

You can also dine in at one of the small indoor or outdoor tables. They make delicious small-batch ice cream as well, perfect for some quick pit-stopping; flavors can range from tiramisu to top-selling toasted coconut.

CHINATOWN BBQ — CHINESE $

Map p273 (604-428-2626; www.chinatownbbq.com; 130 E Pender St; mains $10-19; 11am-8pm Tue-Sun; 3) A modern-day version of this historic neighborhood's once-ubiquitous barbecue shops, this retro-feel eatery (vinyl booths, checkerboard floor and monochrome wall photos) serves simple, perfectly prepared platters of meat and rice plus more (we like the beef-brisket curry). Expect a soundtrack of traditional Chinese music and the thud of meat cleavers from the old dudes in the open kitchen.

RAMEN BUTCHER — RAMEN $

Map p273 (604-806-4646; www.theramenbutcher.com; 223 E Georgia St; mains $10-13; 11am-3pm & 5-10pm Mon-Thu, 11am-10pm Fri-Sun; ; 3) One of several Asian-themed restaurants arriving in Chinatown in recent years, this is the first North American foray of a well-known Japanese ramen franchise. The signature thin noodles come in several broth-bowl varieties with slabs of slow-cooked pork; we recommend the garlicky Red Spicy Ramen. Still have some soup in your bowl? They'll toss in a second serving of noodles for free.

It's mostly about the ramen here, but there are also several gyoza varieties to fill you up (including an unusual pork-and-cheese version).

UMALUMA

GELATO $

Map p273 (☎604-559-5862; www.umaluma.com; 235 E Pender St; single scoop from $6; ⏰4-9pm Tue-Thu, 4-11pm Fri, 2:30-11pm Sat, 2:30-9pm Sun; 📶🥕; 🚌3) A bright, pastel-hued nook serving utterly delicious dairy-free gelato. There are usually 10 or so house-made flavors to choose from here. The decadent Drunken Cherry is a regular top-seller, alongside tempting alternatives including Mucho Matcha and Coffee Toffee, all served in cups or waffle cones. Arrive off-peak in summer for one of the sought-after little tables.

★CAMPAGNOLO

ITALIAN $$

Map p273 (☎604-484-6018; www.campagnolorestaurant.ca; 1020 Main St; mains $18-25; ⏰11:30am-2:30pm Mon-Fri & 5:30-10pm daily; 🥕; 🚌3) Eyebrows were raised when this contemporary, rustic-style Italian restaurant opened in a hitherto sketchy part of town. But Campagnolo has lured locals and inspired a miniwave of other restaurants in the vicinity. Reserve ahead and dive into reinvented comfort dishes such as shrimp gnocchetti and a fennel sausage-topped pizza that may induce you to eat your body weight in thin-crust.

There are several great vegetarian options here. Save some room for a buzz-triggering after-dinner glass of grappa or consider heading to the hidden gem **Campagnolo Upstairs** bar. With a separate street entrance, this woodsy, comfortably hip haunt serves great cocktails, craft beers and its own food menu. Don't miss the famous 'dirty burger' here; it's arguably the best in town.

PHNOM PENH

VIETNAMESE, CAMBODIAN $$

Map p273 (☎604-682-5777; www.phnompenhrestaurant.ca; 244 E Georgia St; mains $8-18; ⏰10am-9pm Mon-Thu, 10am-10pm Fri-Sun; 🚌3) The dishes at this bustling, local-legend joint are split between Cambodian and Vietnamese soul-food classics. It's the highly addictive chicken wings and their lovely pepper sauce that keep regulars loyal. Once you've piled up the bones, dive back in for round two: papaya salad, butter beef and spring rolls show just how good a street-food-inspired Asian menu can be.

Don't leave without sampling a steamed rice cake, stuffed with pork, shrimp, coconut and scallions, and washed down with an ice-cold bottle of Tsingtao. This is the kind of place that makes Vancouver Canada's most authentic ethnic-food city.

SAI WOO

ASIAN $$

Map p273 (☎604-568-1117; www.saiwoo.ca; 158 E Pender; mains $13-23; ⏰5pm-midnight Tue-Sat, 5-9pm Sun; 🚌3) There's a film-set look to the exterior of this contemporary restaurant that resembles a replica of an old Hong Kong restaurant. But the long, slender interior is a candlelit cave with a lounge-like vibe. Expect a wide array of Asian dishes, from Szechuan spicy-beef noodles to Korean-style barbecued-pork pancakes, and consider the happy hour (5pm to 6pm) with half-price dumplings.

Save time to snap a photo of the neon rooster sign outside; it's a replica of the original one that graced the building for many years.

JUKE FRIED CHICKEN

CHICKEN $$

Map p273 (☎604-336-5853; www.jukefriedchicken.com; 182 Keefer St; mains $7-28; ⏰11am-10:30pm Mon-Thu, 11am-11:30pm Fri & Sat, 11am-10pm Sun; 📶; 🚌3) Behind its striking red-panel facade, one of Vancouver's best fried-chicken joints serves up a wood-lined, diner-comfy room (plus chatty patio) and a wide array of utterly irresistible comfort dishes. Crunchy-coated chicken is the staple, of course, but there are also finger-licking pork ribs and sweet-and-sour wings. Save room for sides (fried Brussels sprouts recommended).

RAILTOWN RISING

Radiating six blocks east from the foot of Main St, a former gritty industrial area has become one of Vancouver's coolest new minihoods in recent years. Increasingly colonized by indie shops and restaurants, the old warehouses and workshops of Railtown are luring the hipsters to an area where few feared to tread just five years ago. If you're in Gastown or Chinatown, it's worth detouring for a quick wander around the area. Highlights to look out for here include top eateries St Lawrence Restaurant (p87) and Ask for Luigi (p87).

BAO BEI CHINESE **$$**

Map p273 (☎604-688-0876; www.bao-bei.ca; 163 Keefer St; small plates $6-23; ⊙5:30pm-midnight Mon-Sat, 5:30-11pm Sun; 🚌3) Reinterpreting a Chinatown heritage building with hipsteresque flourishes, this Chinese brasserie is a seductive dinner destination. Bringing a contemporary edge to Asian cuisine are tapas-sized, MSG-free dishes such as *shao bing* (stuffed Chinese flatbread), delectable dumplings and spicy-chicken steamed buns. There's also an enticing drinks menu guaranteed to make you linger, especially if you dive into the inventive cocktails.

Reservations are not accepted and tables can be hard to come by, so try to avoid peak dining times (7pm to 9pm).

DRINKING & NIGHTLIFE

Home to some of Vancouver's best bars, Gastown's atmospheric old brick buildings have been revitalized with distinctive watering holes in recent years, making this an ideal spot for an easy pub crawl. And don't forget about Chinatown, which also has a choice bar or two of its own.

Gastown

★ALIBI ROOM PUB

Map p272 (☎604-623-3383; www.alibi.ca; 157 Alexander St; ⊙5-11:30pm Mon-Thu, 5pm-12:30am Fri, 10am-12:30am Sat, 10am-11:30pm Sun; 📶; 🚌4) Vancouver's best craft-beer tavern pours a near-legendary roster of 50-plus drafts, many from celebrated BC breweries including Four Winds, Yellow Dog and Dageraad. Hipsters and veteran-ale fans alike love the 'frat bat:' choose your own four samples or ask to be surprised. Check the board for new guest casks and stick around for a gastropub dinner at one of the chatty long tables.

Food-wise, the jalapeno chicken 'samwich' lures heat fans but weekend brunch is also recommended (arrive early). There's a slender patio for alfresco summer quaffing, and the cavelike downstairs area is ideal for rainy-day hunkering. Also ask about Brassneck (p138), Alibi's affiliated and arguably even-more-popular microbrewery location on Main St.

★GUILT & CO BAR

Map p272 (www.guiltandcompany.com; 1 Alexander St; ⊙7pm-late; ⓈWaterfront) This cave-like subterranean bar, beneath Gastown's brick-cobbled sidewalks, is also a brilliant venue to catch a tasty side dish of live music. Most shows are pay-what-you-can and can range from trumpet jazz to heartfelt singer-songwriters. Drinks-wise, there's a great cocktail list plus a small array of draft beers (and many more in cans and bottles). Avoid weekends when there are often lineups.

In-the-know locals love this place and it's easy to slide into the vibe and stick around far longer than you had planned.

REVOLVER COFFEE

Map p272 (☎604-558-4444; www.revolvercoffee.ca; 325 Cambie St; ⊙7:30am-6pm Mon-Fri, 9am-6pm Sat; 📶; 🚌14) Gastown's coolest see-and-be-seen coffee shop, Revolver has never lost its hipster crown. But it's remained at the top of the Vancouver coffee-mug tree via a serious commitment to serving expertly prepared top-quality java. Aim for a little booth table or, if they're taken (they usually are), hit the large communal table next door.

DIAMOND COCKTAIL BAR

Map p272 (www.di6mond.com; 6 Powell St; ⊙5:30pm-1am Sun-Thu, 5:30-2am Fri & Sat; 🚌4) Head upstairs via the unassuming entrance to discover one of Vancouver's warmest little brick-lined cocktail bars. A glowing, wood-floored heritage room studded with sash windows – try for a view seat – it's popular with local coolsters but is rarely pretentious. A list of perfectly nailed premium cocktails ($11 to $15) helps, coupled with a diverse tapas menu, tasty flatbreads included.

Check out the lovely crystal chandeliers here, antiques from a bygone age, and try to spot the statue of Gassy Jack atop a whiskey barrel across the square. If you have enough to drink, he might even talk to you. During the 5:30pm to 7:30pm daily happy hour, some cocktails are reduced by $4.

SIX ACRES BAR

Map p272 (☎604-488-0110; www.sixacres.ca; 203 Carrall St; ⊙11:30am-11:30pm Sun-Thu, 11:30am-12:30am Fri & Sat; 📶; 🚌4) Gastown's coziest tavern, you can cover all the necessary food groups via the carefully chosen draft- and bottled-beer list here. There's a small, animated summer patio out front but inside (especially upstairs) is great for hiding in a chatty, candlelit corner and working

LOCAL KNOWLEDGE

VANCOUVER'S BEST ART FEST

Some locals claim that Vancouver doesn't have much of an arts scene. But if you're visiting in November and you know where to look, you'll have possibly the artiest weekend of your life. During the annual **Eastside Culture Crawl** (www.culturecrawl.ca; ⌚mid-Nov), hundreds of local artists open up their studios, houses and workshops for free to art-loving visitors who wander from site to site. People spend their days meeting the creators, hanging with artsy chums and even buying the occasional well-priced gem. Festival locations stretch eastwards from the north end of Main St and visitors spend their time walking the streets looking for the next hot spot, which is typically just around the corner.

During this cultural treasure hunt you'll find full-time artists working on commissioned installations as well as artisans noodling away in their spare bedrooms. There's an almost partylike atmosphere in the streets during the weekend, especially if the rain holds off. Look out for the occasional street performer keeping things lively and incorporate a coffee-shop pit stop or two along the way. The event is a great opportunity to buy one-of-a-kind artwork souvenirs for that difficult person back home (you know the one).

Head to the website to plan your route, although we recommend just wandering and following the crowds to see what you find. Printed programs with maps are also available at most of the galleries involved.

your way through the brews – plus a shared small plate or three (we like the sausage board).

It seems right and proper to also have a whiskey here; that's Gassy Jack's statue outside, perched atop a barrel, and he started the city with his first bar just a few steps from where you are now. The history doesn't end there, though. Six Acres is located in the Alhambra Building, one of the city's oldest structures.

SALT TASTING ROOM — WINE BAR

Map p272 (☎604-633-1912; www.salttastingroom.com; 45 Blood Alley; ⌚3:30pm-midnight; 🚌4) Nestled along a cobbled back alley reputedly named after one of the area's former butchers, this atmospheric little brick-lined wine bar offers dozens of interesting tipples, mostly available by the glass. From your communal table, peruse the large blackboard of house-cured meats and regional cheeses, then go for a $16 tasting plate of three, served with piquant condiments including British style piccalilli.

You can also extend the tasting approach to your libations: three-glass tasting flights of wine, mead or sherry are $15.

REVEL ROOM — BAR

Map p272 (☎604-687-4088; www.revelroom.ca; 238 Abbott St; ⌚4pm-1am Tue-Thu, 4pm-2am Fri & Sat, 4pm-midnight Sun; 🚌4) Tucked along a little Gastown side street, the red-painted facade fronts one of the city's most intimate live music venues. This brick-lined cave features small tables, a tiny performance area and the kind of immersive cocktail list that will have you settling in for a fun night of old fashioned Southern-style bacchanalian fun. Jazz, blues and more hits the corner 'stage' six nights a week.

Reservations are recommended and there's a supper club approach here that includes a menu of Cajun-influenced comfort food.

IRISH HEATHER — PUB

Map p272 (☎604-688-9779; www.irishheather.com; 210 Carrall St; ⌚11:30am-midnight Sun-Thu, 11:30am-2am Fri & Sat; 📶; 🚌4) Belying the clichés about evry expat Irish bar in the world (except for its reclaimed Guinness barrel floor), the Heather is one of Vancouver's best gastropubs. Alongside lovingly prepared sausage and mash, and corned beef with braised cabbage, you'll find good craft beers and, of course, some well-poured stout.

PINBALL WIZARD

One of the neighborhood's greasiest dive bars, **Pub 340** (Map p272; ☎604-602-0644; www.pub340.ca; 340 Cambie St, Gastown; ⏰9am-2am Sun-Thu, 9am-3am Fri & Sat; 📶; 🚌14) has cleaned up its act somewhat in recent years. But it's not the cosmetic paint job and karaoke nights that have lured back some locals. It's the addition of arguably the city's best pinball room. A dozen or so shiny machines – from 1980s classics to new favorites – attract flipping fanatics in their droves. Regular tournaments welcome newbies and veterans alike to show off their skills on machines including Terminator 2 and the Addams Family. Games cost $1 and, if you lose everything, you can cheer yourself up with a karaoke warble of that slightly well-worn Who song in the main bar area; a few glasses of Old Style Pilsner will help persuade you.

Looking for happy hour? Whiskey fans will also be gobsmacked by the wide array of tipples available in the back-room **Shebeen** bar. It's the kind of place where you could settle in for hours and still be there a week later — merry, if not a little worse for wear.

EAST VAN ROASTERS COFFEE

Map p272 (☎604-629-7562; www.eastvanroasters.com; 319 Carrall St; ⏰10am-5pm Mon-Fri, noon-5pm Sat; 📶; 🚌14) Blink and you'll miss the entrance to this small but perfectly formed mosaic-floored cafe, which includes a coffee roastery. It's worth popping in to combine an excellent espresso with some delectable single-origin chocolate treats, also made on-site. It's a social enterprise that's aimed at providing training and employment for women who live in this area, and the service is always sparklingly friendly.

STEAMWORKS BREW PUB BREWERY

Map p272 (☎604-689-2739; www.steamworks.com; 375 Water St; ⏰11:30am-midnight Sun-Thu, 11:30am-1am Fri & Sat; Ⓢ Waterfront) This huge brewpub on the edge of Gastown serves several own-made beers, including crisp pilsners, hoppy IPAs and small-batch seasonals. But the best of the bunch is the malty pale ale, ideal for slow afternoon quaffing at an alfresco table (aim for a view of the mountains). Popular with tourists and clocked-off office workers, there's also an inviting pub-grub menu.

LOCAL PUBLIC EATERY PUB

Map p272 (☎778-737-4277; www.localgastown.com; 3 Alexander St; ⏰11am-1am Mon-Thu, 11am-2am Fri, 10am-2am Sat, 10am-1am Sun; 📶; 🚌4) A large, loud and fun exposed-brick tavern dominating one side of Maple Tree Sq, this is Gastown's best summer-patio spot. There's a good array of locally brewed craft beers to plunge into (anything from Parkside to Parallel 49) plus a hearty burger-dominated menu that adds heaping brunch options on weekends. It's jammed on Friday and Saturday nights, so maybe consider a weekday visit instead.

Chinatown

BACK AND FORTH BAR BAR

Map p272 (☎604-564-7664; www.backandforthbar.com; 303 Columbia St; ⏰4pm-2am Sun-Thu, 4pm-3am Fri & Sat; 📶; 🚌14) There's a distinctly inviting, den-like feel to this cool-but-friendly games-room bar where six ping-pong tables combine perfectly with a 12-tap beer selection (obligatory local microbrews and 'ironic' Lucky Lager included). An ideal late-night hangout; book ahead for a table (from $10 to $25 per hour, with lowest rates from Sunday to Tuesday) or just indulge in some giggle-triggering Jenga and Pictionary.

Take a breather on one of the vintage sofas in the elevated side-nook (its baboon-themed wallpaper is impressive, and the simians have been known to provide tips on your ping-pong technique, depending on how much booze you've imbibed). Snacks are available if you need to fuel up but there are also some top-notch Gastown and Chinatown eateries nearby for more substantial sustenance.

BRICKHOUSE PUB

Map p273 (☎604-689-8645; 730 Main St; ⏰8pm-2am Mon-Sat, 8pm-midnight Sun; 🚌3) Vancouver's most original pub, this old-school hidden gem is a welcoming, windowless tavern lined with Christmas lights, fish tanks and junk-shop couches. It's like hanging out in someone's basement, and is popular with artsy locals and in-the-know young hipsters. Grab an ale at the bar, slide onto a chair and start chatting; you're bound to meet someone interesting.

There's no food here (except chips), and bicycle-shorts-wearing owner and barman Leo is committed to the idea that bars should be places where you hang out, socialise and connect. There's also a full-size pool table here if you've somehow managed to run out of things to say. Chinatown redevelopment is rapidly transforming older buildings like this so be sure to visit while you can, before it's too late.

VANCOUVER URBAN WINERY WINE BAR

(☎604-566-9463; www.vancouverurbanwinery.com; 55 Dunlevy Ave, Railtown; ⏰11:30am-11pm Mon-Wed, 11:30am-midnight Thu & Fri, 10am-midnight Sat, 10am-11pm Sun; 🚌4) Vancouver's only winery is a cavernous, barrel-lined warehouse serving tipples from BC and beyond. It has a public tasting bar (on-tap wine flights available), while also serving beers from the site's popular Postmark Brewing operation. Drop by on Friday night when the place is a popular nightlife spot for those in the know.

There's also a full menu of West Coast small plates and main dishes available, including charcuterie boards and wagyu meatballs. Happy hour is 3pm to 6pm, Monday to Thursday.

KEEFER BAR COCKTAIL BAR

Map p273 (☎604-688-1961; www.thekeeferbar.com; 135 Keefer St; ⏰5pm-1am Sun-Thu, 5pm-2am Fri & Sat; SStadium-Chinatown) This dark, narrow and atmospheric Chinatown bar has been claimed by local cocktail-loving coolsters since the day it opened its doors. Drop in for a full evening of liquid taste-tripping and you'll have a guaranteed blast. From perfectly prepared rosemary gimlets and tart blood moons to an excellent whiskey menu and some tasty tapas (we like the steam buns), it all adds up to the makings of a great night out.

There are also cool extras here every night – including Wednesday's funk and hip-hop – which are always combined with drinks specials. In summer, grab one of the tiny seats outside and watch the Chinatown world go by.

FORTUNE SOUND CLUB CLUB

Map p273 (www.fortunesoundclub.com; 147 E Pender St; ⏰9:30pm-3am Fri & Sat, plus special events; 🚌3) This club has managed to transform what was once a tired Chinatown spot into a slick space that lures a loyal band of party goers. Slide inside and you'll find a huge dance floor popping with cool locals just out for a good time. Expect long weekend queues, and check out Happy Ending Fridays, when it's highly possible that you'll be compelled to spend the evening dancing your ass off.

Reputedly home to one of the city's best sound systems, Fortune also hosts a roster of regular live acts.

☆ ENTERTAINMENT

Gastown is more about the bars but Chinatown is home to some decent entertainment options, including a couple of local-fave live venues. Converse with a few Vancouverites here and ask for recommendations about what's coming up and who's about to hit the stage.

FIREHALL ARTS CENTRE THEATER

Map p272 (☎604-689-0926; www.firehallartscentre.ca; 280 E Cordova St; tickets from $30; 🚌14) One of the leading players in Vancouver's independent-theater scene, this intimate studio-sized venue is located inside a historic former fire station. It presents culturally diverse contemporary drama and dance, with a particular emphasis on showcasing young and emerging talent. A key venue during July's annual Dancing on the Edge festival (www.dancingontheedge.org), it also has a convivial licensed lounge on-site.

Check out the artworks lining the brick walls before you go in for your show; there's typically a focus on intriguing local artists.

RICKSHAW THEATRE LIVE MUSIC

Map p273 (☎604-681-8915; www.liveatrickshaw.com; 254 E Hastings St; tickets from $15; 🚌14) Revamped from its grungy 1970s incarnation, the funky Rickshaw shows that Eastside gentrification can be positive. The stage of choice for many punk and indie acts, it's an excellent place to see a band. There's a huge mosh area near the stage and rows of theater-style seats at the back.

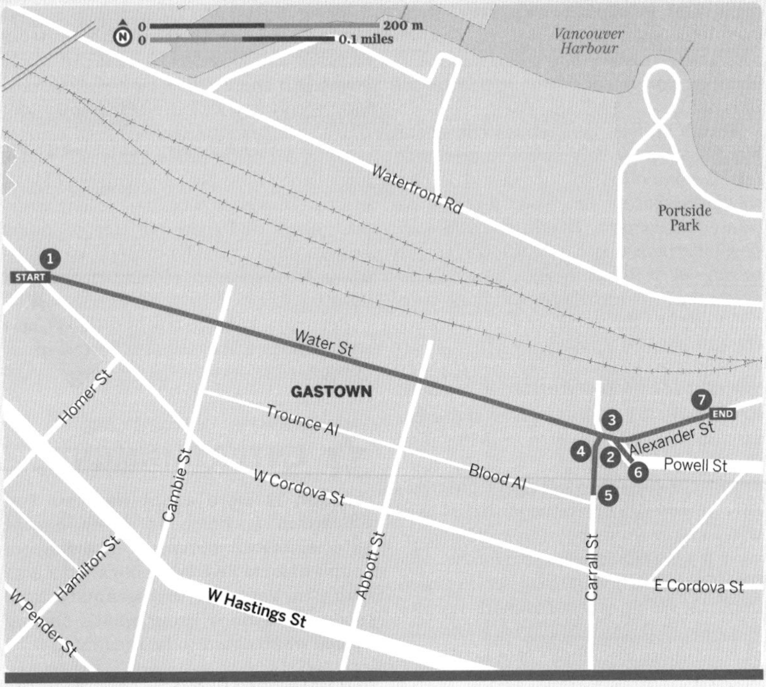

Neighborhood Walk
Gastown Bar Crawl

START STEAMWORKS BREW PUB
END ALIBI ROOM
LENGTH 1KM (TIME DEPENDS ON HOW FAST YOU DRINK...)

This short walk will take you on a merry weave around Gastown's best watering holes and give you a glimpse of the city's nightlife scene.

Start your crawl at the western end of Gastown (near Waterfront SkyTrain station) with an oatmeal stout at **1 Steamworks Brew Pub** (p92), one of the city's few brewpubs. Enjoy the downhill slope east along Water St and you'll soon arrive at Maple Tree Sq. This is where Gassy Jack triggered the city by building his first saloon – tip your hat at the **2 statue** (p82) of him here, then duck underground to **3 Guilt & Co** (p90) for a bottled beer and a board game.

Back outside, nip across the square to **4 Six Acres** (p90), one of the area's coziest hangouts. You'll be tempted to stick around, but the spirit of Gassy will be calling you back to the streets.

Stroll across Carrall St and duck into the **5 Irish Heather** (p91). It's the best spot in town for a Guinness. If you're still walking by this stage, return to Carrall, walk north for a few seconds and turn right onto Powell St. A street sign will point you to the unassuming stairwell that leads to the **6 Diamond** (p90), a great spot for perfect cocktails. Look for Gassy's statue through the window. If he doffs his hat, you've probably had too much to drink.

But if not, head back out and take Alexander St eastwards. Within a couple of minutes you'll reach the **7 Alibi Room** (p90). This is the city's favorite craft-beer bar, and a great spot to end your evening with a 'frat bat' of sampler brews.

Check the schedule to see who's on; many nights there are several bands on the roster.

PAT'S PUB LIVE MUSIC

Map p273 (604-255-4301; www.patspub.ca; 403 E Hastings St; 11am-midnight Mon-Thu, 11am-1am Fri & Sat, 11am-10pm Sun; 14) The Downtown Eastside's most-accessible dive bar started a century ago and, in recent years, it's dusted off the jazz chops that saw Jelly Roll Morton play here back in the day. Monday night sees no-cover jazz shows from 7:30pm, while there are often other cover-free jazz and blues happenings throughout the week. Check the pub's website calendar for events.

The good-value beer menu includes house-made ales from Hastings Mill Brewing; check out any available seasonals or dive straight into their Skid Road IPA. The food here is a cut above typical pub fare – pulled pork poutine, for example – with almost everything on the menu priced under $12.

CINEPLEX ODEON INTERNATIONAL VILLAGE CINEMAS CINEMA

Map p273 (604-806-0799; www.cineplex.com; 88 W Pender St; tickets from $12; S Stadium-Chinatown) Incongruously located on the 3rd floor of a usually half-empty Chinatown shopping mall, this popular Vancouver theater combines blockbuster and art-house offerings and is often used for film festivals. Comfy stadium seating is the norm here, and it's ideal for sheltering on a rainy Vancouver day with a large coffee and a case of Glosette Raisins.

SHOPPING

Once lined with tacky souvenir stores (there are still a few here), Gastown has been increasingly colonized by designer boutiques, making this area a downtown rival to Main St in the indie shopping stakes. While Chinatown's ever-colorful streets used to be more for looking at than actually shopping – how many live frogs do you usually buy? – it's also home to its own cool indie stores.

★ **MASSY BOOKS** BOOKS

Map p273 (604-721-4405; www.massybooks.com; 229 E Georgia St; 10am-6pm Sun-Wed, 10am-8pm Thu-Sat; 3) A former pop-up favorite with a now-permanent Chinatown location, this delightful bookstore is lined with tall stacks of well-curated, mostly used titles. There's an impressively large selection of indigenous-themed books, alongside good selections covering travel, history and literature – plus a bargain $1 cart outside. Love mysteries? Try finding the store's secret room, hidden behind a pushable bookcase door.

★ **EASTSIDE FLEA** MARKET

Map p273 (www.eastsideflea.com; 550 Malkin Ave, Eastside Studios; $3-5; 11am-5pm Sat & Sun, once or twice a month; 22) A size upgrade from its previous venue has delivered a cavernous market hall of hip arts and craftsisans hawking everything from handmade chocolate bars to intricate jewelry and a humungous array of cool-ass vintage clothing. Give yourself plenty of time to hang out here; there's a pool table and retro arcade machines plus food trucks and a long bar serving local craft beer.

It's $3 for entry but $5 buys you an all-weekend pass.

JOHN FLUEVOG SHOES SHOES

Map p272 (604-688-6228; www.fluevog.com; 65 Water St, Gastown; 10am-7pm Mon-Wed & Sat, to 8pm Thu & Fri, noon-6pm Sun; S Waterfront) Like an art gallery for shoes, this alluringly cavernous store showcases the famed footwear of local designer Fluevog, whose men's and women's boots and brogues are what Doc Martens would have become if they'd stayed interesting and cutting-edge. Pick up that pair of thigh-hugging dominatrix boots you've always wanted or settle on some designer loafers that would make anyone walk tall.

Seasonal sales can be amazing and your new look will have everyone staring at your feet.

NOIZE TO GO MUSIC

Map p273 (604-428-7887; www.facebook.com/noizetogo; 243 Union St, Chinatown; 2:30-6:30pm Mon, 12:30-6:30pm Tue-Sat, 1-5:30pm Sun; 3) Like hanging out with a buddy and checking out his cool record collection, dropping in for a chat with store-owner Dale at this tiny, vinyl-lined store is a delight. Peruse the jam-packed racks of brilliantly curated albums yourself or ask for help to find that 7-inch Inspiral Carpets picture disk you let slip through your hands all those years ago.

BOOKSTORE RENAISSANCE

When Massy Books (p95) opened as an under-the-radar pop-up bookstore on Main Street in 2017, digital-embracing locals wondered how a place selling what seemed to be an old-fashioned, even obsolete item could possibly last. But the store was a huge success and, when its temporary lease later expired, they reopened in a permanent Chinatown storefront location in 2018. But they're not the only bookstore that's doing well in Vancouver: don't miss downtown's Paper Hound (p76), Kitsilano's giant Kidsbooks (p175) and the three branches of **Pulpfiction Books** (http://pulpfictionbooksvancouver.com) dotted around the city.

MAIN STREET MIXED BAG MARKET

Map p273 (www.facebook.com/mainstreetmixedbag; 1024 Main St, Chinatown; ⏰11am-6pm Sun, monthly; 🚌3) Occupying the barn-like old wooden building popularized by the now-relocated Eastside Flea (p95), this monthly free-entry artisan market features an ever-changing array of dozens of cool stands. Selling everything from handmade jewelry to sweary cross-stitch art, there's a hip-but-friendly vibe here, aided by the craft-beer bar occupying one corner. Head upstairs for more stands, including pop-culture antiques.

HERSCHEL SUPPLY CO FASHION & ACCESSORIES

Map p272 (☎604-620-1155; www.herschel.com; 347 Water St, Gastown; ⏰10am-7pm Mon-Wed & Sat, 10am-9pm Thu & Fri, 11am-6pm Sun; SWaterfront) The friendly flagship store of this hot, Vancouver-based bags-and-accessories brand is a must-see for Herschel fans. Inside a beautifully restored, artwork-lined Gastown heritage building (check out the waterfront views from the back windows), you'll find a huge array of the company's signature daypacks, plus wallets, totes, pouches and recently added clothing lines. Give yourself plenty of perusing time; you're gonna need it.

ERIN TEMPLETON FASHION & ACCESSORIES

Map p273 (☎604-682-2451; www.erintempleton.com; 511 Carrall St, Chinatown; ⏰11am-5pm Mon & Tue, 11am-6pm Wed-Sat; SStadium-Chinatown) Known for recycling leather into hip, supple bags, belts, hats and purses, this eponymous store has a cult following. Erin herself is often on hand and happy to chat about her creations (she trained in shoe-making at a London college). They're the kind of must-have, one-of-a-kind items that are hard to resist, no matter how many bags you already have back home.

The idea here is to marry form and functionality; locals rave about how long their purses last, and if anything does break, it's often fixed for free by Erin herself. Check the website for the full range and all her most recent designs. Near the front of the store, there are also some racks of carefully curated vintage clothes to check out.

COMMUNITY THRIFT & VINTAGE FROCK SHOPPE VINTAGE

Map p272 (☎604-629-8396; www.communitythriftandvintage.com; 311 Carrall St, Gastown; ⏰11am-7pm Mon-Sat, noon-5pm Sun; 🚌14) A nonprofit social enterprise selling a cornucopia of vintage women's clothing, from 1970s print dresses to elegant silk tops to printed T-shirts of old bands you may never have heard of. Spend plenty of time browsing and trying out a few new looks here, and don't forget to peruse the quirky local-made jewelry as well.

BASEMENT CLOTHING

Map p272 (☎604-688-0955; www.thebasementvan.com; 235 Cambie St, Gastown; ⏰11am-6pm Tue & Wed, 11am-7pm Thu & Fri, noon-6pm Sat & Sun; 🚌14) Keep your eyes peeled for the easily missed doorway that leads downstairs to this exposed-brick subterranean store. You'll find artfully arranged racks of cool, mostly women's, clothing by independent, predominantly Canadian creators. Artisan jewelry, bath products, clever knickknacks and more round out the display; a great spot to find one-of-a-kind items from small-scale producers and supersmart crafty-types.

COASTAL PEOPLES FINE ARTS GALLERY ARTS & CRAFTS

Map p272 (☎604-684-9222; www.coastalpeoples.com; 332 Water St, Gastown; ⏰10am-7pm May-Sep, 10am-6pm Oct-Apr; SWaterfront) This two-level museum-like store showcases an eye-popping array of Inuit and Northwest Coast indigenous jewelry, carvings and prints. On the high-art side of things, the exquisite items here are ideal if you're looking for an extra-very-special souvenir for

LAWRENCE WORCESTER/LONELY PLANET ©

Alibi Room (p90)

someone back home. Don't worry; they can ship the totem poles if you can't fit them in your suitcase.

BLIM ARTS & CRAFTS

Map p273 (☎604-872-8180; www.blim.ca; 115 E Pender St, Chinatown; ⌚11am-6pm Mon-Sat, noon-5pm Sun; 🚌14) Crammed with locally made bright-hued T-shirts, backpacks and ball caps, Blim's main business is the roster of workshops on everything from patch-making to ceramic screen printing. Check to see what's on – or just buy someone else's handiwork from the shop and pretend it's yours. Look out for resident cat Pounce, who likes to bolt for the door whenever possible.

Blim also stages craft markets at sites around the city; they're a great way to meet local artisans and pick up unique souvenirs. Check the website.

SPORTS & ACTIVITIES

A WOK AROUND CHINATOWN WALKING

(☎604-736-9508; www.awokaround.com; tour $80, minimum 2 people) A guided four-hour wander with third-generation Chinese-Canadian Vancouverite Robert Sung, this entertaining walk explores the culinary and cultural sides of Chinatown. The good-value fee includes visits to local landmarks and traditional stores as well as a dim-sum lunch and entry to the Dr Sun Yat-Sen Classical Chinese Garden (p83). There's also a Granville Island Public Market (p100) tour, samples included, for $50.

SINS OF THE CITY WALKING TOUR WALKING

Map p272 (☎604-665-3346; www.sinsofthecity.ca; 240 E Cordova St, Vancouver Police Museum, Chinatown; adult/student $18/14; ⌚Apr-Oct; 🚌14) If your criminal interests are triggered by the Vancouver Police Museum & Archives (p82), take one of their excellent Sins of the City walking tours, which weave through Gastown and Chinatown in search of former brothels, opium dens, gambling houses and more. The tours last up to two hours and are a great way to see the far-less-salubrious side of the shiny, glass-towered metropolis.

Yaletown & Granville Island

Neighborhood Top Five

❶ **Granville Island Public Market** (p100) Wandering the deli stands and gathering some goodies before heading outside to catch a busker or two and watch the boats slide by in twinkling False Creek.

❷ **Rodney's Oyster House** (p105) Shucking and scoffing some of the freshest bivalves you've ever eaten at this local favorite restaurant.

❸ **Liberty Distillery** (p109) Diving into island-made-liquor cocktails during a taste-tastic happy hour.

❹ **Vancouver Whitecaps** (p111) Joining the cheering crowds for a pro-soccer game at BC Place Stadium; face-painting optional.

❺ **Vancouver Foodie Tours** (p114) Eat your way through the city on a gastronomic walking tour hosted by ever friendly guides. Make sure to arrive hungry!

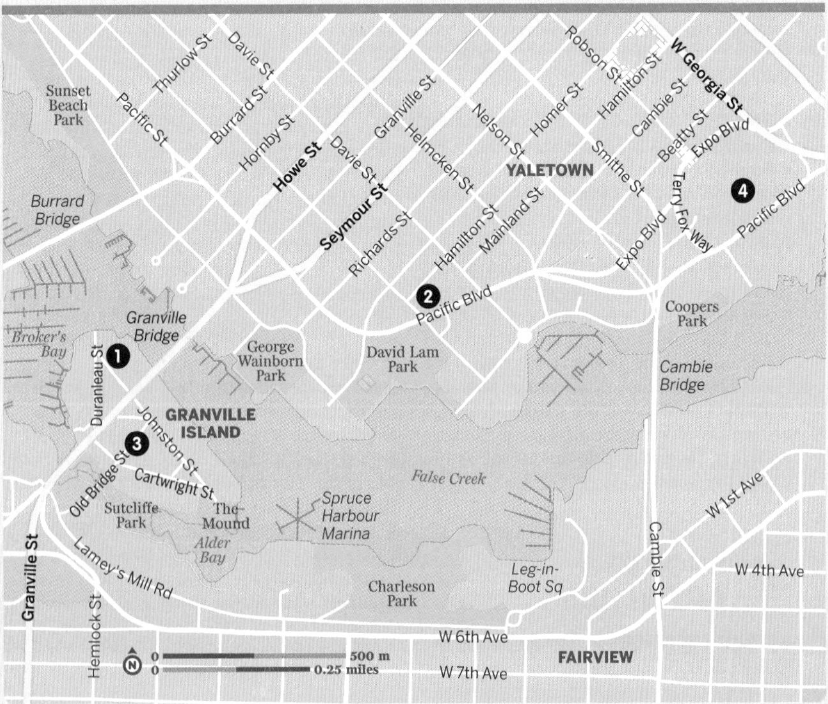

For more detail of this area see Map p274 and p275

Explore Yaletown & Granville Island

Yaletown and Granville Island face each other across False Creek but you can easily see both in one day. Give more of your time to Granville Island. Its entrance is under the south end of Granville Bridge, where Anderson St takes you right onto the island. Strolling the entire area, you'll find cool artisan studios and will escape the summer crowds that jam the busy market end. Johnston St, Cartwright St and Railspur Alley are particularly worth exploring.

Yaletown is a short miniferry (p246) ride from Granville Island. Compact and easy to explore, it radiates a block or two either side of Hamilton St. There are some worthwhile shopping options here, and if you want to join the locals you can stay for dinner. The redbrick buildings house some of Vancouver's finest restaurants; book ahead at the fancier Yaletown joints.

Local Life

- **Doughnuts** The stalls and stands of Granville Island Public Market (p100) are crammed with tasty temptations, but if you only have belly room for one treat, make it a Honey Dip from legendary Lee's Donuts.
- **Steam train** The first transcontinental passenger train to arrive in Vancouver in 1887 was pulled by Engine 374 (p102), now housed in its own free-entry Yaletown pavilion. Drop by on May's Victoria Day for a cake celebration.
- **Theater** Granville Island is the heart of Vancouver's theater scene and hosts several stages and festivals. Locals save money on shows by checking the daily half-price deals at www.ticketstonight.ca.

Getting There & Away

- **Bus** The number 50 from downtown stops near Granville Island's entrance. Bus 10 is also popular and stops on the south side of Granville Bridge – meaning a five-minute stroll under the bridge to reach the island.
- **Train** The Canada Line runs from downtown to Yaletown-Roundhouse Station, a short walk to all of Yaletown's main attractions.
- **Car** There is metered parking in Yaletown. There's parking on Granville Island, but availability is severely limited at peak times.
- **Miniferries** Granville Island is accessible by miniferry service from the West End and Yaletown side of False Creek.

Lonely Planet's Top Tip

Granville Island is great for urban birding. Visit the pond behind the Kids Market for ducks, springtime chicks included. On the island's quieter southern tip, you might spot herons eyeing the water for fish. And don't miss the iron-girder underside of Granville Bridge, where cormorants nest and raise their young.

Best Places to Eat

- Blue Water Cafe (p105)
- Bistro 101 (p107)
- Go Fish (p106)
- MeeT (p105)
- DD Mau (p103)

For reviews, see p103.

Best Places to Drink

- Liberty Distillery (p109)
- Granville Island Brewing Taproom (p110)
- Small Victory (p109)

For reviews, see p109.

Best Places to Shop

- Karameller Candy Shop (p111)
- Granville Island Broom Company (p112)
- Karen Cooper Gallery (p112)
- Circle Craft (p112)

For reviews, see p111.

TOP EXPERIENCE

SNACK YOUR WAY AROUND GRANVILLE ISLAND PUBLIC MARKET

A foodie extravaganza specializing in deli treats and pyramids of shiny fruit and vegetables, this is one of North America's finest public markets. It's ideal for whiling away an afternoon, snacking on goodies in the sun among the buskers outside or sheltering from the rain with a market tour. You'll also find side dishes of (admittedly inedible) arts and crafts.

Taste-Tripping

Come hungry: there are dozens of food stands to weave your way around at the market. Among the must-see vendors are **Oyama Sausage Company**, replete with hundreds of smoked sausages and cured meats; **Benton Brothers Fine Cheese**, with its full complement of amazing curdy goodies from British Columbia (BC) and around the world (look for anything by Farm House Natural Cheese from Agassiz, BC); and **Granville Island Tea Company** (Hawaiian rooibos recommended), with its tasting bar and more than 150 steep-tastic varieties to choose from. Baked goodies also abound: abandon your diet at **Lee's Donuts** and **Siegel's Bagels**, where the naughty cheese-stuffed baked varieties are not to be missed. And don't worry: there's always room for a wafer-thin album-sized 'cinnamon record' from **Stuart's Baked Goods**. French-themed **L'Epicerie Rotisserie and Gourmet Shop** (pictured) has been a popular addition to the market. It sells vinegars, olive oils and delicious house-cooked dishes to go.

In the unlikely event you're still hungry, there's also a small international food court: avoid off-peak dining if you want to snag a table and indulge in a good-value selection

DON'T MISS

- Oyama Sausage Company
- Lee's Donuts
- Granville Island Tea Company
- Guided market tours
- Seasonal farmers market

PRACTICALITIES

- Map p275, C1
- 604-666-6655
- www.granvilleisland.com/public-market
- Johnston St, Granville Island
- 9am-7pm
- 50, miniferries

that runs from Mexican tacos to German sausages. And if you want to dive into some regional seasonal produce, there's a **farmers market** just outside the market building between June and October where you can sample BC-made booze.

Arts & Crafts

Once you've eaten your fill, take a look at some of the market's other stands. There's a cool arts and crafts focus here, especially among the collection of day vendors that dot the market and change every week. Hand-knitted hats, hand-painted ceramics, framed art photography and quirky carvings will make for excellent one-of-a-kind souvenirs. Further artisan stands are added to the roster in the run-up to Christmas, if you happen to be here at that time. For more information on the sorts of day vendors that appear at the market, visit www.gidva.org.

Insider's Tour

If you're a hungry culinary fan, the delicious guided market walk organized by Vancouver Foodie Tours (p114) is the way to go. This leisurely stomach-stuffer (adult/child $70/60) weaves around the vendors and includes several tasting stops that will quickly fill you up. It also caters to vegetarians if you mention it when you book. The company runs friendly tasting tours in other parts of the city too, if you're keen to keep eating.

Forgotten Past

The Public Market is the centerpiece of one of Canada's most impressive urban regeneration projects – and the main reason it has been so successful. Built as a district for small factories in the early part of the last century, Granville Island – which has also been called Mud Island and Industrial Island over the years – had declined into a paint-peeled no-go area by the 1960s. But the abandoned sheds began attracting artists and theater groups by the 1970s, and the old buildings slowly started springing back to life with some much-needed repairs and upgrades. Within a few years, new theaters, restaurants and studios had been built and the Public Market quickly became an instantly popular anchor tenant. One reason for the island's popularity? Only independent, one-of-a-kind businesses operate here.

MARKET TIPS

- ➡ In summer, arrive early to sidestep the crowds, which peak in the afternoons.
- ➡ If you're driving, weekdays are the easiest times to find on-island parking.
- ➡ The food court is the island's best-value dining, but tables are scarce at peak times.
- ➡ A visiting bird-watcher? Look for the cormorants nesting under the Granville Bridge span.
- ➡ Gather a great picnic then find a quiet spot to dine; the grassy knoll at the island's opposite end is ideal, while Vanier Park is a short stroll along the seawall.
- ➡ Arrive in style; both **Aquabus** (Map p275) and False Creek Ferries (p246) operate mini-ferry services to the island.

If you're out enjoying the buskers on the market's waterfront exterior, you'll notice your False Creek view is sandwiched between two famous Vancouver bridges. The ironwork Granville Bridge is the third version of this bridge to span the inlet. The more attractive art-deco Burrard Bridge, opened in 1932, is nearby. During its opening ceremony, a floatplane was daringly piloted under the bridge's main deck.

SIGHTS

Granville Island is a self-guided sight unto itself – and it's not just about the market. Add a miniferry hop across False Creek and you can include some history- and sport-themed attractions from Yaletown on your grand day out.

Yaletown

ENGINE 374 PAVILION — MUSEUM

Map p274 (www.roundhouse.ca; 181 Roundhouse Mews, Roundhouse Community Arts & Recreation Centre; 10am-4pm, reduced hours off-season; ; Yaletown-Roundhouse) FREE May 23, 1887, was an auspicious date for Vancouver. That's when Engine 374 pulled the very first transcontinental passenger train into the fledgling city, symbolically linking the country and kick-starting the eventual metropolis. Retired in 1945, the engine was, after many years of neglect, restored and placed in this splendid pavilion. The friendly volunteers here will show you the best angle for snapping photos and share a few yesteryear railroading stories at the same time.

Administered by the West Coast Railway Heritage Park in Squamish (a good excursion for rail buffs), the engine is kept in sparkling condition and is occasionally wheeled out onto the outside turntable, part of the beautifully restored heritage roundhouse that recalls Yaletown's gritty rail-yard history. Visit on Victoria Day (last Monday before May 25) for the pavilion's annual celebration; free cake included.

BC PLACE STADIUM — STADIUM

Map p274 (604-669-2300; www.bcplace.com; 777 Pacific Blvd; P; Stadium-Chinatown) Vancouver's main sports arena is home to two professional teams: the **BC Lions** Canadian Football League team and the **Vancouver Whitecaps** soccer team. Also used for international rugby sevens tournaments, major rock concerts and a wide array of consumer shows, the renovated stadium – with its huge, crown-like retractable roof – also hosted the opening and closing ceremonies for the 2010 Olympic and Paralympic Winter Games.

BC SPORTS HALL OF FAME & MUSEUM — MUSEUM

Map p274 (604-687-5520; www.bcsportshallofame.com; 777 Pacific Blvd, Gate A, BC Place Stadium; adult/child $15/12; 10am-5pm; ; Stadium-Chinatown) Inside BC Place Stadium, this expertly curated attraction showcases top BC athletes, both amateur and professional, with an intriguing array of galleries crammed with fascinating memorabilia. There are medals, trophies and yesteryear sports uniforms on display (judging by the size of their shirts, hockey players were much smaller in the past), plus tons of hands-on activities to tire the kids out. Don't miss the **Indigenous Sport Gallery**, covering everything from hockey to lacrosse to traditional indigenous games.

CANADA'S HERO

The most poignant gallery at the BC Sports Hall of Fame & Museum is dedicated to national legend Terry Fox, the young cancer sufferer whose one-legged 1980 Marathon of Hope run across Canada ended after 143 days and 5373km, when the disease spread to the Port Coquitlam resident's lungs. When Fox died the following year, the funeral was screened live across the country and the government ordered flags to be flown at half-mast. A memorial was later constructed outside BC Place Stadium but it was replaced in 2011 by a new and much more impressive one created by Vancouver artist and writer Douglas Coupland, who had already penned his own celebrated book, *Terry*, in tribute to Fox. The new statue is a series of running figures showing Fox in motion during his cross-country odyssey. When Fox started his run he received very little attention, but by the time he was forced to stop, it felt as if the entire country was behind him. Every year since his death, fundraising runs have been held in Canada and around the world to remember his bravery. The Terry Fox Foundation (www.terryfox.org) estimates that these have now raised more than $500 million for cancer research.

DAVID LAM PARK PARK

Map p274 (www.vancouverparks.ca; cnr Drake St & Pacific Blvd; Yaletown-Roundhouse) A crooked elbow of landscaped waterfront at the neck of False Creek, Yaletown's main green space is sometimes used for free alfresco summer movie screenings. It's an ideal launch point for a seawall walk, running along the north bank of False Creek to Science World; you'll pass intriguing public artworks and the glass condo towers that transformed the neighborhood in the 1990s.

Keep a look out for birdlife while you're strolling along the route, especially the herons that keep their beady eyes on the waters here and the cormorants who typically nest further along False Creek under the Granville Bridge.

ROUNDHOUSE COMMUNITY ARTS & RECREATION CENTRE ARTS CENTER

Map p274 (604-713-1800; www.roundhouse.ca; 181 Roundhouse Mews, cnr Davie St & Pacific Blvd; 9am-9:45pm Mon-Fri, to 4:45pm Sat & Sun; Yaletown-Roundhouse) The home of the Engine 374 Pavilion, Yaletown's main community gathering space colonizes a handsomely restored heritage railway roundhouse. It offers a full roster of events and courses for locals and visitors alike, including popular drop-in running classes and Philosopher's Cafe debating events. Check the website calendar to see what's on.

Granville Island

GRANVILLE ISLAND PUBLIC MARKET MARKET

See p100.

KIDS MARKET MARKET

Map p275 (604-689-8447; www.kidsmarket.ca; 1496 Cartwright St; 10am-6pm; ; 50) A kaleidoscopic mini shopping mall for under-10s (there's even a special child-size entrance door), the Kids Market is crammed with 25 family-friendly stores, mostly of the toy variety. If your child's interests extend beyond Lego, there is everything from top-quality kites to books, puppets and educational wooden toys to consider here. Afterwards, why not cool the sprogs down at the popular Granville Island Water Park (p115) out back.

RAILSPUR ALLEY AREA

Map p275 (btwn Old Bridge & Cartwright Sts; 50) Located seemingly far from the madding crowds of the Public Market – at least on summer days when every tourist in town seems to be there – this back-alley strip offers up a more relaxing alternative. Here you'll find a short string of unique artisan stores, everything from painters to jewelers. Be sure to check out the Artisan Sake Maker (p110).

There's often a busker here on summer afternoons, so it's worth hanging around the alley for a bit.

EATING

A favored haunt for the more conspicuously wealthy Vancouverites, Yaletown has a good array of splurge-worthy dining options, especially along Hamilton and Mainland Sts. But not everything here is worth the price, so choose carefully. Many of this area's restaurants also have patios to sit out on and dine al fresco. Granville Island has plenty of places to eat, too, but you'll need to do a little digging to avoid the tourist restaurants.

Yaletown

DD MAU VIETNAMESE $

Map p274 (604-684-4446; www.ddmau.ca; 1239 Pacific Blvd; sandwiches $5-13; 11am-4pm Mon-Sat; ; Yaletown-Roundhouse) At the forefront of Vancouver's love affair with Vietnamese *banh mi* sandwiches, this tiny, often-busy spot serves up daily specials (always check these first) alongside five made-to-order regulars. Expect crisp baguette sandwiches (in either large or half-order options) with a range of diverse fillings including barbecue pork and lemongrass chicken. Seating is extremely limited so aim for takeout or visit its larger Chinatown branch.

Hunger still not satisfied? It also boasts heaping rice bowls as well as some pretty tempting side dishes, including spring rolls and tasty kale salads (this is Vancouver after all).

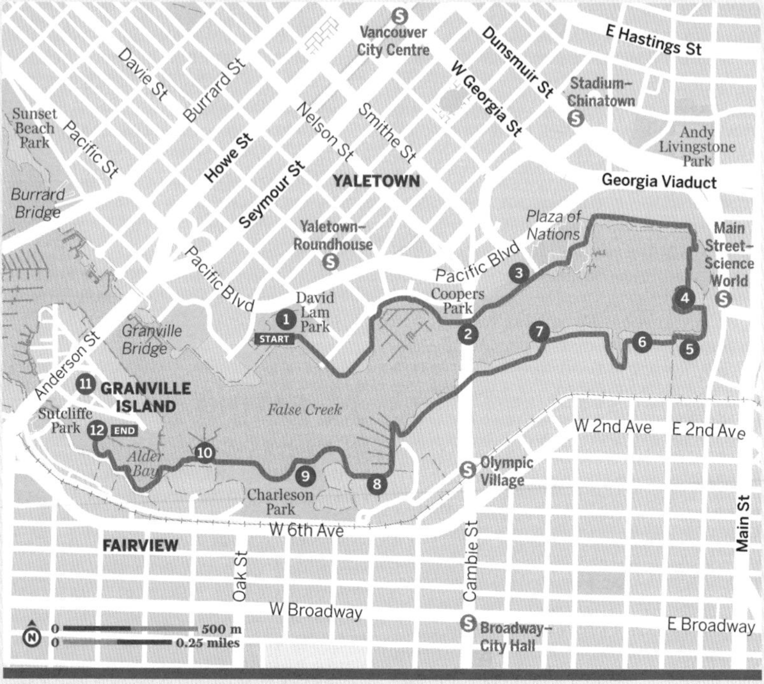

Neighborhood Walk
False Creek Seawall Stroll

START DAVID LAM PARK
END GRANVILLE ISLAND
LENGTH 6KM; THREE HOURS

Start on the north side of False Creek at Yaletown's 1 **David Lam Park** (p103) and head east alongside several public artworks before passing under 2 **Cambie Bridge**. This area housed 3 **Expo '86**, the world exposition that put Vancouver on the international map. From here to 4 **Science World** (p133), you'll see Expo reminders, including, in the distance, the SkyTrain line.

Follow the seawall past Science World to 5 **Olympic Village** (p134). Home to athletes during the 2010 Olympic and Paralympic Winter Games, it's now a neighborhood of condo towers, eateries and two giant bird sculptures. Hungry? 6 **Tap & Barrel** (p138) has a great mountain-view patio.

Continue west along the seawall, crossing a canoe-shaped bridge, and you'll spot 7 **Habitat Island**, an artificially constructed shrub-lined creation that's a pit stop for passing birds.

From here, pass under the Cambie Bridge again before reaching 8 **Leg-in-Boot Square**. Built in the 1980s, the low-rise homes and condos here are a stark contrast to the glassy residential towers that now face the area from the opposite shoreline.

Passing through the neighborhood and alongside 9 **Charleson Park**, you'll arrive at 10 **Spruce Harbour Marina**, a live-aboard boat community. 11 **Granville Island** is ahead. Enter it from the quiet back route and look for the 12 **totem pole** (Map p275, C3; Granville Island; 50). Erected in 1999, it recalls the First Nations residents who once fished here.

SALSA & AGAVE MEXICAN GRILL MEXICAN $

Map p274 (604-408-4228; www.salsaandagave.com; 1205 Pacific Blvd; mains $7-12; 11am-3pm Mon, to 9pm Tue-Thu & Sun, to 9:30pm Fri & Sat; S Yaletown-Roundhouse) You can expect warm service (plus nachos and salsa) when you snag a table at this laid-back, family-run favorite (sunny-day patio seats recommended). Allow plenty of time to peruse the extensive menu of authentic, house-made burrito and enchilada dishes, then dive right in with a four-selection soft taco order ($11), each piled high with pork, chorizo or beef (plus other choices).

MEET VEGAN $$

Map p274 (604-696-1165; www.meetonmain.com; 1165 Mainland St; mains $10-17; 11am-11pm Sun-Thu, to 1am Fri & Sat; ; S Yaletown-Roundhouse) A hip vegan eatery that lures many carnivores with an array of meaty-seeming comfort-grub classics that emulate the flavors and textures of burgers, chicken and more. The Yaletown branch of this Vancouver mini-chain is often busy with chatty diners – which can mean waiting for peak-time tables. If you're starving, go for the bulging crispy barbecue burger or butter 'chicken' poutine.

The fries are excellent here but the main menu isn't just about fake meat dishes. The heaping salads (beet recommended) and satisfying huge rice bowls are justifiably popular, while there's also a good selection of locally brewed craft beers to quench your thirst.

BAKE49 BAKERY $$

Map p274 (www.bake49.com; 1066 Mainland St; desserts $5-27; 1-6pm Tue-Sun; S Yaletown-Roundhouse) A tiny bakery that specializes in various Japanese cheesecakes and pastries. You'll have to arrive early or expect to be greeted by the 'sold out' sign on the door. It's worth rearranging your day, though, just for the chance to sink your teeth into delicate, cream-filled treats or an entire double-fromage cheesecake; only a dozen of these are made every day and it might be tough, but they're specifically designed for sharing.

Cash not accepted; it's a debit- or credit-card-only joint.

RODNEY'S OYSTER HOUSE SEAFOOD $$

Map p274 (604-609-0080; www.rohvan.com; 1228 Hamilton St; mains $16-32; 11:30am-11pm; S Yaletown-Roundhouse) A popular pilgrimage spot for oyster fans, Rodney's is always buzzing. And it's not just because of the convivial room with its nautical flourishes; these folks really know how to do seafood. While the fresh-shucked oysters with a huge array of sauces (try the spicy vodka) never fail to impress, everything from chunky chowders to sautéed garlic shrimp is also served.

You can drop by from 3pm to 6pm (Sundays excluded) for special deals on several dishes including oysters, clams, mussels and more; and don't forget to add an order of the finger-licking pan-fried oysters to your table.

BLUE WATER CAFE SEAFOOD $$$

Map p274 (604-688-8078; www.bluewatercafe.net; 1095 Hamilton St; mains $30-45; 5-11pm; S Yaletown-Roundhouse) Under celebrated executive chef Frank Pabst, this is one of Vancouver's best high-concept seafood restaurants. Gentle music fills the brick-lined, blue-hued interior, while top-notch char, sturgeon and butter-soft scallops grace the tables inside and on the patio. Not a seafood fan? There's also a small array of meaty 'principal plates' to sate your carnivorous appetite, including Kobe-style short ribs.

The service here is perfect: warm, gracious and ever-friendly. Reservations are required.

FLYING PIG CANADIAN $$$

Map p274 (604-568-1344; www.theflyingpigvan.com; 1168 Hamilton St; mains $20-58; 11am-midnight Mon-Fri, 10am-midnight Sat, 10am-11pm Sun; S Yaletown-Roundhouse) A warm and woodsy bistro that has managed to master the art of friendly service and saliva-triggering, gourmet comfort food. Dishes focus on seasonal and locally sourced ingredients and are virtually guaranteed to make your belly smile. Wine-braised short ribs and roast chicken served with buttermilk mash top our to-eat list, but it's best to arrive off-peak to avoid the crowds.

PROVENCE MARINASIDE FRENCH, SEAFOOD $$$

Map p274 (604-681-4144; www.provencemarinaside.ca; 1177 Marinaside Cres, Yaletown; mains $26-59; 8am-10pm; S Yaletown-Roundhouse) There's a serious seafood fixation at this elegant, French-approach restaurant situated just across from Yaletown's False Creek waterfront. But if you're not in the mood for marine-based treats, there are also lamb and

VANCOUVER'S BRICK-BUILT SOHO

Aesthetically unlike any other Vancouver neighborhood, Yaletown has a trendy warehouse-district appearance today because it was built on a foundation of grungy, working-class history. Created almost entirely from red bricks, the area was crammed with railway sheds and goods warehouses in the late 1800s after the Canadian Pacific Railway (CPR) relocated its main Western Canada operation from the British Columbia (BC) interior town of Yale. Along with the moniker, the workers brought something else with them: a tough-as-nails, hard-drinking approach that turned the waterfront area into one where the taverns usually served their liquor with a side order of fistfights. But at least the rough-and-ready workers kept the area alive: when the rail operations were closed down a few decades later, Yaletown descended into a half-empty mass squat filled with homeless locals and marauding rats. But that wasn't the end of the story.

When plans were drawn up for Vancouver to host the giant Expo '86 world exposition, there were few areas of town with the space – and the absence of other businesses – to host it. But Yaletown fit the bill. The area became part of the planned Expo grounds along the north shoreline of False Creek, and was cleared, refurbished and given a new lease on life. After the summer-long fair, its newly noticed historic character made Yaletown the ideal spot for urban regeneration. Within a few years the old brick warehouses had been repaired, scrubbed clean and recolonized with a sparkling array of boutiques, fancy restaurants and swish bars – serving tipples that are a far cry from the punch-triggering beers that used to be downed here.

chicken dishes. Feeling aquatically inclined? Why not face-plant into the feast-tastic seafood platter that includes everything from clams to scallops; it's simply prepared and utterly delicious. During the summer, patio dining is especially recommended.

This restaurant is also one of Yaletown's most popular weekend brunch spots (don't miss the seafood crepes). And if you're in the area and suddenly thirsty for an afternoon libation, the 2pm to 5pm Tappy Hour includes a huge array of by-the-glass wine deals.

Granville Island

★GO FISH SEAFOOD $

Map p275 (604-730-5040; 1505 W 1st Ave; mains $8-14; 11:30am-6pm Mon-Fri, noon-6pm Sat & Sun; 50) Just a short stroll westward along the seawall from the Granville Island entrance, this almost-too-popular seafood stand is one of the city's favourite fish-and-chip joints, offering up halibut, salmon and cod encased in crispy golden batter. The smashing fish tacos are also recommended, while the ever changing daily specials – brought in by the nearby fishing boats – often include scallop burgers or ahi tuna sandwiches.

Expect long queues and sometimes borderline oppressive waits during the summer months; arrive as off-peak as you can. The seating area has been expanded from its original limited selection, but it's still best to continue along the seawall to Vanier Park for a sunset picnic alongside the ever-watchful seagulls.

A BREAD AFFAIR BAKERY $

Map p275 (604-695-0000; www.abreadaffair.com; 1680 Johnston St; sandwiches $8-12; 8:30am-7pm Mon-Thu, to 7:30pm Fri-Sun; 50) A beloved Granville Island mainstay and must-visit for true afficionados of great bread. Alongside its sandwich bar (French ham and Havarti recommended) plus racks of fresh-baked loaves, there's always sure to be an irresistible array of treats, from cookies to croissants to rich chocolate brownies. Be sure not to miss the hearty apple-cheddar-walnut galette; it's enough to feed two but that doesn't mean you have to share.

Little free samples are offered up most days; you might want to consider donning disguises and returning at least 27 times. And if you happen to find yourself at a farmers market around the city, you'll often spot this bakery's stalls; they're the ones with the inevitably gigantic queues.

PUBLIC MARKET FOOD COURT INTERNATIONAL $

Map p275 (1661 Duranleau St, Granville Island Public Market; mains $8-14; ⏲9am-7pm; ✍; 🚌50) A budget dining option that's very busy in summer; you could nearly auction off your table to the highest bidder when you're ready to depart (just kidding). Arrive off-peak to be sure of a seat (aim for the upstairs mezzanine) and you'll have the pick of some excellent vendors hawking everything from German sausages to pad Thai to vegetarian rice bowls.

If you're here at the end of the day, some counters have specials to clear their inventory. Hover around like a vulture and you might manage to snag yourself a bargain pizza slice.

TONY'S FISH & OYSTER CAFE SEAFOOD $$

Map p275 (☎604-683-7127; www.tonysfishandoystercafe.com; 1511 Anderson St; mains $11-23; ⏲11:30am-8pm Mon-Sat, to 7pm Sun; 🚌50) A chatty spot that's popular with both locals and visitors alike, this small spot complete with blue-checkered-tablecloth serves up top notch fish and chips (cod, salmon or halibut), along with generous dollops of house-made coleslaw and tartar sauce. The food is good value, and it's not just about fish and chips; the BBQ-sauced oyster burger is almost a local legend. Service is fast and friendly.

BISTRO 101 CANADIAN $$

Map p275 (☎604-734-4488; www.picachef.com; 1505 W 2nd Ave; prix fixe from $24; ⏲11:30am-1:15pm & 6-8:30pm Mon-Fri; 🚌50) The training restaurant of the Pacific Institute of Culinary Arts is a popular spot with in-the-know locals, especially at lunchtime, when $24 gets you a delicious three-course meal (typically three options for each course) alongside service that's earnestly solicitous. Dinner costs $8 more. There are also regular buffet options, typically on Fridays (lunch $28; dinner $38). Reservations are highly recommended.

Decor-wise, the restaurant is slightly dated, with a 1980s feel. There's an outdoor-seating patio to the side, but the views of Granville Island from inside the restaurant are much better.

POPINA FAST FOOD $$

Map p275 (www.popinacanteen.com; 1691 Johnston St; mains $12-26; ⏲11am-10pm, reduced hours in winter; 🚌50) Like a static food truck on steroids, this quirky, bright-painted freight container serves elevated burgers and hot sandwiches (crispy chicken with fries recommended). Need a seat away from the greedy gulls? The small, covered patio where you pick up your order has tables with waterfront views to Burrard Bridge. BC wines and Vancouver craft beers add to the fun.

GRANVILLE ISLAND'S INDUSTRIAL SIDE

Many visitors spend their time on Granville Island at the Public Market end, nipping between the myriad shops and studios. But heading a few minutes along Johnston St offers some reminders of the time when this human-made peninsula (since it's joined to the mainland, it's not actually an island) was home to dozens of hard-toiling factories making everything from chains to iron hinges.

One million cubic yards of landfill was tipped into False Creek to create the island in the early 20th century, but almost all the reminders of its gritty first few years have been lost. Almost. The area's oldest tenant, **Ocean Concrete**, is a cement maker that began here in 1917 and now cranks out enough product to build a 10-story tower block every week. It also does a great job of being a good neighbor. A Vancouver Biennale initiative saw the company's six gigantic waterfront silos transformed into huge multicolored figures, while its annual April **open house** event is hotly anticipated by local families.

Continue along Johnston a little further and you'll come to a second monument to the past: a landmark **yellow dock crane** that's been preserved from the old days. Nip across to the waterfront here for a final 'hidden' Granville Island view: a string of large and comfy-looking **houseboats** that many Vancouverites wish they lived in.

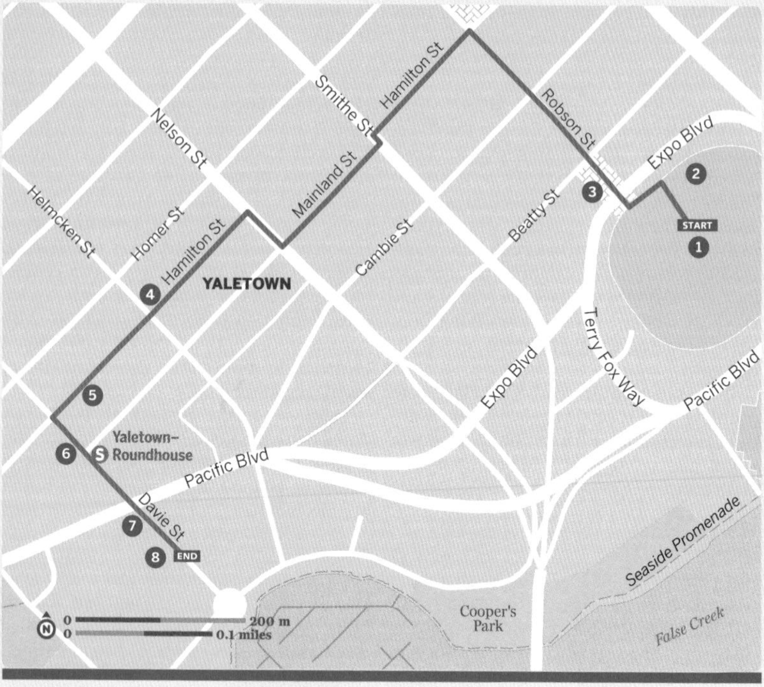

Neighborhood Walk
Yaletown Indulgence

START BC PLACE STADIUM
END ENGINE 374 PAVILION
LENGTH 2KM; ONE HOUR

Start at Vancouver's largest sports venue, 1 **BC Place Stadium** (p102), checking out the 2 **BC Sports Hall of Fame & Museum** (p102) located inside and the 3 **Douglas Coupland public artwork** outside – it celebrates Canadian hero Terry Fox.

Next, head up Robson St and turn left onto Hamilton. Scope out some dinner options for later here, from 4 **Blue Water Cafe** (p105) to 5 **Flying Pig** (p105). Notice the elevated redbrick sidewalks and old rails embedded in the roads, remnants of the neighborhood's former incarnation as a train yard and warehouse district. The Expo '86 world exposition transformed the district with temporary pavilions, laying the foundation for new businesses and sleek condo towers.

When you reach Davie St, turn left. It's all downhill from here, but if it's time for a pit stop, pop into 6 **Caffe Artigiano** for a restorative latte. It's in the Opus Hotel building, one of the city's coolest boutique sleepovers: spot the beautiful people gliding in and out of the lobby.

Continue down Davie, then cross over busy Pacific Blvd to the 7 **Roundhouse Community Arts & Recreation Centre** (p103). It occupies a refurbished former railroad facility. Check to see if there are any events, then dig out your camera for the neighborhood's historic highlight. Attached to the side of the community center, the free-entry 8 **Engine 374 Pavilion** (p102) houses the restored steam engine that pulled the first transcontinental passenger train into the city in 1887.

DRINKING & NIGHTLIFE

Yaletown is where the city's wealthy set come to sip martinis and exchange lap-dog stories. You're sure to find something worth checking out amid the warehouse renovations. Granville Island offers several bars that are perfect for winding down after a day spent weaving around the Public Market and artisan stores.

Yaletown

MATCHSTICK — COFFEE

Map p274 (www.matchstickyvr.com; 1328 Richards St; 7am-9pm; ; 23) Neatly tucked into the bottom of a super-modern shimmering glass condo building, this cool coffee-shop oasis manages to combine a communal table and wood-block perches with stylish houseplant-heavy bookcases tastefully arrayed with vintage vinyl and well-curated paperbacks. But it's not all about looks; the friendly staff serve excellent coffee, irresistible sweet treats (gooey chocolate cookies recommended) and hearty sandwiches (go for the tuna melt).

There's also a small breakfast menu featuring poached eggs if you happen to find yourself in this part of town early.

SMALL VICTORY — COFFEE

Map p274 (604-899-8892; www.smallvictory.ca; 1088 Homer St; 7:30am-6pm Mon-Fri, 8am-6pm Sat & Sun; ; S Yaletown-Roundhouse) The kind of austere, granite-countered coffee shop you might not feel cool enough to enter (or maybe that's just us), Small Victory is a favorite daytime hangout for hip Yaletowners. Sip your perfect cappuccino and standout flaky croissant (there's also an artful array of additional bakery treats) under the geometric wall-mounted artwork and you'll fit right in.

More substantial savory fare of the salads and sandwiches variety is also available if your sweet tooth has momentarily deserted you.

YALETOWN BREWING COMPANY — BREWERY

Map p274 (604-681-2739; www.mjg.ca/yaletown; 1111 Mainland St; 11:30am-midnight Sun-Wed, to 1am Thu, to 3am Fri & Sat; ; S Yaletown-Roundhouse) There's a brick-lined, tavernesque brewpub, complete with beer keg light fittings, on one side plus a humongous dining room with Yaletown's largest patio on the other. Both serve this long-established brewery's own-made beers, but the restaurant adds a huge menu of comfort food to the mix. Ask about the latest unusual small-batch brews or hit one of the classics: IPAs recommended.

If you really want to try something out of the ordinary, ask about the eye-popping Oud Bruin sour beer. It's guaranteed to put a few hairs on your chest, but only if you're brave enough to finish it. Happy hour is 3pm to 5pm Sunday to Thursday, which means $5 beer, wine and highball specials. And there's a long-standing Sunday dining deal where all pizzas are priced at $12.

CAFFE ARTIGIANO — COFFEE

Map p274 (604-336-4766; www.caffeartigiano.com; 302 Davie St; 6am-6pm; ; S Yaletown-Roundhouse) One of Vancouver's most popular local coffee chains serves up arguably Yaletown's best java. Tucked away into a corner of the Opus Hotel building, this spot takes pride in its drinks and is great if you're looking for a chat; go for a latte and the barista will implant a nice little design into the foam (yes, we're easily pleased). Sandwiches and baked treats also available.

Granville Island

★LIBERTY DISTILLERY — DISTILLERY

Map p275 (604-558-1998; www.thelibertydistillery.com; 1494 Old Bridge St; 11am-9pm; 50) Gaze through internal windows at the shiny, steampunk-like booze-making equipment when you visit this handsome saloon-like tasting room. It's not all about looks, though. During happy hour (Monday to Thursday, 3pm to 6pm and after 8pm), sample house-made vodka, gin varieties, vodka and several whiskeys plus great $6 cocktails. Tours are also available ($10, 11:30am and 1:30pm Saturday and Sunday).

The start of happy hour is announced by a steam whistle, so you'll know exactly when to start imbibing. Don't miss a hit or two of the rich, copper-colored Endeavour Old Tom Gin.

ISLAND'S BEST FEST

It might feel like an invasion but it's probably more accurate to call the 11-day **Vancouver Fringe Festival** (www.vancouverfringe.com; Granville Island; tickets from $12; 50) an energetic occupation of Granville Island. Running every September, the event includes a multitude of enthusiastic performers from Canada and around the world staging hundreds of shows – from comedy reviews to poignant dramas – at venues large and small. Naturally, the island's surfeit of theaters is well utilized, but shows are also sometimes staged in less conventional venues, from floating mini-ferries to pop-up stages on every street corner.

Tickets hover around the $12 to $15 mark but deals are plentiful and free shows are common. Book ahead for shows before you arrive, but note that just strolling the island during the event can be equally entertaining, as buskers and fly-posting performers try to catch your attention. Finally, consider hanging out with the performers themselves: usually one bar is set aside during the festival for the thesps to chill out with audience members between shows – it's the perfect opportunity for you to dust off that jaunty musical version of *Waiting for Godot* you've written that just needs a producer.

GRANVILLE ISLAND BREWING TAPROOM — PUB

Map p275 (604-687-2739; www.gib.ca; 1441 Cartwright St; noon-8pm; 50) You can sample the company's main beers in this often busy pub-style room, although most are now made in a far larger out-of-town facility. Of these, Cypress Honey Lager, Lions Winter Ale and False Creek Raspberry Ale are among the most popular. But the small-batch brews, made right here on the island, are even better; ask your server what's available.

Tours (p115) of the small brewery are offered and the taproom's food menu has been seriously improved. Takeout beers and growler refills are available in the liquor store next door, where souvenirs such as T-shirts and beer soap are also sold.

ARTISAN SAKE MAKER — BREWERY

Map p275 (604-685-7253; www.artisansakemaker.com; 1339 Railspur Alley; 11:30am-6pm; 50) Using locally grown rice, this tiny craft sake producer (the first of its kind in Canada) should be on everyone's Granville Island to-do list. Twinkle-eyed sake maker Masa Shiroki creates tempting tipples; you can dive in for a bargain $5 three-sake tasting. It's an eye-opening revelation to many drinkers who think sake is a harsh beverage. Takeout bottles also available.

Consider buying a jar of *kasu*; the lees left over from the fermenting process are a great exotic cooking ingredient and are even used in the small array of chocolaty bonbons for sale on the counter.

DOCKSIDE BREWING COMPANY — BAR

Map p275 (604-685-7070; www.docksidevancouver.com; 1253 Johnston St, Granville Island Hotel; 11am-10pm Sun-Thu, to midnight Fri & Sat; ; 50) Often overshadowed by the other brewers in town (being stuck on the quiet end of Granville Island doesn't help), Dockside's beers are made on-site and include the crisp, nicely malted Cartwright Pale Ale. Sup on the waterfront patio for tranquil views of False Creek's boat traffic and you may have to be forcibly removed by the end of the night.

☆ ENTERTAINMENT

Granville Island is home to several theaters, and is a hotbed of performance art and theatrical and cultural festivals.

GRANVILLE ISLAND STAGE — THEATER

Map p275 (604-687-1644; www.artsclub.com; 1585 Johnston St, Granville Island; tickets from $29; Sep-Jun; 50) The Granville Island arm of Vancouver's leading theater company, this intimate, raked-seating venue is the perfect spot to feel really connected to the action on stage. Cutting-edge homegrown shows as well as new versions of established hits populate the season here and you're close to several restaurants if you fancy a dinner-and-show night out.

If you're curious about the West Coast theatrical scene, look out for plays by Morris Panych, one of BC's favorite playwright sons.

VANCOUVER WHITECAPS SOCCER

Map p274 (604-669-9283; www.whitecapsfc.com; 777 Pacific Blvd, BC Place Stadium, Yaletown; tickets from $45; Mar-Oct; ; Stadium-Chinatown) Using BC Place Stadium (p102) as its home, Vancouver's professional soccer team plays in North America's top-tier Major League Soccer (MLS). Their on-field fortunes have ebbed and flowed since being promoted to the league in 2011, but they've been finding their feet (useful for soccer players) lately. Save time to buy a souvenir soccer shirt to impress everyone back home.

BC LIONS FOOTBALL

Map p274 (604-589-7627; www.bclions.com; 777 Pacific Blvd, BC Place Stadium, Yaletown; tickets from $20; Jun-Nov; ; Stadium-Chinatown) Founded in 1954, the Lions are Vancouver's team in the Canadian Football League (CFL), which is arguably more exciting than its US counterpart, the NFL. The team has had some decent showings lately, but hasn't won the all-important Grey Cup since 2011. Tickets are easy to come by – unless the boys are laying into their arch enemies, the Calgary Stampeders.

Catching a game at the stadium includes plenty of schmaltzy razzmatazz, from cheerleaders to half-time shows. It's family friendly and a lot cheaper than catching an NHL hockey game.

VANCOUVER THEATRESPORTS COMEDY

Map p275 (604-738-7013; www.vtsl.com; 1502 Duranleau St, Improv Centre, Granville Island; tickets from $15; Wed-Sun; 50) The city's most popular improv group stages energetic romps – sometimes connected to themes like Tinder dating – at this purpose-built theater. Whatever the theme, the approach is the same: if you're sitting at one of the tables near the front, expect to be picked on. The late-night (11:15pm) shows are commendably ribald and probably not something to bring your parents to.

If you fancy your skills as a performer, try not to rush the stage; Theatresports offers regular drop-in Saturday-afternoon workshops ($20) for those keen to give improv a try – you'll likely find out it's much harder than it looks.

CAROUSEL THEATRE THEATER

Map p275 (604-669-3410; www.carouseltheatre.ca; 1412 Cartwright St, Waterfront Theatre, Granville Island; tickets adult/child $35/18; ; 50) Mostly performing at Granville Island's Waterfront Theatre, with some shows at the alternate Performance Works space nearby, this child-focused drama company stages some great productions that adults often end up enjoying as much as their kids. Adaptations of children's classics like *The Wind in the Willows* have previously featured, with clever reinterpretations of Shakespearean works added to the mix for older children.

SHOPPING

Colonizing the area's evocative old brick warehouses, chichi Yaletown has some interesting stores and designer boutiques. But for craft fans, it has to be Granville Island. It's teeming with studios where artisans throw clay, blow glass and silversmith jewelry. Head to the Net Loft (p114), Railspur Alley (p103) or Public Market (p100) if you're lacking direction, but make sure you explore as much as possible and duck along the back alleys to see artists at work in their studios. Buskers also hang out here on summer afternoons, making this Vancouver's most convivial shopping area.

Yaletown

★KARAMELLER CANDY SHOP FOOD

Map p274 (604-639-8325; www.karameller.com; 1020 Mainland St; 11am-8pm Mon-Sat; Yaletown-Roundhouse) Grab a paper bag and some tongs then dive into the pick-your-own drawers of brightly colored treats at this slender, white-walled gem dedicated to Swedish candy. Among the 75 varieties, you'll find everything from caramel circles and mixed sour lips to peppermint licorice chalk and raspberry boats (the owner's favorite). Create a grab bag to-go for your walk around Yaletown.

WOO TO SEE YOU FASHION & ACCESSORIES

Map p274 (☎604-559-1062; www.wootoseeyou.com; 1061 Mainland St; ⊙10am-7pm Mon-Sat, 11am-6pm Sun; SYaletown-Roundhouse) Smily, genuinely friendly service is the approach at this tiny womenswear boutique where you should give yourself plenty of time to browse the racks of carefully curated, independent labels. There's a Korean-Canadian fusion approach to the tops, jackets and pants on display, as well as a tempting selection of artisan jewelry that would please any passing magpie.

BROOKLYN CLOTHING CLOTHING

Map p274 (☎604-683-2929; www.brooklynclothing.com; 418 Davie St; ⊙10am-9pm Mon-Sat, 11am-7pm Sun; SYaletown-Roundhouse) Proving that Yaletown men are just as aesthetically focused as women, this hip menswear boutique is the perfect spot to upgrade your style from that snow-washed-jeans look you've been sporting since 1984. Local designers are well represented – check out the achingly cool T-shirts – and there are dozens of jeans styles so you can finally nail that perfect fit.

Drop by on Sunday night when it's quiet and you can try on everything in the store. Twice.

Granville Island

★KAREN COOPER GALLERY ART

Map p275 (☎604-559-5112; www.karencoopergallery.com; 1506 Duranleau St; ⊙10am-6pm, reduced hours in winter; 🚌50) You'll feel like you've entered a tranquil forest clearing when you open the door of this delightful nature-themed photography gallery. Cooper's striking work focuses on BC's jaw-dropping wild beauty, from coniferous trees to grizzly bears. Take your time and don't be surprised if you fall in love with a handsome image of a bald eagle perched on a mountain tree.

PAPER-YA ARTS & CRAFTS

Map p275 (☎604-684-2531; www.paper-ya.com; 1666 Johnston St, Net Loft; ⊙10am-7pm Apr-Dec, to 6pm Jan-Mar; 🚌50) A magnet for slavering stationery fetishists (you know who you are), this store's treasure trove of trinkets ranges from natty pens to traditional *washi* paper. It's not all writing-related ephemera, though. Whoever does the buying also curates an eclectic, changing roster of hard-to-resist goodies that can include cool journals, quirky books and cute greeting cards emblazoned with everything from cats to owls.

There's also a back wall of seals and sealing wax if you happen to be corresponding with someone from the Middle Ages.

GRANVILLE ISLAND BROOM COMPANY HOMEWARES

Map p275 (☎604-629-1141; www.broomcompany.com; 1406 Old Bridge St; ⊙10am-6pm, reduced hours off-season; 🚌50) Ever since Harry Potter, locals have been entranced by this Granville Island fave, which makes its own beautifully handcrafted Shaker-style straw brooms right in the store (you can watch the mesmerizing process in action). But these gnarly-handled lovelies aren't just for decoration. You can pick up cobwebbers, golf-shoe brushes and car whisks that will easily fit in your luggage.

And just in case you're wondering, the brooms – which can take anywhere from 20 minutes to several hours to produce – are all fashioned from broom corn, which grows in northern Mexico.

MAKE ARTS & CRAFTS

Map p275 (☎604-684-5105; www.makevancouver.com; 1648 Duranleau St; ⊙10am-6pm Sun-Fri, 9:30am-6pm Sat; 🚌50) It's hard not to blow your holiday budget at this store, which showcases a huge array of quirky, often nerdy gifts and creations, from Sasquatch-themed socks to fox-patterned wooden earrings to periodic-table hoodies. It's a great spot to find the kind of souvenir Vancouver T-shirts you might actually wear, including retro beer adverts and depictions of angry 'wet coast' rain clouds.

If you can't find a T-shirt you like, you can design your own at the busy counter at the back of the store. And if you're looking for Vancouver's ultracool Herschel bags and daypacks, they have a good selection here as well.

CIRCLE CRAFT ARTS & CRAFTS

Map p275 (☎604-669-8021; www.circlecraft.net; 1666 Johnston St, Net Loft, Granville Island; ⊙10am-7pm Apr-Dec, to 6pm Jan-Mar; 🚌50) This large, bright cooperative gallery hawks a highly diverse and ever-changing array of BC arts and crafts, which could include

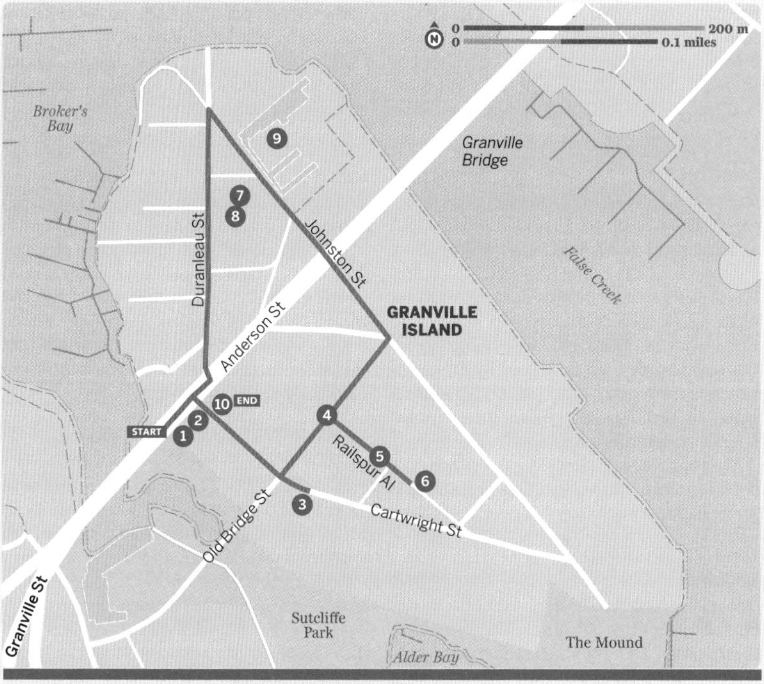

Neighborhood Walk
Granville Island Artisan Trawl

START GRANVILLE ISLAND LICORICE PARLOUR
END GRANVILLE ISLAND BREWING
LENGTH 1KM; ONE HOUR

This stroll covers some of Granville Island's favorite artisan stops and craft booze producers. Entering the island at Anderson St, nip into the 1 **Licorice Parlour** (p114) for a bag of salty-sweet snacks to-go. Continue along Anderson to the corner of Cartwright St. Explore the 2 **Kids Market** (p103) here and consider a Muppet-like puppet for a child back home.

Next weave eastward along Cartwright. You'll see theaters, shops and 3 **Crafthouse** (p114) gallery, with its kaleidoscopic array of regionally made creations, including jewelry and ceramics.

In front of the store, cross over and walk along the right side of Old Bridge St. At the first intersection, you'll find 4 **Liberty Distillery** (p109), a saloon-like room serving house-crafted liquors. If you've timed your visit for the Monday to Thursday 3pm-to-6pm happy hour, indulge in a lip-smacking $6 cocktail. Then, head outside and turn right onto 5 **Railspur Alley** (p103). Peruse the excellent little stores here, including the 6 **Artisan Sake Maker** (p110). Try a tasting or two.

Return to Old Bridge St, continue northeast, and turn left onto Johnston St. Here you'll find the 7 **Net Loft** (p114). It's lined with arts and crafts stores, including the ever-popular 8 **Paper-Ya**. Diagonally across the street from here is the entrance to the 9 **Public Market** (p100). Dominating the area, it specializes in deli-style food stalls – cheese-filled bagels recommended. When you've had your fill, weave southward from the market along Duranleau St. Within a couple of minutes you'll be at the intersection with Cartwright St and the entrance to 10 **Granville Island Brewing** (p115). Take a tour or hit the taproom for a well-deserved pint.

bat-patterned ceramics, sculptures made from twigs and sleek jewelry that echoes bird feathers. Prices vary considerably but there's usually something here to suit most budgets. Even if you're not buying, just looking around is fun.

CRAFTHOUSE ARTS & CRAFTS

Map p275 (☎604-687-7270; www.craftcouncilbc.ca; 1386 Cartwright St; ⏲10am-5:30pm; 🚌50) At this bright and friendly nonprofit gallery run by the Craft Council of British Columbia (CCBC), the shelves hold everything from glass goblets and woven scarves to French butter dishes and lathe-turned arbutus wood bowls – all produced by dozens of artisans from across the region. It's a great place to pick up something different for friends and family back home.

On your way out, check the flyers near the door for more info on local gallery and art-scene happenings.

GRANVILLE ISLAND LICORICE PARLOUR FOOD

Map p275 (☎604-428-0111; 1496 Cartwright St; ⏲10am-6pm; 🚌50) A satellite branch of Commercial Dr's popular candy store, this sweet-tooth pilgrimage spot boasts several dozen jars of serious licorice (anyone for salty *salmiak* from Scandinavia?) alongside a kaleidoscopic array of various other sweeties and bonbons such as jelly babies and saltwater taffy. There are also lots of gelatin-free and gluten-free options plus a super-cool sideline in brightly colored Hula-Hoops.

SEARCH & RESCUE DENIM COMPANY CLOTHING

Map p275 (☎778-379-6479; www.searchandrescuedenim.com; 1420 Old Bridge St; ⏲10am-6pm Mon-Sat, 11am-5pm Sun; 🚌50) You'll walk into this busy workshop thinking you don't need an apron. Then you'll fall in love. These handmade, sometimes punkish and always sturdily functional items are worn by coolsters from chefs to tattoo artists, but they work well for anyone aiming for a serious artisan look. Tote bags and holdalls complete the collection, nestled on shelves between retired sewing machines.

NET LOFT MARKET

Map p275 (☎604-666-6655; 1650 Johnston St; ⏲10am-6pm; 🚌50) An indoor array of creative boutiques just across from the far-busier Public Market. Highlight stores include arts-and-crafty Paper-Ya (p112), cave-like Granville Island Hat Shop and the Wickaninnish Gallery, where indigenous designs adorn everything from jewelry to framed prints to cool water bottles.

SILK WEAVING STUDIO ARTS & CRAFTS

Map p275 (☎604-687-7455; www.silkweavingstudio.com; 1531 Johnston St; ⏲10am-5pm; 🚌50) Almost hidden in a back alley maze of buildings, this beloved local favorite is a crafter's delight. It's hard not to stroke every strand of silk in sight, with a rainbow of colored threads and yarns calling your name. Watch out for weaving demonstrations. You'll find this store tucked down a nameless alley immediately under the bridge.

GANDHARVA LOKA WORLD MUSIC STORE MUSICAL INSTRUMENTS

Map p275 (☎604-683-7733; www.gandharvaloka.ca; 1650 Johnston St; ⏲10am-7pm; 🚌50) From rainsticks to mandolins, visitors are encouraged to try out the unusual instruments in this welcoming, family-friendly store. Need a new instrument for your collection? The knowledgeable staffers will have plenty of suggestions. If you're lucky, they'll encourage you to sit in the Sound Cradle, a kind of harp-rocking-chair combo where you'll feel the vibrating pluck of every string.

VANCOUVER STUDIO GLASS ARTS & CRAFTS

Map p275 (☎604-681-6730; www.vancouverstudioglass.com; 1440 Old Bridge St; ⏲10am-6pm Tue-Sat, to 5pm Sun & Mon; 🚌50) Peer through the windows at this intriguing artisan glass studio and watch the team blow and twirl their stuff. There are plenty of works to purchase in the adjoining store; just remember that you'll need an effective strategy for transporting purchases home without breaking them into a million pieces. Classes are offered if you fancy giving it a try yourself.

SPORTS & ACTIVITIES

★ VANCOUVER FOODIE TOURS TOURS

(☎604-295-8844; www.foodietours.ca; tours from $65) A popular culinary-themed city stroll operator running three taste-tripping tours in Vancouver; choose between Best

Granville Island Brewing

of Downtown, Gastronomic Gastown and Granville Island tours. Friendly red-coated guides lead you through belly-pleasing wanders with plenty to eat and drink; the trick is not to dine before you arrive.

GRANVILLE ISLAND BREWING BREWERY

Map p275 (GIB; 604-687-2739; www.gib.ca; 1441 Cartwright St; tours $11.50; tours 12:30pm, 2pm, 4pm & 5:50pm; 50) One of Canada's oldest microbreweries (established in 1984), GIB offers short tours on which smiling guides walk you through the tiny brewing nook. The brewery has grown exponentially since opening and most of its beers are now made off-site, although some excellent small-batch brews are still made here on the island. The tour concludes with samples in the Taproom (p110).

GRANVILLE ISLAND WATER PARK WATER PARK

Map p275 (Granville Island; May-Sep; ; 50) FREE Vancouver's biggest and best water park is conveniently located near Granville Island's Kids Market (p103), which means you'll have the perfect lure for enticing your sprogs away from the toy shops. There's also a large pond nearby that's often filled with friendly ducks and geese; in May and June, you'll often spot fuzzy babies of the feathered variety here.

RECKLESS BIKE STORES CYCLING

Map p274 (604-648-2600; www.reckless.ca; 110 Davie St, Yaletown; per 2/5hr $22.50/34.50; 9:30am-6pm Mon-Fri, 10am-5pm Sat, 11am-5pm Sun; S Yaletown-Roundhouse) Popular bike rental store with three branches across the city. This one also specializes in high-performance road bikes. Rentals include helmet, bike lock, basket and map.

CHRISTELWISE L/SHUTTERSTOCK ©

1. Queen Elizabeth Park (p150) 2. False Creek Seawall (p104) 3. Grizzly Bear on Grouse Mountain (p182) 4. Spanish Banks is a series of beaches in Vancouver

ERIC BUERMEYER/SHUTTERSTOCK ©

Vancouver Outdoors

Vancouver's sparkling natural setting is a key reason many visitors fall in love with this city. Plunge in at beaches, mountain promontories and perfect trails, both urban and on the city's tree-lined fringes.

Beaches

You're never far from great beaches in Vancouver, such as the busy, sandy swathes of Kits Beach and English Bay Beach or more tranquil gems such as Stanley Park's Third Beach and rustic Spanish Banks. Consider a picnic and plan for a sunset vista.

Grouse Mountain

It's hard not to take a deep breath when you step onto the smile-triggering summit of Grouse. Alpine trails, a grizzly bear refuge and some of the most spectacular natural views of the city shimmering in the water far below will have you itching to click that camera.

Queen Elizabeth Park

Stunning Stanley Park is hard to measure up to, but don't overlook these manicured gardens, jaw-dropping panoramic views of the city framed by mountains, and a tropical botanical garden teeming with beady-eyed, neon-hued birds.

False Creek Seawall

Vancouver's shimmering waterfront has a spectacular seawall trail linking more than 20km of coastline, from downtown through Stanley Park and out to UBC. Don't miss the False Creek stretch; it's crammed with public art and water-to-city views.

Parks & Gardens of UBC

Pacific Spirit Regional Park rivals Stanley Park for stature and tree-hugging glory but it's UBC's manicured green spaces that attract the crowds. From a symbolic traditional Japanese garden to the verdant themed areas of the huge Botanical Garden, green-thumbed visitors will have a ball here.

Commercial Drive

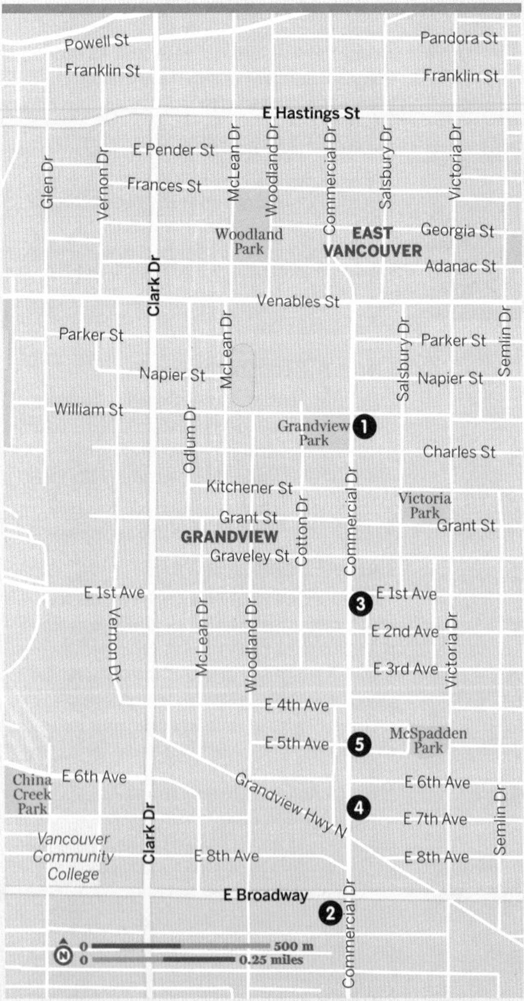

For more detail of this area see Map p276

Neighborhood Top Five

❶ **Rio Theatre** (p127) Making new friends while hanging out with the locals at a late-night cult movie screening; costume and singing along optional.

❷ **Downlow Chicken Shack** (p120) Sinking your choppers into a juicy, hot-sauce-slathered southern-style sandwich; deck seat recommended.

❸ **Bench Bakehouse** (p120) Picking up a crisp, oven-warm croissant or three to fuel your extensive night out on the Drive.

❹ **Mintage** (p129) Rummaging the multitudinous racks for that perfect vintage prom dress, plus matching sunglasses and floppy hat.

❺ **Cafe Deux Soleils** (p125) Taking the stage (after a few beers) and regaling the locals with your flowery magnum opus at the city's favorite poetry-slam night.

Explore Commercial Drive

Take the SkyTrain from downtown, and when you hop off at Commercial-Broadway station a few minutes later, the Drive will be just steps away. Walk north toward the mountains and everything unfolds in a linear fashion: the Drive's main stores, restaurants and bars run on either side for about 17 blocks until Venables St. If it's too far to walk, bus 20 trundles along much of the main drag so you can jump aboard when you feel tired. Better still, just take a coffee-shop pit stop and you'll be back on your feet in no time. If you're exploring both of East Vancouver's top thoroughfares – Main St and Commercial Drive – take the 99B-Line express bus along Broadway: it links the two streets in around 10 minutes.

A lively, colorful strip, the Drive is said to be at its best on sunny summer afternoons. For others, it's languid summer evenings when the Drive thrives. This is the time when its abundant patios are at their most animated. If you're planning to eat, wander along the strip for a few blocks before you settle on a place that truly whets your appetite. The same goes for the chatty bars and coffee shops, where you'll meet everyone from pixie-chick bohemians to chin-stroking poets and old-school dope smokers.

Local Life

- **People watching** Watch locals with naughty cigarettes and hand-holding lovers strolling past from a sidewalk cafe seat or a Grandview Park (p120) perch.
- **Coffee quaffing** Vancouver's java-sipping hub, the Drive is lined with esoteric independent coffee shops, many of them tracing their roots to the area's Italian-style early days.
- **Shopping** The opposite of Robson St's slick chain stores, the Drive is teeming with one-of-a-kind indie shops always worth perusing.
- **Dining** It often seems as if every cuisine on the planet is available here, and the locals tuck right in.

Getting There & Away

- **Train** Board the Expo SkyTrain line from downtown to Commercial-Broadway station.
- **Bus** The 99B-Line express and regular bus 9 stop at the Broadway and Commercial intersection; bus 20 trundles along much of the Drive.
- **Car** There is metered parking on the Drive and nonmetered parking on its side streets.

Lonely Planet's Top Tip

While exploring the Drive, glance along the side streets. Almost every building just off the main drag seems to have an eye-popping mural to entice your camera. There's an especially excellent one – a huge, purple-hued crow (a popular East Vancouver visual symbol) – just around the corner on Venables St.

Best Places to Eat

- Caffè La Tana (p120)
- Downlow Chicken Shack (p120)
- Tangent Cafe (p120)
- Kulinarya (p122)
- Havana (p125)
- Sweet Cherubim (p121)

For reviews, see p120.

Best Places to Drink

- Storm Crow Tavern (p125)
- East Van Brewing Company (p125)
- St Augustine's (p127)
- Cafe Calabria (p126)
- Bump n Grind (p126)
- Cafe Deux Soleils (p125)

For reviews, see p125.

Best Places to Shop

- Mintage (p129)
- Licorice Parlour (p129)
- La Grotta Del Formaggio (p129)
- Attic Treasures (p129)
- Canterbury Tales (p129)

For reviews, see p129.

SIGHTS

The Drive itself is the main attraction here, acting as a bohemian promenade of cool stores and coffee shops. The center of the strip is Grandview Park, a handy green pit stop in your stroll.

GRANDVIEW PARK — PARK

Map p276 (Commercial Dr, btwn Charles & William Sts; 🐾; 🚌20) The Drive's grassy alfresco neighborhood hangout is named after the sterling views peeking between its trees: to the north are the looming North Shore mountains and to the west is a cityscape vista of twinkling glass towers. Teeming with buskers, dreadlocked drummers and impromptu sidewalk sales, the park is a big summertime lure for locals and Drive visitors.

EATING

The Drive is a strollable smorgasbord of independent and adventurous dining options. Fusing ethnic soul-food joints, cheap-but-good pizza spots, chatty street-side cafes and the kind of convivial pub-style hangouts that give the concept of 'neighborhood bar' a very good name, this is the city's most sociable dine-out district. It's also Vancouver's patio capital, so if the weather's good, drop by for an alfresco meal.

★CAFFÈ LA TANA — ITALIAN $

(☎604-428-5462; www.caffelatana.ca; 635 Commercial Dr; mains $12-16; ⏲8am-6pm; 🚌20) Like a 1950s neighborhood cafe in Rome, this handsome little hidden gem looks like it's been here for decades. But it's a relatively new addition to this quiet stretch of the Drive, luring delighted locals with its delicate house-made pastries and fresh pastas (watch the mesmerizing pasta production at the counter). Check the daily special and peruse the shelves of Italian groceries, too.

DOWNLOW CHICKEN SHACK — CHICKEN $

Map p276 (☎604-283-1385; www.dlchickenshack.ca; 905 Commercial Dr; mains $8-32; ⏲11am-9pm Tue-Sat, 11am-4:30pm Sun; 📶; 🚌20) Spicy, deep-fried, southern-style chicken is the menu foundation at this bright and buzzing spot with its surprisingly happy grinning-bird logo. Choose from a variety of cuts, including wings, boneless thighs and the popular-but-messy chicken-breast sandwich, then add your heat level plus tasty sides. Aim for a summertime deck seat and don't miss their $2 Wing Wednesday deal.

Downlow occupies a spot that once housed a popular vegetarian restaurant; they've cheekily retained the old hand-painted 'Best Vegetarian Cuisine' sign above the patio.

TANGENT CAFE — DINER $

Map p276 (☎604-558-4641; www.tangentcafe.ca; 2095 Commercial Dr; mains $11-19; ⏲8am-3pm Mon & Tue, 8am-midnight Wed & Thu, 8am-1am Fri & Sat, 8am-10pm Sun; 📶🌶; 🚌20) Lined with retro wood paneling, this warm and welcoming Drive hangout combines comfort-classic wraps and burgers with several Malaysian curries and some good vegetarian options. But breakfast, served until mid-afternoon, is when you're most likely to meet the locals. A great craft-beer menu (check the corner chalkboard) and regular live music (mostly jazz) also make this a popular nighttime haunt.

The side patio is busy here in summer. It's the perfect spot for sampling brews from BC ale-making darlings such as Dageraad, Driftwood and Persephone.

BENCH BAKEHOUSE — BAKERY $

Map p276 (☎604-251-0677; www.thebenchbakehouse.com; 1641 Commercial Dr; bakery items $2-4; ⏲7:30am-6pm Tue & Wed, 7:30am-7pm Thu & Fri, 8am-5pm Sat & Sun; 📶; 🚌20) Hidden in the back of an otherwise humdrum mini-mall, this delicious bakery cafe takes a butter-forward French approach, which means perfect croissants plus excellent baguettes and rustic sourdough loaves. But it's the mouthwatering treats that will have you lingering over coffee here, especially if you sample their Morning Bun, a glorious honey-sweet fusion of cinnamon bun softness and croissant-crisp exterior.

PIE SHOPPE — PIES $

(☎604-338-6646; www.thepieshoppe.ca; 1875 Powell St; slices $6-7; ⏲11am-7pm Wed-Fri, 11am-6pm Sat, 11am-5pm Sun; 📶; 🚌4) Relocated from its original hole-in-the-wall spot, this welcoming neighborhood hangout is a pie-hugging local legend. Drop by for coffee and slices of mouthwatering fresh-baked sweet pies in a variety of seasonal flavors (chocolate pecan is the only permanent regular). And if you're staying somewhere with a kitchen, buy a savory whole pie to go

THE DRIVE'S BEST FESTS

In addition to the Pacific National Exhibition (p124) a few blocks away, consider celebrating Commercial Drive's rich Italian heritage at June's annual **Italian Day** (www.italianday.ca), an epic, jam-packed street party of music, *boccie* and plenty of food. Expect to see generations of Italian families flocking to the area during this day-long event, fostering a festive vibe that welcomes all. Check the website for exact dates and information.

Equally popular **Car Free Day** (www.carfreevancouver.org; ⌚Jun & Jul; 👪) sees the street closed to traffic and turned into a massive fiesta of food, music, face-painting and stands selling or demonstrating artsy creations and local nonprofit initiatives.

Also look out for the city's finest homegrown Halloween happening if you're here in October. Staged by the Dusty Flowerpot Cabaret, the **Parade of Lost Souls** (www.dustyflowerpotcabaret.com) invites locals to dress up in their most ghoulish attire, stroll en masse with lanterns around the Commercial Drive area, and congregate for spooky displays and performances that thrill, chill and entertain in equal measure. It's more fun than any zombie out for a good time could ever hope for.

(vegetarian options included) and it'll feed you for days.

If you're craving a unique foodie-focused activity on your Vancouver visit, they also run pie-making workshops here. Check the website for upcoming classes and book ahead: they're extremely popular.

JAMJAR LEBANESE **$**

Map p276 (☎604-252-3957; www.jam-jar.ca; 2280 Commercial Dr; mains $12-18; ⌚11:30am-10pm; 🌶; 🚌20) This superfriendly cafe-style joint has a rustic-chic interior and a folksy Lebanese menu of ethically sourced ingredients, with lots of vegetarian options. You don't have to be a veggie to love the crispy falafel balls or the utterly irresistible deep-fried cauliflower which will have you fighting for the last morsel if you made the mistake of ordering to share.

Drop by between 4pm and 6pm on weekdays for happy-hour specials and add a delightful hibiscus lemonade to the mix.

SWEET CHERUBIM VEGETARIAN **$**

Map p276 (☎604-253-0969; www.sweetcherubim.com; 1105 Commercial Dr; mains $7-12; ⌚10am-10pm Mon-Sat, 11am-10pm Sun; 📶🌶; 🚌20) Many Drive restaurants offer vegetarian options but Sweet Cherubim goes the whole hog with a full-on organic, vegan and veggie menu of hearty, well-priced comfort foods served at its red Formica tables. There's an Indian feel to much of the menu, ranging from bulging baked or fried samosas (go for potato and pea) to good-value thali combos.

This is also a good place for a quick pit stop. Snag a seat on the woodsy patio for a cinnamon bun or a raw hemp, vanilla and blueberry smoothie. And keep in mind that the eatery shares its space with a large health food store; perfect if you're staying in a place with a kitchen and need to stock up.

ELEPHANT GARDEN CREAMERY ICE CREAM **$**

Map p276 (☎604-251-6832; www.elephantgarden.ca; 2080 Commercial Dr; ⌚noon-9pm Wed-Mon; 📶; 🚌20) Arguably Vancouver's most original independent ice-cream store, the ever-intriguing concoctions here are all made on-site by its friendly brother-and-sister owners. Their rolling roster of a dozen-or-so delicious flavors (many with Asian influences) can range from Vietnamese Coffee to Malted Milk Choc to vegan Mango Coconut Sticky Rice. The best way to plunge in? A $12, four-scoop tasting flight.

SPADE CAFE **$**

Map p276 (☎604-428-4092; www.spadecoffee.ca; 1858 Commercial Dr; mains $8-12; ⌚8am-9:30pm Mon-Thu, 8am-10:30pm Fri-Sun; 📶🌶; 🚌20) A sunny oasis routinely animated with chatty, laptop-wielding locals, Spade is more than just another Drive coffeeshop. Alongside the breakfast bowls and lunchtime sandwiches (including a wide array of vegetarian options), there are often bistro-style evening specials and an enticing cocktail menu to match. During the day, this is a warm pit stop for a leisurely latte and bakery treat.

FRATELLI BAKING
BAKERY $

Map p276 (☎604-255-8926; www.fratellibakery.com; 1795 Commercial Dr; bakery items from $3; ⊙9am-4pm Sun & Mon, 9am-5:30pm Tue-Sat; 🚌20) An authentic holdover from the Drive's Italian immigrant era, this ever-busy bakery is stuffed with old-school, fresh-made treats from lemon bars to cream-filled Neapolitan slices. Give yourself plenty of time to choose from the kaleidoscopic glass cabinet displays (be sure to add a cannoli or three to your order) and consider a warm loaf of Asiago cheese bread to go.

To start the makings of a great picnic, you could combine your loaf with some cheese and charcuterie at the Italian deli that's just next door. Once you've got your ad-hoc lunch fully gathered, weave north a few blocks and find a picnic spot in grassy Grandview Park.

CANNIBAL CAFE
BURGERS $

Map p276 (☎604-558-4199; www.cannibalcafe.ca; 1818 Commercial Dr; mains $10-16; ⊙7am-10pm Mon-Thu, 7am-midnight Fri & Sat, 10am-10pm Sun; 📶; 🚌20) This is a punk-tastic diner for fans of seriously real burgers. You'll find an inventive array, from the simple classics to the more adventurous kimchi-infused Korean-BBQ burgers, all made with love. Top-notch ingredients will ensure you never slink into a fast-food chain again. Add a BC craft beer, check for daily specials and keep in mind that there are happy-hour deals from 3pm to 6pm weekdays.

Whatever you do, don't try and tackle the Beast, a stomach-busting eating challenge comprised of an eight-patty burger. Eat it in 30 minutes and you'll receive a T-shirt (and a week's worth of regret).

LA CASA GELATO
ICE CREAM $

(☎604-251-3211; www.lacasagelato.com; 1033 Venables St; s scoop $4.50; ⊙11am-11pm; 📝; 🚌22) If you've been on your feet all day exploring the city, it may be time to cool down with an ice-cold treat. A quick visit to Vancouver's favourite traditional ice-cream joint should hit the spot, although you'll likely get brain-freeze trying to choose from the bewildering kaleidoscope of gelato, sorbetto and frozen yoghurt flavors (238 at last count).

Staffers are more than happy to let you taste your way through the many options here. And there are plenty of vegan, gluten-free, nut-free and dairy-free choices. However you should keep in mind that credit cards are not accepted.

KULINARYA
FILIPINO $$

Map p276 (☎604-255-4155; www.kulinarya.ca; 1134 Commercial Dr; mains $13-18; ⊙11am-3pm & 5-9pm Tue-Sat, to 8pm Sun; 🚌20) It's easy to miss this tiny storefront, unless you spot one of the colourful *kamayan* feasts heaped on the tables inside. But while you need at least six diners to order that particular banquet, there are plenty of other authentic Filipino dishes to discover here. Start with *lumpiang* spring rolls, then explore some dishes with your dining partner. We enjoyed fried milkfish *bangsilog*.

KIN KAO
THAI $$

Map p276 (☎604-558-1125; www.kinkao.ca; 903 Commercial Dr; mains $16-19; ⊙11:30am-3pm & 5-10pm Tue-Sat, 5-10pm Mon; 📶; 🚌20) An austere, white-walled interior belies the warm service and spicy menu at this modern Thai restaurant. You can choose to share a few plates between you (don't miss the deep-fried crispy pork belly) or dive straight into the excellent red-curry duck, with its sweet pineapple and coconut flavors. Booze is not an afterthought here either, hence the generous selection of growlers on shelves behind the counter.

KISHIMOTO JAPANESE RESTAURANT
JAPANESE $$

Map p276 (☎604-255-5550; www.kishimotorestaurant.com; 2054 Commercial Dr; mains $14-25; ⊙5pm-9:45pm Wed-Sun; 🚌20) Reservations are not accepted at this Commercial Drive favorite, so arrive early for a table or prepare yourself for a queue. Even if you have to wait, it'll be worth it: the sushi here uses super fresh ingredients with exquisite presentation and attentive service. The spicy salmon sashimi and vegetarian OMG rolls are recommended but they also do an excellent prawn-packed *okonomiyaki* (Japanese pancake).

Ask for sake recommendations while you're here; the selection includes hot and sparkling choices alongside several popular cold-sake concoctions.

Neighborhood Walk
Beers & Bites

START ST AUGUSTINE'S
END EAST VAN BREWING COMPANY
LENGTH 1KM; AN HOUR OR THREE (DEPENDING ON DRINKING)

From the Commercial-Broadway SkyTrain station, walk north one block to ❶ **St Augustine's** (p127) to find one of the city's biggest arrays of draft microbrews from BC and beyond. If you haven't indulged too much, continue north on Commercial – don't worry, it's a straight line – and sober up with a coffee at ❷ **Prado** (p127), one of many popular Drive java shops.

If you like your booze served with a Tolkienesque side dish, slip on your elf ears at self-proclaimed nerd bar ❸ **Storm Crow Tavern** (p125) a few blocks north. If you don't get sidetracked by their loaner board games, continue north towards the mountains and lie back in the grass at ❹ **Grandview Park** (p120) – but not before checking out the craggy peaks to the north and downtown's twinkling towers to the west.

Peel yourself from the park and nip next door to Euro-style ❺ **BierCraft Tap & Tapas** (p127). Play it safe with a whiskey or work your way down the amazing menu of local and imported beers. Even better, forsake the booze and try a fortifying bowl of brothy, Belgian-style mussels. The side patio here is perfect on sunny days.

If you didn't eat at BierCraft, continue along the same side of the Drive to ❻ **Sweet Cherubim** (p121) for hearty vegan and vegetarian comfort food. Dessert? Nip across the street to the eclectic ❼ **Licorice Parlour** (p129). Aside from dozens of imported varieties, it sells hand-made hula-hoops (an ideal purchase unless your head is still reeling from the beer earlier). Gather a bag of licorice treats to go.

Continue north, perusing the side-street murals, then turn left onto Venables St. Within a minute or two, you'll reach ❽ **East Van Brewing Company** (p125), a microbrewery favorite. Sip a tasting flight and consider your Drive dinner options. Now's the time to make a decision.

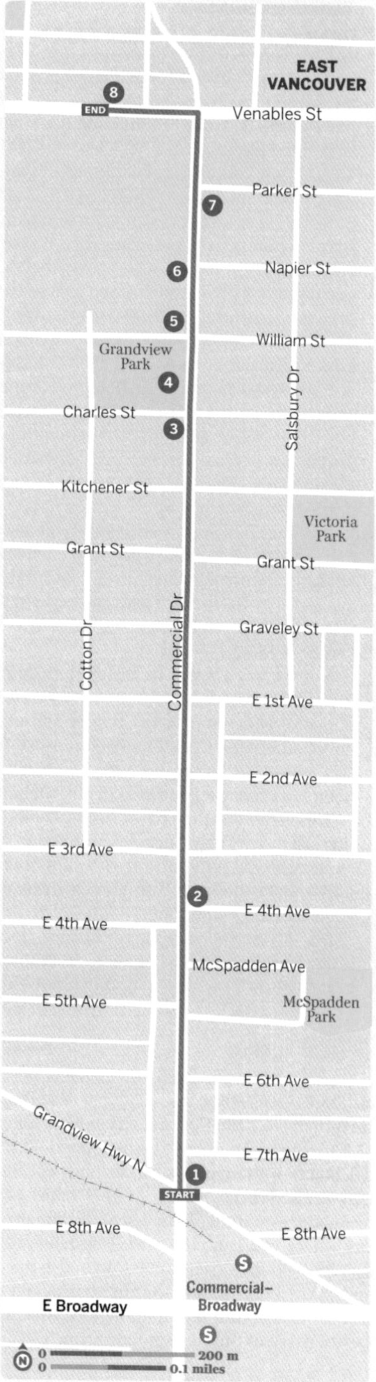

WORTH A DETOUR

VANCOUVER'S SUMMER FAIR

Some of Vancouver's summer events and festivities have been around for several decades, but only one is still going strong after more than a century. Started in 1912, the **Pacific National Exhibition** (www.pne.ca; 2901 E Hastings St, Hastings Park; adult/under-13s $18/free; mid-Aug–Sep; ; 14) – known simply as the PNE by locals – is an August tradition for generations of Vancouverites. It's held just a few blocks from the northern end of Commercial Drive (hop the Hastings St bus 14 for faster access). Starting life as an agricultural fair and community festival, the PNE has done a good job of updating itself over the years. It continues to be a popular, family-friendly day out, and a great way for visitors to rub shoulders with locals; it's hard to imagine an event that caters so well to such a diverse range of interests.

Plan ahead for a successful visit: check the website to see what entertainment you'd like to catch, then arrive as close to opening time as you can. This helps beat the crowds but also gives you the chance to see as much as possible. The parkland site is crammed with exhibition halls and arenas; take time to check out the market halls lined with vendors selling 'miracle' made-for-TV products. Then head to the livestock barns; the PNE is an important agricultural show for regional farmers, and these barns are lined with prize horses, cows, goats and sheep. There are also horse shows in the domed stadium, where you can take a seat and plot the rest of your day using the printed program.

Included with your admission (typically around $18 but cheaper if bought via the PNE website) is a wide array of performances running all day. In recent years, these have included magician shows, motorcycle stunts and the SuperDogs. There's also live music on alfresco stages throughout the day, especially in the evening, with nostalgic acts such as Foreigner and the Goo Goo Dolls adding to the party atmosphere in recent years.

Not everyone wants to stick around and watch their parents dance, though, and there are other attractions. The **Playland fairground** offers more than 50 rides, from dodgems to horror houses, but the top lure for thrill seekers is the 1950s-built wooden rollercoaster. Coaster aficionados from across North America frequently eulogize this scream-triggering boneshaker, which reaches speeds of up to 75km (47 miles) an hour. It's usually a good idea to go on it before indulging in the final big attraction.

This is the one time of year when Vancouverites forget about their yoga-and-rice-cakes regimen, happily loosening their pants and stuffing themselves silly. The midway here is jam-packed with naughty treats from deep-fried ice cream to two-foot-long hotdogs. And don't miss the biggest diet-defying tradition: warm bags of sugar-coated minidonuts.

Don't spend all your money on food, though, because you'll need some for the big lottery. Take a walk through the show home, then enter the draw; you might win a brand new house, furnishings included. Try fitting that in your suitcase.

LA MEZCALERIA — MEXICAN $$

Map p276 (604-559-8226; www.lamezcaleria.ca; 1622 Commercial Dr; 5-10pm Mon-Thu, 11am-11pm Fri, 10am-11pm Sat, 10am-10pm Sun; 20) Expect superb soft tacos topped with delectable ingredients such as pork confit and braised beef cheeks at this superior Mexican restaurant. Take a seat at the long bar where you can chat with twinkle-eyed servers who give friendliness a good name and know exactly how to sate your adventurous mezcal and tequila cravings. Also a great Friday-to-Sunday spot for brunch.

If you fancy trying out this place off-peak, there's also a small but tempting food and drinks happy-hour menu from Monday to Thursday (after 9pm) and Friday to Sunday (2pm to 5pm).

VIA TEVERE — PIZZA $$

Map p276 (604-336-1803; www.viatevere pizzeria.com; 1190 Victoria Dr; mains $15-21; 5-10pm Tue-Thu & Sun, 5-11pm Fri & Sat; ; 20) Just two blocks east from the Drive, it's worth the five-minute walk for what may be East Van's best pizza. Which is saying something, since the Drive is studded with good pizza joints like an over-packed pepperoni pie. Run by a family with true Neapolitan roots, check out the mosaic-tiled, wood-fired oven, then launch yourself into a delicious feast. We highly recommend the capricciosa.

There's a focus on simple but supremely well-made classic pizzas here. But there are also a couple of kid-friendly special options plus an utterly irresistible dessert: Neapolitan fritters made with cinnamon and Nutella.

HAVANA LATIN AMERICAN $$

Map p276 (☎604-253-9119; www.havanavancouver.com; 1212 Commercial Dr; mains $14-25; ⏰11am-11pm Mon-Fri, 10am-11pm Sat & Sun; 🚌20) One of the originators of the Drive's rich international-dining scene. A change of owner has smoothed the gritty edges of this Cuban-themed restaurant. You'll still find the street's best patio, a tiny on-site theater, plus the old graffiti wall on prominent display. The menu retains lots of hearty Latin-inspired dishes as well as a seriously popular brunch menu (we love the Cuban Skillet).

Reservations are not accepted between Friday evenings and Sunday afternoons, when you should expect to wait for a park-view patio table...especially on summer evenings when the mojitos will be calling your name.

Looking for an alternative night out? Check ahead to see what's on at the 60-seat theater where comedy, live music and book launches color an eclectic calendar.

DRINKING & NIGHTLIFE

If you like your drinks served with a frothy head of chatty locals, the Drive has some great neighborhood bars worth considering. Arguably, even more enticing are the coffee joints that make this one of Vancouver's main java destinations. And don't forget the microbrewery district that's accessible from the north end of Commercial; it's the city's best.

★STORM CROW TAVERN PUB

Map p276 (☎604-566-9669; www.stormcrowtavern.com; 1305 Commercial Dr; ⏰11am-1am Mon-Sat, to midnight Sun; 📶; 🚌20) Knowing the difference between Narnia and *Neverwhere* is not a prerequisite at this brilliant Commercial Drive nerd pub. But if you do, you'll certainly make new friends. With displays of Dr Who figures and steampunk ray guns – plus TVs that might screen *Logan's Run* at any moment – dive into the craft beer and settle in for a fun evening.

Alongside the BC brews (plus well-named cocktails including Romulan Ale and Pan Galactic Gargle Blasters), the grub here is of the cheap-and-cheerful burgers and wraps variety. There are also role-play books and a huge wall of board games for the so-inclined (if you know what Elfenland is, that means you). Twice-monthly trivia nights and weekday happy hours also add to the festivities.

EAST VAN BREWING COMPANY MICROBREWERY

Map p276 (☎604-558-3822; www.eastvanbrewing.com; 1675 Venables St; ⏰noon-11pm Sun-Thu, noon-midnight Fri & Sat; 📶; 🚌20) This is a favorite among Commercial Dr locals. Arrive off-peak (weekday afternoons are best) for a sought-after table at this busy microbrewery. Order a tasting flight in a paddle shaped like a crucifix (an East Van symbol) but be sure it includes the lip-smacking Humble Hive brown ale. Save time for sandwiches and snack pickles – plus a whirl on the AC/DC pinball machine.

CAFE DEUX SOLEILS CAFE

Map p276 (☎604-254-1195; www.cafedeuxsoleils.com; 2096 Commercial Dr; ⏰8am-11pm Mon-Wed, 8am-midnight Thu & Fri, 9am-midnight Sat, 9am-11pm Sun; 📶; Ⓢ Commercial-Broadway) This rambling bohemian cafe is a hip, healthy and ever-friendly Drive landmark, serving a good array of local beers and well-priced vegetarian comfort food. The small stage is deployed every evening, with acoustic musicians, performance poets or open-mic wannabes keeping things lively. Aim for a red-vinyl side booth or hit the slender deck out front for a pyrotechnic sunset.

Poetry slams are held on Monday nights ($6 to $10 cover charge) and shows start at 9pm (doors open 8pm). This is your big chance to regale the locals with your leotard-clad retelling of *The Rime of the Ancient Mariner*, perhaps while playing a lute. There are also good-value happy-hour food and drink specials from 4pm to 6pm (weekdays only).

WORTH A DETOUR

CRAWLING YEAST VANCOUVER

If you're a true ale nut, consider checking out a round of little, off-the-beaten-path 'Yeast Vancouver' microbreweries that together constitute one of Canada's best beer districts. Each has its own alluring tasting room and they also offer takeout growlers if you need libations to go. Stay on the Drive and continue walking north for a few minutes past the intersection with Venables St and into an old industrial part of town (it's perfectly safe). When you come to Adanac St, turn left. Just ahead, you'll see **Bomber Brewing** (Map p276; 604-428-7457; www.bomberbrewing.com; 1488 Adanac St; noon-11pm; ; 14), where the windowless little tasting room invites plenty of cozy quaffing; try ESB. Back outside, continue west on Adanac for a couple of minutes; **Off the Rail** (Map p276; 604-563-5767; www.offtherailbrewing.com; 1351 Adanac St; noon-8pm Sun-Thu, noon-10pm Fri & Sat; ; 14) is nearby on the other side of the street. Climb the staircase and you'll find a convivial tasting room serving great beers made in the room next door.

Back on Adanac, continue to Clark Dr, turn right and walk for a few minutes on Clark until you reach Franklin St. Turn right on Franklin and you'll find red-fronted **Callister Brewing** (604-569-2739; www.callisterbrewing.com; 1338 Franklin St; 2-9pm Mon-Thu, 2-10pm Fri, 1-10pm Sat, 1-8pm Sun; ; 14), a shared facility where several excellent nano-breweries concoct their tasty wares. Next, return to Clark, continue north and then turn right onto Powell St. Just ahead of you and across the street is the celebrated **Powell Brewery** (www.powellbeer.com; 1357 Powell St; 2-9pm Mon-Thu, noon-10pm Fri & Sat, noon-9pm Sun; ; 4). Consider the lip-smacking Dive Bomb Porter or an Old Jalopy Pale Ale.

Continue east on Powell and, a couple of minutes later, you'll reach **Andina Brewing Company** (604-253-2400; www.andinabrewing.ca; 1507 Powell St; 11am-11pm; ; 4) with its beacon-like bright-yellow exterior. Check out the Latin American–influenced brews here. Finally, if you still have your wits about you, continue along Powell and turn right onto Victoria Dr then left on Triumph St. Here you'll find **Parallel 49 Brewing Company** (604-558-2739; www.parallel49brewing.com; 1950 Triumph St; 11am-11pm; ; 4) where the large tasting room serves a popular array of quirkily named tipples, including Hoparazzi India Pale Lager and Gypsy Tears Ruby Red Ale. Need to know more? Pick up a copy of *The Growler* ($3), sold at many of these breweries. It'll tell you all you need to know about the province's burgeoning beer scene. And when you're ready to fuel up with another essential food group, the Pie Shoppe (p120) is just a three-minute walk away from Parallel 49.

BUMP N GRIND — COFFEE

Map p276 (604-569-3362; www.bumpngrindcafe.com; 916 Commercial Dr; 7am-7pm Mon-Fri, 8am-7pm Sat & Sun; ; 20) Showing that Drive locals can never get enough good java, this hipster-cool addition to Commercial's coffee-house culture has a loyal following, especially among the laptop-loving, coffee-quaffing devotees of communal tables. There's a strong commitment to well-prepared brews – not always the case on the area's highly competitive scene – as well as top beans provided by local artisanal roasters.

It's not all about coffee here, of course. Among the baked goodies are some hulking, house-made muffins that are well worth skipping lunch for.

CAFE CALABRIA — COFFEE

Map p276 (604-253-7017; www.cafecalabria.ca; 1745 Commercial Dr; sandwiches $6-12; 6am-10pm; 20) When Vancouverites say the Drive is the city's best coffee street, this is one of the places they're thinking of: the frothy top on a brimming mugful of cafes founded here by Italian immigrants. Don't be put off by the chandeliers-and-statues decor (not everyone likes a side order of statuesque genitalia); just order an espresso, sit outside and watch the Drive promenade past.

Hearty (and mostly meaty) *panini* fill out the menu here and there's also a selection of gelato if you need to cool off.

ST AUGUSTINE'S

PUB

Map p276 (☎604-569-1911; www.staugustinesvancouver.com; 2360 Commercial Dr; ⊙11am-1am Sun-Thu, 11am-2am Fri & Sat; 📶; Ⓢ Commercial-Broadway) It resembles a regular, sometimes overly loud, neighborhood sports bar from the outside, but step inside St Aug's and you'll find around 60 on-tap microbrews. It has one of the city's largest selections, mostly from BC. This is your chance to sample ales from regional brewers you don't often see on draft in Vancouver, such as Yellow Dog and Twin Sails.

Check the website to see what's on tap before you arrive; it has a clever 'live beer menu' showing how much of each brew is left. And if you're still not sure what to order, ask for the four-glass tasting flight. The food is of the heaping pub-grub variety here (burgers and fish and chips).

BIERCRAFT TAP & TAPAS

BAR

Map p276 (☎604-254-2437; www.biercraft.com; 1191 Commercial Dr; ⊙11am-midnight Mon-Thu, 11am-1am Fri, 10am-1am Sat, 10am-midnight Sun; 📶; 🚌20) Originally founded with a huge, hangover-triggering Belgian beer menu – it still has lots of rare international ales – BierCraft has since shifted its boozy focus to incorporate the surging BC microbrew scene, including dozens of choice drafts from the likes of Four Winds and Strange Fellows. On sunny days, snag a patio seat and keep drinking until you find your favorite tipple.

They're equally serious about their food here, with a gastropub menu studded with tempting tapas plates and brothy bowls of fresh BC mussels (go for the miso-ginger version). This is also one of the Drive's most popular weekend-only brunch spots.

PRADO

COFFEE

Map p276 (☎604-255-5537; www.pradocafe.co; 1938 Commercial Dr; ⊙7am-8pm Mon-Fri, 7am-6pm Sat & Sun; 📶; 🚌20) A beloved java hangout for laptop-wielding local hipsters, this sunny, wood-floored nook in a handsome redbrick heritage building serves up serious fair-trade coffee alongside an array of tempting baked treats (chunky cookies rock). On long summer days, snag a streetside perch out front; it's the perfect place to watch the Drive in action.

CHARLATAN

PUB

Map p276 (☎604-253-2777; www.thecharlatanrestaurant.com; 1447 Commercial Dr; ⊙11am-1am Sun-Thu, 11am-2am Fri & Sat; 📶; 🚌20) A long-time Drive fixture, this darkly lit neighborhood bar is a perfect rainy-day hunker spot for beer specials and comfort pub grub. But in summer it becomes a different beast with its jam-packed and ever-popular side patio plus open front windows. Beer-wise, you'll find lots of BC taps here, typically including Phillips, Hoyne and Central City.

There's a hearty menu of well-executed pub grub (burgers and tacos included), while the popular weekend brunch, served until 3pm, ranges from eggs-benny options to a calorifically naughty poutine topped with beef brisket and poached eggs.

WILDER JUICE

JUICE BAR

Map p276 (☎778-871-4102; www.wilderjuice.com; 1108 Commercial Dr; ⊙10am-6pm; 🚌20) At this small-batch juice-pressing bar with a loyal clientele of health-minded Drive fans, you'll find an enticing array of house-made cleanses, almond-based mylks and organic fruit-and-vegetable concoctions. Sold in glass bottles from the counter cabinet, juicy favorites include carrot-and-orange-based Root Awakenings and Mean Green, a cucumber, celery, kale and more pick-me-up that's perfect for weary travelers.

☆ ENTERTAINMENT

The Drive is home to some of Vancouver's most eclectic night-out options, from poetry slams to retro bowling, plus one of the city's most popular independent theaters.

★RIO THEATRE

LIVE PERFORMANCE

Map p276 (☎604-879-3456; www.riotheatre.ca; 1660 E Broadway; tickets from $5; Ⓢ Commercial-Broadway) A huge public fundraising campaigning in 2018 saved this beloved theater and cinema venue from possible redevelopment, proving just how important it's become in the cultural lives of locals. But alongside arthouse movie screenings, there's a seriously eclectic array of entertainment here, from burlesque to stand-up and from live music to cult films. Check the calendar to see what's on during your visit.

Regular shows to look out for here include the Gentlemen Hecklers, who narrate big screen movies with their own naughty soundtrack, and Story Story Lie, a kind of

DRIVE PAST

Strolling Commercial Drive today, it's easy to imagine the bohemians have ruled this strip forever. In reality, the street has an unexpected past as one of the city's most historic neighborhoods. Once part of the main transportation link between Vancouver and the city of New Westminster, streetcars trundled down the middle of the Drive from the 1890s, triggering the housing and storefront developments that remain here today. Many of these were later colonized by European families (mostly Italians as well as some Portuguese) who emigrated here in the 1950s. The handful of old-school coffee shops that remain are an evocative reminder of this period.

But the Italians were a later chapter in the Drive's history. While main-drag storefronts catch the eye today, make sure you take a peek down the side streets. They're lined with gabled, wood-built homes constructed for Canadian Pacific Railway (CPR) workers in the first few years of the last century, and many have been restored in recent decades to their bright-painted clapboard glory. In fact, this neighborhood is home to one of the largest collections of **heritage homes** in Vancouver. Architecture fans will likely spot some well-known styles, including Edwardian, Queen Anne, Craftsman and Arts and Crafts.

In recent years, locals have begun to celebrate the area's rich past and a volunteer organization calling itself the **Grandview Heritage Group** (www.grandviewheritagegroup.org) has formed to help preserve the district's architectural treasures. The organization's annual **Centenary Signs Project** sees houses and buildings in the area that are more than 100 years old recognized with cool plaques. Walkers can then trawl the neighborhood spotting the best examples. There's a map of the centenarian houses on the website, where you'll also find some evocative vintage images of the area's past.

gameshow where audiences guess who is telling the truth.

CULTCH — THEATER

Map p276 (Vancouver East Cultural Centre; ☎604-251-1363; www.thecultch.com; 1895 Venables St; tickets from $20; 🚌20) This once-abandoned church has been a gathering place for performers and audiences since being officially designated a cultural space in 1973. Following comprehensive renovations a few years back, the beloved Cultch (as everyone calls it) is now one of Vancouver's entertainment jewels, with a busy roster of local, fringe and visiting companies staging everything from spoken word to puppet shows to Ibsen plays.

Check the online calendar to see what's on stage here during your visit. Following its own sparkling renovation, the nearby **York Theatre** was also added to the Cultch stable in 2013. Check the Cultch's website to see what's on there; look out for the annual East Van Panto, a rip-roaring Christmas show that sells out every year.

VANCOUVER POETRY SLAM — PERFORMING ARTS

Map p276 (www.cafedeuxsoleils.com; 2096 Commercial Dr, Cafe Deux Soleils; tickets $6-10; ⏲9pm Mon; Ⓢ Commercial-Broadway) If you thought that poetry was a tweedy, soporific experience, check out the weekly events organized by the Vancouver Poetry House at Cafe Deux Soleils for a taste of high-speed, high-stakes poetry slamming. The expert performers are sure to blow your socks off with their verbal dexterity, which often bears more than a passing resemblance to rap.

There's an open-mic element to every slam night, so this might just be your big chance to hop on stage and give it all you've got.

WISE HALL — LIVE MUSIC

Map p276 (☎604-254-5858; www.wisehall.ca; 1882 Adanac St; tickets from $20; 📶; 🚌20) This comfortably grungy former church hall is a friendly neighborhood spot, close to the heart of in-the-know locals who flock here to catch live ska, folk, improv shows and the occasional hip-hop DJ night. Check the schedule for events or just hang out in the lounge (ask the bartender to sign you in as a guest).

It's a great place to mix with cool East Vancouverites; the bouncy floor brings out the most reluctant of dancers.

GRANDVIEW LANES BOWLING CENTRE
BOWLING

Map p276 (☎604-253-2747; www.grandviewbowling.com; 2195 Commercial Dr; ⏲10am-11pm Mon-Wed, 10am-midnight Thu, 10am-1am Fri & Sat, 10am-10pm Sun; Ⓢ Commercial-Broadway) Look for the beacon-like neon bowling pin sign outside, then slip on some rented shoes and hit the lanes at this family-run retro joint. There are regular five- and 10-pin options but the big draw is the glow-in-the-dark neon bowling––preferably with a side order of hot dogs and BC craft beers. Check the website for specials and book ahead.

SHOPPING

Like a counterculture department store stretched along both sides of one street, the Drive is Vancouver's 'anti-Robson.' You'll find dozens of interesting, independent shops, ranging from ethical clothing stores to intelligent-minded bookshops. If the area sounds a little too earnest, keep in mind that Commercial also has plenty of frivolous shopping outlets where you can pick up handmade candies and pop-culture gifts for your friends back home.

★LICORICE PARLOUR
FOOD

Map p276 (☎604-558-2422; 1002 Commercial Dr; ⏲11am-6pm Mon-Wed, 11am-6:30pm Thu-Sat, noon-6pm Sun; 🚌20) Just when you think you'll never find that combination licorice and hula-hoop store you've been searching for, here it is. This perky little spot with a serious commitment to the love-it-or-hate-it candy stocks dozens of tempting options, from miniwitches to palate-expanding Scandinavian varieties. Work off your candy belly with a hula-hoop session, then buy some hand-dipped chocolates to go.

Gelatin-free, sugar-free and gluten-free varieties, plus small tins of snorting chocolate, are also available here. Take your time; there's a lot to see.

MINTAGE
VINTAGE

Map p276 (☎604-646-8243; www.facebook.com/MintageClothingCo; 1714 Commercial Dr; ⏲10am-7pm Mon-Sat, 11am-6pm Sun; 🚌20) Drive coolsters add some vintage glam to their look in this Western-saloon-like establishment. But don't be fooled: this is one of the city's most kaleidoscopically eclectic stores. Dominated by womens wear, it has everything from saris to tutus, while the menswear at the back is ideal for finding a velour leisure suit with 'matching' Kenny Rogers T-shirt.

Don't miss the funky costume jewelry and check out the cleverly reworked clothes that give new life to old, otherwise unfashionable pieces.

LA GROTTA DEL FORMAGGIO
FOOD & DRINKS

Map p276 (☎604-255-3911; www.lgdf.ca; 1791 Commercial Dr; ⏲9am-6pm Mon-Thu & Sat, 9am-7pm Fri, 10am-6pm Sun; 🚌20) If you insist on eating something other than chocolate or ice cream, hit this legendary time-capsule deli and sandwich shop, a family-run holdover from the days when this was Vancouver's 'Little Italy.' Peruse the lip-smacking cheese and charcuterie selections, then check out the wall of marzipan, antipasti, olive oil and balsamic vinegar. Almost everything here has been imported from the mother country.

It's a good spot to gather the makings of a mighty fine picnic – try prosciutto and smoked ricotta – to scoff in nearby Grandview Park. But before you leave the store, check out the ceiling: it's painted with clouds, just like the Sistine Chapel (but better). There's often a lineup at the counter, with many locals flocking in for made-to-order deli sandwiches.

ATTIC TREASURES
ANTIQUES

Map p276 (☎604-254-0220; www.attictreasuresvancouver.com; 944 Commercial Dr; ⏲11am-6pm Tue & Thu-Sat, noon-5pm Sun; 🚌20) A Vancouver favorite specializing in antiques and midcentury items, this retro-cool double-room is lined with 1950s-to-1980s furniture and treasures. Peruse the candy-colored coffee pots and kaleidoscopic cocktail glasses and save time for the back area, where bargains sometimes lurk. Much of the furniture has a Danish modern feel and there is often also sparkling Finnish glassware to make your credit cards sweat.

CANTERBURY TALES
BOOKS

Map p276 (☎604-568-3511; www.canterburytales.ca; 2010 Commercial Dr; ⏲10am-6pm Mon-Wed & Sat, 10am-7pm Thu & Fri, 11am-6pm Sun; 🚌20) Serving the area's voracious bookworms, this used and new bookstore is one of several Drive literary nooks. It's a mini-labyrinth of floor-to-ceiling stacks bulging with titles, including some quirky staff picks near the entrance. Sci-fi and fantasy fans should also check the extensive sections at the back of the store. Don't miss the well-curated literary-travel section near the center of the shop.

Consider picking up a Charles Bukowski anthology or two: the infamous American author and poet gave a few notorious live readings on the Drive back in the day. This is also a good spot to buy new books; they're typically 30% cheaper than list price.

AUDIOPILE MUSIC

Map p276 (☎604-253-7453; www.audiopile.ca; 2016 Commercial Dr; ⏰11am-7pm; 🚌20) From classic rock to obscure German metal bands, this local-fave record store takes a no-nonsense approach with its basic racks of new and used vinyl, CD and cassette recordings. Find that rare Joy Division (or not-so-rare New Order) album, check out the bargain selection and staff picks near the front and also take a peak at the outside box of freebie giveaways.

This is the perfect location for an extensive rainy-day rummage. The staff really know their stuff; quiz them on Carter the Unstoppable Sex Machine albums and see if they flinch.

PULPFICTION BOOKS EAST BOOKS

Map p276 (☎604-251-4311; www.pulpfictionbooksvancouver.com; 1744 Commercial Dr; ⏰11am-7pm; 🚌20) The smallest of Pulpfiction's miniempire of three Vancouver bookstores, this spartan-looking shop has little decoration but lots of well-stocked wooden bookshelves. And what that shows, of course, is that it really is all about the books here. This is an easy spot to while away an hour of browsing, and it's almost impossible not to find something you want to buy.

If you're a fast reader, you can try to resell your purchase back to the store before you leave for home: it has an active book-buying program (although apparently not very keen on anything by Dan Brown).

LITTLE MISS VINTAGE VINTAGE

Map p276 (☎604-255-3554; www.littlemissvintage.com; 931 Commercial Dr; ⏰11am-6pm Tue-Sat, noon-5pm Sun & Mon; 🚌20) A jam-packed browser's paradise of mostly women's retro clothes and accessories, this is the perfect store to reinvent your look. Thinking of combining a 1970s tartan vest with a 1950s prom dress? This is the place for you. Rows of shoes and a magpie-worthy surfeit of costume jewelry add to the treasures; check out the old velvet paintings on the walls as well.

KALI CLOTHING

Map p276 (☎604-215-4568; 1000 Commercial Dr; ⏰10am-6pm Mon-Thu & Sat, 10am-7pm Fri, 11am-6pm Sun; 🚌20) Serving up an eclectically diverse array of well-curated women's clothing and crafty housewares and trinkets sourced from around the world, this popular browser's hangout is perfect for squandering a lazy hour or so before dinner. You'll find everything from summer hats to Buddha statues calling your name here.

KALENA'S SHOES SHOES

Map p276 (☎604-255-3727; www.kalenashoes.com; 1526 Commercial Dr; ⏰10am-6pm Mon-Fri, 10am-5:30pm Sat, noon-5pm Sun; 🚌20) True to Commercial Dr's Italian heritage, family-run Kalena's imports handsome top-quality leather shoes and boots from the old country. Well-crafted men's and women's styles can be had for reasonable prices and there's also a big area devoted to sale items. It's the kind of place you'll pay $200 for a pair of brogues and they'll last you for a couple of decades.

Main Street

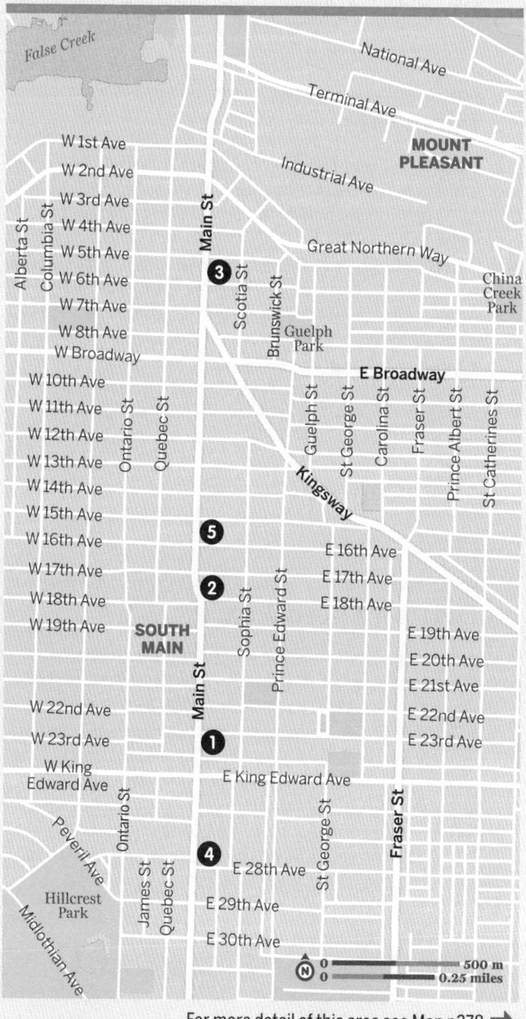

For more detail of this area see Map p278

Neighborhood Top Five

❶ **Regional Assembly of Text** (p142) Composing pithy missives to your loved one on vintage typewriters at the legendary monthly letter-writing club.

❷ **Anh & Chi** (p136) Dining on delightful contemporary Vietnamese dishes (and a glass or three of housemade punch) at this beloved restaurant.

❸ **Brassneck Brewery** (p138) Downing a Passive Aggressive pale ale at Vancouver's favorite neighborhood microbrewery, and adding a growler to go.

❹ **Red Cat Records** (p142) Browsing the racks, buying local gig tickets and finally finding that signed Buttless Chaps album you've been looking for.

❺ **Urban Source** (p143) Planning the perfect craft project at Main's favorite (and most eclectic) supply store, where everything from vintage buttons to reclaimed cassette tapes are just waiting to be repurposed.

Lonely Planet's Top Tip

Head to **Holy Trinity Ukrainian Orthodox Cathedral** (p135) before 5pm on the first Friday of every month. You'll join in-the-know locals queuing for home-cooked pierogi and cabbage rolls. Budget for $17 and you'll be full for days.

Best Places to Eat

- Anh & Chi (p136)
- Fish Counter (p136)
- Dock Lunch (p136)
- Hawkers Delight (p134)
- Federal Store (p134)

For reviews, see p134. ➡

Best Places to Drink

- Brassneck Brewery (p138)
- Key Party (p139)
- Narrow Lounge (p139)
- Shameful Tiki Room (p139)
- Sing Sing Beer Bar (p140)

For reviews, see p138. ➡

Best Places to Shop

- Regional Assembly of Text (p142)
- Mintage Mall (p143)
- Pulpfiction Books (p144)
- Red Cat Records (p142)
- Bird on a Wire Creations (p143)

For reviews, see p142. ➡

Explore Main Street

After Science World and the nearby Olympic Village, the main action on Main takes place further south in two key areas: around the intersection with Broadway and then further south from 18th Ave. These are the twin hearts of Vancouver's hipster scene. The first, the center of the Mount Pleasant neighborhood, is lined with independent bars and coffee shops, while the area past 18th is perfect for airing your credit cards: it's full of unique fashion, arts and vintage stores. Consider an afternoon of window shopping here, followed by dinner and a few beers in either area. Handily, bus 3 runs along Main every few minutes but make sure you hop off regularly for some on-foot exploration. Wherever you stop, check out the side streets; this area has been richly adorned with eye-popping outdoor art murals.

Local Life

- **Coffee shops** Locals spend more time hunched over laptops in cafes here than anywhere else in the city. Join them for a glimpse of what makes the area tick at Gene Cafe (p140).
- **Nightlife** From cocktail bars to microbrewery tasting rooms, Main is dripping with brilliant independent watering holes. Start or end your evening at Key Party (p139), hidden behind a fake accountancy office.
- **Indie shopping** The last place any major big box retailer would move to. Browsing the surfeit of one-of-a-kind boutiques, bookstores and record shops keeps locals happily occupied. First stop? Try Mintage Mall (p143).
- **Vegetarian dining** Main offers a meat-free cornucopia of amazing veggie options, including city favorite Acorn (p136).

Getting There & Away

- **Bus** Number 3 runs the length of Main St. The 99B-Line express bus connects Main and Commercial Dr along Broadway, as does the much slower bus 9.
- **Train** SkyTrain connects to bus 3 services at Main St-Science World Station. But if you're on the Canada Line, alight at Broadway-City Hall and take the 99B-Line along Broadway to Main St.
- **Car** There is some metered parking on Main St, plus lots of side-street parking the further south you drive.

ROSEBC10987/SHUTTERSTOCK ©

TOP EXPERIENCE
LEARN THROUGH PLAY AT SCIENCE WORLD

Vancouver's landmark geodesic dome isn't just a shiny shoreline bauble; it's also home to the city's most popular family-friendly attraction. Teeming with hands-on exhibits, engaging galleries, an eye-popping large-format movie theater and much more, it's the kind of attraction you plan to cover off quickly but find yourself still exploring three hours later.

Start by letting your kids loose in the ground floor **Puzzles & Illusions** gallery, a tactile array of activities from wobble rings to whisper dishes. Consider paying extra ($8) here for **Birdly**, a virtual-reality solo flight over a tower-forested city. Nearby, check out the **Centre Stage** live science demonstrations, then head up to the second level. It's circled by themed galleries bristling with hands-on action, including the nature-themed **Sara Stern Gallery** (with fossils and live critters) and the brilliant **BodyWorks**, which explores the engineering marvels of the human body.

There's a full array of activities for all ages here – we could easily spend hours playing at the humongous water table – but, if the weather's fine, save time for the outdoor **Ken Spencer Science Park** (pictured). Focused on sustainable communities, it's a quirky collection of climbing frames, rugged interactive games and stage demonstrations plus a coop-full of beady-eyed chickens.

DON'T MISS

- BodyWorks
- Centre Stage shows
- Omnimax
- Ken Spencer Science Park
- After Dark

PRACTICALITIES

- Map p278, B1
- ☎604-443-7440
- www.scienceworld.ca
- 1455 Quebec St
- adult/child $27.15/18.10
- ⏲10am-6pm Jul & Aug, reduced hours off-season
- P 👪
- S Main St-Science World

SIGHTS

A leisurely weave between Main's indie stores and cafes is the prime activity for most locals and visitors here, but there are also lots of striking street murals and a highly popular science center to look out for.

SCIENCE WORLD — MUSEUM

See p133.

OLYMPIC VILLAGE — AREA

Map p278 (Athletes Way; S Main St-Science World) Built as the home for 2800 athletes during the 2010 Olympic and Paralympic Winter Games, this glassy waterfront development became the city's newest neighborhood once the sporting types went home. New shops, bars and restaurants – plus some cool public art – have made this an increasingly happening area. Worth a look on your seawall stroll.

Don't forget to photograph the area's two gigantic **bird sculptures** – preferably with the mountains behind them.

EATING

Main St is an intriguing area for eclectic, one-of-a-kind dining experiences. Many options radiate out from the intersection with Broadway. Make sure you also peruse the local bar listings since many of the drinkeries here also have worthwhile dining menus.

HAWKERS DELIGHT — ASIAN $

Map p278 (604-709-8188; www.facebook.com/hawkersdelightdeli; 4127 Main St; mains $5-13; noon-9pm Mon-Sat; ; 3) It's easy to miss this cash-only hole-in-the-wall, but it's worth retracing your steps for authentic Malaysian and Singaporean street food, made from scratch at this family-run favorite. Prices are temptingly low, so order to share – from spicy *mee pok* to noodle-heavy *mee goreng* and shrimp-packed *laksa*. Check the counter for addictive veggie fritters (just $1.45 for two).

This is one of the city's best and most enduring budget eats; there's not much room, so consider arriving off peak, unless you're planning a takeout picnic.

LOCAL KNOWLEDGE

STREET ART MURALS

Main Street and its surrounding tributaries are like a walk-through kaleidoscope of eye-popping street-art installations. The center of the annual **Vancouver Mural Festival** (www.vanmuralfest.ca; Main St; Aug) features dozens of striking, richly colored works that have been applied to the blank-canvas alfresco walls of large local buildings, encouraging lots of selfie-snapping wanderers to explore the area and hunt down the cool creations. Visit the Mural Festival's website for guided summer walks as well as a handy online map of local works and tips where to find them. Our favorite cluster? We love the dozen or so creations on the walls of Industrial Ave and Southern St, between Western St and Station St.

FEDERAL STORE — CAFE $

Map p278 (778-379-2605; www.federalstore.ca; 2601 Quebec St; mains $4-12; 8am-6pm; 3) Revitalizing an old mom-and-pop corner store into a funky little community cafe, this warmly welcoming checker-floored charmer serves coffee, light breakfasts and delicious lunch sandwiches (go for the juicy porchetta). Among the bakery treats, a boutique array of artisan groceries and knick-knacks, and lots of chatty locals, you'll feel like you're in the heart of the neighborhood.

They've chosen not to have wi-fi here so you might feel encouraged to start a conversation with someone on the sunny seats outside; Vancouver's eye-watering apartment-rental rates are a good topic to begin with, but be aware that chairs might start flying through the air.

TRAFIQ — CAFE $

Map p278 (604-648-2244; www.trafiq.ca; 4216 Main St; mains $7-10; 9am-6pm; ; 3) This sometimes clamorously busy French-influenced bakery-cafe is a lunchtime magnet with its quesadillas, house-made soups and bulging grilled sandwiches (California club on cranberry pecan recommended). But the best time to come is off peak, when you can snag a table and take on one of the large, belly-busting cake slabs. Miss the salted-caramel slice at your peril.

If there are two of you – or you're just greedy – add a slice of Chunky Monkey, a rich, cake-bread-pudding fusion combo that simulaneously triggers equal feelings of delight and guilt.

BUDGIE'S BURRITOS TEX-MEX $

Map p278 (604-874-5408; www.budgiesburritos.com; 44 Kingsway; mains $7-10; 11am-midnight; ; 8) It's a rare vegetarian eatery that has a loyal clientele of carnivores, and this is one of them. The bulging, good-value burritos at this quirky, well-hidden neighborhood haunt keep locals coming back for a seat among the Elvis, conquistador and creepy-clown velour 'artworks.' First time here? Go for the tofu-sausage-packed Henry and snag a booth in the slightly grungy subterranean basement. Vegan options also available.

If you're still hungry, why not chase it with a bowl of house-made tortilla soup. It's often busy here, so arrive off peak to avoid the line-ups.

PUREBREAD BAKERY $

Map p278 (604-336-9001; www.purebread.ca; 5 E 5th Ave; bakery items $3-6; 8am-6pm; ; 3) The Mount Pleasant branch of this wildly popular Whistler-started bakery is a walk-in treasure chest of truly irresistible treats. Try not to drool too much while you're perusing the counter's eye-popping array of chocolate-almond croissants, raspberry-lemon drizzle cakes, salted-caramel brownie pies and more. Regardless of what you feast on at your table, the stuff here is so good that you'll want to make sure you also pick up something to go before you leave.

ARBOR VEGETARIAN $

Map p278 (604-620-3256; www.thearborrestaurant.ca; 3941 Main St; mains $11-16; 11am-midnight; ; 3) Contrary to what the white-walled aesthetic might suggest, this is a warm and casual cafe, especially in the evenings when it becomes a popular neighborhood hangout. The elevated comfort grub will make an instant vegetarian of anyone who's hungry – particularly if you dive into the burgers, pizzas or the deliciously spicy Southern-fried artichoke sandwich. Add BC craft beers from Strathcona or Four Winds for the full effect.

They make sure to cater for a few different diets here, and there's always a good array of vegan and gluten-free options marked on the menu. There's also a very tempting twice-daily (3pm to 6pm, 10pm to midnight) happy-hour selection of drinks and food to dive into.

TOSHI SUSHI JAPANESE $

Map p278 (604-874-5173; 181 E 16th Ave; mains $8-17; 4:30-9:45pm Tue-Sat; ; 3) There are no reservations and the place is tiny, but this unassuming sushi joint situated just off Main is hands down the best place in the neighborhood for Japanese dining. Expect to have to queue (try to arrive off peak) before tucking into outstanding fresh-made dragon rolls, crunchy tempura and succulent sashimi platters; why not just order a selection and everyone at the table will be delighted.

The service can be hit-and-miss – they're sometimes overwhelmed by the crowd – but this family-run joint is usually all smiles and welcomes diners with kids.

HOLY TRINITY UKRAINIAN ORTHODOX CATHEDRAL UKRAINIAN $

Map p278 (604-876-4747; www.uocvancouver.com; 154 E 10th Ave; mains $10-17; 5-8pm 1st Fri of the month; ; 3) Guaranteed to fill you for a full day of walking around Vancouver, this monthly Friday Night Supper is well known to locals. Line up for takeout or grab a table inside the church hall for heaping plates of delicious pierogi, cabbage rolls and sausage sections lovingly prepared and served by a smiling gathering of matronly women. There's also a vegetarian platter available.

EARNEST ICE CREAM ICE CREAM $

Map p278 (778-379-0697; www.earnesticecream.com; 1829 Quebec St; ice cream from $5; 10am-10pm; 3) The Olympic Village branch of this popular artisan ice-cream shop is neatly tucked into a redbrick former warehouse building. There's typically a dozen or so flavors, split between regulars including salted caramel and whiskey hazelnut, and seasonals such as the utterly delicious lemon poppy seed. All are available in cone or cup form – plus the option of tempting to-go pint jars.

There's plenty of seating here if you need to rest up. Otherwise, you can grab your cone and walk toward a waterfront seat at the nearby Olympic Village; you're likely to finish long before you get there, though. Vegan options are available as well.

BILLY BUTTON DESSERT BAR
DESSERTS $

Map p278 (604-423-3344; www.billybuttondessertbar.com; 141 E Broadway; desserts $9-12; 2-11pm; 9) There's a serious commitment to delicious, photo-friendly desserts at this dark, cave-like cafe that's not much bigger than a train carriage. There are usually six delicately constructed treats to choose from, including one made with panna cotta 'udon noodles' and another concocted from a red-wine-poached pear atop a slender disc of chocolate cake. Add tea or house-made ginger ale.

It's easy to miss the tiny, unassuming storefront as you're walking along Broadway. The place really gets going in the evening, when the dozen or so little tables fill up and a sugar high fuels the buzzy crowd.

SLICKITY JIM'S CHAT 'N' CHEW
DINER $

Map p278 (604-873-6760; www.skinnyfatjack.com; 3475 Main St; mains $9-15; 8:30am-4pm Mon-Fri, to 5pm Sat & Sun; ; 3) This good-value local favorite gets jam-packed with bleary-eyed locals soothing their hangovers, but it's worth the wait for a quirky, darkened room lined with the kind of oddball art David Lynch probably favors. Menu-wise, they've nailed breakfast here, with traditional as well as inventive (and heaping) plates enlivened with quirky names like the Breakfast of Broken Dreams.

If you're looking for lunch, burgers and hearty sandwiches are on the menu, and there are plenty of vegetarian options, too.

★ANH & CHI
VIETNAMESE $$

Map p278 (604-878-8883; www.anhandchi.com; 3388 Main St; mains $16-25; 11am-11pm; ; 3) You'll find warm and solicitous service at this delightful contemporary Vietnamese restaurant whose authentic, perfectly prepared dishes are a must for local foodies. Not sure what to order? Check out the menu's 'bucket list' dishes, including the highly recommended prawn-and-pork-packed crunchy crepe. Reservations are not accepted and waits here can be long; consider mid-afternoon weekday dining instead.

There are good options here for vegetarians. If tables are not available, you can dine at the small bar; under its glowing, leaf-patterned stained-glass window, you can also plunge into the cocktail list.

★ACORN
VEGETARIAN $$

Map p278 (604-566-9001; www.theacornrestaurant.ca; 3995 Main St; mains $18-22; 5:30-10pm Mon-Thu, to 11pm Fri, 10am-2:30pm & 5:30-11pm Sat, to midnight Sun; ; 3) One of Vancouver's hottest vegetarian restaurants – hence the sometimes long wait for tables – the Acorn is ideal for those craving something more inventive than mung-bean soup. Consider seasonal, artfully presented treats such as beer-battered haloumi or vanilla-almond-beet cake and stick around late-night: the bar serves until midnight if you need to pull up a stool and set the world to rights.

DOCK LUNCH
INTERNATIONAL $$

Map p278 (604-879-3625; www.facebook.com/docklunch; 152 E 11th Ave; mains $10-18; noon-4pm Tue-Thu, noon-4pm & 7-10pm Fri, 11am-4pm Sat & Sun; 3) Like dining in a cool hippie's home, this charming room in a side-street house serves a daily changing menu of one or two soul-food mains (think spicy tacos or heaping weekend brunches). Arrive early and aim for one of the two window seats and you'll soon be chatting with the locals or browsing the cookbooks and novels on the shelves.

One of Vancouver's most unusual eateries, this is as far from a restaurant dining experience as you can get. No reservations.

FISH COUNTER
SEAFOOD $$

Map p278 (604-876-3474; www.thefishcounter.com; 3825 Main St; mains $10-22; 10am-8pm; 3) Main's best fish and chips. This busy spot combines a seafood wet counter and a bustling fry operation. Order from the cashier, snag a spot at the stand-up table inside or sit-down benches outside and wait to be called. Battered halibut and cod are popular, but we love the wild salmon, served with fries and a mound of 'slaw.

There's much more to the menu than fish and chips, though. Check the regularly changing special (steamed halibut dumplings on our visit) or consider the fish tacos, oyster po'boys and a stomach-warming chowder that will fill you for a week. Add a beverage from the excellent array of artisan pop bottles.

Neighborhood Walk **Main Street Hipster Stroll**

START NEPTOON RECORDS
END SHAMEFUL TIKI ROOM
LENGTH 1KM; ONE TO THREE HOURS

Vancouver's hippest strip is ideal for those who like to browse around some of the city's coolest indie stores.

Hop off southbound bus 3 around 18th Ave. Start at indie-favorite 1 **Neptoon Records** (p143) for some cool vinyl that's way more hip than you are. Then nip across the street to the smashing little designer shop 2 **Smoking Lily** (p143) – especially if you're an intellectual clotheshorse. The staff here are ever friendly and they'll have plenty of additional suggestions for what to see on your walk.

Further south, you can dip into the vintage clothing racks at 3 **Front & Company** (p143). If you've always wanted a 1950s crushed-velvet smoking jacket to wear with your jeans, this is the place to find it. But it's not only togs: the store does a cool line in kitsch giftware, too. At this point, you should also begin to notice your surroundings: check the painted murals on the sides of many buildings just off Main and look out for the steaming coffee-cup motifs etched into the sidewalk concrete.

From here, re-cross to the west side of the street, and if it's time to eat, join the throng at the 4 **Fish Counter** (p136), home to arguably the city's best fish and chips. Grab a perch outside in the sun.

Across the street, a couple of minutes south, you'll find one of the city's most eclectic stores: the 5 **Regional Assembly of Text** (p142), where you can indulge your fetish for sumptuous writing paper, old-fashioned typewriters and all manner of stationery items. Pick the right day for your visit and join the hipsters at the monthly letter-writing social club.

Continue south to the area's other top indie record shop, 6 **Red Cat Records** (p142). Peruse the CDs and vinyl and ask the staff for tips on bands to see in town – tickets are available here for many area shows. End your crawl with a cocktail at the delightful 7 **Shameful Tiki Room** (p139).

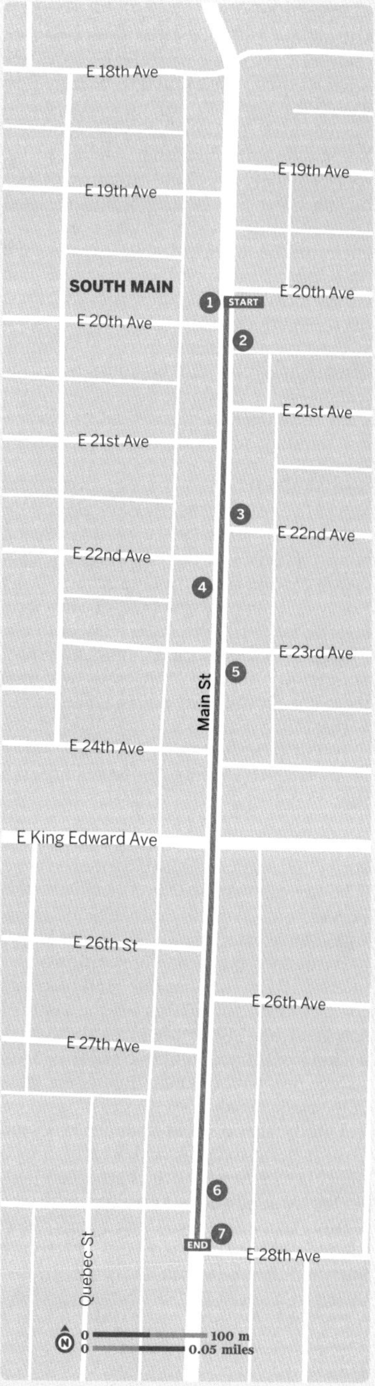

FABLE DINER DINER $$

Map p278 (☎604-563-3463; www.fablediner.com; 151 E Broadway; mains $8-19; ⏰7:30am-10pm Mon-Thu, 7:30am-11pm Fri, 9:30am-11pm Sat, 9:30am-10pm Sun; 📶✎; 🚌9) Transforming a former greasy spoon in the landmark Lee Building into a casual satellite of Fable's popular Kitsilano restaurant, this hipster diner is a favorite Mount Pleasant hangout. Snag a window booth or swivel chair at the kitchen-facing counter and dive into elevated all-day breakfasts and comfort grub, including the smashing roast duck and kimchi pancake.

Finish with a naughty round of mini-doughnuts or dive into the stomach-busting peanut-butter chocolate milkshake – especially recommended if you need to add several thousand more calories to your diet.

SUN SUI WAH CHINESE $$

Map p278 (☎604-872-8822; www.sunsuiwah.ca; 3888 Main St; mains $8-22; ⏰10:30am-3pm & 5-10pm; 🚌3) One of the best places in Vancouver for dim sum, this large, chatty Hong Kong–style joint has deservedly been a local favorite for years. Order an array of treats, then sit back for the feast – although expect to fight over the lazy Susan to see who gets the last mouthful. Seafood is a huge specialty (hence the live tanks).

If it's a special occasion and you want to push out the boat, gorge on some king crab legs.

BURGOO BISTRO NORTHWESTERN US $$

Map p278 (☎604-873-1441; www.burgoo.ca; 3096 Main St; mains $16-23; ⏰11am-10pm; 🚌3) Burgoo, an incongruous rustic-chic shack with a huge exterior wall mural and Main's best summer patio, has a warm, woodsy interior that matches its international comfort-food approach. Check the seasonal specials, then dive into a tasty fall-back position of gumbo, butter chicken or irresistible beef bourguignon. End with a glass of BC-made mead.

This is also a great spot for weekend brunch (11am to 3pm); arrive early to beat the crowds and go for the barbecued pork skillet. And if you're traveling with the family, the kids' menu is a cut above dinosaur-shaped chicken bites. There are four additional Burgoo branches around the city.

TAP & BARREL NORTHWESTERN US $$

Map p278 (☎604-685-2223; www.tapandbarrel.com; 1 Athletes Way; mains $16-23; ⏰11am-midnight Mon-Sat, 10am-midnight Sun; SMain St-Science World) In the heart of Olympic Village, this popular neighborhood haunt serves gourmet comfort nosh such as Cajun chicken burgers and pineapple-and-pulled-pork pizzas. In summer, it's all about the views from the expansive, mountain-facing waterfront patio (the area's best alfresco dining). Add some BC beer or wine and you'll have to be forcibly removed at the end of the night. An ideal spot for a long, languid alfresco dinner.

BOB LIKES THAI FOOD THAI $$

Map p278 (☎604-568-8538; www.boblikesthaifood.com; 3755 Main St; mains $13-18; ⏰11:30am-2:30pm & 5-10pm; 🚌3) Take a seat beneath the giant wooden spoon and fork paintings at this laid-back joint and tuck into satisfying Thai comfort grub. The papaya salad and green-curry chicken are hugely popular, but consider the exotic *miang kham* (six bites) starter dish, a cornucopia of flavors from peanut and ginger to lime and coconut shavings, all wrapped in vine leaves.

And don't bother asking who Bob is. He's a made-up person and the staff are well used to explaining 'he's not here' without rolling their eyes too much.

DRINKING & NIGHTLIFE

Combining excellent microbrewery tasting rooms with independent bars and coffeehouses, Main St is the kind of area where you can nurse a drink all afternoon while you type your latest travel-blog entry on your device. Bus 3 makes bar-hopping easy here; the service runs every few minutes up and down Main and also links you to downtown Vancouver.

★**BRASSNECK BREWERY** MICROBREWERY

Map p278 (☎604-259-7686; www.brassneck.ca; 2148 Main St; ⏰2-11pm Mon-Fri, noon-11pm Sat & Sun; 🚌3) A beloved Vancouver microbrewery with a small, wood-lined tasting room. Peruse the ever-changing chalkboard of intriguing libations with names like Pinky

Promise, Silent Treatment and Faux Naive, or start with a delicious, highly accessible Passive Aggressive dry-hopped pale ale. It's often hard to find a seat here, so consider a weekday afternoon visit for a four-glass $8 tasting flight.

Hungry? Couple your libations with cured sausages from the counter or takeout from the food truck outside. And don't forget to peek through the holes punched in the wood-planked walls for a glimpse of the brewery beyond. Pick up a Brassneck growler to go (filled of course) at the front; it'll keep you going for the rest of your visit.

★KEY PARTY BAR

Map p278 (www.keyparty.ca; 2303 Main St; ⏲5pm-1am Mon-Thu, to 2am Fri & Sat, to 1am Sun; 🚌3) Walk through the doorway of a fake storefront that looks like an accountancy office and you'll find yourself in a candlelit, boudoir-red speakeasy dominated by a dramatic mural of frolicking women and animals. Arrive early to avoid the queues, then fully explore the entertaining cocktail program (Kir Royale champagne jello shooters included).

Despite the playful name, this is not a swingers party joint, although there's a cheeky bowl of stuck-down keys by the entrance and you'll also be given a chewy sour-candy key when you leave. If you can't wait that long, there's a small array of bar snacks to fortify you as well.

SHAMEFUL TIKI ROOM BAR

Map p278 (www.shamefultikiroom.com; 4362 Main St; ⏲5pm-midnight Sun-Thu, to 1am Fri & Sat; 🚌3) This windowless snug instantly transports you to a Polynesian beach. The lighting – including glowing puffer-fish lampshades – is permanently set to dusk and the walls are lined with tiki masks and rattan coverings under a straw-shrouded ceiling. But it's the drinks that rock; seriously well-crafted classics from zombies to blue Hawaii's to a four-person Volcano Bowl (don't forget to share it).

Arrive early on weekends; there's only space for around 50 people. The worst thing about this perfect little tiki bar? When someone opens the door and lets the light in from the outside, it reminds you that reality is waiting. Block it out with another Volcano Bowl.

NARROW LOUNGE BAR

Map p278 (☎778-737-5206; www.narrowlounge.com; 1898 Main St; ⏲5pm-1am Mon-Fri, to 2am Sat & Sun; 🚌3) Enter through the doorway on 3rd Ave – the red light tells you if it's open or not – then descend the graffiti-lined stairway into one of Vancouver's coolest small bars. Little bigger than a train carriage and lined with taxidermy and junk-shop pictures, it's an atmospheric nook that always feels like 2am. In summer, try the hidden alfresco bar out back.

Work your way through the craft beer and classic cocktails, but if the mangy bear head on the wall starts talking to you, it's probably time to call it a night.

KAFKA'S COFFEE

Map p278 (☎604-569-2967; www.kafkascoffee.ca; 2525 Main St; ⏲7am-10pm Mon-Thu, 7am-8pm Fri, 8am-8pm Sat & Sun; 📶; 🚌3) Kafka's has more MacBooks than an Apple Store courtesy of the locals who fill the tables here, silently updating their social media statuses as if their lives depended on it. But, despite appearances, this is a warm and welcoming hangout. The single-origin coffee is excellent and there's a serious commitment to local artworks on the walls; it's like quaffing in a cool gallery.

All the art is for sale, making this the perfect spot to pick up a unique Vancouver souvenir that beats anything you'll find in the usual places. If you're lucky, you might even meet the artist supping an espresso in the corner and trying to look nonchalant.

WHIP PUB

Map p278 (☎604-874-4687; www.thewhiprestaurant.com; 209 E 6th Ave; ⏲10am-1am Mon-Thu, 10am-2am Fri, 9am-2am Sat, 9am-1am Sun; 🚌3) The laid-back, wood-floored Whip fuses a friendly neighborhood bar ambience with a gastropub menu and a good array of classic cocktails. But many regulars are here for the BC craft beers and hulking bison or salmon burgers (yam fries recommended). Beer nuts should not miss Sunday afternoon's guest keg, tapped at 4pm, ideally combined with a sunny patio seat.

Check out the rotating exhibitions of local artists featured on the walls. If you're here in late May, look out for the Whip's annual Show and Shine event where vintage cars park up outside.

THE RETURN OF BREWERY CREEK

Mainland Brewery, Red Star Brewery, San Francisco Brewery and, of course, Vancouver Brewery. The names of the city's long-gone beer producers recall a time when Brewery Creek – an area radiating from Main St around 7th Ave – concocted the suds quaffed by many ale-loving Vancouverites. The area was named after a rolling creek that once powered water wheels at area breweries, but there are now few reminders of this beer-making golden age. But don't despair: Brewery Creek is back, with a tasty crop of brand new microbreweries popping up in recent years. And all of them have highly inviting tasting rooms.

Tucked into a refurbished space at one of the few remaining Vancouver Brewery buildings, Main Street Brewing combines an industrial-chic tasting room with a tempting roster of regular beers and ever-changing casks. Just around the corner on Main, Brassneck Brewery (p138) is many locals' number-one Vancouver beermaker; afternoons are a great time to avoid the crowds. A short walk away, 33 Acres Brewing Company has a white-walled tasting room that may be the chattiest bar in town. A short downhill stroll away, R&B Brewing has a rec-room vibe and great pizzas.

SING SING BEER BAR — BAR

Map p278 (604-336-9556; www.singsingbeerbar.com; 2718 Main St; 11am-1am; ; 3) This bright, white-walled, plant-accented bar would look at home on a Singapore side street. Snag a communal table and dive into the 20 or so BC craft beer taps (often including lesser-known libations from celebrated microbreweries such as Twin Sails and Fuggles & Warlock). Food-wise, there's an unusual combination of pizzas and hearty pho bowls on the menu.

There's also a good array of cocktails to explore. Since it's often clamorously busy on weekend evenings, consider checking the place out during the daily 3pm to 6pm happy hour, complete with beer, wine and cocktail specials.

CASCADE ROOM — PUB

Map p278 (604-709-8650; www.thecascade.ca; 2616 Main St; 4pm-1am Mon-Thu, to 2am Fri & Sat, to midnight Sun; ; 3) The perfect reinvention of a trad neighborhood bar, this is arguably Mount Pleasant's merriest watering hole. The ale list includes some great craft beers, including own-brand Main Street Brewing tipples, produced just a few blocks away. Hungry on the weekend? Indulge in the area's best Sunday evening roast ($19), plus a naughty Scotch egg side dish.

There's an excellent cocktail menu here; check the board above the bar for your options, then decamp to a back table to sip your prize. Happy-hour drink-and-dine specials run from 4pm to 6pm every day and there are additional daily specials to consider as well; ask your server for the latest info.

R&B BREWING — MICROBREWERY

Map p278 (604-336-0275; www.randbbrewing.com; 54 E 4th Ave; 11am-11pm Sun-Tue, to midnight Wed-Sat; ; 3) One of the neighborhood's best brewery lounges (hence the peak-time line-ups) combines a hip-but-cozy rec-room vibe with a look that includes random taxidermy and Bill Murray portraits. There's a wide array of own-made beers to sample but don't miss the deliciously malty East Side Bitter. Food here is also a cut above, with pizzas recommended.

On warm days, aim for a perch on R&B's long but slender patio.

GENE CAFE — COFFEE

Map p278 (604-568-5501; http://genecoffeebar.com; 2404 Main St; 7:30am-7pm Mon-Fri, 8:30am-7pm Sat & Sun; ; 3) Colonizing a flatiron wedge of bare concrete floors and oversized windows, locals treat Gene as their living-room hangout, especially if they manage to monopolize one of the three tiny tables overlooking Main and Kingsway. Coffee is artfully prepared and the menu has expanded to include flake-tastic croissants plus Aussie-style meat pies and all-day breakfast wraps.

On sunny afternoons, bask on a wood-block perch outside and don't miss the cafe's striking First Nations' mural exterior, one of many super-cool murals dotted around the neighborhood.

JUICE TRUCK — JUICE BAR

Map p278 (604-620-6768; www.thejuicetruck.ca; 4236 Main St; 9am-6pm Mon-Sat, 10am-5pm Sun; ; 3) The largest branch of this metro Vancouver all-vegan beverage joint is a bright and welcoming spot with a communal table, a menu of 20 or so made-to-order smoothies and cold-pressed juices, and a family-friendly approach that includes toys and mom-and-kid events. Drinks-wise, the Green Protein smoothie is a bestseller and there are also salad-and-rice bowls to dive into.

Take your time perusing the above-the-counter menu before you order; there's a lot to choose from. Save some time to check out the shelves of products made in-house and also brought in from favored producers, including Vancouver-made vegan chocolate from Beta5, and vegan cheese made by Main St's Blue Heron Creamery (p144).

MAIN STREET BREWING MICROBREWERY

Map p278 (604-336-7711; www.mainstreetbeer.ca; 261 E 7th Ave; 2-11pm Mon-Thu, noon-11pm Fri-Sun; 3) Tucked into a historic, yellow-painted old brewery building, Main Street Brewing has a chatty, industrial-chic tasting room and a booze roster divided into regular beers and seasonal casks. Start with a four-flight tasting sampler, then dive in with a larger order. The malty Smash Pale Ale is our favorite, but there's usually a pithy IPA or two worth quaffing too.

Main Street also has a larger food menu than many Vancouver microbreweries, ranging from tacos to chicken wings, and a recommended grilled-cheese sandwich.

33 ACRES BREWING COMPANY MICROBREWERY

Map p278 (604-620-4589; www.33acresbrewing.com; 15 W 8th Ave; 9am-9pm Mon & Tue, 9am-11pm Wed-Fri, 10am-11pm Sat, 10am-9pm Sun; ; 9) A rec room for hipsters, this white-walled brewery-bar reverberates with chatter in the early evening when tech workers disgorge from nearby offices. By 8pm, it's usually more mellow. Aim for a glass of lightly hoppy Ocean pale ale, served in a mason jar. The food menu has been pumped up to include breakfast and pizzas, and weekend-only brunches are popular.

If you're a true beer buff, check out its 33 Brewing Experiment bar next door, where up to 20 taps of test and small-batch brews jostle for attention. Four-glass tasting flights cost around $10 and you can expect some truly unusual tipples (anyone for sea salt IPA?).

BREWHALL BEER HALL

Map p278 (604-709-8623; www.brewhall.com; 97 E 2nd Ave; 11am-midnight; ; 3) A modern-day reinvention of Bavarian beer halls, this cavernous heritage building serves own-made beers plus drafts from top BC microbreweries. Order and pick up at the bar (Neon Lights Pale Ale recommended) before decamping to a chatty long table. Pub grub from burgers to bowls is also available and there's a 'barcade' area of pinball and video games, too.

ENTERTAINMENT

The Biltmore and Fox Cabaret are the area's favorite options for a night out alternative to downtown's Granville St. But there are several regular events worth keeping your calendar open for.

★FOX CABARET LIVE MUSIC

Map p278 (www.foxcabaret.com; 2321 Main St; 3) One of North America's last remaining porn cinemas has been transformed (and fully pressure-washed) into a brilliantly eclectic independent nightlife venue, ditching the dodgy flicks in favour of live bands, rib-tickling comedy and Saturday night dance fests with disco or '90s themes. Check the online calendar; there's always something different on stage in this narrow, high-ceilinged venue.

BILTMORE CABARET LIVE MUSIC

Map p278 (604-676-0541; www.biltmorecabaret.com; 2755 Prince Edward St; tickets from $15; 9) One of Vancouver's favorite alt venues, the intimate Biltmore is a firm fixture on the local indie scene. A low-ceilinged, good-vibe spot to mosh to local and touring musicians, it also has regular event nights; check the online calendar for upcoming happenings, including trivia nights and stand-up comedy shows.

BMO THEATRE CENTRE THEATER

Map p278 (604-687-1644; www.artsclub.com; 162 W 1st Ave; tickets from $29; 3) The studio venue of the city's Arts Club theater empire hosts more challenging and intimate productions in a space that's cleverly and sometimes dramatically reconfigured for each show. There are often three or four productions per season as well as on-stage

MAIN'S BEST FEST

If you make it to the annual Car Free Day (p121) – staged along Main St, south of the Broadway intersection, for at least 30 blocks – you'll realize there's much more diversity in this area than you thought. Taking over the streets for this family-friendly community fest are live music, craft stalls, steaming food stands and a highly convivial atmosphere that makes for a party-like afternoon with the locals.

readings of new works in progress, which are typically free; check the Arts Club website for information on these.

CELLULOID SOCIAL CLUB CINEMA

Map p278 (www.celluloidsocialclub.com; 3 W 8th Ave, ANZA Club; tickets $5-10; 7:30pm mid-month; 9) Visiting movie nuts with a penchant for making their own flicks – or just chewing the fat with those who do – should unspool their film at one of Vancouver's coolest underground hangouts. Held every month at the ANZA Club, it's a drop-in for local filmmakers and video artists who like showing their shorts to anyone who turns up.

ANZA CLUB LIVE MUSIC, CABARET

Map p278 (604-876-7128; www.anzaclub.org; 3 W 8th Ave; tickets from $10; 4pm-midnight Mon & Tue, 4pm-2am Wed-Fri, 2pm-2am Sat, 6pm-midnight Sun; 9) This yellow-painted, wood-built community hall – which has the look of a worker's club without the edge – is popular with local cool kids as well as old-school hippies who've been coming here for decades. Staging an eclectic roster of weekly events (many of them in the upstairs lounge), it also has regular live shows and DJ nights.

SHOPPING

This is Vancouver's must-see area for locally owned independent stores. Many showcase the exciting creative skills of hot regional designers, but there are also some perfect spots to buy that unique souvenir no one else will have back home. The two main shopping areas on Main are around the Broadway intersection and south of the intersection with 18th Ave – this second area is full of options and is especially recommended.

★REGIONAL ASSEMBLY OF TEXT ARTS & CRAFTS

Map p278 (604-877-2247; www.assemblyoftext.com; 3934 Main St; 11am-6pm Mon-Sat, noon-5pm Sun; 3) This ironic antidote to the digital age lures ink-stained locals with its journals, handmade pencil boxes and T-shirts printed with typewriter motifs. Check out the tiny under-the-stairs gallery showcasing global zines and don't miss the monthly Letter Writing Club (7pm, first Thursday of every month), where you can hammer on vintage typewriters, crafting erudite missives to far-away loved ones.

If you have time, make your own pin badge or just browse the racks of hyper-cool greeting cards, mostly fashioned by the store's friendly art-school-grad co-owners. One of Vancouver's most original stores, it also sells handmade self-published mini-books near the front window – where else can you read *One Shrew Too Few* and *Secret Thoughts of a Plain Yellow House*?

★RED CAT RECORDS MUSIC

Map p278 (604-708-9422; www.redcat.ca; 4332 Main St; 11am-7pm Mon-Thu, to 8pm Fri & Sat, to 6pm Sun; 3) Arguably Vancouver's coolest record store and certainly the only one named after a much-missed cat... There's a brilliantly curated collection of new and used vinyl and CDs, and it's co-owned by musicians; ask them for tips on where to see great local acts such as Loscil and Nick Krgovich or peruse the huge list of shows in the window.

You can buy show tickets here, and listen to albums before you buy. If you're curious about the red cat, his name was Buddy and, although he passed away in 2006, he's fondly commemorated via the handsome portrait poster behind the counter.

★MOUNTAIN EQUIPMENT CO-OP SPORTS & OUTDOORS

Map p278 (604-872-7858; www.mec.ca; 111 E 2nd Ave; 10am-7pm Mon-Wed, 10am-9pm Thu & Fri, 9am-6pm Sat, 10am-6pm Sun; 9) Grown hikers weep at the amazing selection of clothing (including lifestyle wear for urban hipsters), kayaks and clever camping gadgets at this cavernous store. You'll need to be a member to buy, but that costs just $5.

You can also rent gear such as canoes, snowshoes and sleeping bags, and there's a good selection of regional and international maps and guidebooks, plus a climbing wall to test your new shoes. Check the noticeboard at the front of the store; it's a great place to see what the local hiking/cycling brigades are up to.

URBAN SOURCE — ARTS & CRAFTS

Map p278 (☎604-875-1611; www.urbansource.bc.ca; 3126 Main St; ⌚10am-5:30pm Mon-Sat, 11am-5:30pm Sun; 👪; 🚌3) From used postcards and insect rubber stamps to ladybug stickers and map pages from old books, this brilliant store offers a highly eclectic, ever-changing array of reclaimed materials and alternative arts-and-crafts supplies to a loyal band of locals. In this browser's paradise you'll suddenly be inspired to make an oversized pterodactyl model from glitter and discarded cassette tapes.

This is the perfect spot to gather all the supplies for making your own postcards. Your friends back home will be mightily impressed – or they may think you have too much time on your hands.

MINTAGE MALL — VINTAGE

Map p278 (☎604-428-6732; 245 E Broadway; ⌚11am-7pm Mon-Sat, to 6pm Sun; 🚌9) Comprising seven super-cool vintage vendors offering everything from 1970s outfits (at Thirteen Moons) to antique taxidermy (Salamander Salt Curio), this eclectic, labyrinthine upstairs 'mall' is one of the best ways to spend an hour in Mount Pleasant. Don't miss the ever-changing pop-up unit. Add a tarot reading to keep things lively and check out its Instagram account for after-hours events.

SMOKING LILY — CLOTHING

Map p278 (☎604-873-5459; www.smokinglily.com; 3634 Main St; ⌚10:30am-6:30pm Mon-Sat, noon-5pm Sun; 🚌3) Art-school cool rules at this mostly womens wear boutique, with skirts, belts and halter-tops whimsically accented with prints of rabbits, narwhals and the periodic table. Anatomically correct heart motifs are also popular, appearing on shirts, jewelry and cushion covers. And there's a great array of accessories, including quirky purses and shoulder bags beloved of the local pale-and-interesting set.

Everything is designed and made in BC. Quirky kids' clothes are also available, from hats to onesies to diaper covers. Expect friendly service.

FRONT & COMPANY — CLOTHING, ACCESSORIES

Map p278 (☎604-879-8431; www.frontandcompany.ca; 3772 Main St; ⌚11am-6:30pm; 🚌3) You could easily spend a couple of hours perusing the new and vintage clothing in the main space of Front & Company, which colonizes a row of storefronts along Main and threatens to become a hipster department store in the process. There's also knowingly cool housewares and must-have gifts and accessories (anyone for manga nightlights and unicorn ice trays?).

The ideal store to pick up a quirky souvenir for that difficult person back home who hates maple syrup (does such a person exist?); make sure you buy something cool for yourself as well.

BIRD ON A WIRE CREATIONS — ARTS & CRAFTS

Map p278 (☎604-874-7415; www.birdonawirecreations.com; 2535 Main St; ⌚10am-6pm Mon-Sat, 11am-5pm Sun; 🚌3) Specializing in BC artisans, there's an eminently browsable and surprisingly diverse array of tasteful handmade goodies at this ever-friendly store. Your credit cards will start to sweat as you move among the cute jewelry, artsy T-shirts, ceramic tea tankards and fiber arts kids' toys (that adults want, too). But it's not just for show; there are regular craft classes here too.

Class themes can range from fibre art figures to cross-stitching with naughty slogans.

NEPTOON RECORDS — MUSIC

Map p278 (☎604-324-1229; www.neptoon.com; 3561 Main St; ⌚11am-6:30pm Mon-Sat, noon-5pm Sun; 🚌3) Vancouver's oldest independent record store is still a major lure for music fans, with its *High Fidelity* ambience and time-capsule feel. But it's not resting on its laurels: you'll find a well-priced array of new and used vinyl and CD recordings, plus some serious help with finding that obscure Mighty Wah! recording you've been looking for.

Unlike some record stores, there's no attempt to be hip here, making it arguably the most comfortable spot in town for a browse, whether or not you're a geeky muso. It also sells tickets for local shows; ask the knowledgeable staff for recommendations.

LOCAL KNOWLEDGE

DON'T MISS THE MARKETS

Vancouverites love markets and there are many to keep them busy throughout the city. The summertime Main Street Station Farmers Market is perfect for picking up seasonal BC-grown peaches, blueberries and luscious cherries. There are usually more than a few baked treats to indulge in while you're mulling over your produce options. It's one of many markets organized by Vancouver Farmers Markets (VFM); check its website (www.eatlocal.org) for additional locations.

Purchases of the nonedible variety are offered over in Yaletown at the quarterly, weekend-long **Portobello West** (Map p274; www.portobellowest.com; 181 Roundhouse Mews, Roundhouse Community Arts & Recreation Centre; adult/child $5/free; 10am-5pm; ; Yaletown-Roundhouse) arts, crafts and fashion market. Expect an eclectic blend of handmade, one-of-a-kind goodies and locally designed togs to take back home, or just enjoy the live music and family-friendly vibe.

Even more eclectic is the new permanent location for the super-cool Eastside Flea (p95), which has grown to become the city's favorite hipster market in recent years. With dozens of new and vintage vendors plus food trucks, a long bar and live music, you'll be sure to have a good time.

LUCKY'S BOOKS & COMICS — BOOKS

Map p278 (604-875-9858; www.luckys.ca; 3972 Main St; noon-6pm Mon-Fri, 11am-6pm Sat, noon-5pm Sun; ; 3) Don't be put off by the unassuming windowless exterior of this local favorite; instead nip inside for a cornucopia of esoteric storybooks, graphic novels, oddball zines and homemade chapbooks at one of Vancouver's coolest independent stores. There's a rich originality to almost everything here and staff are highly adept at matching your interests to something cool you haven't yet discovered.

The store is a great place to bring bookish kids craving something new.

BLUE HERON CREAMERY — CHEESE

Map p278 (604-283-7534; www.blueheroncheese.com; 2410 Main St; noon-5pm Sat, to 3pm Sun; 3) A tiny, small-batch vegan cheese shop that'll challenge your deepest dairy attachments. Arrive early to avoid the crush during its limited opening hours. Samples are readily offered and there's a wide array of approaches and flavours. There's typically a special batch of something unusual to buy too, and these super-friendly folks also operate next door's **vegan cafe** (Map p278; 604-428-5859; 2408 Main St; mains $12-20; 11am-8pm Wed-Fri, 10am-4pm Sat & Sun; ; 3).

PULPFICTION BOOKS — BOOKS

Map p278 (604-876-4311; http://pulpfictionbooksvancouver.com; 2422 Main St; 10am-8pm Mon-Wed, 10am-9pm Thu-Sat, 11am-7pm Sun; 3) One of the city's best used-book stores (there are also plenty of new tomes in the front room), this is the ideal haunt for the kind of serious browsing where you forget what time it is. You'll find good literature and sci-fi sections, as well as a travel area at the back for planning your next big trip.

It also buys used books so if you happen to be traveling with your personal library in several steamer trunks, this is the place to offload it and cash it in for dinner. If they don't buy, just hang around the stacks for a few more hours looking morose.

HILL'S NATIVE ART — ARTS & CRAFTS

Map p278 (604-685-4249; www.hills.ca; 120 E Broadway; 10am-7pm; 9) One of Vancouver's oldest and most respected indigenous galleries has moved to this huge new storefront, whose two floors are crammed with often strikingly beautiful traditional and contemporary carvings, jewelry, paintings and more. Dozens of artists from the northwest coast and beyond are represented. This is an excellent place to find authentic and unique artworks to take home.

Look out for imited-edition prints by Andy Everson, especially works that fuse *Star Wars* themes with indigenous iconography.

8TH & MAIN — CLOTHING

Map p278 (604-559-5927; www.8main.ca; 2403 Main St; 10am-8pm Mon-Wed, to 9pm Thu-Sat, to 7pm Sun; 3) Vancouver's largest hipster clothing store, with Herschel daypacks and ironic cropped T-shirts, offers a cornucopia of men's and women's fashions as well as footwear and accessories. Prices cover every budget but don't miss the sale rails if you're keen to find that bargain neon plaid mankini you've been searching for.

Before you leave, pick up some of the indie magazines and weekly newspapers by the door. There's also a smaller satellite of this popular store on downtown's Granville Street.

SPORTS JUNKIES — SPORTS & OUTDOORS

Map p278 (☎604-256-4139; www.sportsjunkies.com; 102 W Broadway; ⏰10am-7pm Mon-Wed, to 8pm Thu & Fri, to 6pm Sat, to 5pm Sun; 🚌9) Along with the shelves of used boots and shoes near the entrance of this outdoor gear and sports equipment consignment store, you'll find racks of end-of-range new togs. Upstairs is a cornucopia of new and used equipment, from skis to snowshoes. If you know your prices, you can save a bundle here.

If you're inspired to take to the city's surfeit of cycling lanes on your visit but don't want to rent, there's always a good selection of well-priced used bikes on offer here, including some good-value mountain bikes.

BREWERY CREEK LIQUOR STORE — DRINKS

Map p278 (☎604-872-3373; www.brewcreek.ca; 3045 Main St; ⏰11am-11pm; 🚌3) The bottled-beer selection at this private liquor store (ie not run by the government, like many in the city) is among Vancouver's best. Alongside seasonal and stalwart favorites from celebrated BC brewers like Four Winds and Twin Sails, there's a wide array of international tipples to keep you merry. There's also a boutique selection of BC and global wines and liquors.

This local favorite is often busy with Main Streeters stocking up for their house parties.

MAIN STREET STATION FARMERS MARKET — MARKET

Map p278 (www.eatlocal.org; 1100 Station St, Thornton Park; ⏰2-6pm Wed Jul-Sep; SMain St-Science World) 🌿 Transforming the south side of the park that fronts Pacific Central Station, this convivial farmers market is also handily located across from a SkyTrain station. Drop by for artisan bread, food-cart treats and stalls selling produce from farms around the region; seasonal fruit is the main lure, so keep your taste buds primed for BC peaches, cherries, blueberries and more.

From melt-in-your-mouth fresh-crop peaches to juicy BC-grown blueberries, it's not hard to overindulge here.

GIVING GIFTS & COMPANY — ARTS & CRAFTS

Map p278 (☎604-831-7780; www.givinggifts.ca; 4570 Main St; ⏰11am-6pm Mon-Fri, 10am-6pm Sat, noon-5pm Sun; 🚌3) Despite the twee name, this is a five-room cooperative representing local craft vendors and artisan businesses under one roof. From sock puppets to rustic candles, handmade chocolate bars to upcycled antiques, it's a great one-stop shop for unique local souvenirs. New products (and occasionally new vendors) pop up all the time.

ALBERTART/SHUTTERSTOCK ©

1. Denman Street 2. Chinese New Year (p20) parade
3. Totem poles and long houses, Museum of Anthropology (p164)
4. Chinatown (p82)

2

GABI ROSE/SHUTTERSTOCK ©

4

Multicultural Vancouver

Canada's most multicultural metropolis, Vancouver offers uncountable ways to dive into the food, traditions and artistic side of nations near and far. For many visitors, this rich international accessibility is a highlight of their trip.

Festivals

From giant Chinese New Year parades to grassroots events such as Greek Day, Italian Day and Caribbean Days, Vancouver serves up a heady mix of great cultural fests. Dive right in, and be sure to eat as much as you can.

Chinatown

Canada's largest historic Chinatown is in transition but it still remains a vital part of the city. It's not just about the visuals of dragon-topped street lamps and terracotta-tiled heritage buildings, though. The bustling grocery stores indicate a neighborhood grounded in tradition.

Denman Street

This West End thoroughfare is lined with mid-priced dining options showcasing cuisines from around the world. From authentic *izakayas* (Japanese neighborhood pubs) to Spanish tapas restaurants, you can eat in a different country here every night.

First Nations Art

The region's first inhabitants have a rich heritage of creativity for visitors to discover. From thrilling carvings at UBC's Museum of Anthropology (p164) to a stunning collection at the Bill Reid Gallery of Northwest Coast Art (p57). And don't forget the airport; it's filled with monumental First Nations works.

Commercial Drive

Coffee is a way of life on the Drive, where generations of Italian families have been serving the city's best java since arriving in the 1950s. You'll find elderly Italian grandparents and cool-ass hipsters enjoying a perfect cup to see them through the day here.

Fairview & South Granville

FAIRVIEW | CAMBIE VILLAGE | SOUTH GRANVILLE

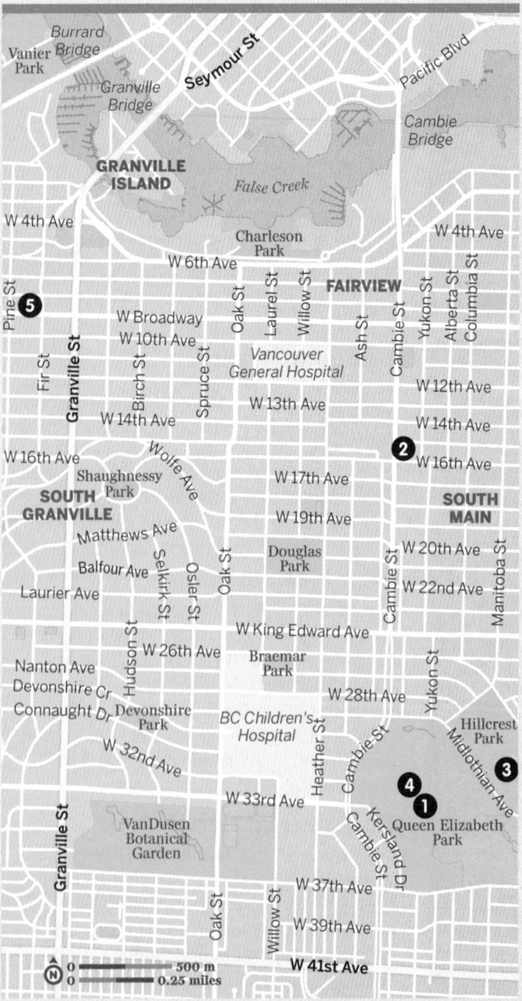

For more detail of this area see Map p280

Neighborhood Top Five

❶ **Bloedel Conservatory** (p150) Feeding the rainbow-hued tropical birds from a bowl as the parrots around you call loudly to each other; exploring the surrounding park with panoramic city views.

❷ **Pacific Arts Market** (p159) Perusing the work of dozens of regional artists and artisans, and finding great local-made souvenirs at this upstairs, shared gallery space.

❸ **Vij's** (p153) Rubbing elbows with the locals while face-planting into Vancouver's (and maybe Canada's) finest Indian food; lamb popsicles included.

❹ **Vancouver Canadians** (p158) Basking in the sun with a beer and a hot dog while catching an afternoon baseball game at Nat Bailey Stadium.

❺ **Storm Crow Alehouse** (p157) Practicing your Vulcan hand gestures while sipping a Romulan Ale or three, then beating everyone at a role-playing card game.

Explore Fairview & South Granville

Start your exploration in Queen Elizabeth Park, then stroll north down Cambie St into shop-and-restaurant-lined Cambie Village. It's not heavily touristed, so you'll get a good glimpse of local life. Peruse the heritage houses on the side streets or catch bus 15 to speed your course. Either way, you'll soon reach City Hall and the superbusy Cambie and Broadway intersection.

It's a 30-minute walk west along Broadway to South Granville. There are plenty of shops, eateries and coffee shops en route to the heart of Fairview. Alternatively, backtrack one block and walk in the same direction on tranquil, tree-lined W 10th Ave. Your other option is transit. The 99B-Line express bus zips from here to South Granville in under 10 minutes.

At the Broadway and Granville St intersection, turn left and explore South Granville's upmarket boutiques, private galleries and enticing dining options. It's full of browsable fashion stores and home-decor shops and has the feel of a European high street.

From here, you can hop on bus 10 and you'll be back downtown in minutes via Granville Bridge (scenic views included).

Local Life

- **Shopping** South Granville is busy with well-to-do locals buzzing around its designer boutiques, shopping bags in hand.
- **Night out** Cambie Village is popular for dinner at a local restaurant followed by an artsy flick at the one-screen Cineplex Park Theatre (p159).
- **Parklife** Summertime cooldown means Queen Elizabeth Park (p150), where you can picnic on the grass and feel as if you're far from the city.

Getting There & Away

- **Train** Cambie Village's shopping and dining area is sandwiched between the Canada Line SkyTrain stations at Broadway-City Hall and King Edward. The rest of Fairview also radiates along Broadway from the Broadway-City Hall station.
- **Bus** Service 15 runs along Cambie St; bus 10 runs along South Granville. The two streets are linked along Broadway by the 99B-Line express and the slower bus 9.
- **Car** There is metered parking on Cambie and South Granville, with some limited street parking available throughout both areas.

Lonely Planet's Top Tip

On rainy days, escape to **Bloedel Conservatory** (p150). At this great warm-up spot, step inside the glass-roofed dome (expect your spectacles to fog up) for tropical flowers, a balmy climate and dozens of bright-plumed free-flying birds.

Best Places to Eat

- Vij's (p153)
- Salmon n' Bannock (p151)
- Heritage Asian Eatery (p152)
- Heirloom Vegetarian (p155)
- Paul's Omelettery (p153)

For reviews, see p151.

Best Places to Drink

- Storm Crow Alehouse (p157)
- Grapes & Soda (p158)
- The Marquis Grill (p158)
- Kino (p159)
- Small Victory (p155)

For reviews, see p156.

Best Places to Shop

- Pacific Arts Market (p159)
- Walrus (p160)
- Bacci's (p159)
- Meinhardt Fine Foods (p161)
- Turnabout (p161)

For reviews, see p159.

SIGHTS

Parks and botanical attractions are the main visitor sights in this area and they're easily accessible via transit along Cambie St and Oak St.

★VANDUSEN BOTANICAL GARDEN — GARDENS

Map p280 (☎604-257-8335; www.vandusengarden.org; 5251 Oak St; adult/child Apr-Sep $11.25/5.50; ⏲9am-8pm Jun-Aug, 9am-6pm Apr & Sep, 9am-7pm May, hours reduced Oct-Mar; P 🚸; 🚌17) This highly popular green-thumbed oasis is a 22-hectare, 255,000-plant idyll that offers a strollable web of pathways weaving through specialized garden areas: the Rhododendron Walk blazes with color in spring, while the Korean Pavilion is a focal point for a fascinating Asian collection. Save time to get lost in the hedge maze and look out for the herons, owls and turtles that call the park and its ponds home. Informative guided tours are also offered here daily from April to October.

There's an excellent onsite gift shop plus a popular cafe. If you're here from the start of December onwards, you'll also find one of the city's top Christmastime lures, complete with thousands of twinkling fairy lights and shimmering installations strung on and around the wintering plants. Visiting with nature-loving kids? VanDusen offers a wide range of short summer camps for children.

★BLOEDEL CONSERVATORY — GARDENS

Map p280 (☎604-257-8584; www.vandusengarden.org; 4600 Cambie St, Queen Elizabeth Park; adult/child $6.75/3.30; ⏲10am-5pm Jan-Mar & Nov-Dec, 10am-6pm Apr & Sep-Oct, 10am-8pm May-Aug; P 🚸; 🚌15) Cresting the hill in Queen Elizabeth Park, this domed conservatory is a delightful rainy-day warm-up. At Vancouver's best-value paid attraction, you'll find tropical trees and plants bristling with hundreds of free-flying, bright-plumaged birds. Listen for the noisy resident parrots but also keep your eyes peeled for rainbow-hued Gouldian finches, shimmering African superb starlings and maybe even a dramatic Lady Amherst pheasant, snaking through the undergrowth. Ask nicely and the attendants might even let you feed the smaller birds from a bowl.

Pick up a free bird-watcher's checklist from the front desk and record how many you see. The walkways are accessible for strollers, so this is a good place to bring the family.

QUEEN ELIZABETH PARK — PARK

Map p280 (www.vancouverparks.ca; entrance cnr W 33rd Ave & Cambie St; P; 🚌15) The city's highest point – 167m above sea level and with panoramic views over the mountain-framed downtown skyscrapers – this 52-hectare park claims to house specimens of every tree native to Canada. Sports fields, manicured lawns and formal gardens keep the locals happy, and you'll likely also see wide-eyed couples posing for their wedding photos in particularly picturesque spots. This is a good place to view local birdlife: keep your eyes peeled for chickadees, hummingbirds and huge bald eagles whirling high overhead.

Check out the synchronized fountains at the park's summit – home to the Bloedel

BEHIND THE DECO FACADE

The Great Depression caused major belt-tightening among the regular folks of 1930s Vancouver. But despite the economic malaise, mayor Gerry McGeer spared no expense when it came time to build a new City Hall (p151) in 1936 (50 years after Vancouver was incorporated as a city). Defending the grand art-deco edifice he planned as a make-work project for the idled construction industry, the $1 million project (a very large sum for the time) was completed in just 12 months.

But while the jobs were appreciated by some locals, McGeer showed no additional sympathy for the the city's working class. Believing that radicalism was taking hold among out-of-work Vancouverites, he ordered that police officers should crack down on protests whenever they emerged. When hundreds gathered to call for jobs in East Vancouver's Victory Sq, McGeer turned up personally to read them the riot act. A few weeks later, police and an estimated 1000 protesters fought a three-hour street battle with rocks, clubs and tear gas. Rumors at the time said the police were preparing to use machine guns against the crowd when it began to disperse. The most famous incident in Vancouver labor history was later named the Battle of Ballantyne Pier.

Conservatory – where you'll also find a hulking Henry Moore bronze called *Knife Edge – Two Piece*. If you want to be taken out to the ball game here, the park's beloved Nat Bailey Stadium is also a popular summer hangout for catching games of the Vancouver Canadians (p158) baseball team.

CITY HALL HISTORIC BUILDING

Map p280 (604-873-7000; www.vancouver.ca; 453 W 12th Ave, Fairview; 8:30am-5pm Mon-Fri; P; S Broadway-City Hall) FREE Architecture fans should save time for one of Vancouver's best art-deco buildings. Completed in 1936, its highlights include a soaring, Gotham-style exterior as well as an interior of streamlined signs, cylindrical lanterns and embossed elevator doors. Snap some photos of the statue of Captain George Vancouver outside, then check out the handsome wooden heritage mansions on surrounding Yukon St and W 12th Ave. Finally, snag a table at the public plaza next to City Hall for some grand mountain-framed cityscape views.

If you're on a deco roll, make sure you also hit downtown's magical Marine Building (p57).

EATING

Fairview and Cambie Village mostly offer welcoming casual eateries where the neighbors drop by to chill out, while higher-end South Granville has a couple of top spots as well as some good midrange options. Linking the two is Broadway, which is lined on both sides with good-value restaurants of every variety, from steaming pho (Vietnamese noodle soup) spots to popular breakfast joints.

Fairview

TRACTOR CAFETERIA $

Map p280 (604-343-2712; www.tractorfoods.com; 601 W Broadway; mains $8-14; 7am-9:30pm; ; 9) A branch of Vancouver's favorite healthy fast-food minichain, with a tasty selection of house-made soups, stews and sandwiches, alongside a highly enticing array of fresh-prepared salads (curried cauliflower or mushroom ditalini recommended). Order at the counter and add a craft beer or an own-made lemonade to the mix.

LA TAQUERÍA PINCHE TACO SHOP MEXICAN $

Map p280 (604-558-2549; www.lataqueria.com; 2450 Yukon St; tacos $3-6; mains $14-17; 11am-11pm Mon-Thu, 11am-midnight Fri & Sat, 11am-9pm Sun; ; 9) The latest finger-licking edition of this wildly popular Mexican minichain combines communal tables, a large patio and an inviting bar area with a full menu of favorites. Order a selection of meat and/or veggie tacos for the table (*al pastor* and *asada* recommended) and add some beers from Vancouver-based South American brewery Andina. Ask about afternoon and late-night happy-hour specials here.

K CAFE CAFE $

Map p280 (778-737-9295; 2533 Heather St; mains $6-12; 7:30am-4pm Mon-Fri, 9am-2:30pm Sat; 9) Superfriendly family-run cafe loved by those working at nearby Vancouver General Hospital. You can grab a coffee on the run here or – better still – linger over lunch. The menu combines Korean comfort dishes such as bibimbap rice bowls with home-made soups and toasted sandwiches. Sitting on an off-Broadway side street, this cafe is a great value option.

Also a good spot for a traditional eggs-and-bacon breakfast if you're in the area.

MARULILU CAFE BREAKFAST $

Map p280 (604-568-4211; www.marulilu.com; 451 W Broadway; mains $4-13; 8am-6pm Mon-Fri, 8:30am-6pm sat & Sun; ; S Broadway City-Hall) Don't be put off by the grubby exterior; this tiny homestyle cafe specializing in good-value all-day breakfasts, brunches and lunches is hugely popular. The eclectic menu ranges from traditional eggs and bacon to a wide array of Japanese options, such as *katsu* sandwiches and curry-rice bowls. Service is exceptionally friendly and you'll meet lots of loyal regulars.

There aren't many tables here so it can fill up quickly; consider dining off-peak, especially on weekends.

★SALMON N' BANNOCK NORTHWESTERN US $$

Map p280 (604-568-8971; www.facebook.com/SalmonNBannockBistro; 1128 W Broadway; mains $16-32; 5-10pm Mon-Sat; 9) Vancouver's only First Nations restaurant is an utterly delightful art-lined little bistro on an unassuming strip of Broadway shops. It's worth the easy bus trip, though, for fresh-made indigenous-influenced dishes made with local ingredients. The juicy salmon 'n' bannock burger has been a staple here for years but more elaborate, feast-like options include game sausages and bison pot roast.

Be sure to order some bannock, a traditional flatbread introduced by Scottish settlers that's now a staple of First Nations BC dining. This is also a golden opportunity to sample some wines from two local First Nations wineries; ask the ever-friendly servers for recommendations.

HERITAGE ASIAN EATERY ASIAN **$$**

Map p280 (☎604-559-6058; www.eatheritage.ca; 382 W Broadway; mains $12-18; ⏰11am-8pm; 📶✎; 🚌9) Bigger than its Pender St sibling, this bright, cafeteria-style spot serves a small, well-curated menu of comfort-food rice and noodle bowls. Serving top-notch dishes such as velvety pork belly and spicy lamb shank, it also offers a couple of flavor-hugging vegetarian options; go for the lip-smacking eggplant rice bowl. On your way out, add a warm egg custard bun to your day.

The heaping bowls can be quite filling; snag a takeout box from the stack on the cart if you fancy finishing it later on. And if you're not quite hungry enough for a big meal, the $5 bao sandwiches are an excellent savory snack (pulled duck leg recommended).

SUIKA JAPANESE **$$**

Map p280 (☎604-730-1678; www.suika-snackbar.com; 1626 W Broadway; mains $9-18; ⏰11:30am-2pm & 5:30-11:30pm Sun-Thu, 11:30am-2pm & 5:30-12:30am Fri & Sat; 🚌9) A contemporary *izakaya* (Japanese neighborhood pub) with a playful edge, Suika is all about sliding alongside a moodlit table under the sake-bottle chandelier and sharing inventive dishes of unagi pizza, deep-fried *hellz* chicken (recommended for ultra-spice fans) and the naughty-but-delicious Chinese poutine – fries topped with mozzarella and ground-pork gravy. Drinks-wise, try a refreshing white-lychee sangria.

This is not a place for a quiet, intimate meal; expect a constant chorus of friendly Japanese hollers from the staff as they welcome and wave goodbye to diners.

TOJO'S JAPANESE **$$$**

Map p280 (☎604-872-8050; www.tojos.com; 1133 W Broadway; mains $28-45; ⏰5-10pm Mon-Sat; 🚌9) Hidekazu Tojo's legendary skill with the sushi knife launched Vancouver's Japanese dining scene; his sleek restaurant is still a pilgrimage spot. Among his exquisite dishes are favorites such as lightly steamed monkfish, sautéed halibut cheeks and fried red tuna wrapped in seaweed and served with plum sauce. This is a sophisticated night out; book ahead for a seat at the *omakaze* sushi bar.

If Tojo is there on your visit, consider asking him about his Tojo tuna roll, created to introduce 1970s North American audiences to the pleasures of eating raw fish. Legend says that his creation later became known as the California roll. And the rest, of course, is sushi history.

Cambie Village

MIGHTY OAK CAFE **$**

Map p280 (☎604-243-9322; www.themightyoak.ca; 198 W 18th Ave; sandwiches $7-8; ⏰8am-5pm Mon-Fri, 9am-5pm Sat & Sun; 🚌15) A beloved and well-hidden neighborhood corner cafe tucked among handsome wooden heritage homes. Snag a sunny-day street-side seat here and sip on perfectly prepared java and delicious bakery treats, including luscious cinnamon buns and thick-cut chocolate-banana bread. Sandwiches and wraps lure the lunch crowd (goat cheese and fig recommended).

RAIN OR SHINE ICE CREAM **$**

Map p280 (☎604-876-9986; www.rainorshineicecream.com; 3382 Cambie St; ⏰noon-10pm; 👪; 🚌15) You might have to queue under the gaze of a cone-crowned purple cow on the wall at this finger-licking ice-cream emporium. That will give you time to mull the multitudinous flavors, ranging from – on our visit – honey lavender to coffee toffee. All are made on-site and served in cups or cones, although perhaps staff will shovel it straight into your mouth if you ask nicely.

Alongside the flavor mainstays, there are always some seasonal additions to the roster, while glutinous milkshakes (Earl Grey lavender recommended) are also available if you still need a few thousand more calories to round out your day. If you're in Kitsilano, find the original Rain or Shine (p172) on W 4th Ave.

DUTCH WOODEN SHOE CAFE BREAKFAST **$$**

Map p280 (☎604-874-0922; 3292 Cambie St; mains $12-16; ⏰8am-2:30pm Mon-Fri, 8am-4pm Sat & Sun; 🚌15) A homestyle Dutch-themed

CHRISTMAS IN VANCOUVER

While summer remains a favorite time of year for many Vancouver-bound visitors, the city is also gaining a reputation as a sparkling Christmastime destination. From mid-November onwards, dozens of Yuletide offerings pop up around the city, from seasonal markets to festive stage shows to an annual parade (p25). Many year-round attractions also convert themselves into magical Christmas hot spots, including Grouse Mountain (p182), FlyOver Canada (p57) and Capilano Suspension Bridge Park (p182). One of the best places to slide into the Yuletide spirit, though, is VanDusen Botanical Garden (p150), which transforms its walkways into a colorful winter wonderland of fairy lights and shimmering musical dioramas. Considering a festive-season visit to the city? See what's on at www.vancouverchristmasguide.com.

breakfast and lunch hangout lined with wall-mounted clogs and a huge collection of beer glasses (despite there being no liquor license), this old-school charmer hasn't changed in years. Expect plate-sized *pannekoek* pancakes, slightly thicker and spongier than their French counterparts, topped with a vast array of options; go for the Windmill, complete with spinach, sausage slices and melted edam.

On a budget? Drop by on Tuesdays for the restaurant's regular buy-one-get-one-half-price pancake deal. And if your sweet tooth needs a fix, add a serving of sweet *poffertjes* pancake bites to your order. Service here is famously friendly; don't forget to pick up a piece of salty Dutch licorice from the counter on your way out.

LANDMARK HOT POT HOUSE CHINESE **$$**

Map p280 (☎604-872-2868; www.landmarkhotpot.com; 4023 Cambie St; mains $8-24; ⏰5pm-2am; Ⓢ King Edward) Pull up a black-laquered chair and dive into the menu at this Hong Kong–style hot-pot spot. It's a surprisingly large, long-established place that is often bustling with locals from the Chinese-Canadian community – usually a good sign of authenticity – and they're mostly here for plates of meat and veggies that you cook yourself at your table via a pot of boiling broth.

A good place to come for a feast, this is also an accessible introduction to the city's traditional Chinese dining scene.

★**VIJ'S** INDIAN **$$$**

Map p280 (☎604-736-6664; www.vijs.ca; 3106 Cambie St; mains $23-36; ⏰5:30-10pm; 🖉; 🚌15) Spicy aromas scent the air as you enter this warmly intimate dining space for Vancouver's finest Indian cuisine. Exemplary servers happily answer menu questions, while bringing over snacks and chai tea. There's a one-page array of tempting dishes but the trick is to order three or four to share (mains are all available as small plates and orders come with rice and naan).

Alongside popular meat dishes (including near-legendary lamb popsicles), there's an excellent array of vegetarian options; eggplant in yoghurt curry is a highlight. A limited number of reservations are available daily here, with tables always kept back for walk-ins.

South Granville

★**PAUL'S OMELETTERY** BREAKFAST **$**

Map p280 (☎604-737-2857; www.paulsomelettery.com; 2211 Granville St; mains $6-19; ⏰7am-3pm; 🖉; 🚌10) You'll be jostling for space with chatty locals at this breakfast and lunch joint near the south side of Granville Bridge. But it's worth it: the cozy, superfriendly place is superior to most bacon-and-eggs destinations. The menu is grounded on signature omelets, while also offering excellent eggs Benedict and heaping 'lumberjack breakfasts.' Reservations are not accepted; arrive early on weekends.

It's not just about breakfast here; they also serve all-day lunches including salads, burgers and grilled cheese sandwiches. It's the perfect place to fuel up before exploring nearby Granville Island.

BEAUCOUP BAKERY & CAFE BAKERY **$**

Map p280 (☎604-732-4222; www.beaucoupbakery.com; 2150 Fir St; baked items $3-5; ⏰7am-5pm Tue-Fri, 8am-5pm Sat & Sun; 📶; 🚌4) The expertise and allure of this French-approach bakery is second to none, serving what are arguably the best croissants and *pain au chocolat* in the city. Add coffee and extra

Neighborhood Walk South Granville Stroll

START PAUL'S OMELETTERY
END BUMP N GRIND
LENGTH 1.5KM; ONE HOUR

Hop on bus 10 from downtown. Pull the bell when you're halfway over Granville Bridge, then alight at the first stop on the other side. On the right side of Granville St, fuel up for the walk ahead at 1 **Paul's Omelettery** (p153). Don't weigh yourself down, though; you still have to hoof it uphill from here. When you reach Broadway, cross to the other side, turn left and walk for a minute or two. You'll soon reach the 2 **Pacific Arts Market** (p159); take the stairs to the 2nd floor and explore the eclectic arts and crafts of dozens of local creatives.

Retrace your steps along Broadway and turn left onto Granville Street, which is lined on both sides with boutiques, restaurants and coffee shops. Spend plenty of time exploring the stores here. At the intersection with W 11th Ave, you'll find Vancouver's largest chocolate purveyor 3 **Purdy's Chocolates** (p160). Consider a well-deserved ice-cream bar here or some treats for later.

Cross over and head east on W 11th Ave for half a block. On your right is 4 **Rangoli** (p155); add this delicious Indian curry joint to your dinner possibilities list, then rejoin Granville St and continue south. After a few steps, you'll reach the 5 **Stanley Theatre** (p158), a handsome heritage venue that stages some of Vancouver's most popular plays. At the end of the block, you'll also come to 6 **Bacci's** (p159); nip inside to peruse the funky home wares and trendy fashions.

A couple more blocks delivers you to 7 **Meinhardt Fine Foods** (p161) where you can spend a giddy half hour perusing the posh groceries. Finally, if all that strolling has your blisters throbbing, nip next door to 8 **Bump n Grind** (p158) for a restorative java. It's an excellent spot to reflect on your leisurely South Granville exploration. And if you're aiming to head back downtown, you can hop the northbound bus 10 anywhere along Granville; you'll soon be back in the city center.

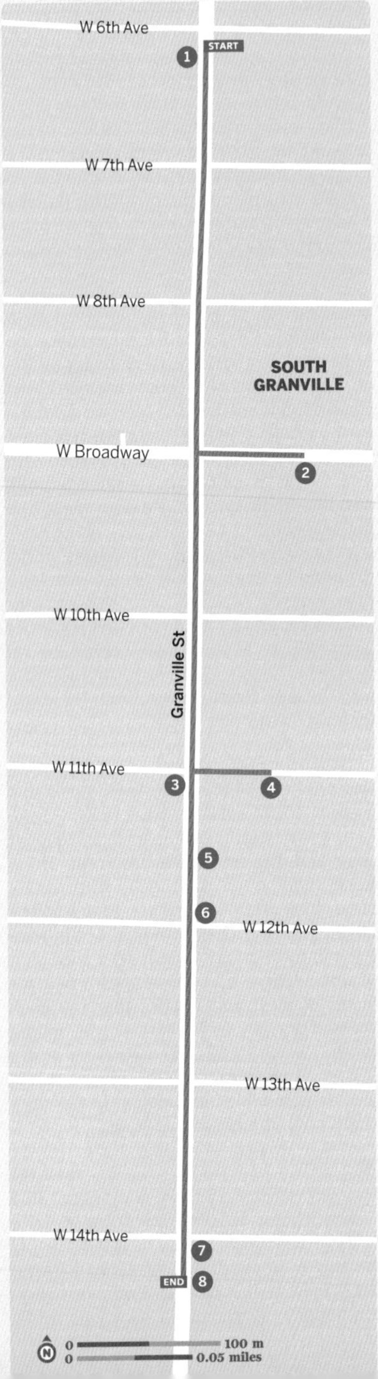

treats (bite-sized *kouign-amann* pastries recommended) then tackle the lovely Arbutus Greenway (p166) walking route that starts across the street. Before you go, buy a copy of owner Betty Hung's page-turning *French Pastry 101.*

SMALL VICTORY CAFE **$**

Map p280 (☎604-742-1737; www.smallvictory.ca; 3070 Granville St; mains $6-13; ⏰8am-6pm; 📶; 🚌10) A large, chic, see-and-be-seen cafe that serves great coffee, a huge array of dainty pastries, desserts, and light breakfast and lunch dishes. Spend some time perusing the glass cabinets of treats here before you order. Whatever you go for, add a naughty takeout order just before you leave. Looking for avocado toast in Vancouver? Here's where you'll find it.

HEIRLOOM VEGETARIAN VEGETARIAN **$$**

Map p280 (☎604-733-2231; www.heirloomrestaurant.ca; 1509 W 12th Ave; mains $11-22; ⏰9am-10pm; 🌿; 🚌10) With a white-walled cafeteria-meets-rustic-artisan look (hence the farm forks on the wall), this is one of Vancouver's best vegetarian eateries, serving mostly locally grown and organic seasonal ingredients fused with international influences. Dinner-wise, the bulging burger and cashew coconut curry are definite winners, but the all-day brunch has risen to prominence in recent years, especially the utterly delicious avocado eggs Benedict.

Alongside a good wine, beer and cocktail list, there's a diverse array of tempting non-alcoholic options; this is the place to have that beet, carrot and orange detox juice you know you need.

RANGOLI INDIAN **$$**

Map p280 (☎604-736-5711; www.vijsrangoli.ca; 1480 W 11th Ave; mains $16-32; ⏰11:30am-1am Sun-Thu, 11:30am-2am Fri & Sat; 🌿; 🚌10) This small, cafe-like satellite of Cambie St's landmark Vij's restaurant (p153) is a favorite among South Granville locals. Service is brisk and famously friendly and the menu takes a gourmet-comfort-food approach to Indian dishes such as their delicious lamb in cumin-and-cream curry. Add some addictive *pakoras* to share but make sure you snag the last one for yourself.

There are daily happy-hour deals to plunge into here between 3pm and 5pm as well as after 10pm. One caveat: there are no reservations, so you'll likely have to wait for a table during peak dining periods.

WHAT'S IN A NAME?

In 1870, the Earl of Granville generously lent his grand title to the search for a new name for the community that had grown up around what is now known as Maple Tree Sq. The locals had begun calling it 'Gastown' but the colonial administration wanted something of its own. Virtually no-one used the name 'Granville' to describe the settlement and it was replaced with 'Vancouver' after the seafaring British captain who had set foot on the forested shoreline in 1792. 'Granville Street' was later adopted for the moniker of one of the city's busiest thoroughfares.

STABLE HOUSE BISTRO **$$**

Map p280 (☎604-736-1520; www.thestablehouse.ca; 1520 W 13th Ave; mains $19-24; ⏰11am-3pm Tue-Fri, dinner from 5pm daily; 🚌10) This modern reinvention of a European bistro has a loyal band of South Granville regulars. They're usually the ones hogging the weirdly angular window table, chatting over shareable plates of cheese and charcuterie or gourmet comfort dishes such as pork loin or parmesan gnocchi. Weekend brunch adds to the allure, with the delicious sausage-and-fig-jam breakfast sandwich highly recommended.

There's a lively by-the-glass wine program here as well, including some themed wine-flight tasting options.

WEST NORTHWESTERN US **$$$**

Map p280 (☎604-738-8938; www.westrestaurant.com; 2881 Granville St; mains $28-43; ⏰11:30am-2:30pm & 5:30-10pm; 🚌10) This sleek but never snobbish fine-dining favorite is committed to superb West Coast meals with ultra-attentive service and a great wine selection. Ideal for a classy night out, its seasonally changing highlights often include duck breast or braised lamb shank, while the pastry chef delivers some of Vancouver's best desserts. Arrive early for a seat at the bar and sup some excellent cocktails.

Before you leave, ask to try the sliding ladder attached to the wine shelves: staff usually (okay, always) say 'no.' If you're looking for a romantic dinner destination – and maybe a place to pop the question – West is ideal: you likely won't be the first to propose here.

DRINKING & NIGHTLIFE

Not renowned for its big-night-out credentials, this neighborhood has a couple of spots that are perfect for parking your thirst. Java-wise, there are also some excellent neighborhood coffeehouses dotted on the main drags of Cambie and South Granville, plus some hidden spots just off the beaten path.

Fairview

ELYSIAN COFFEE COFFEE

Map p280 (www.elysiancoffee.com; 590 W Broadway; 7am-7pm; ; 9) Just to prove not all the hipsters hang out on Main St, this chatty neighborhood joint lures every skinny-jeaned local in its vicinity. They come for the excellent coffee plus a small array of baked treats (go for a naughty slab of shortbread). Take a seat at the front-window perch and watch Broadway bustle past.

You won't be the only one flicking through a copy of the *Georgia Straight* and planning your weekend at one of the tables here; there's a box just outside where you can pick up a free copy. If you really love the coffee, you can buy blend bags to go.

CAFFÈ CITTADELLA COFFEE

Map p280 (604-568-5909; www.caffecittadella.com; 2310 Ash St; 7am-7pm Mon-Fri, 8am-7pm Sat, 8am-6pm Sun; ; S Broadway-City Hall) Don't tell anyone you found this place, since the regulars will be very upset. This cute two-floored cafe incongruously tucked into a restored clapboard heritage home is perfect for a morning of java-supported newspaper reading. There are some tables scattered around the building outside, but on sunny days, the doors are thrown open and it feels alfresco inside anyway.

Alongside the excellent house-made cakes and inventive treats (lavender-cashew clusters are excellent), there are light breakfast dishes such as frittatas and egg-and-bacon wraps as well as a good array of soups and sandwiches (go for the Jamaican jerk wrap).

APERTURE COFFEE BAR COFFEE

Map p280 (604-620-8065; www.aperturecoffeebar.com; 243 W Broadway; 8am-9:30pm; ; 9) A sometimes clamorously busy spot, this neighborhood coffee shop is ideal for hanging out on a rainy day – especially if you dip into their groaning shelves of loaner books, ranging from Albert Camus to Stephen King. The coffee is good here while light meals including wraps and sandwiches are available if that paperback you're reading isn't sustenance enough.

Warm and friendly (despite the animal-skull artworks on the whitewashed walls), it's a local hipster haunt without the too-cool edge that some similar-looking cafes have.

ROGUE KITCHEN & WET BAR BAR

Map p280 (604-568-9400; www.roguewetbar.com; 602 W Broadway; 11:30am-midnight Mon-Thu, 11:30am-1am Fri & Sat, 11:30am-11pm Sun; ; 9) A casual West Coast restaurant on one side and a funky lounge bar on the other, the main reason to go to Rogue is the excellent craft-beer selection. Expect drafts from celebrated Vancouver brewers including Powell Street and Strange Fellows plus cocktails, whiskey flights and a good by-the-glass wine menu. There are also extensive happy-hour drink-and dine-deals here.

There is a large menu of elevated pub grub to dive into, from tacos to burgers to poke bowls. On sunny days, aim for an alfresco table on the adjoining side-street patio.

Cambie Village

XING FU TANG BUBBLE TEA

Map p280 (604-707-0275; www.xingfutang.ca; 3432 Cambie St; noon-10pm; ; 15) Bubble-tea joints have swept across the Lower Mainland in recent years (especially in Richmond) but this sometimes clamorous Taiwanese cafe is one of the hottest. Their tapioca pearls are stir-fried in brown sugar at the counter and added to many of the most popular drinks. Thirsty? Go for the creamy Brown Sugar Pearl Milk Tea.

While you're queuing to order your beverage, pick up a fortune stick and discover your future from one of the little wooden drawers in the wall-mounted cabinet – it may change the course of your life...or at least your choice of bubble-tea flavor.

BIERCRAFT BISTRO BEER HALL

Map p280 (604-874-6900; www.biercraft.com; 3305 Cambie St; 11:30am-midnight Mon-Thu, 11:30am-1am Fri, 10am-1am Sat, 10am-midnight Sun; 15) With a chatty, wood-lined interior

PARK LIFE

Vancouver's urban green spaces are home to a surprising array of critters. Many of them roam the city's streets after dark, foraging for extra food. During your visit, you'll find **black squirrels** everywhere, but don't be surprised to also spot **raccoons**. Common in several parks, they are often bold enough to hang out on porches and root through garbage bins. **Skunks** are almost as common, but the only time you'll likely see them is after an unfortunate roadkill incident (a fairly common occurrence around area parks).

Every spring, several Vancouver neighborhoods post notices of **coyote** spottings (there are an estimated 3000 living in and around the city). This is the time of year when these wild dogs build dens and raise pups, often in remote corners of city parks – and they become more protective of their territory in the process. This can lead to problems with domesticated pets. Vancouverites are warned to keep pets inside when coyotes are spotted in their neighborhoods, and to report any sightings to authorities. Many locals will tell you they've only seen a coyote once or twice; these animals are very adept at avoiding humans.

Animal encounters are an even bigger problem for areas that back directly on to wilderness regions. The North Shore is shadowed by a forest and mountain swathe that's long been a traditional home for **bears** – mostly black bears. Residents in North Vancouver and West Vancouver know how to secure their garbage so as not to encourage bears to become habituated to human food. But every year – often in spring when the hungry furballs are waking from hibernation – a few are trapped and relocated from the area.

At the other end of the scale, Vancouver is a great city for bird spotters. In Queen Elizabeth Park, keep your eyes peeled for **bald eagles** whirling overhead. On Granville Island, glance up under Granville Bridge and you'll spot **cormorants** treating the girders like cliffside roosts. And if you're near a pond anywhere around the city, you might see **coots**, **wood ducks** and statue-still **blue herons** alongside the ubiquitous **Canada geese**. Head to Stanley Park's Lost Lagoon and you'll likely see them all in fairly short order.

It's not all about waterbirds, though. On streets around the city, look out for **Northern flicker woodpeckers** (known for their red cheeks and black-spotted plumage) as well as **finches, chickadees**, **American robins** and **Steller's jays**, a blue feathered friend that's also BC's provincial bird. If you're really fast, you'll even spot what many regard as an unlikely bird here: the delightful little **Anna's hummingbird** is a year-round resident in Vancouver. And, in spring and summer, it's joined by the migrating **rufous hummingbird**. They're the reason you'll spot sugar-water feeders on balconies across the city.

For more information on wildlife (and guided nature walks) in the city, click on www.stanleyparkecology.ca.

plus two popular street-side patios, this beer-forward resto-bar is a great spot for ale aficionados. Dive into the astonishing array of Belgian tipples and compare them to some choice microbrews from BC and the US. Save time for food; the slightly pricey gastropub menu here ranges from steak *frites* to bowls of locally sourced mussels in several brothy iterations.

You'll see many of the same locals back here on the weekend, enjoying brunch, which is served until 3:30pm. Poached eggs on cornbread is a popular choice.

South Granville

★STORM CROW ALEHOUSE PUB

Map p280 (☎604-428-9670; www.stormcrowalehouse.com; 1619 W Broadway; ⏰11am-1am Sun-Thu, 11am-2am Fri & Sat; 📶; 🚌9) The larger sibling of Commercial Drive's excellent nerd bar, this pub welcomes everyone from the Borg to beardy *Lord of the Rings* dwarfs. They come to peruse the memorabilia-studded walls (think Millennium Falcon models and a TARDIS washroom door), check out the role-playing games and dive into refreshments including Romulan Ale and Pangalactic Gargleblaster cocktails. Hungry? Miss the chunky chickpea fries at your peril.

It's not all about geek-based affectation here. This is a seriously good pub with an excellent array of BC craft beers and a menu of hearty pub fare. Drop in during happy hour (2pm to 5pm weekdays) for specials and your pick of the back-wall board games. And if the drinkers at the next table happen to be speaking Klingon, it's probably best to avoid eye contact.

★GRAPES & SODA WINE BAR

Map p280 (☎604-336-2456; www.grapesandsoda.ca; 1541 W 6th Ave; ⊙5:30-11pm Tue-Sat; 🚌10) A warm, small-table hangout that self-identifies as a 'natural wine bar' (there's a well-curated array of options from BC, Europe and beyond). This local favorite also serves excellent cocktails: from the countless bottles behind the small bar, they can seemingly concoct anything your taste buds desire, whether or not it's on the menu. Need help? Slide into a Scotch, ginger and walnut Cortejo.

There's a small menu of dinner dishes to explore here (many of them with Asian influences) but elevated bar snacks are the way to go, especially the excellent cheese and charcuterie board. Also consider dropping by for the 5pm to 6:30pm daily happy hour, complete with cocktail special.

THE MARQUIS GRILL BAR

Map p280 (☎604-568-0670; www.themarquis.ca; 2666 Granville St; ⊙4pm-2am Mon-Sat, 4pm to midnight Sun; 🚌10) Don't blink or you'll miss the entrance to this cave-like, speakeasy-sized nook that's popular with locals launching their evenings out or dropping by for a laid-back nightcap before bedtime. Find a moodlit perch at the high tables facing the bar and tuck into a menu of classic martinis and flirty cocktails, plus brews from BC producers such as Driftwood and Four Winds.

The menu includes a good array of mains, from gourmet burgers to fish and chips and a flavourful beef bourguignon.

BUMP N GRIND COFFEE

Map p280 (☎604-558-4743; www.bumpngrindcafe.com; 3010 Granville St; ⊙7am-7pm Mon-Fri, 8am-7pm Sat & Sun; 📶; 🚌10) The South Granville branch of this two-outlet local coffee chain has a great long table at the back where you can settle down with a java and peruse the tiny wall-mounted library of handmade zines. Alternatively, press your face against the glass cabinet of bakery treats at the front and try to levitate a muffin or cookie into your mouth.

This is a popular spot for local hipsters so there can be lineups at peak times.

☆ ENTERTAINMENT

This area offers some laid-back entertainment options away from the crowds of downtown. You're much more likely to meet the locals at these events and there are plenty of nearby dining options if you want to add a meal to your big night out.

★STANLEY THEATRE THEATER

Map p280 (☎604-687-1644; www.artsclub.com; 2750 Granville St, South Granville; tickets from $29; ⊙Sep-Jul; 🚌10) Popular musicals dominate early summer (usually the last show of the season) at this heritage theater, but the rest of the year sees new works and adaptations of contemporary hits from around the world. Officially called the Stanley Industrial Alliance Stage (a moniker that not a single Vancouverite uses), the Stanley is part of the Arts Club Theatre Company, Vancouver's biggest.

The heritage 1200-seat theater was opened as a movie house and live venue in 1931, and its interior is an unusual mix of the era's architectural fashions, from Moorish to art deco. If you're reading this in 2107, it's time to open the time capsule of contemporary street photographs that was buried in 2007 outside the theater.

VANCOUVER CANADIANS BASEBALL

Map p280 (☎604-872-5232; www.milb.com/vancouver; 4601 Ontario St, Nat Bailey Stadium; tickets from $15; ⊙Jun-Aug; 👪; 🚌33, Ⓢ King Edward) Minor-league affiliates of the Toronto Blue Jays, the Canadians play at the charmingly old-school Nat Bailey Stadium. It's known as 'the prettiest ballpark in the world' thanks to its mountain backdrop. Afternoon games – called 'nooners' – are perfect for a nostalgic bask in the sun. Hot dogs and beer rule the menu, but there's also sushi and fruit – this is Vancouver, after all.

KINO CABARET

Map p280 (☎604-875-1998; www.thekino.ca; 3456 Cambie St, Cambie Village; tickets from $5; ⏰5pm-1am Mon-Fri, 3pm-1am Sat, 3pm-midnight Sun; 🚌15) Vancouver's only flamenco cafe is a great place to chill on a summer evening. If it's really warm, bask in the sun with a beer outside. But be sure to trip back in when the show starts: there's live dancing on the little wooden side stage from Wednesday to Saturday, with jazz, bluegrass and comedy also popping up regularly on other nights.

Whether or not you think you like flamenco, it's hard not to be caught up in the energy of the performances and you'll likely be tapping your own toes on the hardwood floor within minutes. Order some tapas for your table to keep everyone in the mood. If you're here on Friday and Saturday, expect a crowd: this room can really buzz on weekends.

PACIFIC THEATRE THEATER

Map p280 (☎604-731-5518; www.pacifictheatre.org; 1140 W 12th Ave, South Granville; tickets from $30; 🚌10) This unusual fringe-style venue stages a broad mixture of shows during its September-to-June season, mostly with a light undercurrent of Christian themes. There's usually a different one every month, ranging from contemporary retellings of Shakespeare to new or classic dramas. The intimate setting – seats are configured 'alley style' on either side of the stage – can make for especially involving performances.

Tickets are around the $35 mark (discounted on Wednesday evenings). The Christmas show is usually the busiest of the year; it's typically an uplifting affair with plenty of Yuletide cheer.

CINEPLEX PARK THEATRE CINEMA

Map p280 (☎604-709-3456; www.cineplex.com; 3440 Cambie St, Cambie Village; tickets from $8.25; 🚌15) The last holdout of a popular Vancouver independent theater chain that succumbed to a takeover by the big boys a few years back. But the Park is still a one-screen neighborhood charmer where you'll be rubbing shoulders with the locals at new releases or classic old flicks. Be sure to check out the cool deco-esque neon sign on top of the building.

YUK YUK'S COMEDY CLUB COMEDY

Map p280 (☎604-696-9857; www.yukyuks.com; 2837 Cambie St, Fairview; tickets from $10; ⏰Tue-Sun; 📶; Ⓢ Broadway-City Hall) Although there are other comedy nights in bars and theaters around the city, Yuk Yuk's is one of Vancouver's few dedicated stand-up venues. Check ahead to see what's on: open mic and amateur nights are the best deals but there's also a roster of journeyman comedians rolling in from across Canada and the US.

Don't be put off by the unassuming exterior, which resembles the stage door at the back of a regular theater. Food-wise: stick to the drinks.

SHOPPING

The main retailing activity here is on South Granville, which – especially between Broadway and 16th Ave – recalls a boutique-packed English high street in a well-to-do town. It makes for a pleasant hour or two of strolling as you nose around fashion stores and slick homeware emporiums. Art fans should also check out the handful of private galleries on Granville, mostly north of Broadway. Cambie Village is also worth a poke around, with some cool indie stores nestled between the restaurants and coffeehouses.

★**PACIFIC ARTS MARKET** ARTS & CRAFTS

Map p280 (☎778-877-6449; www.pacificartsmarket.ca; 1448 W Broadway, South Granville; ⏰noon-5:30pm Tue & Wed, noon-7pm Thu & Fri, 11am-7pm Sat, 1-5pm Sun; 🚌9) Head upstairs to this large, under-the-radar gallery space and you'll find a kaleidoscopic array of stands showcasing the work of 40+ Vancouver and BC artists. From paintings to jewelry and from fiber arts to handmade chocolate bars, it's the perfect spot to find authentic souvenirs to take back home. The artists change regularly and there's something for every budget here.

One of Vancouver's best art spaces, check the website for their monthly free-entry social gatherings, complete with live music, free snacks, artist meet-and-greets and a cash bar; this event has a great atmosphere and it's an ideal way to connect with the local art scene. They also host regular workshops and other art happenings; check ahead before you arrive in the city.

BACCI'S HOMEWARES, CLOTHING

Map p280 (☎604-733-4933; www.baccis.ca; 2788 Granville St, South Granville; ⏰9:45am-5:45pm Mon-Sat; 🚌10) Combining designer women's

LOCAL KNOWLEDGE

TAKE ME OUT TO THE BALL GAME

If you can't get tickets to a **Vancouver Canucks** game, there's another local option to scratch your itch for spectator sports. It's a tradition for many Vancouverites to catch a summertime baseball game with the minor league Vancouver Canadians (p158). Tickets cost from just $15 to catch a game at the nostalgic **Nat Bailey Stadium**, an idyllic 1950s wooden stadium (capacity around 5000). Naturally, nosh is a big draw – especially if the action flags a little – and, for many, that means sitting in the stands munching on a hot dog and gulping a few cold beers. Adding to the fun are the non-baseball shenanigans ranging from kiss cams trained on the crowd to mascot races. And, several times during the season, the nighttime action ends with a fun fireworks display. Catching a game here is arguably the most fun you can have at a spectator sport in Vancouver – and it's also one of the most budget-friendly options (depending on how many hot dogs you put away).

clothing on one side with a room full of perfectly curated trinkets piled high on antique wooden tables on the other, Bacci's is a dangerous place to browse. Before you know it, you'll have an armful of chunky luxury soaps, embroidered cushions and picture-perfect coffee mugs to fit in your suitcase.

Before you leave, check out the shelves of clearance goodies near the door, proof that you can be fashionably tasteful without killing your credit cards.

WALRUS HOMEWARES

Map p280 (☎604-874-9770; www.walrushome.com; 3408 Cambie St, Cambie Village; ⏰10am-6pm Mon-Fri, 10am-5pm Sat, noon-5pm Sun; 🚌15) A small but brilliantly curated store teeming with must-have accessories and home wares, mostly from Canadian designers. Form meets function with everything on the shelves here, so give yourself plenty of time to browse the perfect pottery knick-knacks, quirky artisan jewelry and raft of irresistible bags from Vancouver favorites Herschel Supply Co. Your credit card will soon be sweating.

BOOK WAREHOUSE BOOKS

Map p280 (☎604-872-5711; www.bookwarehouse.ca; 632 W Broadway, Fairview; ⏰9am-8pm Mon-Tue & Sat, 9am-9pm Wed-Fri, 10am-6pm Sun; 👪; 🚌9) Locals routinely beeline to this browse-worthy bookstore for discounts on new and just-released titles. If you're not sure what you're looking for, it's also an excellent spot for great staff recommendations; check out the extensive Staff Picks near the counter and chat to the friendly front-deskers for personalized suggestions. Whatever you buy, save time for the red bargain bins outside.

You'll find good selections of fiction, children's books and travel guides here. This is also a great spot to pick up BC-focused tomes in the Local Interest section (nature fans should consider the *Vancouver Tree Book* or *The Birder's Guide to Vancouver*).

IAN TAN GALLERY ARTS & CRAFTS

Map p280 (☎604-738-1077; www.iantangallery.com; 2342 Granville St, South Granville; ⏰10am-6pm Mon-Sat, noon-5pm Sun; 🚌10) Now in its third South Granville location in the space of a few years, this popular stop on the city's one-time gallery row focuses its chin-scratching gaze on contemporary Canadian artists. You'll find lots of bold, often bright, paintings and installations on the walls here, and it's a great place to put your finger on the pulse of Canada's modern art scene.

There's usually an intriguing mix of styles and approaches on display, including large paintings, smaller-scale photography (Vancouver is renowned for its contemporary photoconceptualism) and even a plinth or two of ceramics or sculpted figures.

PURDY'S CHOCOLATES CHOCOLATE

Map p280 (☎604-732-7003; www.purdys.com; 2705 Granville St, South Granville; ⏰10am-6pm Mon-Sat, noon-5pm Sun; 🚌10) Like a sweet beacon to the weary, this purple-painted chocolate purveyor stands at the corner of Granville and W 11th Ave calling your name. It's a homegrown BC business with outlets dotted like candy sprinkles across the city, and it's hard not to pick up a few treats: go for chocolate hedgehogs, orange meltie bars or sweet Georgia browns – pecans in caramel and chocolate.

It's a great spot to pick up distinctive, Vancouver-made souvenirs for your friends and family back home; rush to the sales racks after Christmas and Valentine's Day for dramatic bargains. And on sunny days, drop in and treat yourself: the nut and chocolate-covered ice-cream bars here are a local legend.

MEINHARDT FINE FOODS FOOD

Map p280 (604-732-4405; www.meinhardt.com; 3002 Granville St, South Granville; 7am-9pm Mon-Sat, 9am-8pm Sun; 10) The culinary equivalent of a sex shop for food fans, this swanky deli and grocery emporium's narrow aisles are lined with international condiments, luxury canned goods and the kind of tempting treats that everyone should try at least once. Build a perfect picnic from the tempting bread, cheese and cold cuts, or snag one of the house-made deli sandwiches (paprika chicken recommended).

It's worth spending some time browsing the towering shelves for that unexpected item: where else are you going to find that essential jar of fig mustard, for example? But it's not all sophisticated edibles: treat yourself to a smiley-face cookie and savor it as you stroll down the street.

TURNABOUT VINTAGE

Map p280 (604-754-5313; www.turnabout.com; 3135 Granville St, South Granville; 10am-6pm Mon-Sat, noon-6pm Sun; 10) The original branch of a popular Lower Mainland mini-chain, this high-end used-clothing consignment store is perfect for a spot of leisurely browsing. Expect luxury women's-wear labels from Prada to Alexander Wang and don't miss the shoe shelves near the front. It's worth visiting a couple of times during your stay since the stock changes continually.

BAU-XI GALLERY ARTS & CRAFTS

Map p280 (604-733-7011; www.bau-xi.com; 3045 Granville St, South Granville; 10am-5:30pm Mon-Sat, 11am-5:30pm Sun; 10) One of the oldest established of Vancouver's private galleries, Bau-Xi – pronounced 'bo-she' – showcases the best in local artists and generally has prices to match its exalted position. The main gallery selection changes monthly and the focus is usually on original paintings – although prints, drawings and sculpture are also added to the mix on occasion.

Look out for works by favored Vancouver contemporary painters such as Jack Shadbolt, who is one of Canada's most collectible modern artists.

RESTORATION HARDWARE HOMEWARES

Map p280 (604-731-3918; www.restorationhardware.com; 2555 Granville St, South Granville; 10am-8pm Mon-Fri, 10am-7pm Sat, 11am-6pm Sun; 10) Filled with furnishings and interior flourishes that you wish you had in your house, this upmarket favorite has lots of design ideas for transforming your pad when you get back home. Even if you don't buy anything, it's a great place to poke around and get some ideas for your summer house in the south of France.

Kitsilano & University of British Columbia (UBC)

Neighborhood Top Five

❶ **Museum of Anthropology** (p164) Exploring Vancouver's best museum, with its immersive array of regional indigenous art and artifacts, as well as fascinating, sometimes mysterious exhibits from cultures around the world.

❷ **Bard on the Beach** (p173) Watching a great Shakespeare show in a tented Vanier Park theater, as the sun sets over the mountains behind the stage.

❸ **West 4th Avenue** (p167) Shopping for outdoor gear, vinyl records and great travel books.

❹ **Museum of Vancouver** (p166) Noodling around the nostalgic displays illuminating the yesteryear city, before adding the two other nearby museums to your day out.

❺ **Kitsilano Beach** (p166) Sunning yourself with the locals on the area's best beach before catching a free show at the Kitsilano Showboat stage.

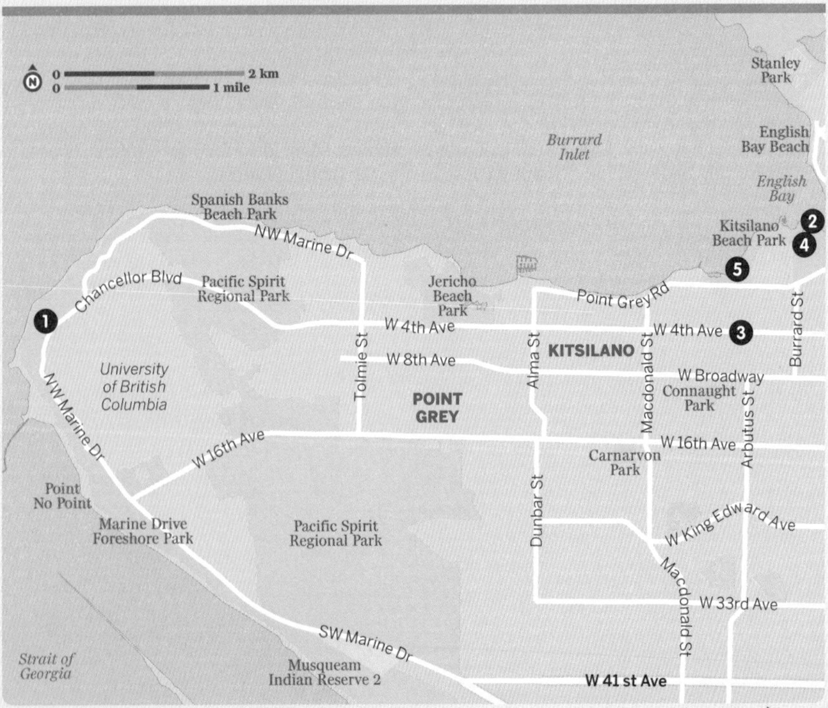

For more detail of this area see Map p282 and p286

Explore Kitsilano & University of British Columbia (UBC)

Kitsilano and UBC occupy the same peninsula, but you'll hit Kits first when traveling from downtown. The number 4 bus trundles along West 4th Ave, which is Kitsilano's best shopping district (especially west of Cypress St). Walk five blocks south and you'll come to Broadway, the other main Kits artery. West of Trafalgar St, it has its own village-like feel (and number 9 bus service), with many restaurants and boutique stores. Add the three museums in Vanier Park plus dinner for a full Kitsilano day out.

From Kits, hop back on a westbound bus to reach the end of the peninsula and the sprawling UBC campus. A great day-trip destination, UBC has museums, galleries and garden attractions to explore. There are even live music and theater venues if you fancy extending your visit. Frequent buses from UBC make it easy to return downtown at the end of the day.

Don't forget the beaches, either: the peninsula is lined with great sandy hangouts, from summertime-packed Kits Beach to UBC's naturist Wreck Beach.

Local Life

- **Cycling** The Arbutus Greenway (p166) takes you all the way to Marpole's Fraser River shoreline; watch for birds en route.
- **Hangouts** In summer, everyone in Vancouver seems to soak up the rays at Kitsilano Beach (p166).
- **Free shows** The Kitsilano Showboat (p175) is an annual tradition. Snag a bleacherlike perch and watch acts from Morris dancers to brass bands.
- **Markets** Peruse seasonal fruit and veg at the festival-like Kitsilano Farmers Market (p175).

Getting There & Away

- **Bus** Services 4 and 9 run through Kitsilano to UBC. The 99B-Line express also runs on Broadway to UBC.
- **Train** Take Canada Line SkyTrain from downtown to Broadway-City Hall, then hop on bus 9 or 99B-Line to UBC.
- **Car** There is metered parking on W 4th and Broadway in Kitsilano as well as surrounding side streets. UBC has metered parking and parking lots.

Lonely Planet's Top Tip

Many of Kitsilano's best restaurants are packed on weekends and finding a table can be a problem. Consider dining off-peak or coming on a weekday, when you'll have your pick of the best options. Breakfast and brunch are almost as popular as dinner among weekending locals, so follow the same rule for your first meal of the day; come early or late or wait for a weekday.

Best Places to Eat

- Fable Kitchen (p171)
- Linh Cafe (p171)
- Naam (p171)
- Maenam (p171)
- Sophie's Cosmic Cafe (p171)

For reviews, see p169.

Best Places to Drink

- Koerner's Pub (p173)
- Corduroy (p173)
- Wolf & Hound (p173)
- Galley Patio & Grill (p173)
- 49th Parallel Coffee (p172)

For reviews, see p172.

Best Places to Shop

- Kidsbooks (p175)
- Kitsilano Farmers Market (p175)
- Zulu Records (p176)
- Wanderlust (p176)
- Stepback (p176)

For reviews, see p175.

ALEXANDER HOWARD/LONELY PLANET ©

TOP EXPERIENCE

WANDER THE WORLD AT THE MUSEUM OF ANTHROPOLOGY

Vancouver's best museum is the main reason many visitors come to the University of British Columbia campus. The MOA is home to one of Canada's finest and most important collections of Northwest Coast indigenous art and artifacts. But that's just the start; the ambitious collection here goes way beyond local anthropological treasures, illuminating diverse cultures from around the world.

DON'T MISS

- Great Hall
- Free tours
- Multiversity Galleries
- Gallery of Northwest Coast Masterworks
- MOA gift shop

PRACTICALITIES

- MOA
- Map p286, A2
- ☎604-822-5087
- www.moa.ubc.ca
- 6393 NW Marine Dr, UBC
- adult/child $18/16
- ⏲10am-5pm Fri-Wed, 10am-9pm Thu, closed Mon Oct-May
- P
- 🚌99B-Line, then 68

MOA 101

The highlight of the Arthur Erickson–designed museum, the grand **Great Hall** (pictured) is a forest of dozens of towering totem poles plus a menagerie of carved ceremonial figures, house posts and delicate exhibits – all set against a giant floor-to-ceiling window facing the waterfront and mountains. Many of the ornate carvings are surprisingly vibrantly colored: look out for some smiling masks as well as a life-size rowing boat containing two figures that look ready to head straight out to sea on an adventure. The Great Hall is everyone's introduction to the museum – it's the first part you stroll into after paying your admission – and it's also where the **free tours** depart from several times a day: these are highly recommended since they provide an excellent overview of what else there is to see here.

Getting Lost

If you miss the tour or just want to go at your own pace, this is also a good museum in which to get lost. The **Gallery of Northwest Coast Masterworks** combines breathtaking smaller creations from the region, such as intricate ceremonial headdresses and a pipe shaped like an open-mouthed baby bird, with the recorded voices of Indigenous artisans contextualizing the exhibits. Nearby, the jam-packed **Multiversity Galleries** teem with more than 10,000 fascinating and often eye-popping ethnographic artifacts from cultures around the world. Closely packed into display cabinets, they're a sensory immersion: you'll find everything from Kenyan snuff bottles to Maori stone knives and ancient Greek jugs to Swedish lace doilies.

There's so much to see in this part of the museum that it can be a little overwhelming, but you can calm your brain in the soothing **European Ceramics Gallery**. Sometimes overlooked by visitors clambering to see the totem poles, it's a subtle stunner, created from a private collection of hundreds of pieces of delicately beautiful pottery and porcelain made between the 16th and 19th centuries. This gallery is rarely crowded, so you can usually peruse in relative tranquility: look out for detailed porcelain figures, ornate tea sets and a hulking tile-covered oven that once graced a busy kitchen.

Value-Added Extras

Aside from the regular permanent galleries, there are some diverse temporary exhibitions during the year. Do not leave before you've checked these out. Recent visiting shows have included photography from Nairobi, contemporary art from Papua New Guinea and puppets from around the world. Check MOA's website calendar before you arrive and for show openings and additional events. If it's a fine day, don't forget to walk around MOA's **Outdoor Exhibits** area as well; it includes two evocative Haida houses and some striking Musqueam house posts.

Before You Leave

The final part of anyone's visit should be the **gift shop**. While many museum stores are lame afterthoughts offering cheesy trinkets at inflated prices, MOA's version is far superior. And while you can certainly pick up T-shirts and art books here, the best purchases are the authentic indigenous arts and crafts created by local artisans. Look out for unique carved masks as well as intricately engraved gold and silver jewelry. In fact, you could start your own anthropology museum when you get back home.

MOA TOP TIPS

- ➡ Admission is cut to $10 from 5pm to 9pm every Thursday.
- ➡ There are free tours, included with entry, on most days. Check at the front desk for times.
- ➡ Entry to the Outdoor Exhibits area is free and does not require a ticket.
- ➡ There are several other attractions on campus; ask at the front desk for combined ticket options that include entry to some of these other UBC sites.

The museum was founded in the basement of the main campus library in 1949 and moved to its current purpose-built space in 1976. Architect Arthur Erickson's design was inspired by traditional post-and-beam structures built by regional Northwest Coast Indigenous communities. Since moving to its own space and undergoing some major renovations, the museum has almost doubled in size. Appropriately, it stands on traditional Musqueam land.

SIGHTS

Kitsilano's Vanier Park is home to a triumvirate of museums, and some of the city's best beaches stretch from here along the shoreline to the University of BC. The campus itself has more than enough attractions of its own to justify an alternative day out from the city center.

Kitsilano

★ARBUTUS GREENWAY PARK

Map p282 (www.vancouver.ca/parks; W 6th Ave & Fir St; 👪; 🚌4) A former disused urban rail line that's being transformed by the city into a cool linear park, this 8.5km-long flora-fringed walking and cycling route is already paved and open to the public. Running south to the Fraser River, it's a popular and accessible nature-hugging weave where you can expect to spot birdlife, butterflies and lots of wildflowers. There are Mobi public-bike share stations en route if you fancy hopping in the saddle.

You don't have to walk the whole thing; popular stops include the shops and restaurants of Kerrisdale and also **Marpole Museum**, an evocative little house furnished as a working-class residence of the early 1900s. Keep your eyes peeled for new additions to this park; public art and cool gathering places are being considered.

KITSILANO BEACH BEACH

Map p282 (cnr Cornwall Ave & Arbutus St; 🚌2) Facing English Bay, Kits Beach is one of Vancouver's favorite summertime hangouts. The wide, sandy expanse attracts buff Frisbee tossers and giggling volleyball players, and those who just like to preen while catching the rays. The ocean is fine for a dip, though serious swimmers should consider the heated **Kitsilano Pool** (Map p282; ☎604-731-0011; www.vancouverparks.ca; 2305 Cornwall Ave; adult/child $6.10/3.05; ⏰7am-evening mid-Jun–Sep; 👪), one of the world's largest outdoor saltwater pools.

Perch on a log on a summer afternoon and catch the breathtaking view of: one of the region's signature panoramas. You'll be treated to shimmering seafront backed by the twinkling glass towers of downtown and the North Shore mountains beyond. It's one of those vistas that will have you considering your emigration options.

MUSEUM OF VANCOUVER MUSEUM

Map p282 (MOV; ☎604-736-4431; www.museumofvancouver.ca; 1100 Chestnut St; adult/child $20.50/9.75; ⏰10am-5pm Sun-Wed, to 8pm Thu, to 9pm Fri & Sat; P 👪; 🚌2) The MOV serves up cool temporary exhibitions alongside in-depth permanent galleries of fascinating First Nations artifacts and evocative pioneer-era exhibits. But it really comes to life in its vibrant 1950s pop culture and 1960s hippie counterculture sections, a reminder that Kitsilano was once the grass-smoking centre of Vancouver's flower-power movement. Don't miss the shimmering gallery of vintage neon signs collected from around the city; it's a favorite with locals.

There are plenty of hands-on exhibits, including push-button tunes from local 1960s bands such as Mock Duck and Seeds of Time. The museum shop also has a well-curated array of T-shirts, local history books and indigenous-themed arts and gifts. Admission is by donation after 5pm on the last Thursday of every month.

HR MACMILLAN SPACE CENTRE MUSEUM

Map p282 (☎604-738-7827; www.spacecentre.ca; 1100 Chestnut St; adult/child $19.50/14; ⏰10am-5pm Jul & Aug, reduced hours off-season; P 👪; 🚌2) Focusing on the wonderful world of space, admission to this kid-favorite museum includes a gallery of hands-on exhibits (don't miss the Mars section where you can drive across the surface in a simulator) as well as a menu of live science demonstrations in the small theatre and a cool 45-minute planetarium show upstairs. Check the daily schedule of shows and presentations online before you arrive. The Saturday-night planetarium performances are popular with locals and typically draw a more adult crowd.

Peruse the website for a lively roster of additional special events, often including visits to the facility's observatory, a short walk from the main building.

VANIER PARK PARK

Map p282 (1000 Chestnut St; P; 🚌2) Winding around Kitsilano Point toward Kits Beach, waterfront Vanier Park is more a host than a destination. Home to three museums, it's also the venue for the tents of the annual Bard on the Beach (p173) Shakespeare festival. Bring takeout from Granville Island (a 10-minute stroll away via the seawall) to this popular picnic spot, and watch the local birdlife and kite-flyers do their thing.

SAVE YOUR DOSH

The **Vanier Park Explore Pass** costs adult/child $42.50/36.40 and covers entry to the Museum of Vancouver (MOV), Vancouver Maritime Museum and HR MacMillan Space Centre. It's available at each of the three attractions and can save you around $10 on individual adult entry. There is also an alternate **Dual Pass** (adult/child $31.50/18.50) that covers the MOV and the Space Centre only.

You can also save with two separate passes at the university. The **UBC Museums Pass** (adult/child/family $25/20/60) includes entry to the Museum of Anthropology (MOA) and Beaty Biodiversity Museum, while the **UBC Gardens and MOA Pass** (adult/child/family $27/23/65) covers the Museum of Anthropology, UBC Botanical Garden and Nitobe Memorial Garden.

WEST 4TH AVENUE AREA

Map p282 (www.shopwest4th.com; 4th Ave; 4) This strollable smorgasbord of stores and restaurants may have your credit cards whimpering for mercy after a couple of hours. Since Kits is now a bit of a middle-class utopia, shops that once sold cheap groceries are now more likely to be hawking designer yoga gear, hundred-dollar hiking socks and exotic (and unfamiliar) fruits from around the world.

OLD HASTINGS MILL STORE MUSEUM MUSEUM

Map p282 (604-734-1212; www.hastingsmillmuseum.ca; 1575 Alma St; by donation; 1-4pm Tue-Sun Jun-Sep, 1-4pm Sat & Sun Feb-May; 4) Built near Gastown in 1865, this gabled wooden structure is Vancouver's oldest surviving building. Originally a store for sawmill workers, it made it through the Great Fire of 1886 and was used as a makeshift morgue on that tragic day. Saved from demolition by locals, it was floated here in the 1930s and now houses an eclectic array of pioneer-era and First Nations exhibits.

VANCOUVER MARITIME MUSEUM MUSEUM

Map p282 (604-257-8300; www.vancouvermaritimemuseum.com; 1905 Ogden Ave; adult/child $13.50/10; 10am-5pm Fri-Wed, to 8pm Thu; P; 2) Teeming with salty seafaring artifacts, dozens of intricate ship models and a couple of walk-through recreated boat sections, the prize exhibit at this waterfront A-frame museum is the *St Roch,* a 1928 Royal Canadian Mounted Police Arctic patrol vessel that was the first to navigate the Northwest Passage in both directions. Entry includes timed access to this celebrated boat and you can also try your hand at piloting it via a cool wheelhouse simulator.

UBC

MUSEUM OF ANTHROPOLOGY MUSEUM

See p164.

UBC BOTANICAL GARDEN GARDENS

Map p286 (604-822-4208; www.botanicalgarden.ubc.ca; 6804 SW Marine Dr; adult/child $10/5; 10am-4:30pm; 99B-Line, then 68) You'll find a huge array of rhododendrons, a fascinating apothecary plot and a winter green space of off-season bloomers in this 28-hectare complex of themed gardens. Among the towering trees, look for northern flicker woodpeckers and chittering little Douglas squirrels. Also save time for the attraction's April-to-October Greenheart TreeWalk (p169), which elevates visitors up to 23m above the forest floor on a 310m guided ecotour. The combined garden and Greenheart ticket costs adult/child $23/10.

Check the garden's website Events page before your visit; themed walking tours are available on selected days. Make sure you drop into the gift shop before you leave, for its brilliantly curated collection of green-thumbed books and trinkets. Here in October? The annual UBC Apple Festival (p172) is also staged right here; it's the highlight of the year for the kind of locals and visitors who love munching on Cox's Orange Pippins.

BEATY BIODIVERSITY MUSEUM MUSEUM

Map p286 (604-827-4955; www.beatymuseum.ubc.ca; 2212 Main Mall; adult/child $14/10; 10am-5pm Tue-Sun; 99B-Line) A family-friendly museum showcasing a two-million-item natural-history collection including birds, fossils and herbarium displays. The highlight is the 25m blue-whale skeleton, artfully displayed in the two-story entranceway. Don't miss the first display case, which is crammed with a beady-eyed menagerie of tooth-and-claw taxidermy. Consider visiting on the third Thursday of the month when

BLAST FROM THE PAST

Kitsilano was named after Chief Khatsahlano, leader of the First Nations village of Sun'ahk, which occupied the area now designated as Vanier Park. In 1901 the local government displaced the entire community, sending some families to the Capilano Indian Reserve on the North Shore and others to Squamish.

The first Kits streetcar service in 1905 triggered an explosion of housing development, but by the 1960s many of these homes had been converted for university students, sparking the 'beatnik ghetto' that soon defined Kits. Fueled by pungent BC bud, counterculture political movements mushroomed – including a little group of antinuclear protesters that a few years later became Greenpeace. But Khatsahlano has not been completely forgotten: every July, the neighborhood's biggest community festival is a day-long celebration on 4th Ave featuring more than 50 live bands. It is the area's most popular (and best attended) event, called the **Khatsahlano Street Party** (www.khatsahlano.com; 4th Ave, btwn Burrard & Macdonald Sts, Kitsilano; ⌚Jul; 🚌4).

entry is by donation after 5pm and the museum stays open until 8:30pm; there's often a special theme or live performance for these monthly Nocturnal events.

Many of the exhibits are in pullout drawers, so you can spend hours poking around. There's also a surprisingly well-stocked gift shop with some excellent nature-themed books and cool wildlife-themed knickknacks (bird-species stuffies recommended). And if you're curious about that humongous whale, start your visit by viewing *Raising Big Blue;* the free movie that tells its story is screened in the museum's auditorium throughout the day.

PACIFIC MUSEUM OF EARTH — MUSEUM

Map p286 (☎604-822-6992; www.pme.ubc.ca; 6339 Store Rd; by donation; ⌚10am-5pm Mon-Fri; 👪; 🚌99B-Line) Across from the Beaty Biodiversity Museum (p167), this sparkling little attraction has really upped its game in recent years. The cabinets of shimmering minerals come with handset audio narrations, while its darkened **Globe & Gem Gallery**, centered on an Earth-shaped projection screen, is surrounded by gold and jewelry exhibits. But 'George,' the wall-mounted duck-billed dinosaur skeleton, is the museum's star – perfect for a 75-million-year-old selfie. Nearby, there's also a large dino bone that you're encouraged to (gently) touch.

It's great for kids who love rocks, gems and dinosaurs. Don't miss the tornado machine where they can also create their own twister at the touch of a button. The museum has been on an expansion kick that should see it become a much more popular UBC attraction in the future; check its website for the latest developments.

PACIFIC SPIRIT REGIONAL PARK — PARK

Map p286 (☎604-224-5739; www.pacificspiritparksociety.org; cnr Blanca St & W 16th Ave; ⌚dawn-dusk; P; 🚌99B-Line) This stunning 763-hectare park stretches from Burrard Inlet to the North Arm of the Fraser River, a green buffer zone between the UBC campus and the city. A smashing spot to explore with a wide array of walking, jogging and cycling trails, it includes **Camosun Bog wetland** (accessed by a boardwalk at 19th Ave and Camosun St), a bird and plant haven.

Some of the more dense forest trails give an indication of what Vancouver would have looked like before it was developed: a rich, verdant jungle of huge ferns, unencumbered birdlife (including bald eagles) and towering trees arching overhead.

CHUNG COLLECTION — MUSEUM

Map p286 (☎602-822-2521; http://chung.library.ubc.ca; 1961 East Mall, Irving K Barber Learning Centre; ⌚10am-4pm Mon-Fri; 🚌99B-Line) FREE Leave your photo ID at the front desk of the lower level of UBC's main library building, and then wander around a roomful of exhibits chronicling the early days of BC's Chinese history plus the golden age of the Canadian Pacific Railway Company. Check out the romantic travel posters and brochures, sparkling steamship dinner services and intricate scale model of the *Empress of Asia* vessel. Free public tours are offered on Thursdays at 11am.

Traveling bookworms should also drop by the library on Wednesdays at 11am when there's a free one-hour public tour of the Rare Books and Special Collections department, Harry Potter artifacts included.

GREENHEART TREEWALK AMUSEMENT PARK
Map p286 (☎604-822-4208; www.botanicalgarden.ubc.ca; 6804 SW Marine Dr, UBC Botanical Garden, UBC; adult/child $23/10; ⏰Apr-Oct; P 👪; 🚌99B-Line, then 68) One of the best ways to commune with nature is to pretend you're a squirrel. While costumes are not required for this cool canopy walkway (you may win a raised eyebrow if you chance it), visitors love swaying across the steel bridges and noodling around the wooden platforms up to 23m from the forest floor. Located inside UBC Botanical Garden (p167), Greenheart admission includes entry to that attraction.

NITOBE MEMORIAL GARDEN GARDENS
Map p286 (☎604-822-6038; www.botanicalgarden.ubc.ca/nitobe; 1895 Lower Mall; adult/child $7/4 Apr-Oct, by donation Nov-Mar; ⏰10am-4:30pm Apr-Oct, 10am-2pm Mon-Fri Nov-Mar; 🚌99B-Line, then 68) Exemplifying Japanese horticultural philosophies, this is a delightfully tranquil green oasis of peaceful pathways, small traditional bridges and a large, moss-banked pond filled with plump koi carp. It's named after Dr Inazo Nitobe, a scholar whose mug appears on Japan's ¥5000 bill. Consider a springtime visit for the florid cherry blossom displays and keep your eyes peeled for the occasional turtle basking in the sun.

WRECK BEACH BEACH
Map p286 (☎604-224-5739; www.wreckbeach.org; via Trail 6; 🚌99B-Line, then 68) Follow Trail 6 into the woods and down the steep steps to find Vancouver's only official naturist beach, complete with a motley crew of counterculture locals, independent vendors and sunburned regulars. The pants-free bunch are a generally welcoming group, so long as you're not just there to gawk; start your visit on the right foot by quickly peeling off in solidarity.

Time your visit well and you can take part in August's annual **Bare Buns Fun Run**. And if you fancy connecting with other local naturists during your stay, check in with the Van Tan Nudist Club (www.vantan.ca) for events, including regular swimming meets at local pools.

MORRIS & HELEN BELKIN ART GALLERY GALLERY
Map p286 (☎604-822-2759; www.belkin.ubc.ca; 1825 Main Mall; ⏰10am-5pm Tue-Fri, noon-5pm Sat & Sun; 🚌99B-Line, then 68) FREE This ever-intriguing gallery specializes in contemporary and often quite challenging pieces, with chin-stroking new exhibitions opening in its high-ceilinged, white-walled spaces throughout the year. Check ahead for workshops and presentations, often covering key or emerging themes in avant-garde art.

EATING

Kitsilano's two main arteries – W 4th Ave and Broadway – offer a healthy mix of places to eat: it's well worth the trek here to lounge on a beach or stroll the shopping areas, then end your day with a rewarding meal. The neighborhood's hippie past has left a legacy of vegetarian-friendly restaurants, but Kits' more recent wealth means there are also some top-notch high-end options well worth a splurge. If you're at UBC, there are some good dining options available; alternatively, hop on a bus to nearby Kitsilano for a far superior selection.

Kitsilano

★**UNO GELATO** ICE CREAM $
Map p282 (☎604-733-5884; www.unogelato.com; 2579 W Broadway; 1/2 scoops $6/7.50; ⏰noon-9pm; 🌱; 🚌9) Globally feted Vancouver gelato maestro James Coleridge has reinvented his business with a cool new brand and an endlessly tempting array of perfectly executed flavors. The menu changes with the seasons but often features unmissable classics such as salted caramel, chocolate brownie and an utterly delightful (and vegan) lemon that may make you weep with pleasure.

Ingredients are routinely sourced from local farms and dairies and many are also organic.

CAFE LOKAL CAFE $
Map p282 (☎604-739-0098; www.cafelokal.ca; 2610 W 4th Ave; mains $8-10; ⏰7:30am-6pm; 📶 👪; 🚌4) A highly welcoming neighborhood hangout lined with mismatched wooden seating and soundtracked with warm jazz recordings. Drop by for coffee, house-baked treats (cinnamon buns recommended) or a freshly prepared panini and you'll likely find yourself staying much longer than you

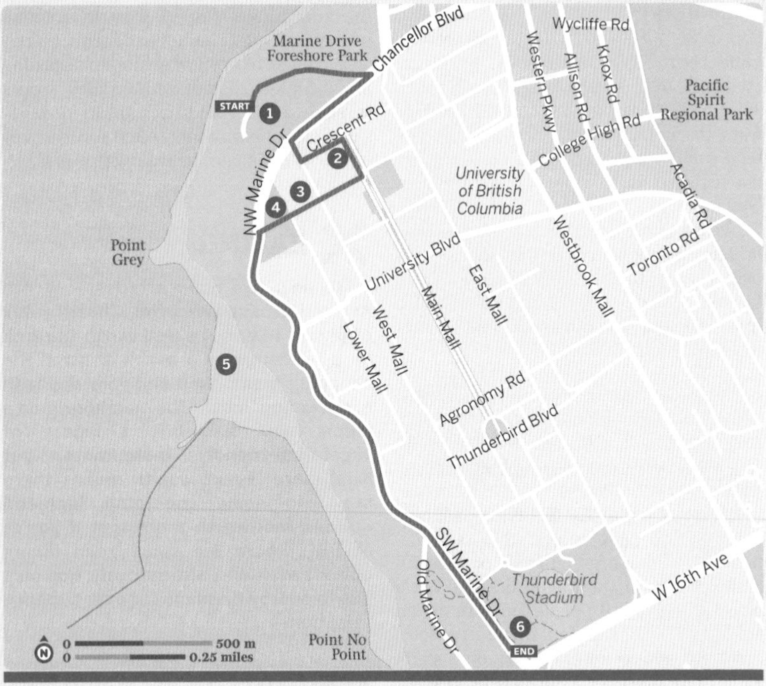

Neighborhood Walk
UBC Campus & Gardens Walk

START MUSEUM OF ANTHROPOLOGY
END UBC BOTANICAL GARDEN
LENGTH 3KM; 1½ HOURS

This walk introduces you to UBC's leading cultural attractions and celebrated gardens. Keep your camera ready for the many public artworks that dot the campus.

Start at Vancouver's best museum, the **1 Museum of Anthropology** (p164), where you'll gain an appreciation for the culture and artistry of the region's original residents. Make sure you take some photos of the towering totem poles in the main atrium.

Cross NW Marine Dr and head down West Mall, turning left on Crescent Rd then right onto Main Mall. On your right is the free-entry **2 Morris & Helen Belkin Art Gallery** (p169), which stages changing and sometimes challenging exhibitions of contemporary art.

Continue southwards along Main Mall, then turn right onto Memorial Rd. Continue downhill until you come to the rock garden of the **3 UBC Asian Centre**, on your right. The boulders here are inscribed with Confucian philosophies.

Continue along Memorial to the oasis-like, Japanese-themed **4 Nitobe Memorial Garden** (p169). Immerse yourself in the site's subtle yet meaningful design – and look for turtles in the pond.

Return to NW Marine Dr and continue southeastwards for about 1km. If you're feeling adventurous, look for the signs for Trail 6. Follow this to the waterfront, where you can disrobe – you're on **5 Wreck Beach** (p169), Vancouver's official naturist beach.

Continue along NW Marine Dr (make sure you've put your clothes back on first) until it becomes SW Marine Dr. Near the intersection with W 16th Ave, you'll find **6 UBC Botanical Garden** (p167). Wander through the verdant site and save time for the Greenheart TreeWalk, an elevated stroll through the trees via platforms and suspension bridges.

anticipated. Traveling with kids? There's also a shelf of games and toys, plus several child-sized options on the menu.

NAAM VEGETARIAN **$**

Map p282 (☎604-738-7151; www.thenaam.com; 2724 W 4th Ave; mains $9-17; ⊙24hr; ; 4) An evocative relic of Kitsilano's hippie past, this vegetarian restaurant has the feel of a comfy farmhouse. It's not unusual to wait for a table at peak times, but it's worth it for the huge menu of hearty stir-fries, nightly curry specials, bulging quesadillas and ever-popular fries with miso gravy. It's the kind of veggie spot where carnivores delightedly dine.

There's live music several nights a week, as well as good beers (go for Nelson Brewing's Organic IPA) and a popular patio – it's covered, so you can cozy up here and still enjoy the rain. Happy hour is 3pm to 6pm weekdays and typically includes good food specials.

LINH CAFE FRENCH, VIETNAMESE **$$**

Map p282 (☎604-559-4668; www.linhcafe.com; 2836 W 4th Ave; mains $14-45; ⊙11am-9pm Wed-Fri, 10am-9pm Sat & Sun; ; 4) Arrive off-peak (limited reservations are also available) at this chatty locals' favorite, a friendly, red-tabled restaurant serving French bistro classics and enticing Vietnamese specialties. You'll find everything from escargot to steak frites on the eclectic menu, but we recommend the deliciously brothy beef pho. On your way out, add a shiny little palmier pastry and a Vietnamese coffee to go.

This is also a highly popular brunch spot, serving generously portioned dishes including a delicious Brittany Breakfast of seafood-infused scrambled eggs.

FABLE KITCHEN CANADIAN **$$**

Map p282 (☎604-732-1322; www.fablekitchen.ca; 1944 W 4th Ave; mains $21-28; ⊙11am-2:30pm & 5:30-10pm Tue-Fri, 10am-2pm & 5-10pm Sat & Sun; 4) One of Vancouver's favorite farm-to-table restaurants is a lovely rustic-chic room of exposed brick, wood beams and prominently displayed red rooster logos. But looks are just part of the appeal. Expect perfectly prepared bistro dishes showcasing local seasonal ingredients such as duck, pork and scallops. It's great gourmet comfort food with little pretension, hence the packed room most nights. Reservations recommended.

The lunch and brunch menu – including an excellent *croque madame* – is invitingly priced if you're planning to be in Kits earlier in the day.

MAENAM THAI **$$**

Map p282 (☎604-730-5579; www.maenam.ca; 1938 W 4th Ave; mains $22-30; ⊙noon-2pm Tue-Sat, 5-10pm daily; ; 4) Kitsilano's best Thai restaurant is a contemporary reinvention of the concept, with subtle, complex influences flavoring the menu in a warm, wood-floored room with an inviting ambience. You can start with the familiar (although even the Pad Thai here is eye-poppingly different), but save room for something new, such as the utterly delicious lamb shank with red cumin curry.

SOPHIE'S COSMIC CAFE DINER **$$**

Map p282 (☎604-732-6810; www.sophiescosmiccafe.com; 2095 W 4th Ave; mains $14-19; ⊙8am-2:30pm Mon & Tue, 8am-8pm Wed-Sun; ; 4) Slide between the oversized knife and fork flanking the entrance and you'll find one of Vancouver's best retro-look diners, its kitsch-lined walls studded with everything from Village People albums to Charlie's Angels lunch boxes. Burgers and huge milkshakes dominate the menu, but breakfast (try the bulging Spanish omelet) is the best reason to snag a booth. Expect weekend queues.

LA CIGALE FRENCH BISTRO FRENCH **$$**

Map p282 (☎604-732-0004; www.lacigale.ca; 1961 W 4th Ave; mains $19-35; ⊙11:30am-2:30pm & 5-10pm Tue-Fri, 10:30am-2:30pm & 5-10pm Sat & Sun; 4) A charming neighborhood bistro with a casual contemporary feel, La Cigale's menu combines traditional French recipes with local ingredients and simple, flavor-revealing preparations. Expect hearty nosh including practically perfect filet mignon and velvet-soft braised beef cheeks. We recommend the three-course Sunday-to-Thursday $32 *prix-fixe* special. In summer, the garage-like front windows are thrown open so it feels like you're dining alfresco.

BISHOP'S NORTHWESTERN US **$$$**

Map p282 (☎604-738-2025; www.bishopsonline.com; 2183 W 4th Ave; mains $36-45; ⊙5:30-11pm; 4) Behind its anonymous exterior, Bishop's pioneered West Coast 'locavore' dining long before the farm-to-table movement arrived. Legendary chef-owner John Bishop is still

LOCAL KNOWLEDGE

UBC'S BEST FEST

From Salish to Aurora Golden Gala and from Gravensteins to Cox's Orange Pippins, fans of the real king of fruit have plenty to bite into at the autumnal, weekend-long **Apple Festival** (604-822-4208; www.ubcbotanicalgarden.org/events; 6804 SW Marine Dr, UBC Botanical Garden, UBC; adult/child $5/free; mid-Oct; ; 99B-Line, then 68). Staged every October at the UBC Botanical Garden (p167), it's one of Vancouver's most popular community events. Along with live music and demonstrations on grafting and cider-making, there are lots of smile-triggering children's activities. But the event's main lure is the chance to nibble on a vast array of around 18,000kg of BC-grown treats that make most supermarket apples taste like hockey pucks.

The best way to sample as many as possible is to pay an extra $5 and dive into the **Tasting Tent**. Here, dozens of locally grown heritage and more recent varieties are available for considered scoffing, including rarities such as Crestons and Oaken Pins. Before you leave, follow your nose to the sweet aroma of perhaps the best apple pie you'll ever taste. The deep-dish, golden-crusted slices for sale here are a highlight of the festival, and an indulgence you could happily eat until you explode – with an apple-flavored smile on your face.

at the top of his game, serving outstanding dishes in a warm, elegant room where white tablecloths and silver candlesticks are de rigueur. Expect a seasonally changing menu that could include Haida Gwaii halibut or Fraser Valley lamb.

The service here is pitch-perfect, so stay a little longer and indulge in dessert. And look out for the man himself; he'll almost certainly drop by your table to say hi and will sign a copy of his cookbook *Fresh* if you wave it in front of him. Reservations recommended.

UBC

JAMJAR CANTEEN — LEBANESE $

Map p286 (604-620-5320; www.jamjarcanteen.ca; 6035 University Blvd; mains $10-12; 10:30am-10pm Mon-Fri, to 9pm Sat & Sun; ; 99B-Line) Visiting Canteen, a simplified version of the city's highly popular Jamjar Lebanese comfort-food restaurants, means choosing from four mains (lamb sausages or deep-fried cauliflower recommended) then adding the approach: rice bowl, salad bowl or wrap. Choices of olives, veggies, hummus and more are then requested before you can dive into your hearty lunch or dinner.

RAIN OR SHINE — ICE CREAM $

Map p286 (604-620-2004; www.rainorshineicecream.com; 6001 University Blvd; scoop single/double $4.50/6; 11am-10pm Mon-Fri, 10am-10pm Sat & Sun; 99B-Line) Tucked around the corner from a row of eateries serving everything from noodle bowls to Lebanese dishes, this small outpost of one of Vancouver's favorite artisan ice creameries is the perfect place for dessert. Expect to queue on sunny days; it's worth it for an ever-changing array of lip-smacking varieties often including such exotics as honey lavender and blueberry balsamic.

If you can't make it to UBC or Cambie Village (p152), there's another Rain or Shine in Kitsilano, located at 1926 W 4th Ave.

DRINKING & NIGHTLIFE

You can only hang out at the beach and wander the shops in Kits for so long. After a while, the bars will start calling your name. Don't be afraid to listen. UBC has a couple of good watering holes, which are great if you need a drink on campus, but there's a wider selection a short bus ride away.

49TH PARALLEL COFFEE — COFFEE

Map p282 (604-420-4901; www.49thcafe.com; 2198 W 4th Ave; 7am-7pm Sun-Thu, to 8pm Fri & Sat; ; 4) Kitsilano's favorite coffee shop hangout. Sit with the locals in the glass-enclosed conservatory-like area (handy in the deluge-prone Raincouver) while sipping your latte in a turquoise cup and scoffing as many of the own-brand Luckys Doughnuts as you can manage; just because they're artisanal, that doesn't mean you should have only one. Need a recommendation? How about trying an apple-bacon fritter. Or two.

This company also roasts its own beans, which means that you're unlikely to leave disappointed. The tables here are often dominated by fashionable young parents and their strollers, so maybe visit off-peak or stroll along shop-lined W 4th with a take-out cup.

CORDUROY — BAR

Map p282 (☎604-733-0162; www.corduroyrestaurant.com; 1943 Cornwall Ave; ⊙4pm-2am Mon-Sat, to midnight Sun; 📶; 🚌2) Situated near the first bus stop after the Burrard Bridge (coming from downtown), this intimate, cave-like hangout is arguably one of Kitsilano's best late-night haunts. Slide yourself onto a seat and peruse the beady-eyed taxidermy before ordering a pitcher of the house beer from the shingle-backed bar. A lively show roster (check ahead via its Facebook page) often includes bands, comedy or open-mike shenanigans.

Comfort food ranging from burgers to pierogi dominates the dining menu here, but we can't recommend the pizza enough (go for the spicy lamb).

GALLEY PATIO & GRILL — PUB

Map p282 (☎604-222-1331; www.thegalley.ca; 1300 Discovery St, Jericho Sailing Centre; ⊙10am-10pm Mon-Fri, 9am-10pm Sat & Sun, reduced hours off-season; 📶👪; 🚌4) At sunset, plop yourself down on one of the plastic patio chairs and then spend your evening eyeballing the sailboats steering toward shore as the pyrotechnic sky unfolds. There are usually a couple of BC wine offerings available, along with tasty local beers from R&B Brewing (Red Devil Pale Ale recommended). Grub is of the beer-battered fish-and-chips variety, but the salmon burger is recommended.

This 2nd-floor spot is a family-friendly joint where you'll mostly meet locals. They're always up for a chat and you can quiz them about other sunset-viewing spots around the city (they'll likely mention Third Beach in Stanley Park).

KOERNER'S PUB — PUB

Map p286 (☎604-827-1443; www.koerners.ca; 6371 Crescent Rd, UBC; ⊙11:30am-10:30pm Mon & Tue, to midnight Wed-Fri; 🚌99B-Line) UBC's best pub makes for a welcoming spot with its communal tables, foliage-fringed patio and clientele of nerdy professors and hipster regulars. There's an excellent booze list; dive into BC craft beers from the likes of Driftwood and Strange Fellows. Food-wise, the Koerner Organic Burger is a staple, but also try the crunchy UBC Farm Harvest Salad, largely sourced from the university's own farm.

There are $4 beer deals during the 2pm-to-4pm daily happy hour, plus additional specials throughout the week; ask your server for details. It's a bit hard to find Koerner's; just head along West Mall toward NW Marine Dr and you'll find the entrance located up a slight incline on the last driveway.

WOLF & HOUND — PUB

Map p282 (☎604-738-8909; www.wolfandhound.ca; 3617 W Broadway; ⊙4-10:30pm Mon, noon-midnight Tue-Thu, noon-1am Fri & Sat, 11am-11pm Sun; 📶; 🚌4) At UBC's nearest good pub and one of Vancouver's best Irish watering holes, you'll be sure to find plenty of students avoiding their assignments. They come to down some pints, watch TV sports or catch free live music, often of the lyrical Celtic persuasion. Harp and Smithwick's join Ireland's fave stout on the beer list alongside some good BC craft brews.

Try comparing the delicious Vancouver-made Storm Black Plague Stout with a more traditional glass or two of Guinness and you'll soon be singing a merry ballad. Food-wise, you'll find all the usual heaping pub grub classics, from fish and chips to bangers and mash.

☆ ENTERTAINMENT

From cinema to live shows to Vancouver's favorite summertime theatrical event, there's a small but excellent array of things to do on a night out here.

★BARD ON THE BEACH — PERFORMING ARTS

Map p282 (☎604-739-0559; www.bardonthebeach.org; 1695 Whyte Ave, Vanier Park, Kitsilano; tickets from $24; ⊙Jun-Sep; 👪; 🚌2) Watching Shakespeare performed while the sun slowly sets over the mountains beyond the tented main stage is one of Vancouver's summertime highlights. There are usually three Shakespeare plays, plus one Bard-related work (*Rosencrantz and Guildenstern*

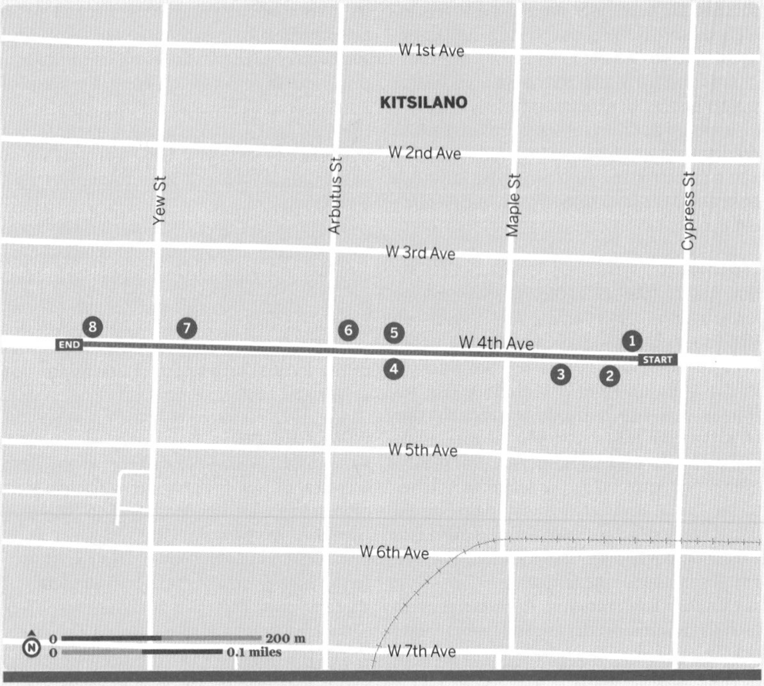

Neighborhood Walk Kitsilano Food-for-Thought Hop

START WANDERLUST
END GRAVITY POPE
LENGTH 1KM; ONE HOUR

This walk will introduce you to Kitsilano's W 4th Ave neighborhood and two of its main obsessions: shopping and dining.

Kick things off with a pre-lunch visit to 1 **Wanderlust** (p176), Vancouver's biggest travel bookstore (check out the display of 1970s Lonely Planet editions). Then, nip across the street and continue west on W 4th for a brunch at 2 **Fable Kitchen** (p171), a popular farm-to-table joint.

Once you're full, continue on to nearby 3 **Zulu Records** (p176), a *High Fidelity*–style music-store legend. Browse the vinyl among the local musos here, and ask the all-knowing staff about Vancouver bands to discover during your visit (concert tickets are available here).

You're now in the heart of the Kits shopping district. On the next block, that includes leaf-loving 4 **Silk Road Tea** (p176) and, across the street, 5 **Arc'teryx** (p177), a Vancouver premium outdoor clothing brand. If all that shopping requires a midafternoon pick-me-up, snag a diner perch among the kitsch-tastic decor at 6 **Sophie's Cosmic Cafe** (p171); apple pie recommended.

It's unlikely you'll be hungry at this stage, but peruse a few restaurant window menus during your wander. Be sure to include 7 **Bishop's** (p171) as a potential dinner option. Check its fine-dining seasonal menu and, if you like what you see, call ahead to reserve a table. It will likely be one of your trip's most memorable meals.

But since it's not dinnertime yet, continue west and salve your appetite for fashion instead at 8 **Gravity Pope** (p176). Women and men are treated as clothes-loving equals here, but it's the shoes that stand out: buy a pair and work them in with a little more Kitsilano strolling.

are Dead, for example), to choose from during the season. Q&A talks are staged after some of the Tuesday performances; also opera, fireworks and wine-tasting special nights are held throughout the season.

Expect Christopher Gaze – the festival's effervescent public figurehead – to hop on stage to introduce the show. He's the kind of old-school actor-manager that Shakespeare himself would have appreciated. And make sure you save some time to hit the on-site gift shop; it's the perfect place to pick up that Shakespearean insult T-shirt you've always wanted, you poisonous bunch-backed toad.

KITSILANO SHOWBOAT — CONCERT VENUE

Map p282 (☎604-734-7332; www.kitsilanoshowboat.com; 2300 Cornwall Ave, Kitsilano; free; ⏰7pm Mon, Wed, Fri & Sat Jun-Aug; 👪; 🚌2) An 80-year-old tradition that generations of locals know and love, this alfresco waterfront stage near Kits Pool offers free shows and concerts in summer. Grab a bleacher-style seat facing the North Shore mountains and prepare to be entertained by singers, musicians, dancers and more; check the online schedule to see what's coming up. A great way to mingle with the friendly and ever chatty locals.

JERICHO FOLK CLUB — WORLD MUSIC

Map p282 (www.jerichofolkclub.ca; 1300 Discovery St, Jericho Sailing Centre, Kitsilano; $10; ⏰7pm Tue twice-monthly May-Sep; 🚌4) These fun folkie meet-up nights include everything from an open-stage session, support act, jam time and the 9pm main act. Local and visiting performers may be scheduled and you can check the online calendar to see who's coming up. The definition of folk here is pretty loose and can include anything from Celtic and bluegrass to guitar-wielding singer-songwriters, but you're almost always guaranteed a great time. Cash only.

CINEPLEX FIFTH AVENUE CINEMAS — CINEMA

Map p282 (☎604-734-7469; www.cineplex.com; 2110 Burrard St, Kitsilano; tickets $13.50; 🚌44) Kitsilano's biggest movie house, popular Fifth Avenue screens indie films, foreign flicks and blockbuster Hollywood schlock (those locals might look like intellectuals, but they enjoy Marvel movies as much as anyone else). This is one of Cineplex' adult-focused cinemas, which means there's an on-site bar and you must be 19-plus to watch a movie here.

SHOPPING

West 4th Avenue is one of Vancouver's best strollable shopping strips, especially on the stretch west of Cypress Street, where outdoor gear is among the area's specialties. There are also several large bike, board and skate shops between Pine Street and Burrard Street. Nip five blocks south to Broadway for another round of good local stores and bookshops, especially west of Trafalgar Street.

★KITSILANO FARMERS MARKET — MARKET

Map p282 (www.eatlocal.org; 2690 Larch St, Kitsilano Community Centre, Kitsilano; ⏰10am-2pm Sun May-Oct; 🚌9) 🍃 This seasonal farmers market is one of the city's most popular and is Kitsilano's best excuse to get out and hang with the locals. Arrive early for the best selection and you'll have the pick of freshly plucked local fruit and veg, such as sweet strawberries or spectacularly flavorful heirloom tomatoes. You'll likely never want to shop in a mainstream supermarket again.

Save some tummy room for the baked treats and peruse the arts and crafts; there may be something here of the handmade variety that will serve as a perfect souvenir of your West Coast visit.

KIDSBOOKS — BOOKS

Map p282 (☎604-738-5335; www.kidsbooks.ca; 2557 W Broadway, Kitsilano; ⏰9:30am-6pm Mon-Thu & Sat, 9:30am-9pm Fri, 11am-6pm Sun; 👪; 🚌9) From *Dolphin Boy* to *The Wonky Donkey,* this huge, highly inviting store – reputedly Canada's biggest children's bookshop – has thousands of novels, picture books and anything else you can think of to keep your bookish sprogs happy. There are regular author events (check ahead via the website) plus quality toys and games to provide a break from all that strenuous page-turning.

And if *Creepy Pair of Underwear* is not your idea of a great read (you're wrong, by the way), there's also a cleverly curated array of books for adults to explore.

THE DOPE ON LOCAL POT SHOPS

Just a couple of years ago, Vancouver had dozens of storefront marijuana dispensaries operating in a gray area of law that accepted the personal use of cannabis for medical reasons. But when national legislation changed to allow recreational use of the drug, the city and the province moved to regulate this 'Wild West' industry. Rather than navigate through the rigorous new licensing laws, many of these weed stores suddenly shut down.

The 2.0 version of Vancouver's pot shops is now emerging, with licensed shops and mini-chains including City Cannabis Co, Hobo Recreational Cannabis and Evergreen Cannabis Society now serving curious customers around the city. And where do they get their grass from? The province's BC Liquor Distribution Branch, longtime controller of booze sales in the region, is now the only legal way for private pot shops to source supplies for recreational resale. It remains to be seen if this new business model will thrive, or if Vancouver's long-time 'BC bud' users will simply keep buying from their friendly (and cheaper) neighborhood suppliers. Need more info? Check out the province's BC Cannabis Stores website at www.bccannabisstores.com.

WANDERLUST SPORTS & OUTDOORS

Map p282 (☎604-739-2182; www.wanderlustore.com; 1929 W 4th Ave, Kitsilano; ⊙10am-7pm Mon-Fri, 10am-6pm Sat, noon-5pm Sun; 🚌4) Divided between Vancouver's best selection of guidebooks and travel literature (plus maps) on one side and a huge array of luggage, backpacks and travel accessories on the other, the chatty, ever-friendly staffers here have been inspiring itchy feet for years. Peruse the money belts and mosquito nets, then wonder how you ever traveled without quick-drying underwear.

Check out the vintage guidebooks on display here, including some very early Lonely Planet *Shoestring* titles.

ZULU RECORDS MUSIC

Map p282 (☎604-738-3232; www.zulurecords.com; 1972 W 4th Ave, Kitsilano; ⊙10:30am-7pm Mon-Wed, 10:30am-9pm Thu & Fri, 9:30am-6:30pm Sat, noon-6pm Sun; 🚌4) Kitsilano's fave indie music store has downsized in recent years, but it's still easy to blow an afternoon here with the vinyl and CD nerds, flicking through the new, used and hard-to-find albums. It also sells local show tickets, while the knowledgeable staffers can point you to essential Vancouver recordings worth buying (ask for a copy of *Last Call*).

STEPBACK HOMEWARES

Map p282 (☎604-731-7525; www.stepback.ca; 2936 W Broadway, Kitsilano; ⊙11am-5:30pm Mon-Fri, 10am-6pm Sat, noon-5pm Sun; 🚌9) If your to-buy list includes taxidermy, vintage cameras and old hotel matchbooks, this cleverly curated, highly browsable shop is the place for you. Among the new and used trinkets, homewares and accessories, look out for old pulp-fiction paperbacks and yesteryear postcards of historic Vancouver. There are usually far more people looking than buying; this place almost feels like a museum.

SILK ROAD TEA TEA

Map p282 (☎778-379-8481; www.silkroadteastore.com; 2066 W 4th Ave, Kitsilano; ⊙10am-6pm Mon-Sat, to 5pm Sun; 🚌4) Plunging into the scalding hot Kitsilano tea-boutique wars, this satellite branch of Victoria's favorite fancy-tea emporium combines superbly friendly staff with a lip-smacking array of hundreds of leafy varieties. A bag of Berry Victoria is a recommended souvenir, while the fragrant Angelwater has a cult local following and is reputedly a perfect antidote to jet lag.

GRAVITY POPE SHOES

Map p282 (☎604-731-7673; www.gravitypope.com; 2205 W 4th Ave, Kitsilano; ⊙10am-9pm Mon-Fri, 10am-7pm Sat, 11am-6pm Sun; 🚌4) This unisex footwear temple is a dangerous place to come if you have a shoe fetish; best not to bring more than one credit card. Quality and designer élan are the key here and you can expect to slip into Vancouver's best selection of fashion-forward clogs, wedges, mules and classy runners, many of them arranged like a fashion-show runway.

Next door there's a smaller but equally tempting designer clothing store under the same Gravity Pope banner. It's stuffed with stylish must-have men's and women's clothing.

ARC'TERYX SPORTS & OUTDOORS

Map p282 (☎604-737-1104; www.arcteryx.com; 2033 W 4th Ave, Kitsilano; ⏰10am-7pm Mon-Sat, 11am-6pm Sun; 🚌4) Flagship branch of Vancouver's high-end outdoor-gear store. Expect to pay a premium for the best waterproof jackets and weather-resistant pants. The upside is they'll last for ages and you'll be joining a cool group of outdoorsy types wearing a highly regarded logo. Keen to save? It also has a factory outlet in North Vancouver (see the company's website for details).

SPORTS & ACTIVITIES

WINDSURE ADVENTURE WATERSPORTS WATER SPORTS

Map p282 (☎604-224-0615; www.windsure.com; 1300 Discovery St, Jericho Sailing Centre, Kitsilano; ⏰8:30am-8:30pm mid-Apr–Sep; 👪; 🚌4) For those who want to be at one with the sea breeze, Windsure specializes in windsurfing, skimboarding and stand-up paddleboarding rentals and courses for a variety of skill levels. Prices are reasonable (for example, one-day skimboard rental is under $27) and the venue is inside the Jericho Sailing Centre, home of the city's recreational aquatic community.

Novices are more than welcome here: the two-hour windsurfing introductory group lesson ($65) is recommended. There are also lots of classes and activities for children.

DIVING LOCKER DIVING

Map p282 (☎604-736-2681; www.divinglocker.ca; 2745 W 4th Ave, Kitsilano; dives from $50; ⏰10am-6pm Mon-Fri, to 5:30pm Sat, to 4pm Sun; 🚌4) A long-established favorite with local snorkelers and scuba divers, the Diving Locker is not just for experienced practitioners. Along with its regular series of training courses, there's a great introductory scuba course ($99, including equipment) for first-timers. Staff also lead weekly, good-value guided dives around the area at Whytecliff Park, Porteau Cove and beyond.

JERICHO SAILING CENTRE BOATING

Map p282 (☎604-224-4177; www.jsca.bc.ca; 1300 Discovery St, Kitsilano; ⏰9:30am-sunset; 🚌4) The salty heart of Vancouver's aquatic community, this bustling center is home to several operators that can teach or rent equipment to those interested in everything from surfing to sailing. There's also an on-site resto-bar with a great water-view patio for relaxing and exchanging stories about your ocean-going shenanigans while the sun sets dramatically to your left.

MAC SAILING BOATING

Map p282 (☎604-224-7245; www.macsailing.com; 1300 Discovery St, Jericho Sailing Centre, Kitsilano; rental per hour from $40; ⏰9am-7pm Mon-Fri, noon-6pm Sat & Sun, reduced hours off-season; 👪; 🚌4) This excellent operation at the Jericho Sailing Centre caters to sailing veterans and newbies who want to learn the ropes. There are several boats available for rent – the super-fast and easy-to-sail *Hobie Getaway* is fun – and lessons (including introductory courses) are also offered, some tailored specifically for children.

1

2

1. Lions Gate Bridge
Officially known as the First Narrows Bridge, this suspension bridge connects downtown Vancouver with the North Shore through Stanley Park (p58).

2. Grouse Mountain (p182)
In summer, your admission ticket also includes access to lumberjack shows, alpine hiking, bird-of-prey displays and a grizzly bear refuge.

3. Steam Clock (p82)
Gastown's oddly popular tourist magnet lures the cameras with its tooting steam whistle.

4. Cafe Deux Soleils (p125)
This rambling bohemian cafe is a hip, healthy and ever-friendly Drive landmark.

4

I VIEWFINDER/SHUTTERSTOCK ©

North Shore

NORTH VANCOUVER | WEST VANCOUVER

Neighborhood Top Five

❶ **Capilano Suspension Bridge Park** (p182) Inching across the gently swaying wooden deck at this celebrated attraction, jelly legs included.

❷ **Grouse Mountain** (p182) Skiing or snowboarding the winter powder with the locals or dropping by in summer for a full day of hiking and zip-lining.

❸ **Polygon Gallery** (p182) Scratching your chin meaningfully as you peruse the striking contemporary artworks at this dramatic waterfront public gallery.

❹ **Deep Cove Kayak Centre** (p189) Sighing deeply as you slide across glassy, mountain-shadowed waters in a kayak, seemingly a million miles from any city.

❺ **Sewell's Marina** (p189) Communing with the cavorting orcas, lolling seals and beady-eyed shorebirds, on a face-spraying boat tour.

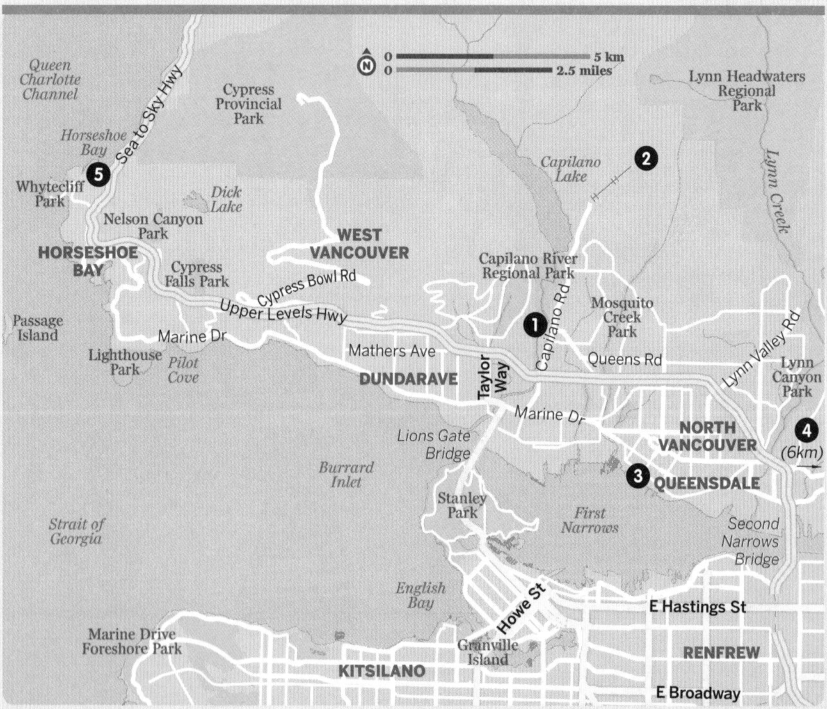

For more detail of this area see Map p284

Explore North Shore

The North Shore comprises North Vancouver and West Vancouver, with most visitors arriving from downtown via the 15-minute SeaBus ferry from Waterfront Station. You'll have an easy couple of hours of on-foot exploration straight off the boat: Lonsdale Quay Public Market is steps from the dock and the waterfront has been reclaimed from its grungy shipyard past. Next door to the market is the new Polygon Gallery (p182), while nearby Lonsdale Ave is hopping with stores and restaurants.

Once you're done with Lower Lonsdale (or you've just had enough of how steep the street is), hop on a bus from Lonsdale Quay. The 236 will take you to the region's two main attractions: Capilano Suspension Bridge Park (p182; 20 minutes from Lonsdale Quay) and Grouse Mountain (p182; 10 minutes further along). Grouse is the end of the line, so don't worry about getting off at the right stop. You can do both attractions in one day: start with Capilano (before it gets too crowded), then continue to Grouse (where you'll want to take more time). Both attractions also run free shuttle buses from downtown Vancouver.

To explore West Vancouver, catch bus 250 from downtown Vancouver. It'll take you through Stanley Park (p58), over the Lions Gate Bridge and then along Marine Dr, which is the heart of West Van. It's a little further out than North Van, but most attractions here are accessible via transit.

Local Life

- **Alternative Suspension Bridge** Capilano is a huge draw for many visitors but locals prefer the smaller, less-crowded 'other bridge' at Lynn Canyon Park (p183). It's also free.
- **Night Market** Everyone in the area seems to hang out at the Friday evening May-to-September Shipyards Night Market (p186) where live music and food trucks foster a festive vibe.
- **Birding** A delightful nature escape surprisingly close to the city, Maplewood Flats Conservation Area (p183) is a rustic tangle of trees and pathways where you'll often spot eagles, ospreys and more.

Getting There & Away

- **SeaBus** From downtown's Waterfront Station, it takes around 15 minutes to reach Lonsdale Quay on the transit network's ferry service.
- **Bus** Lonsdale Quay has a bus terminal where services depart for North and West Vancouver. Bus 236 is key: it runs to both Capilano and Grouse Mountain.

Lonely Planet's Top Tip

If you're fit (or just really keen to save money), you can access the attractions atop **Grouse Mountain** (p182) without having to pay the whole pricey gondola fee. The catch? You'll have to do it by hiking the steep, sweat-triggering Grouse Grind. But you'll still have to pay the $15 gondola charge to get back down.

Best Places to Eat

- Lift Breakfast Bakery (p185)
- Meat at O'Neill's (p184)
- Burgoo Bistro (p185)
- Wooden Fish (p185)

For reviews, see p184.

Best Places to Drink

- Gull Bar & Kitchen (p186)
- Buddha-Full (p186)
- West of Java (p186)

For reviews, see p186.

Best Places to Shop

- Shipyards Night Market (p186)
- Lonsdale Quay Market (p186)
- Mo's General Store (p186)
- Mountain Equipment Co-op (p188)

For reviews, see p186.

SIGHTS

The North Shore is home to some of Metro Vancouver's favorite outdoor attractions. But North Van, in particular, is also starting to buzz as an urban visitor lure, especially at the shoreline end of Lonsdale Ave. You'll find shoreline walks, public art, a summer night market and a striking new contemporary art gallery here.

North Vancouver

★CAPILANO SUSPENSION BRIDGE PARK — PARK

Map p284 (☎604-985-7474; www.capbridge.com; 3735 Capilano Rd; adult/child $47/15; ⏰8am-8pm May-Aug, reduced hours off-season; P 👪; 🚌236) As you inch gingerly across one of the world's longest (140m) and highest (70m) pedestrian suspension bridges, swaying gently over roiling Capilano Canyon, remember that its thick steel cables are firmly embedded in concrete. That should steady your feet – unless there are teenagers stamping across. Added park attractions include a glass-bottomed **cliffside walkway** and an elevated **canopy trail** through the trees.

This is a hugely popular attraction (hence the summer tour buses); try to arrive early during peak months so you can check out the historic exhibits, totem poles and tree-shaded nature trails on the other side of the bridge in relative calm. On your way out, peruse what must be BC's biggest souvenir shop for First Nations artworks, 'moose-dropping' choccies and a full range of T-shirts and ball caps. And if you're here during the winter holidays, the park is transformed with a sparkling array of more than one million fairy lights. If you're not sure how to get to Capilano, there's also a free year-round shuttle bus from downtown; check the website for scheduling details.

★POLYGON GALLERY — GALLERY

Map p284 (☎604-986-1351; www.thepolygon.ca; 101 Carrie Cates Ct; by donation; ⏰10am-5pm Tue-Sun; ⛴Lonsdale Quay Seabus) North Van's former Presentation House Gallery renamed itself and relocated to this dramatic, sawtooth-roofed waterfront landmark in 2017, providing greatly increased wall space for the multiple exhibitions staged here throughout the year. Photoconceptualism remains a focus but expect thought-provoking contemporary art installations and evocative indigenous exhibits as well. There are free 45-minute tours every Saturday at 2pm. On our visit, a new North Vancouver Museum was also under construction across the street.

Check out the panoramic second-floor views over the water and save time to visit the bookstore and lobby-level gift shop, complete with Polaroid cameras, artisan jewelry and papaya-themed jigsaws shaped like – you guessed it – papayas.

GROUSE MOUNTAIN — PARK

Map p284 (☎604-980-9311; www.grousemountain.com; 6400 Nancy Greene Way; adult/child $56/29; ⏰9am-10pm; P 👪; 🚌236) The self-proclaimed 'Peak of Vancouver,' this mountain-top playground, accessed via Skyride gondola (included with admission), offers spectacular views of downtown glittering in the water below. In summer, your ticket also includes access to lumberjack shows, alpine hiking, bird-of-prey displays and a grizzly bear refuge. Pay extra for zip-lining and Eye of the Wind, a 20-story, elevator-accessed turbine tower with a panoramic viewing pod that will have your camera itching for action.

Reduce the admission fee by hiking the ultra-steep **Grouse Grind** (Map p284; www.grousemountain.com; Grouse Mountain, North Shore; 🚌236) up the side of the mountain; it's one-way only and costs $15 to return via the Skyride. Grouse lures visitors from downtown from May to September by offering a free shuttle from Canada Place. And in winter, it's all about skiing and snowboarding at this popular powdery playground.

MAPLEWOOD FARM — FARM

Map p284 (☎604-929-5610; www.maplewoodfarm.bc.ca; 405 Seymour River Pl; adult/child $8.51/5; ⏰10am-4pm Apr-Oct, 10am-4pm Tue-Sun Nov-Mar; 👪; 🚌239 then 212) This popular farmyard attraction includes plenty of hands-on displays, plus a collection of more than 200 birds and domestic farm animals. Your wide-eyed kids can pet some critters, watch the milking demonstrations and feed some squawking, ever-hungry ducks and chickens; don't miss Petunia the pot-bellied pig. The highlight is the daily round-up (3:30pm), when hungry critters streak back into their barn for dinner.

Book ahead for a behind-the-scenes tour where your sprogs can learn what it's like

SURFING THE SEABUS

Sashaying between downtown Vancouver's Waterfront Station and the North Shore's Lonsdale Quay, the 400-seat SeaBus (www.translink.ca) vessels easily divide the locals from the tourists. Vancouverites barely raise a glance when the boats arrive in their little docks to pick up passengers for the 15-minute voyage across Burrard Inlet. In contrast, wide-eyed visitors excitedly crowd the automatic doors as if they're about to climb onto a theme-park ride.

Once on board, it's a similar story: locals shuffle to the back and attach themselves to their phone screens, while out-of-towners glue themselves to the front seats for a panoramic view of the glittering crossing, with the looming North Shore mountains growing in stature ahead of them as the voyage unfolds.

The boxy, low-slung catamarans first hit the waves in 1977. But they weren't the first boats to take passengers over the briny. The first regular private ferry covering this route launched in 1900. It was taken over and run as a public service by the City of North Vancouver a few years later, when the route's two vessels were imaginatively renamed *North Vancouver Ferry 1* and *North Vancouver Ferry 2*. No prizes for guessing what the third ferry was named when it was added in 1936. The opening of the Lions Gate Bridge, linking the two shores by road a couple of years later, slowly pulled the rug from under the ferry service, and the last sailing took place in 1958. It would be almost 20 years before a new public service was restored to the route, when *Burrard Beaver* and *Burrard Otter* hit the water. In recent years, two shiny new vessels have also been added to the fleet: *Burrard Pacific Breeze* and *Burrard Chinook*.

to be a farmer, from grooming to collecting the eggs and preparing the feed. The $28 fee covers one adult and one child.

MT SEYMOUR PROVINCIAL PARK — PARK

Map p284 (www.bcparks.ca; 1700 Mt Seymour Rd; dawn-dusk) FREE A popular rustic retreat from the downtown clamor, this huge, tree-lined park is suffused with summertime **hiking trails** that suit walkers of most abilities (the easiest path is the 2km Goldie Lake Trail). Many trails wind past lakes and centuries-old Douglas firs. This is also one of the city's main winter playgrounds.

The park is a great spot for **mountain biking** and has many dedicated trails. It's around 30 minutes from downtown Vancouver by car; drivers can take Hwy 1 to the Mt Seymour Pkwy (near the Second Narrows Bridge) and follow it east to Mt Seymour Rd.

LYNN CANYON PARK — PARK

Map p284 (www.lynncanyon.ca; Park Rd, North Vancouver; 10am-5pm Jun-Sep, noon-4pm Oct-May; P; 228 then 227) FREE Amid a dense bristling of century-old trees, the main lure of this popular park is its **Suspension Bridge**, a free alternative to Capilano. Not quite as big as its tourist-magnet rival, it nevertheless provokes the same jelly-legged reaction as you sway over the river that tumbles 50m below – and it's always far less crowded. Hiking trails, swimming areas and picnic spots will keep you busy, while there's also a cafe to fuel you up.

The park's **Ecology Centre** (Map p284; 604-990-3755; www.lynncanyonecologycentre.ca; by donation; 10am-5pm Jun-Sep, 10am-5pm Mon-Fri & noon-4pm Sat & Sun Oct-May; ; 227) houses interesting displays, including dioramas on the area's rich biodiversity. There are also some fascinating free history-themed walking tours in the park on Wednesdays and Thursdays in July and August; check www.nvma.ca/programs for details.

MAPLEWOOD FLATS CONSERVATION AREA — NATURE RESERVE

Map p284 (604-929-2379; www.facebook.com/MaplewoodFlats; 2645 Dollarton Hwy; P; 215) FREE Managed by the Wild Bird Trust of BC, this delightful nature escape is surprisingly accessible from Vancouver yet it feels like a million miles from the city. Its tangle of trees, winding paths and protected wetland beach lure swallows, ospreys and bald eagles – and there are free guided nature walks the second Saturday of every month (10am); check their Facebook page for upcoming themes and other events.

LOCAL KNOWLEDGE

NORTH SHORE'S BEST FEST

Late July is the time when everyone on the North Shore finds their party groove at one of Metro Vancouver's best community events. The weekend-long **Caribbean Days Festival** (☎604-515-2400; www.caribbeandays.ca; Waterfront Park, North Vancouver; 👪; SeaBus Lonsdale Quay Station) FREE in the city's Waterfront Park – not far from the SeaBus dock – includes a street parade; live music and dance; a food fair of epic, spicy proportions; and a popular art and clothing market. Attracting thousands to the area, it never fails to put smiles on faces.

West Vancouver

LIGHTHOUSE PARK PARK

Map p284 (www.lighthousepark.ca; 4902 Beacon Ln; ⊙dawn-dusk; P; 🚌250) FREE Some of the region's oldest trees live within this accessible 75-hectare park, including a rare stand of original coastal forest and plenty of gnarly, copper-trunked arbutus trees. About 13km of hiking trails crisscross the area, including a recommended trek that leads to the rocky perch of Point Atkinson Lighthouse, ideal for capturing shimmering, views over Burrard Inlet.

Accessible via transit bus from downtown Vancouver, if you're driving here turn left on Marine Dr after crossing the Lions Gate Bridge to reach the park.

WHYTECLIFF PARK PARK

Map p284 (7100-block Marine Dr; ⊙dawn-dusk; 🚌257) Just west of Horseshoe Bay, this is an exceptional little waterfront green space. Trails lead to vistas and a gazebo, from where you can watch the Burrard Inlet boat traffic. The rocky beach is a great place to scamper over the large rocks protruding from the beach. It's also one of the region's favorite dive spots for scuba fans.

WEST VANCOUVER SEAWALL WATERFRONT

Map p284 (🚌250) Take bus 250 from downtown Vancouver and hop off on Marine Dr at the intersection with 24th St. Peruse the stores and coffee shops in Dundarave Village, then stroll downhill to the waterfront. Take in the panoramic coastline from Dundarave Pier, then weave eastwards along the shore-hugging Centennial Seawalk route, West Van's favorite promenade. You'll pass joggers, herons and public artworks.

After 2km, the trail comes to a halt. From here, head back up to the Marine Dr shops or weave over to Ambleside Park, where you'll find a dramatic First Nations carved welcome figure facing the water.

FERRY BUILDING ART GALLERY GALLERY

Map p284 (☎604-925-7290; www.ferrybuildinggallery.com; 1414 Argyle Ave, West Vancouver; ⊙11am-5pm Tue-Sun; 🚌255) FREE Housed in a cute wooden heritage building, which was once a ferry terminal when transit boats plied the waters between West Van and Vancouver, this popular waterfront community gallery is well worth a look if you're in the Ambleside Park vicinity. Shows change frequently and there's a strong commitment to showcasing local artists.

EATING

North Shore's dine-out options range from popular brunch spots to elevated seafood joints. You'll find a concentrated cluster radiating up Lonsdale Ave from the waterfront, with many more dotted around both North and West Van.

★MEAT AT O'NEILL'S SANDWICHES $

Map p284 (☎604-987-1115; www.facebook.com/meatatoneillsnvan; 144 Lonsdale Ave, North Vancouver; mains $6-13; ⊙11:30am-4:30pm Mon, from 9:30am Tue, Wed & Sat, 9:30am-10pm Thu & Fri; ⛴Lonsdale Quay SeaBus) A top-quality sandwich emporium fueling the local takeout crowd with satisfying all-day breakfast sandwiches and a mouthwatering array of slow-roasted meat sandwiches (pork loin or Mexican meatloaf recommended). There's a handful of seats at the counter if you need a pit-stop break, but your best bet is to keep rolling down the hill to the waterfront for an alfresco picnic.

Thursday and Friday dinners feature an expanded menu of hearty house-made curries or stews. You'll also find a good selection of BC craft beers, typically including some from the North Shore.

ARTISAN BAKE SHOPPE BAKERY $

Map p284 (☎604-990-3530; www.artisanbakeshoppe.ca; 108 E 2nd St, North Vancouver; mains $7-9; ⏰7am-5:30pm Mon-Sat; 🚌230) The house-baked German-style breads here are about as far from factory-made products as possible. Be sure to pick up an ancient grains loaf (it'll keep you going all week) then indulge in some instant treats, many of which are vegan; don't miss the butter pecan bars. It's not just takeout; soups and sandwiches are also served in this yellow-hued bakery cafe.

If you still have room (or even if you don't), consider some eye-rollingly-good apple strudel for the road.

EARNEST ICE CREAM ICE CREAM $

Map p284 (☎604-770-4136; www.earnesticecream.com; 127 W 1st St, North Vancouver; 1/2 scoop $5/7; ⏰noon-10pm; 🚌239) This is a busy outpost of the popular Vancouver artisan ice-cream fave. Sidle up to the striped-wood counter and pretend you're buying cones for two people. That'll give you the chance to scoff one in each hand, but you'll still have to choose from a highly tempting array of flavors that often includes salted caramel, whiskey hazelnut, matcha green tea and many more.

Better yet, snag a pint of the good stuff and eat it outside at one of the little round seats; no-one will judge you.

LIFT BREAKFAST BAKERY CAFE $$

Map p284 (☎778-388-5438; www.liftonlonsdale.ca; 101 Lonsdale Ave, North Vancouver; mains $14-26; ⏰7am-4pm Mon, Wed & Thu, to 10pm Fri & Sat, 9am-10pm Sun; 📶; 🚌239) A popular heritage building corner cafe with little square tables and a woodsy, sun-dappled patio, Lift lures locals for coffee and bakery treats throughout the day. But it's also a hugely popular daily brunch hangout, serving classic breakfasts as well as bowls, pancakes, French toast and more. Friday-to-Sunday dinner adds fresh-made pasta to the mix (reservations recommended).

WOODEN FISH VIETNAMESE $$

Map p284 (☎604-926-6789; www.thewoodenfish.ca; 1403 Marine Dr, West Vancouver; mains $14-25; ⏰11am-9pm Mon-Fri, from 10am Sat & Sun; 🚌250) The staffers are almost as warm as the steaming pho bowls at this North Shore hidden gem, which is superior to the mom-and-pop Vietnamese joints that have operated in Metro Vancouver for decades. Menu highlights include duck confit rice bowls and crisp salad rolls, but it's the Hanoi beef noodle soup that stands out: rich, intense and fortifyingly delicious.

BURGOO BISTRO BISTRO $$

Map p284 (☎604-904-0933; www.burgoo.ca; 3 Lonsdale Ave, North Vancouver; mains $14-18; ⏰11am-10pm; ⛴SeaBus Lonsdale Quay) With the feel of a cozy rustic cabin – complete with a large stone fireplace – Burgoo's menu of elevated international comfort dishes warms up even the coolest North Van nights: juicy beef bourguignon, gooey grilled cheese sandwiches or chicken-and-shrimp-packed farmers gumbo recommended. There's also a wide array of house-made soups and salads.

Drinks-wise, dive into local craft beer or sip on a boozy Spanish coffee. There's often live music on Sunday evenings and if you fancy copying some of Burgoo's best dishes when you get back home, it also sells its own cookbook. It's handily close to the SeaBus terminal.

PALKI RESTAURANT INDIAN $$

Map p284 (☎604-986-7555; www.palkirestaurant.com; 116 E 15th Street, North Vancouver; mains $13-24; ⏰11:30am-2:30pm & 4:30-10pm; 🌿; 🚌242) Don't be discouraged by the drab, gray-brick exterior of this Indian restaurant: inside, it's cozy and welcoming with a swish contemporary look. Budget-watchers should check out the daily all-you-can-eat buffet, but it's worth coming back in the evening for a more considered approach. Start with a mixed platter of samosas and pakoras, then graduate to the excellent lamb rogan josh.

It's a good idea to share a few dishes here; note that there's a Northern Indian feel to much of the menu.

SALMON HOUSE ON THE HILL SEAFOOD $$$

Map p284 (☎604-926-3212; www.salmonhouse.com; 2229 Folkestone Way, West Vancouver; mains $27-48; ⏰11am-2:30pm Sat & Sun, 5-9:30pm Sun-Thu, 5-10pm Fri & Sat; 🚌256) West Vancouver's old-school destination restaurant has been luring locals for special-occasion dinners for years. But Salmon House doesn't rest on its laurels – if laurels can be defined as a gable-roofed wooden interior and floor-to-ceiling windows with sunset cliff-top city views. Instead, you'll find a menu of delectable seasonal BC seafood with serious gourmet credentials.

There are also top-notch duck and lamb dishes for non-aquatic scoffers. And if you just want to check it out without the top-end dinner price, drop by for weekend brunch (crab eggs Benedict recommended).

DRINKING & NIGHTLIFE

The North Shore isn't a great place for a destination night out, but there are some standouts worth pulling over for (with a designated driver, of course).

WEST OF JAVA — COFFEE

Map p284 (604-983-3467; 105 E 1st St, North Vancouver; 6:30am-6pm Mon-Fri, 7am-5pm Sat, 8am-5pm Sun; ; 229) This tiny, darkened hole-in-the-wall just off Lonsdale Ave is the locals' favorite fuel-up spot, so you'll be lucky to find a seat inside. But on sunny days, when you're craving a huge milky latte and a chance to soak up some rays, a row of alfresco tables pops up along the street outside; it's perfect for eavesdropping on juicy North Van gossip.

GULL BAR & KITCHEN — PUB

Map p284 (604-988-5585; www.thegull.ca; 175 E 1st St, North Vancouver; 11:30am-10pm Tue-Fri, from 11am Sat & Sun; ; 239) A phoenix-like reinvention of the old Rusty Gull neighborhood pub, the gray-painted clapboard facade hides a long drink-and-dine area now serving the kind of craft beers and cocktails former quaffers wouldn't even recognize. A gastropub menu of charcuterie plates and brie-infused burgers completes the transformation. Curious about the former drinkers? Peruse the wall-mounted yesteryear photos of gritty shipyard workers.

BUDDHA-FULL — JUICE BAR

Map p284 (604-973-0231; www.buddha-full.ca; 106 W 1st St, North Vancouver; 8am-8pm; ; SeaBus Lonsdale Quay) North Van's favorite juice bar is a thirst-quenching pit stop that also serves a huge array of hearty vegan and vegetarian dishes, from *pakoras* to wraps to heaping 'buddha bowls.' But its the luscious smoothies that many locals snag a seat for. Slurp a Peaceful Warrior or a Green Detox and your belly will feel at one with the world.

SHOPPING

Outdoor stores are a specialty here but it's not all about action. There are also plenty of food and artisan emporiums to tempt your wallet, as well as a year-round public market and a popular summer night market.

★SHIPYARDS NIGHT MARKET — MARKET

Map p284 (www.northshoregreenmarket.com; Shipbuilders Sq, North Vancouver; 5pm-10pm Fri May-Sep; ; Lonsdale Quay SeaBus) Muscling in on the region's summertime night-market scene, North Van's is a few steps east of Lonsdale Quay. It's a fun way to spend a balmy Friday evening, with the ocean lapping nearby. Dive into the food trucks (Tacofino recommended), tap your toes to live bands and sip a brew or three in the ever-clamorous beer garden.

This is an easy spot to end your North Shore day out; the SeaBus back to the city is a short stroll away.

LONSDALE QUAY MARKET — MARKET

Map p284 (604-985-6261; www.lonsdalequay.com; 123 Carrie Cates Ct, North Vancouver; 9am-7pm; ; SeaBus Lonsdale Quay) A SeaBus hop from downtown Vancouver, this is the region's second most popular public market (after Granville Island). Look for BC wines and fresh fish plus trinkets and clothing one floor up. There's also a microbrewery bar; sober up at the nearby C41 Coffee stand. Finish with an ice cream and linger over the boardwalk views of Vancouver's glass-towered skyline.

If you're still hungry, the market has a food court plus several other tasty options, including a legendary local soup stand. But if you're really starving, **Sharky's** is the way to go: $9.95 for a heaping plate of meat and veggies that easily feeds two. There's also a Saturday farmers market on-site here from May to October.

MO'S GENERAL STORE — GIFTS & SOUVENIRS

Map p284 (604-928-7827; www.mosgeneralstore.com; 51 Lonsdale Ave, North Vancouver; 8am-6pm Mon, to 8pm Tue-Sat, 9am-6pm Sun; Lonsdale Quay SeaBus) This is a browser's paradise of quirky gifts, arts and crafts, and must-have trinkets you never thought you needed. The heritage building once housed North Van's first full-time grocery

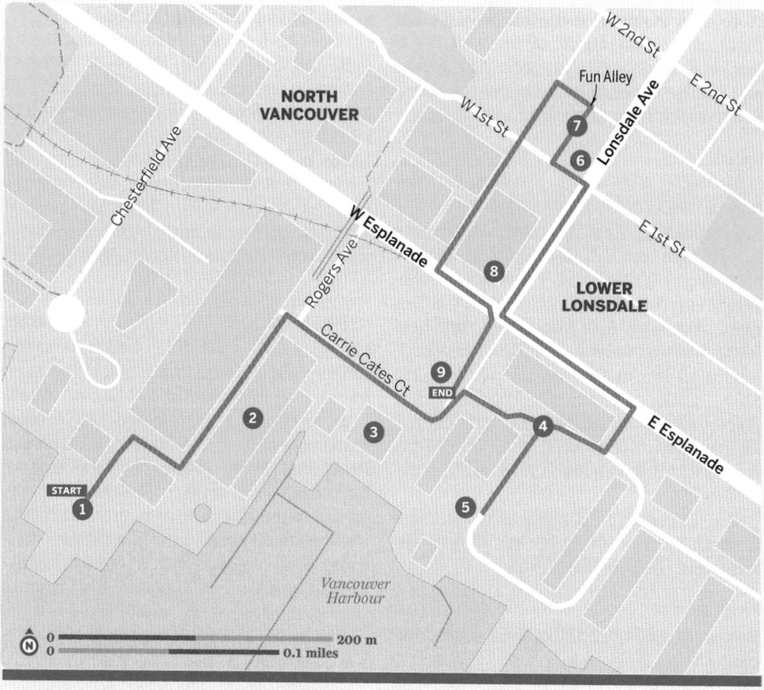

Neighborhood Walk
Lower Lonsdale Wander

START LONSDALE QUAY SEABUS STATION
END BURGOO BISTRO
LENGTH 1KM; ONE HOUR

This easy loop will take you into the heart of North Van's reinvented shipyards area, complete with gritty history, oceanfront attractions and tasty pit stops.

After a 15-minute SeaBus hop from Vancouver's Waterfront Station, disembark at ❶ **Lonsdale Quay**, walk up the ramp and turn right. You'll quickly reach ❷ **Lonsdale Quay Market** (p186). But before entering, swivel to the shoreline for panoramic photos of Vancouver's waterfront skyline.

Enter the market, giving yourself plenty of time to explore its food stands and artisan stores, then exit through the back doors onto Carrie Cates Ct. Turn right and the dramatic ❸ **Polygon Gallery** (p182) is just ahead. This sparkling contemporary art museum is a must-see.

Next, follow the curve of Carrie Cates Ct and, on your right, you'll reach a huge photo mural of yesteryear shipyard workers, marking the entrance to the old ❹ **Wallace Shipyards site**. Its former sheds now house halls and restaurants, while its outdoor plaza hosts summer's ❺ **Shipyards Night Market** (p186). Read the history plaques and stroll the pier alongside passing cormorants.

From here, return to the shipyard mural and turn right onto Lonsdale Ave. This steep main thoroughfare is lined with stores and restaurants. Hungry? Walk up Lonsdale to 1st St and ❻ **Lift Breakfast Bakery** (p185), a popular brunch spot. Check out ❼ **Fun Alley** next door; it's a kaleidoscopically painted back-lane art installation.

Return down Lonsdale to ❽ **Mo's General Store** (p186) for quirky trinket shopping. On the next block is a row of dinner options. Choose one for later, ❾ **Burgoo Bistro** (p185) recommended, then keep exploring until you work up an appetite. After dinner, return to Vancouver via the nearby SeaBus terminal.

store; check out the evocative large-format photo of the 1903 interior on one wall. Looking for avocado socks, unicorn snow globes and whale-shaped salt and pepper shakers? You're at the right place.

MOUNTAIN EQUIPMENT CO-OP SPORTS & OUTDOORS

Map p284 (604-990-4417; www.mec.ca; 212 Brooksbank Ave, North Vancouver; 10am-9pm Mon-Fri, 9am-6pm Sat, 10am-6pm Sun, reduced hours winter; 239) Smaller than its Vancouver parent, this MEC branch has a friendlier, more neighborly feel. Almost everyone here – staff and customers – seems to know each other and is a member of the active North Shore outdoor community. It's the perfect place to stock up on gear for your nature-loving adventures; you'll find everything from soft hiking shoes to great waterproof jackets.

You'll need to be a member to purchase from this nonprofit co-op: it's easy to arrange and costs just $5 (for life).

PARK ROYAL MALL

Map p284 (604-922-3211; www.shopparkroyal.com; Marine Dr, West Vancouver; 10am-7pm Mon & Tue, to 9pm Wed-Fri, 9:30am-6pm Sat, 11am-6pm Sun; 250) It's the region's oldest mall but Park Royal does a good job of keeping up with the competition. With 280+ stores (including all the usual suspects), its ever-expanding Village area emulates an outdoor UK high street with strollable big stores and restaurants. The indoor area is a good option when the region's 'Wet Coast' nickname is demonstrated in full force.

Park Royal is easy to access on transit from downtown Vancouver; buses trundle over the picturesque Lions Gate Bridge and stop just outside. Fashion-wise, the **Simons** store is worth a look; it's the only BC branch of the highly popular Quebec clothing and accessories store.

SPORTS & ACTIVITIES

★GROUSE MOUNTAIN SNOW SPORTS

Map p284 (604-980-9311; www.grousemountain.com; 6400 Nancy Greene Way, North Vancouver; lift ticket adult/child $47/42; 9am-10pm mid-Nov–mid-Apr; ; 236) Vancouver's favorite winter hangout, family-friendly Grouse offers four chair lifts plus 33 ski and snowboard runs (including night runs). Classes and lessons are available for beginners and beyond, and the area's forested snowshoe trails are magical. There are also a couple of dining options if you just want to relax and watch the snow with a hot chocolate in hand.

If you're here in December, this is a great place to soak up some Christmas spirit; if you're looking for Santa in Vancouver, this is where you'll find him, along with a reindeer or two.

CYPRESS MOUNTAIN SNOW SPORTS

Map p284 (604-926-5612; www.cypressmountain.com; 6000 Cypress Bowl Rd, West Vancouver; lift ticket adult/youth/child $79/56/36; 9am-10pm mid-Dec–Mar, to 4pm Apr;) Around 8km north of West Van via Hwy 99, **Cypress Provincial Park** (Map p284; www.bcparks.ca; dawn-dusk) FREE transforms into Cypress Mountain resort in winter, attracting well-insulated locals with its 53 runs, cross-country ski access and a family-friendly snow-tubing course. There are also 11km of snowshoe trails, with several guided tours available (the $59 chocolate fondue option is recommended).

There's a large floodlit area here, so it's popular with night-skiers. When you're done, head to the mountain's Crazy Raven Bar for a fireplace-warmed pint of beer; there are several additional places to eat and drink as well. And if you don't want to drive here, consider the seasonal **Cypress Coach Lines shuttle** (www.cypresscoachlines.com; return $25; cash only), which picks up in Vancouver and beyond.

MT SEYMOUR SNOW SPORTS

Map p284 (604-986-2261; www.mountseymour.com; 1700 Mt Seymour Rd, North Vancouver; adult/youth(13–18yr)/child $51/44/24; 9:30am-10pm Mon-Fri, from 8:30am Sat & Sun Dec-Apr) This branch of the region's three main Vancouver-accessible winter playgrounds offers ski and snowboarding areas, plus toboggan and tubing courses. The snowshoe trails and tours are also popular – check out the nighttime snowshoeing and chocolate fondue tour ($59). This is usually the least crowded snowy destination in the region, so you're much more likely to meet the locals here.

Seymour runs a handy winter-season shuttle bus from Vancouver and North Vancouver (round trip $10 to $15).

MOTHER NATURE'S STAIRMASTER

If you're finding your vacation a little too relaxing, head over to North Vancouver and join the perspiring throng snaking – almost vertically – up the Grouse Grind (p182) trail. The entrance is near the parking lot, across the street from where slightly more sane Grouse Mountain (p182) visitors pile into the Skyride gondola and trundle up to the summit without breaking a sweat.

Around 3km in total, this steep, rock-studded forest trek will likely have your joints screaming for mercy within 15 minutes as you focus on the feet of the person in front of you. Most people take around an hour to reach the top, where they collapse like fish gasping on the rocks.

Things to keep in mind if you're planning to join the 100,000+ people who hike the Grind every year: take a bottle of water, dress in thin layers so you can strip down, and bring $15 with you: the trail is one-way, so when you reach the summit you have to take the Skyride back down – your consolation is that you get to enjoy the summit's many attractions for free in exchange for your exploding calf muscles.

DEEP COVE KAYAK CENTRE KAYAKING

Map p284 (☎604-929-2268; www.deepcovekayak.com; 2156 Banbury Rd, Deep Cove, North Vancouver; kayaks per 2hr/day $39/99; ⏰9am-dusk Jun-Aug, reduced hours off-season; 🚌211) Enjoying Deep Cove's sheltered waters, this is an ideal – and idyllic – spot for first-timers to try their hand at paddling. Lessons and tours are available (the $75 Full Moon Evening Tour is recommended), and stand-up paddleboarding (SUP) has also been added to the mix – try it out with a two-hour introductory class ($60).

For those with a little more experience, the center also sponsors Tuesday evening race nights, as well as Thursday night women-only social kayaking if you'd like some company out on the water.

ENDLESS BIKING MOUNTAIN BIKING

Map p284 (☎604-985-2519; www.endlessbiking.com; 1467 Crown St, North Vancouver; rentals from 4hr/$35; ⏰9am-5:30pm Apr-Oct, to 5pm Wed-Sun Nov-Mar; 🚌239) A great first stop for anyone looking to access North Van's brilliant bike scene. The friendly folks here can take you on a guided tour or just rent you a bike and point you in the right direction. Lessons are also available if you're a newbie and you want to learn how to negotiate gnarly tree roots without wiping out.

Beginners should book ahead for the Scenic Tour (from $175 for two hours) which includes a bike, a helmet and a trundle into the wilderness for mountain and waterfront views.

SEWELL'S MARINA BOATING

Map p284 (☎604-921-3474; www.sewellsmarina.com; 6409 Bay St, Horseshoe Bay, West Vancouver; adult/child $93/60; ⏰8am-6pm Apr-Oct; 👪; 🚌257) West Vancouver's Horseshoe Bay is the departure point for Sewell's two-hour Sea Safari boat tours. Orcas are always a highlight, but even if they're not around you'll almost certainly spot harbor seals lolling on the rocks and pretending to ignore you. Seabirds and bald eagles are also big stars of the show.

Staying downtown? They can pick you up and take you home on their shuttle-bus service ($18 return).

EDGE CLIMBING CENTRE CLIMBING

Map p284 (☎604-984-9080; www.edgeclimbing.com; 1485 Welch St, North Vancouver; ⏰1-11pm Mon-Fri, noon-9pm Sat & Sun; 👪; 🚌239) This high-tech North Van facility has a large climbing gym with over 1300 sq meters of climbing surfaces for those who like hanging around. There are plenty of courses, from introductory level to advanced classes where you can learn all about diagonaling and heel-and-toe hooking. And if your kids are keen, there are age-appropriate sign-up classes for them as well.

If you enjoy this, you can drive straight from here to the **Stawamus Chief** in Squamish. This giant granite rock face looming over the town and studded with climbers in summer is an hour's drive north via Hwy 99.

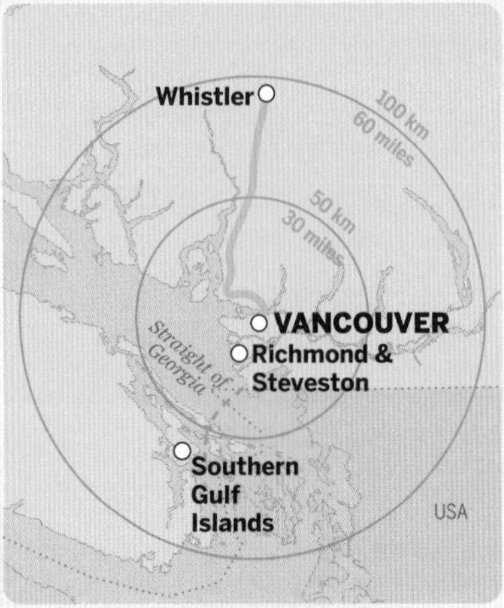

Day Trips from Vancouver

Whistler p191

The region's favorite outdoor wonderland, this mountain-framed ski village offers year-round thrills including skiing, rafting and zip-lining.

Richmond & Steveston p196

Hosting North America's best Asian dining scene, Richmond also incorporates the pretty seaside village of Steveston, home to some great historic attractions.

Southern Gulf Islands p199

On a scenic floatplane or ferry ride from the mainland, islands such as Salt Spring and Galiano will feel as if they're million miles away from the city.

Whistler

Explore

Named for the furry marmots that populate the area and whistle like deflating balloons, this gabled alpine village and 2010 Olympics venue is one of the world's largest, best-equipped and most popular ski resorts. Colonizing two mountains – Whistler and Blackcomb – and lying a mere 90 minutes north of Vancouver, the Village, which dates from the late 1970s, is a poster child for attractive design with nary an ugly building or piece of litter to pierce the natural beauty. Skiing may be Whistler's raison d'être, but these days summer visitors with their BMXs and SUPs outnumber their ski-season equivalents. Adding more diversity, the resort has recently developed an art scene worthy of a small European city. The caveat? Whistler is busy (2.3 million visitors a year) and expensive. For a quieter more economical experience, be selective with your dates and don't follow the herd.

The Best...

- **Sight** Audain Art Museum
- **Place to Eat** Hunter Gather (p194)
- **Place to Drink** Garibaldi Lift Company (p194)

Top Tip

There's a year-round roster of events in Whistler, with new ones being created all the time. Check local newspapers to see what's on during your visit.

Getting There & Away

- **Bus** Skylynx (www.yvrskylynx.com) operates seven services a day between Vancouver International Airport and Whistler Village (from $58.50, three hours). En route, the bus stops at the Hyatt Hotel in downtown Vancouver and, by request, at Whistler Creekside. Snowbus (www.snowbus.com) operates two winter-only services a day from Vancouver International Airport ($40), via Vancouver's Hyatt Hotel.
- **Car** take W Georgia St through Stanley park and over the Lions Gate Bridge then follow the signs to Hwy 99 north. You'll reach Whistler in around 90 minutes.

Need to Know

- **Location** 122km north of Vancouver
- **Tourist Office Whistler Visitors Centre** (Map p192; ☎604-935-3357; www.whistler.com; 4230 Gateway Dr; ⏰8am-8pm, to 10pm Thu-Sat Jun-Aug, reduced hrs Sep-May)
- **Area Code** ☎250

SIGHTS

Over the last decade, Whistler has worked hard to improve its cultural attractions, with extremely positive results.

★AUDAIN ART MUSEUM — GALLERY

Map p192 (☎604-962-0413; www.audainartmuseum.com; 4350 Blackcomb Way; adult/child $18/free; ⏰10am-5pm, to 9pm Fri, closed Tue) The opening of the Audain in 2016 elevated Whistler from 'world-class ski resort' to 'world-class ski resort with serious art credentials.' With two-dozen works by iconic painter Emily Carr, a priceless collection of indigenous masks, and sparkling photoconceptualist images by Jeff Wall, Rodney Graham et al, this is no rainy-day filler. BC artists take center stage. Alongside Carr you'll spot material from the 'Group of Seven' modernists, plus works by contemporary First Nations artists like Robert Davidson.

Everything is beautifully curated and explained using succinct panels in a dramatic angular building that is a piece of art in itself.

SQUAMISH LIL'WAT CULTURAL CENTRE — MUSEUM

Map p192 (☎604-964-0990; www.slcc.ca; 4584 Blackcomb Way; adult/child $18/5; ⏰9:30am-5pm Apr-Sep, 10am-5pm Tue-Sun Oct-Mar) This handsome, wood-beamed facility showcases two quite different First Nations groups – the Lil'wat and the Squamish – who have inhabited this region for eons. Take a tour for the vital context behind the museumlike exhibits and keep your eyes open for on-site artist demonstrations during the summer, when there are also Tuesday-night barbecue dinners. There's also an on-site cafe serving bannock tacos.

WHISTLER MUSEUM & ARCHIVES — MUSEUM

Map p192 (☎604-932-2019; www.whistlermuseum.org; 4333 Main St; suggested donation $5; ⏰11am-5pm, to 9pm Thu) Tucked into an anonymous green shed behind the library

Whistler

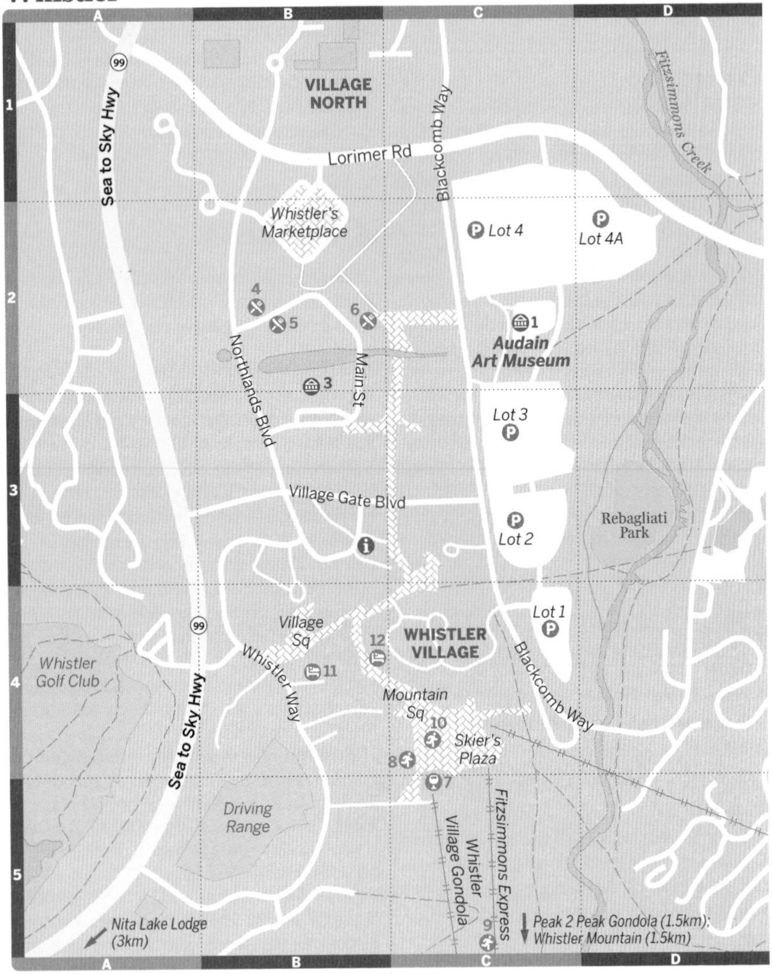

building, this great little museum traces Whistler development from 1970s hippy hangout to 21st century resort. The story is as compelling as it is short, speckled with interesting exhibits such as the original 1965 ski-lift gondola and a 2010 Olympic torch. Don't leave without digesting the story of the infamous 1973 'Toad Hall' photo.

PEAK 2 PEAK GONDOLA CABLE CAR

(☎604-967-8950; www.whistlerblackcomb.com/discover/360-experience; 4545 Blackcomb Way; adult/child $63/32; ⏲10am-5pm) Built to link the area's two main mountaintops, the world's second longest free-span gondola eases passengers along a lofty and ethereally peaceful 4.4km ride that takes around 11 minutes to complete. En route, you can gaze down on forest, crags, skiers and bears – especially if you snag one of the two glass-bottomed cars. The gondola's completion in 2008 effectively joined Whistler and Blackcomb into one giant ski area, making it one of the world's largest.

The gondola is open year-round. Tickets also include up and down rides on the separate Whistler and Blackcomb mountain gondolas.

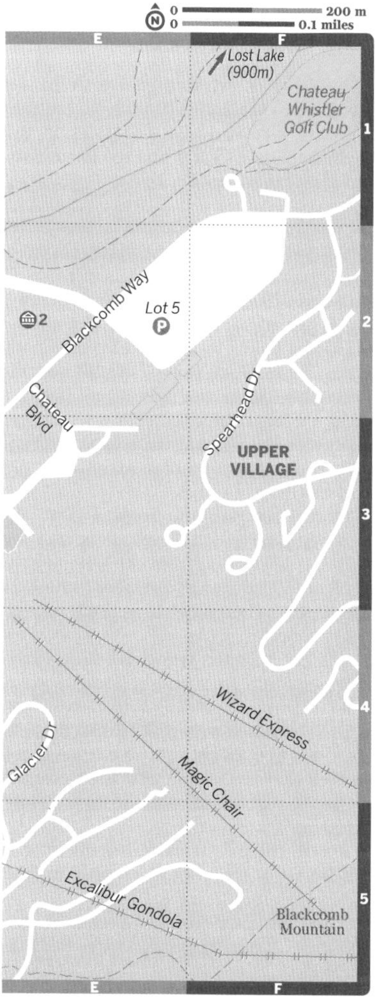

Whistler

CLOUDRAKER SKYBRIDGE BRIDGE

The newest attraction on Whistler Mountain is this 130m-long suspension bridge with a see-through base that connects the top of Whistler Peak with the Raven's Eye viewing platform on the West Ridge. Opened in summer 2018, the bridge is accessed by hiking downhill for 15 minutes from the Roundhouse Lodge and then taking the Peak Empress chairlift to the top of Whistler Mountain. If you are a vertigo sufferer, bear in mind that both chairlift and suspension bridge are mildly exposed.

Entrance is included with the Peak 2 Peak Gondola ticket.

EATING & DRINKING

It's not all pizzas and burgers. Indulge in gourmet dinners in Whistler Village or pick casually at Spanish-style tapas. Diversity is added in the shape of Japanese sushi, Australian pies and French-Canadian crepes.

★ PUREBREAD BAKERY $

Map p192 (☎604-962-1182; www.purebread.ca; 4338 Main St; baked goods $3-6; ⏲8am-6pm) Imagine the best bakery you've ever visited, elevate the quality by the power of 10 and you might just get Purebread. Founded as a pinprick sized business in Whistler's Function Junction business park in 2010, this slice of baking heaven has since expanded to fill this larger cafe in the central village.

It's hard to overstate the ambrosial perfection of the melt-in-your-mouth scones, wonderfully stodgy cakes and doorstep-sized sandwiches. Rather like a Whistler 'black diamond,' it will remain etched in your memory long after you leave.

PEAKED PIES AUSTRALIAN $

Map p192 (☎604-962-4115; www.peakedpies.com; 4369 Main St; pies $7-9; ⏲8am-9pm) Whistler's contingent of seasonal Aussie workers didn't just import their antipodean accents. Fortunately for us, they also brought their food - fresh, flaky and generously filled pies such as butter chicken or pepper steak which can also be enjoyed 'peaked,' ie topped with mashed potato, mushy peas and gravy. If you're having a sweet day, go for the apple crumble or mixed berry.

★HUNTER GATHER CANADIAN $$
Map p192 (☎604-966-2372; www.huntergatherwhistler.com; 4368 Main St; mains $15-29; ⏲noon-10pm) A noisy but cheerful emporium of local food, this new place has quickly become known for its smoked meats (the 'hunter' part) and local veg (the 'gather' part). Relish the beef brisket (smoked for 18 hours) and the golden-brown Pemberton potatoes, pan-fried to a state of crispy deliciousness. Punters must order and pay up-front and then grab a pew.

RED DOOR BISTRO FRENCH $$$
(☎604-962-6262; www.reddoorbistro.ca; 2129 Lake Placid Rd; mains $26-43; ⏲5-10pm) As soon as you know you're coming to Whistler, call for a reservation at this hot little Creekside eatery, largely a local residents' domain. Taking a French-bistro approach to fine, mostly West Coast ingredients means juniper-rubbed elk with mint pesto, or a seafood bouillabaisse - the menu is a changeable feast (check the blackboard). Food presentation is artistic and the service is spot on.

GARIBALDI LIFT COMPANY PUB
Map p192 (☎604-905-2220; 4165 Springs Lane; ⏲11am-1am) The closest bar to the slopes. You can smell the sweat of the skiers (or mountain bikers) hurtling past the patio at this cavernous bar that's known by every local as the GLC. The furnishings have the scuffs and dings of a well-worn pub, and the best time to come is when DJs or bands turn the place into a clubbish mosh pit.

SPORTS & ACTIVITIES

Pack plenty of extra adrenaline. Whistler has black diamond ski runs, a ballistic downhill bike park, bobsled rides in the Olympic Sliding Centre and the longest zip line in North America.

★WHISTLER-BLACKCOMB SNOW SPORTS
(☎604-967-8950; www.whistlerblackcomb.com; day-pass adult/child $178/89) Comprising 37 lifts and crisscrossed with over 200 runs, the Whistler-Blackcomb sister mountains, physically linked by the resort's mammoth 4.4km Peak 2 Peak Gondola (p192) are, indisputably, one of the largest and best ski areas in North America. The variety and quality of the facilities here is staggering and regular upgrades have maintained the resort's Olympian edge.

More than half the resort's runs are aimed at intermediate-level skiers, and the season typically runs from late November to April on Whistler and November to June on Blackcomb - December to February is the peak for both.

You can beat the crowds with an early-morning Fresh Tracks ticket ($23.95), available in advance at the Whistler Village gondola. Coupled with your regular lift ticket, it gets you an extra hour on the slopes (boarding from 7:15pm) and the ticket includes a buffet breakfast at the Roundhouse Lodge up top.

Snowboarders should also check out the freestyle terrain parks, mostly located on Blackcomb, including the Snow Cross and the Big Easy Terrain Garden. There's also the popular Habitat Terrain Park on Whistler.

CROSS-COUNTRY SKIING AROUND WHISTLER

Whistler has 120km of cross-country skiing trails spread over two areas: Lost Lake Park, a short walk from the Village, and the interlinked Olympic Park–Callaghan Country network, 25km by road to the west. Both areas offer groomed trails appropriate for classic and skate skiing and are graded easy (green) to advanced (black). Lost Lake is a pretty but relatively benign area with placid vistas and 30km of trails that partially utilize the snowed-in Chateau Whistler golf course. The Olympic Park has more technical terrain including the Nordic and Biathlon Olympic courses. The adjacent Callaghan Valley has a wilder flavor, including an opportunity to ski to the backcountry Journeyman Lodge, where you can dine and/or spend the night.

WHISTLER MOUNTAIN BIKE PARK MOUNTAIN BIKING

Map p192 (☎604-967-8950; http://bike.whistlerblackcomb.com; half-day lift ticket adult/child $59/32; ⏰May-Oct) Colonizing the melted ski slopes in summer and accessed via lifts at the village's south end, this park offers barreling downhill runs and an orgy of jumps and bridges twisting through well-maintained forested trails. Luckily, you don't have to be a bike courier to stand the knee-buckling pace: easier routes are marked in green, while blue intermediate trails and black-diamond advanced paths are also offered. BYO bike, or hire from **Summit Sport** (Map p192; ☎604-932-9225; www.summitsport.com; 4293 Mountain Sq; downhill/trail per day $150/80; ⏰9am-8:30pm).

Outside the park area, regional trails include Comfortably Numb (a tough 26km with steep climbs and bridges), A River Runs Through It (suitable for all skill levels, it has teeter-totters and log obstacles) and the gentle Valley Trail (an easy 14km loop that encircles the village and its lake, meadow and mountain chateau surroundings, and is recommended for first-timers).

WHISTLER OLYMPIC PARK SNOW SPORTS

(☎604-964-0060; www.whistlersportlegacies.com; 5 Callaghan Valley Rd; trail pass skiing/snowshoeing $28/17; ⏰9am-4:30pm mid-Dec–late-Mar) Just 25km southwest of the village via Hwy 99, the pristine, snow-swathed Callaghan Valley hosted several 2010 Olympic Nordic events. There are essentially two cross-country skiing areas here: the Whistler Olympic Park (where you can sample the Nordic and biathlon courses) and Ski Callaghan, which predates it. One pass covers both.

A modern, rarely overcrowded day lodge at the end of the road rents skis and snowshoes and has an economical cafe. There are 90km of trails leading out from the lodge plus around 40km of snowshoe trails. Several are pet-friendly. For an altogether more unique experience, it is possible to partake in biathlon lessons ($99, weekends only) at the nearby Olympic shooting range and race circuit.

A shuttle bus from Whistler Village ($10 round-trip) serves the park with one drop-off and two pick-ups per day in season. Book via the website.

LOST LAKE SNOW SPORTS

(☎604-905-0071; www.crosscountryconnection.ca; day pass adult/child $22/11; ⏰8am-8pm mid-Dec–Mar) Walking distance from the village, Lost Lake is the hub for 30km of wooded cross-country ski trails in the winter, most of them relatively easy. Approximately 4km of the trail around the lake is lit for additional nighttime skiing. The nexus and place to get kitted out is the PassivHaus, which served as the Austrian team HQ during the 2010 Olympics.

There are also 13km of trails for snowshoeing (day pass $11). The PassivHaus does daily rentals: $20 for snowshoes and $30 for skis.

In the summer, Lost Lake Park is known for hiking and swimming. There's a small beach and a more secluded platform on the lake's east shore that's popular with naturists.

ZIPTREK ECOTOURS ADVENTURE SPORTS

Map p192 (☎604-935-0001; www.ziptrek.com; 4280 Mountain Sq, Carleton Lodge; adult/child from $119/99; 👪) Not content with having one of the world's longest gondolas, Whistler opened North America's longest zip line in 2016, the super-scary Sasquatch (June to September) – a 2.2km-long catapult between Whistler and Blackcomb Mountains where it's possible to attain speeds of up to 100kmh. They also have several less dramatic zip lines, some aimed at kids, plus a great canopy walking tour ($49).

SLEEPING

Accommodation in Whistler is expensive but of a high quality (even the HI hostel is plush). Most hotels offer deluxe rooms with kitchenettes, fireplaces and balconies. Many are also equipped with sofa beds and hot tubs and are classified as studios or suites. The bigger hotels have gyms, spas, outdoor pools and hot tubs. Parking, if available, costs up to $40 extra. Breakfast is seldom included in room rates.

HI WHISTLER HOSTEL HOSTEL $

(☎604-962-0025; www.hihostels.ca/whistler; 1035 Legacy Way; dm/r $43/120; @📶) Built as athlete accommodation for the 2010 Winter Olympics, this sparkling hostel is 7km south of the village, near Function Junction.

WORTH A DETOUR

COWBOY COUNTRY

If you're craving an alternative to tourist-heavy Whistler Village, head for Pemberton – the next community north along Hwy 99. Founded as a farming and cowboy town, it still has a distant-outpost feel, with enough to keep you occupied for a half-day. Plan ahead via www.tourismpemberton.com.

Start with coffee and a giant cinnamon bun at the woodsy little **Blackbird Bakery** (☎604-894-6226; www.blackbirdbread.com; 7424 Frontier St; baked goods & sandwiches $3-8; ⏰6am-8pm, from 7am Sun) in the former train station, then walk over to **Pemberton Museum** (☎604-894-5504; www.pembertonmuseum.org; 7455 Prospect St; by donation; ⏰10am-5pm May-Oct) for the lowdown on how this quirky little town started. Ask them about the Pemberton mascot, a neckerchief-wearing potato dressed like a cowboy.

Next, hit **Pemberton Distillery** (☎604-894-0222; www.pembertondistillery.ca; 1954 Venture Pl; ⏰noon-5pm Wed & Thu, to 6pm Fri & Sat Jun–early Sep, reduced hrs rest of yr). A pioneer of BC's latter-day artisan-booze movement, they have tours and a tasting room; try their wild-honey liqueur. Then – with designated driver at the wheel – weave to to **Joffre Lakes**. There's a lovely two-hour hike from the trailhead here or you can just snap some glacier photos from the parking lot.

Finally, when dinner beckons, weave back into town and find a table at the rustic, red-walled **Pony** (☎604-894-5700; www.theponyrestaurant.ca; 1392 Portage Rd; mains $22-38; ⏰6:30am-late; ✍). It serves an elevated comfort-food menu (pizzas recommended) and BC craft beers.

Transit buses to/from town stop right outside. Book ahead for private rooms (with private baths and TVs) or save by staying in a small dorm. Eschewing the sometimes institutionalized HI hostel feel, this one has IKEA-style furnishings, art-lined walls and a licensed cafe.

PANGEA POD HOTEL HOTEL **$$**

Map p192 (☎604-962-1011; www.pangeapod.com; 4333 Sunrise Alley; pods from $140; ❄📶) Posing as a smarter, more private version of a hostel, Canada's first capsule hotel is based on the Japanese model, offering bed-sized 'pods' equipped with double futons, privacy curtains, individual air-con units, reading lights, lockers and mirrors. Colorfully tiled showers, powder rooms and loos are shared, but kept scrupulously clean.

ADARA HOTEL BOUTIQUE HOTEL **$$**

Map p192 (☎604-905-4009; www.adarahotel.com; 4122 Village Green; r from $219; 📶🏊🐾) Unlike all those lodges now claiming to be boutique hotels, the sophisticated and blissfully affordable Adara is the real deal. With warm wood furnishings studded with orange exclamation marks, the rooms offer spa-like baths, cool aesthetics and 'floating' fireplaces that look like TVs. Boutique extras include fresh cookies and in-room boot dryers. Prices dip significantly in shoulder season.

★**NITA LAKE LODGE** BOUTIQUE HOTEL **$$$**

(☎604-966-5700; www.nitalakelodge.com; 2135 Lake Placid Rd; d $289; 📶🐾) Adjoining the handsome Creekside railway station, this chic timber-framed lodge offers 'suites' rather than mere rooms, the smallest of which is an ample 45 sq m. Hugging the lakeside, the swankier suites feature individual patios, rock fireplaces and baths with heated floors and large tubs; some also have handy kitchens.

Creekside's ski lifts are a walkable few minutes away and there's an on-site spa. The hotel also has an excellent West Coast restaurant and a free shuttle to whisk you to the village if you'd prefer to dine further afield. Check the website for weekday bargains.

Richmond & Steveston

Explore

The region's modern-day Chinatown is easy to reach via Canada Line SkyTrain from Vancouver, making for an easy half-day excursion. There are two distinctly different experiences to be had here. Richmond proper is a utilitarian grid of Asian shopping malls, car parks and (with a bit of delving) some of the best Asian restaurants outside Asia. A little to the south, waterfront Steveston village is second only to Fort Langley in its historical significance, harboring two museums, an afternoon's worth of blustery dyke walks and legendary fish and chips.

The Best...

- **Sight** Richmond Night Market
- **Place to Eat** Shanghai River Restaurant (p199)
- **Place to Drink** Leisure Tea & Coffee (p199)

Top Tip

Ideal for cycling, Richmond's West Dyke Trail runs from Terra Nova Rural Park to Garry Point Park. From here, track east through Steveston on the South Dyke Trail.

Getting There & Away

- **Train** Skytrain Canada Line services zip from downtown Vancouver into Richmond every few minutes throughout the day, taking about 20 minutes from Waterfront Station. Make sure you board a Richmond-Brighouse train, otherwise you'll be heading to the airport instead.
- **Bus** For Steveston, hop on bus 401 or 407 at Richmond-Brighouse Station.

Need to Know

- **Location** 16km south of Vancouver
- **Tourist Office Tourism Richmond Visitor Centre** (Map p198; 604-271-8280; www.tourismrichmond.com; 3811 Moncton St, Steveston; 9:30am-6pm Jul & Aug, 9:30am-5pm Mon-Sat, noon-4pm Sun Sep-Jun; 401, S Richmond-Brighouse)
- **Area Code** 604

SIGHTS

Steveston is home to a couple of excellent museums, while Richmond hosts North America's best Asian night-market scene.

★RICHMOND NIGHT MARKET MARKET

Map p198 (604-244-8448; www.richmondnightmarket.com; 8351 River Rd, Richmond; adult/child $5/free; 7pm-midnight Fri-Sun mid-May–mid-Oct; S Bridgeport) Arguably Richmond's biggest lure is this atmospheric, always busy, Asian-flavored night market that has grown from humble beginnings in 2000 to become the largest night market in North America. Beyond the predictable (but fun) trinket stalls and fairground attractions, the complex is best known for its abundance of steam-billowing food stalls that ply everything from poke bowls to fried octopus. The live entertainment is equally diverse with punk rock alternating with martial arts displays.

It's handily located one block from Bridgeport station and 20 minutes from downtown Vancouver. Arrive early and be prepared to queue.

GULF OF GEORGIA CANNERY MUSEUM

Map p198 (604-664-9009; www.gulfofgeorgiacannery.org; 12138 4th Ave, Steveston; adult/child $12/free; 10am-5pm; ; 401, S Richmond-Brighouse) British Columbia's best 'industrial museum' illuminates the sights and sounds of the region's bygone era of labor-intensive fish processing. Most of the machinery remains and there's an evocative focus on the people who used to work here; you'll hear recorded testimonies from old employees percolating through the air like ghosts, bringing to life the days they spent immersed in entrails as thousands of cans rolled down the production line. Take one of the excellent, free, volunteer-led tours for the full story.

BRITANNIA SHIPYARD MUSEUM

Map p198 (640-718-8038; www.britanniashipyard.ca; 5180 Westwater Dr, Steveston; 10am-5pm, from noon Oct-Apr; 402, S Richmond-Brighouse) FREE A riverfront complex of historic sheds housing dusty tools, boats and reminders of the region's maritime past, this is one of the most evocative, fancy-free historic sites in the region. Check out the preserved Murakami House, where a large Japanese family lived before being unceremoniously interned during the war. Interpretive boards tell the story; well-versed volunteers fill in the gaps.

EATING & DRINKING

Richmond is one of the best places to sample Asian food in North America. The tourist office publishes a 'dumpling trail' leaflet listing around 20 restaurants specializing

Richmond & Steveston

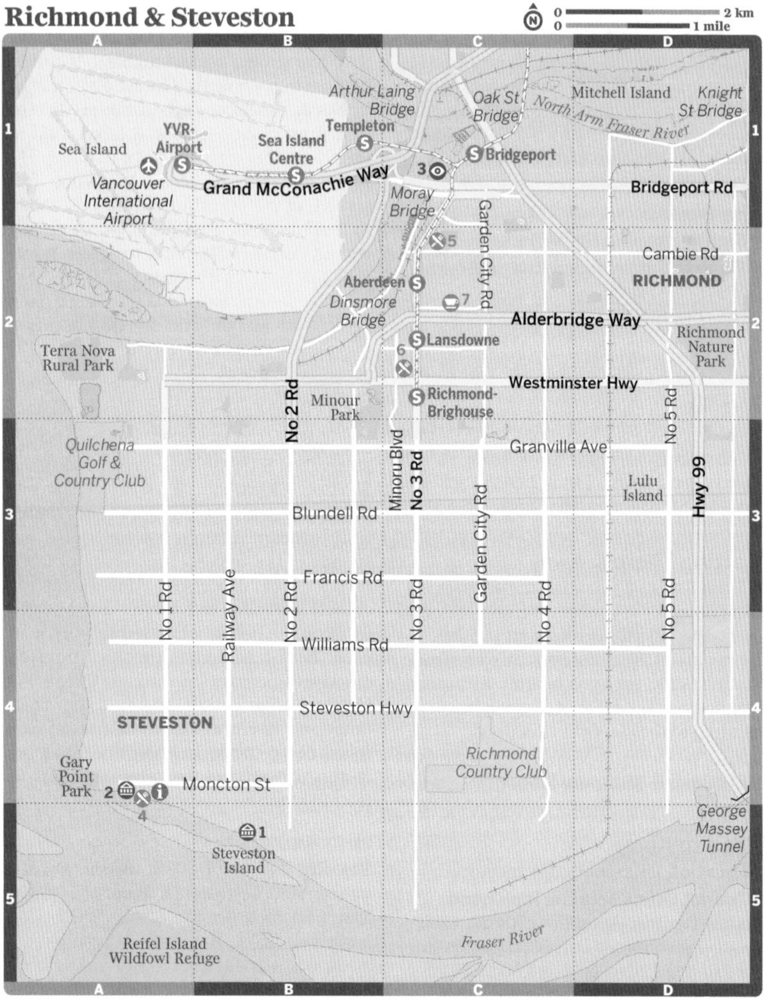

Richmond & Steveston

Sights (p197)
1 Britannia Shipyard B5
2 Gulf of Georgia Cannery A4
3 Richmond Night Market C1

Eating (p197)
4 Pajo's A4
5 President Plaza Food Court C2
6 Shanghai River Restaurant C2

Drinking & Nightlife (p197)
7 Leisure Tea & Coffee C2

in Asian, mostly Chinese dumplings. There are also several hawker-style food courts encased in large shopping malls. The still active fishing port of Steveston is, not surprisingly, a fine purveyor of fish and chips.

PAJO'S SEAFOOD $

Map p198 (☎604-272-1588; www.pajos.com; The Wharf, Steveston; mains $12-20; ⊙11am-8pm, reduced hrs off-season; 🚌401, Ⓢ Richmond-Brighouse) This weather-dependent floating fish shack nestled amid the fishing boats offers a three-way choice of salmon, cod and halibut to have with your chips. They also offer burgers, but seriously you didn't come here for that! If it's raining, try Dave's, a bricks-and-mortar place in Moncton St around the corner.

Pajo's house-made chowder is the ideal warm-up on a chilly day and there are also some good vegetarian and kid-portion options available.

PRESIDENT PLAZA FOOD COURT FOOD HALL $

Map p198 (☎604-270-8677; 8181 Cambie Rd, Richmond; mains $5-8; ⊙10am-7pm; Ⓢ Aberdeen) Richmond's bustling shopping-mall food courts echo the hawker stands found in many Asian cities, and one of the most authentic is this upstairs hidden gem that's lined with independent vendors. Order a few plates to share and you'll soon be diving into savory pancakes, silken-tofu soup and chewy Beijing donut bread.

★**SHANGHAI RIVER RESTAURANT** CHINESE $$

Map p198 (☎604-233-8885; www.shanghairiverrestaurant.com; 7381 Westminster Hwy, Richmond; mains $10-22; ⊙11am-3pm & 5:30-10pm; Ⓢ Richmond-Brighouse) Dining at Shanghai River is like attending a jam-packed Asian-style banquet brimming with an array of food. Fried eel arrives in hot stone bowls, whole fish adorns overstuffed plates, while smaller dishes of crispy pot-stickers, prawns with candied walnuts, Szechuan smoked duck and soup dumplings fly by.

If you've never been here before or aren't well-versed in any of the Chinese languages, it's best to just point at something you like the look of on one of the other (always crowded) revolving tables. Dining here is as much an experience as a feast, yet still manages to feel refined despite the restaurant's massive popularity. Book ahead.

LEISURE TEA & COFFEE TEAHOUSE

Map p198 (☎604-821-9998; 8391 Alexandra Rd, Richmond; ⊙noon-midnight; 📶; Ⓢ Lansdowne) Cultural fusion runs amok at this Asian-owned cafe decked out with a dark-wood German-Dutch–style interior. The menu is equally eclectic with Jamaican 'Blue Mountain' coffee, milk teas and super-sweet deserts all making appearances. Flemish art including several Rembrandt reproductions adorns the walls.

Southern Gulf Islands

Explore

Stressed Vancouverites love escaping into the restorative arms of these laid-back islands, strung like a shimmering necklace between the mainland and Vancouver Island. Formerly colonized by hippies and US draft dodgers, Salt Spring, Galiano, Mayne, Saturna, and North and South Pender deliver on their promise of rustic, sigh-triggering getaways. For more visitor information, see www.sgislands.com.

The Best

➡ **Sight** Salt Spring Island's Saturday Market (p200)

➡ **Place to Eat** Salt Spring Island's Tree House Cafe (p201)

➡ **Place to Drink** Galiano Island's Hummingbird Pub (p201)

Top Tip

Like a mental spa treatment, the whole point of visiting the Southern Gulf Islands is to slow down and stop looking at your watch: island time rules here.

Getting There & Away

➡ **Air** Seair Seaplanes (www.seairseaplanes.com) covers the five main islands, offering short hops from Vancouver. Harbour Air (www.harbourair.com) links Salt Spring Island with Vancouver.

➡ **Ferry** BC Ferries (www.bcferries.com) operates services, some direct, from Vancouver Island's Swartz Bay terminal to all the Southern Gulf Islands. There are also services from the mainland's Tsawwassen terminal. Gulf Islands Water Taxi (www.gulfislandswatertaxi.com) runs a limited walk-on service between some islands in July and August.

WORTH A DETOUR

FORT LANGLEY

Little Fort Langley's tree-lined streets and 19th-century storefronts make it one of the Lower Mainland's most picturesque historic villages, ideal for an afternoon away from Vancouver. Its main historic highlight is the colorful **Fort Langley National Historic Site** (604-513-4777; www.pc.gc.ca; 23433 Mavis Ave; adult/child $7.80/free; 10am-5pm;), perhaps the region's most important old-school landmark.

A fortified trading post since 1827, this is where James Douglas announced the creation of British Columbia (BC) in 1858, giving the site a legitimate claim to being the province's birthplace. With costumed re-enacters, re-created artisan workshops and a gold-panning area that's very popular with kids – who also enjoy charging around the wooden battlements – it's ideal for families.

If you need an introduction before you start exploring, there's a surprisingly entertaining time-travel-themed movie presentation on offer. And make sure you check the website before you arrive: there's a wide array of events that bring the past evocatively back to life, including a summertime evening campfire program that will take you right back to the pioneer days of the 1800s.

If you're driving from Vancouver, take Hwy 1 east for 40km, then take the 232nd St exit north. Follow the signs along 232nd St until you reach the stop sign at Glover Rd. Turn right here, and continue into the village. Turn right again on Mavis Ave, just before the railway tracks. The fort's parking lot is at the end of the street.

Need to Know

- **Location** Southwest from Vancouver; one to three hours by ferry or 20 minutes by plane
- **Tourist Offices Salt Spring Island Visitor Information Centre** (250-537-5252; www.saltspringtourism.com; 121 Lower Ganges Rd, Ganges; 9am-4pm May-Oct, 11am-3pm Nov-Apr); **Galiano Island Visitors Info Booth** (www.galianoisland.com; 2590 Sturdies Bay Rd; 10am-5pm Mon-Sat Jun-Aug, reduced hrs Sep-May)
- **Area Code** 250

SIGHTS

Salt Spring Island

★**SATURDAY MARKET** MARKET
(www.saltspringmarket.com; Centennial Park, Ganges; 9am-4pm Sat Apr-Oct) At the best market in British Columbia, the gigantic cornucopia of produce, edible goodies and locally made artworks lures everyone like a magnet on summer Saturdays. Arrive in the morning; it can be oppressively jam-packed at times. Alternatively, join the locals at the smaller, produce-only Tuesday market. Everything at both markets is made, baked or grown on the island.

SALT SPRING ISLAND CHEESE FARM
(250-653-2300; www.saltspringcheese.com; 285 Reynolds Rd; 11am-5pm, to 4pm Oct-Apr;) A family-friendly farmstead with a strollable garden, wandering chickens and a winery-like tasting room and shop, this quintessential Salt Spring spot produces goat- and sheep-milk chèvres, feta and Camembert styles; the soft goat-cheese rounds in several flavors (the peppercorn one packs a punch) are the farm's specialty. You can watch the handmade production through special windows, but look out for the farm's gamboling goats.

North Pender Islands

SEA STAR VINEYARDS WINERY
(250-629-6960; www.seastarvineyards.ca; 6621 Harbour Hill Dr, North Pender; 11am-5pm May-Sep) Once upon a time you had to fly to France for the kind of idyllic wine-supping experience offered at Sea Star. Water glistens like tin-foil through the trees, vines cling to huge step-like terraces and the handsome tasting room dispenses wine made from nine different varieties of grape. Crisp whites are a specialty.

PENDER ISLANDS MUSEUM MUSEUM
(www.penderislandsmuseum.ca; 2408 South Otter Bay Rd, North Pender; 10am-4pm Sat & Sun Jul & Aug, reduced hrs off-season; P) FREE Colonizing a historic white-clapboard farmhouse

dating from 1908, this volunteer-run museum includes an eclectic array of exhibits tracing the island's early pioneers. Look out for some evocative old photos and a beautiful vintage wool loom (weaving was once a thriving industry on Pender). The museum is located inside a tract of the Gulf Islands National Park Reserve overlooking tiny Roe Islet. A short trail leads to the tip of the tree-covered islet.

EATING

Salt Spring, especially in Ganges, has lots of dining options. The rest of the islands, though small, punch well above their weight, with diminutive rural-style cafes, restaurants affiliated to resorts and the odd more gourmet offering. Beware seasonal closures.

Salt Spring Island

BUZZY'S LUNCHEONETTE JEWISH **$**

(☎250-222-8650; 122 Fulford-Ganges Rd; sandwiches $8-12; ⊙11am-4pm Mon-Sat) It's tempting to suggest that recently opened Buzzy's is creating a buzz around Salt Spring with its Montreal smoked-meat sandwiches, but realistically it's more of a siren than a buzz. The tiny takeout utilizes succulent meat that's been cured for 10 days, smoked for eight hours and steamed for three.

★TREE HOUSE CAFE CANADIAN **$$**

(☎250-537-5379; www.treehousecafe.ca; 106 Purvis Lane, Ganges; mains $12-18; ⊙8am-4pm, to 10pm Wed-Sun, reduced hrs Sep-Jun) At this magical outdoor dining experience, you'll be sitting in the shade of a large plum tree as you choose from a menu of North American–style pastas, Mexican specialties and gourmet burgers and sandwiches. The roasted-yam quesadilla is a local favorite, perhaps washed down with a Salt Spring Island Ales porter. There's live music Wednesday to Sunday nights in summer.

Galiano Island

HUMMINGBIRD PUB PUB FOOD **$$**

(☎250-539-5472; www.hummingbirdpub.com; 47 Sturdies Bay Rd; mains $12-17; ⊙noon-midnight) A beloved rustic pub nestled among the Galiano trees. Look out for wandering deer and, of course, hummingbirds, outside. Fish and chips is the mainstay of the menu but plenty of other satisfying pub grub is also available. They run their own summer shuttle bus to get you to and from the pub, or you can walk along the Sturdies Bay trail paralleling the road.

ATREVIDA RESTAURANT CANADIAN **$$$**

(☎250-539-3388; www.galianoinn.com; 134 Madrona Dr; mains $22-32; ⊙6-9pm Jun-Sep, reduced hrs Oct-May) On busy nights ('Sticky Finger Fridays' are best, with hot finger food including chicken wings) the restaurant in the Galiano Inn (p202) transforms into the island's social hub with live music, loud chatter and plate-loads of lamb burger sliders. Service is pretty informal but the food has gourmet flourishes.

Mayne Island

SUNNY MAYNE BAKERY CAFE CAFE **$**

(☎250-539-2323; www.sunnymaynebakery.com; 472 Village Bay Rd; mains $4-10; ⊙6am-6pm) All Mayne visitors should make a beeline for the island's most reliable eating joint (open year round with earlier closing in the winter), a source of immense muffins, custom cakes, homemade pizzas and thick soups.

BENNETT BAY BISTRO CANADIAN **$$**

(☎250-539-3122; www.bennettbaybistro.com; 494 Arbutus Dr; mains $15-28; ⊙11:30am-8:30pm) You don't have to be a guest of the Mayne Island Resort (p202) to dine at its restaurant, and you'll find a menu combining pubby classics like fish and chips with elevated dinner features like pasta and steaks. Go for the seafood, though – especially the velvet-soft fennel-seared halibut. Reservations recommended.

North Pender Islands

VANILLA LEAF BAKERY CAFE CAFE **$**

(☎250-629-6453; 17/4605 Bedwell Harbour Rd, Driftwood Centre, North Pender; snacks $3-8; ⊙7am-5pm, from 8am Sun; ⓦ) Superb pastries both sweet and savory are served here along with organic coffee. Safeguarded behind a glass partition, you can admire pistachio-cream danish pastries, steak-and-ale pies and the dangerous-looking 'mile-high apple pie.' It's located in the Driftwood Centre with extra seating (and a summer ice-cream trolley) on a square of lawn outside.

JO'S PLACE CANADIAN $$

(☎250-629-6033; www.josplacepender.com; 4605 Bedwell Harbour Rd, North Pender; mains $15-24; ⊙8am-2pm, plus 5-8pm Fri-Sun) It's worth making Jo's your first stop after the ferry, so good is the food, service and ambiance, especially if you're in the mood for brunch when the eclectic menu parades bubble & squeak, and pear and Gorgonzola omelets.

SPORTS & ACTIVITIES

SALT SPRING ADVENTURE CO KAYAKING

(☎250-537-2764; www.saltspringadventures.com; 125 Rainbow Rd, Ganges; rentals/tours from $40/65; ⊙9am-6pm May-Sep) When it's time to hit the water, touch base with this well-established local operator. They can kit you out for a bobbling kayak tour around Ganges Harbour, but they also serve the SUP crowd. Bike rentals and half-day whale-watching tours ($130) are also on the menu.

GALIANO KAYAKS KAYAKING

(☎250-539-2442; www.seakayak.ca; 3451 Montague Rd; per 2hr/day from $35/60, tours from $60) Offering kayak, canoe and SUP rentals to those who fancy exploring on their own, the friendly folk here also run popular guided kayak tours, including early morning jaunts, sunset tours and an immersive (not literally) six-hour Experience Galiano tour.

PENDER ISLAND KAYAK ADVENTURES KAYAKING

(☎250-629-6939; www.kayakpenderisland.com; 4605 Oak Rd, North Pender; rentals/tours from $30/65) Venture out with a paddle (and hopefully a boat) into the calm waters of Port Browning. The marina-based operator also rents SUPs (per hour $25) and bicycles (per two hours $25), and runs popular guided kayak tours; the sunset bliss tour is especially recommended. They also run multiday tours – great if you want to go in-depth (while still remaining in your kayak).

SLEEPING

B&Bs and cabin rentals are the staple on the islands. Salt Spring has a couple of small hotels. Mayne, Galiano and Pender each have a small high-quality resort.

★**GALIANO INN** HOTEL $$

(☎250-539-3388; www.galianoinn.com; 134 Madrona Dr; d from $249;) The island's most deluxe accommodation occupies a small unobtrusive collection of buildings right next to the ferry dock, complete with spa, manicured lawns and the casual-gourmet Atrevida Restaurant (p201). All rooms face the placid water and the one-bedroom villas positively spoil you with multi-jet showers, wine coolers and outdoor patios/decks furnished with hot tubs, barbecues and wood-burning fireplaces.

WOODS ON PENDER CABIN $$

(☎250-629-3353; www.woodsonpender.com; 4709 Canal Rd, North Pender; d/cabin/Airstream from $130/220/275;) With lodge rooms and rustic cabins also available, the stars here are the six self-catering Airstream caravans, each with its own barbecue-equipped deck. The tree-lined site also includes hot tubs, outdoor games and a restaurant serving farm-to-table food. There's a three-night minimum stay in summer.

MAYNE ISLAND RESORT HOTEL $$

(☎250-539-3122; www.mayneislandresort.com; 494 Arbutus Dr; d/villa $159/299;) Superbly inviting option with lots of deluxe flourishes, there are cottages and inn rooms to choose from here. You'll also find a restaurant (p201), on-site spa and beach proximity at this top-notch hotel.

SALT SPRING INN HOTEL $$

(☎250-537-9339; www.saltspringinn.com; 132 Lower Ganges Rd, Ganges; d shared/private bath from $99/175;) This small old-school hotel is located in the heart of Ganges, above a popular bar, in one of the island's oldest buildings. The pricier deluxe rooms have sea views, en suite baths and fireplaces. All are well maintained and well located.

Sleeping

Metro Vancouver has more than 23,000 hotel, B&B and hostel rooms, the majority in or around the downtown core. Airbnb also operates here, although a regulatory crackdown has reduced their number in recent years. Rates peak in July and August, but expect good spring and fall deals. Book far ahead for summer, unless you fancy sleeping rough in Stanley Park.

Hotels

A rash of new hotels, mostly in the boutique and high-end range, has popped up here in recent years, including the EXchange Hotel, Hotel BLU and the Fairmont Pacific Rim. The swish Parq Vancouver downtown casino complex also opened its doors recently and, along with its posh restaurants, has two hotels of its own.

Older 'it' properties such as the Opus Hotel, Loden Hotel and St Regis Hotel have worked hard to maintain their appeal in the face of this competition, often offering enticing off-season rates. There are also plenty of attractive midrange options, many of which offer great-value in-suite kitchens that can save you a considerable amount on dine-out costs. Consider staying downtown: there are lots of options in the area and much of the neighborhood is easily accessed on foot. In the budget range, the popular YWCA Hotel was undergoing a large-scale expansion on our visit. Free wi-fi is common at city accommodations, and most properties are nonsmoking.

B&Bs

The closest B&Bs to downtown are in the West End, and are typically sumptuous heritage homes of the romantic, higher-end sleepover variety. Prices vary more in neighborhoods a little further out – especially Kitsilano and Fairview – where you usually won't be far from a bus or SkyTrain route that can have you downtown in a few minutes. Keep in mind that some B&Bs require a two-night minimum stay – especially on summer weekends – and cancellation policies can cost you an arm and a leg if you decide not to turn up.

Budget Options

There are many low-cost options in the city, but remember that hostels, in particular, are not all created equal. While some offer great value, others can be smelly fleapits that you'll be itching (quite literally) to get out of. Consider the popular YWCA, Samesun or HI hostel options as well as accommodations at the University of British Columbia (UBC). There are also a couple of respectable but low-cost guesthouse-style options. When traveling off-season, your budget will likely stretch to a bargain rate at a midrange property.

Taxes & Fees

Be aware that there will be some significant additions to most quoted room rates. You'll pay an extra 8% Provincial Sales Tax (PST) plus 5% Goods and Services Tax (GST) above the advertised rate. Also, in common with other large British Columbia (BC) cities, Vancouver charges an additional 3% hotel tax (called the Municipal and Regional District Tax). On top of this, some hotels also charge a Destination Marketing Fee and/or a Facilities Fee. Parking fees don't help either: overnight parking, especially at higher-end downtown hotels, can be expensive, sometimes more than $50 per night. B&Bs usually include parking free of charge. Clarify each of these potential extras with your accommodations before you book.

NEED TO KNOW

Price Ranges

The following price ranges refer to a double room with bathroom.

$	less than $100
$$	$100–$250
$$$	over $250

Check-in & Check-out Times

Check-in is typically 3pm, although hotels are often willing to let you in earlier if your room is ready. Check-out time is typically noon.

Tipping

Bellhops typically get tipped $2 to $5 for hailing you a cab at the front of the hotel, and up to $5 for carrying your bags to your room. Housekeepers can be tipped $2 to $5 per night of your stay, although this is entirely optional.

Useful Websites

Tourism Vancouver (www.tourismvancouver.com) Wide range of accommodations listings.

Hello BC (www.hellobc.com) Destination British Columbia (BC) accommodations search engine.

Accredited BC Accommodations Association (www.accreditedaccommodations.ca) Wide range of B&Bs in and around Vancouver.

Lonely Planet (www.lonelyplanet.com/canada/vancouver/hotels) Recommendations and bookings.

Lonely Planet's Top Choices

Victorian Hotel (p206) Downtown historic hotel near all the action.

Sunset Inn & Suites (p208) West End favorite with kitchen-equipped rooms.

St Regis Hotel (p206) I Amenity-packed boutique property with a great central location.

Sylvia Hotel (p208) Ivy-covered heritage charmer with some lovely beachfront views.

Skwachàys Lodge (p210) First Nations art-themed boutique sleepover.

Loden Hotel (p209) Designer boutique hotel steps from the downtown action.

Best by Budget

$

YWCA Hotel (p210) Centrally located tower with comfortable rooms that offer great value (especially for families).

HI Vancouver Downtown (p208) Actually located in the West End, this friendly hostel also has sought-after private and family rooms.

$$

Skwachàys Lodge (p210) New boutique hotel lined with First Nations art.

Sylvia Hotel (p208) Charming beachfront sleepover in the West End, overlooking English Bay.

$$$

Rosewood Hotel Georgia (p207) Vancouver's top 'it' hotel for a stylish stay.

Wedgewood Hotel & Spa (p207) Classic deluxe hotel dripping with elegant flourishes.

Best Boutique Hotels

St Regis Hotel (p206) City-center accommodations with some excellent value-added amenities.

Loden Hotel (p209) A slick and alluring Coal Harbour property just steps from the downtown core.

Opus Hotel (p210) Sexy and chic hotel in the heart of Yaletown; close to many restaurants.

Wedgewood Hotel & Spa (p207) Classic and classy European-feel decor, plus a popular spa.

Best Under-the-Radar Hotels

Sunset Inn & Suites (p208) Tucked into the West End but with a highly loyal following.

Times Square Suites Hotel (p209) Great location near Stanley Park for this hidden-in-plain-sight property.

Granville Island Hotel (p211) Tucked at the quieter end of the island, with great waterfront views.

YWCA Hotel (p210) Downtown budget-friendly tower close to everything.

L'Hermitage Hotel (p207) Slick but discreet sleepover in the heart of downtown.

Where to Stay

NEIGHBORHOOD	FOR	AGAINST
Downtown	Walking distance to stores, restaurants, nightlife and some attractions; great transit links to wider region; good range of hotels	Can be pricey; streets can be clamorous; some accommodations overlook noisy traffic areas
West End	Walking distance to Stanley Park; many midrange restaurants nearby; heart of the LGBT+ district; quiet residential streets	Mostly high-end B&Bs with a couple of additional chain hotels; can be a bit of a hike to the city center and attractions other than Stanley Park
Yaletown & Granville Island	Close to shops and many restaurants; good transport links to other areas	Few accommodations options to choose from
Fairview & South Granville	Quiet residential streets; well-priced heritage B&B sleepovers; good bus and SkyTrain access to downtown	Most options are B&Bs; few local nightlife options
Kitsilano & UBC	Comfy heritage houses and good UBC budget options; direct transit to downtown; on the doorstep of several beaches	Not the center of the action; scant nightlife options; can feel a bit too quiet and laid back
North Shore	Better hotel rates than city center; handy access to downtown via SeaBus; close to popular attractions such as Grouse Mountain and Capilano Suspension Bridge	Away from the heart of the action; takes time to get to other major attractions

Downtown & West End

Most of the city's main hotels are located downtown, many of them in the few blocks that radiate south from the waterfront. The West End is also home to some top-notch heritage B&Bs.

Downtown

HI VANCOUVER CENTRAL HOSTEL $

Map p266 (604-685-5335; www.hihostels.ca/en/destinations/british-columbia/hi-vancouver-central; 1025 Granville St, Downtown; dm/r from $60/120; 10) On the Granville Strip, this warren-like hostel is more of a party joint than its HI Downtown (p208) sibling. Some of the benefits of its past hotel incarnation remain, including air-conditioning and small rooms, some of which are now private, with the rest converted to dorm rooms with up to four beds. There are dozens of two-bedded rooms (some en suite).

Snag a back room to avoid Granville St noise issues. Kitchen facilities are limited to microwaves and toasters but a free continental breakfast is included. There's a brimming roster of social activities, including regular sightseeing tours. Location-wise, this hostel is within staggering distance of many bars and clubs.

SAMESUN BACKPACKERS LODGE HOSTEL $

Map p266 (604-682-8226; www.samesun.com; 1018 Granville St, Downtown; dm/r incl breakfast from $62/180; 10) Vancouver's liveliest hostel is right on the city's nightlife strip. Ask for a back room if you fancy a few hours of sleep or head down to the on-site bar (provocatively called the Beaver) to hang out with the partying throng. Dorms, including some pod beds, are comfortably small, and there are also private rooms plus a large shared kitchen.

Continental breakfast is included. This sociable hostel offers daily events and activities (including tours) as well as a large common room for hanging out with your next best friend from halfway around the world. The downstairs bar is also a good spot to catch a game, along with a few beer specials.

★**VICTORIAN HOTEL** HOTEL $$

Map p266 (604-681-6369; www.victorianhotel.ca; 514 Homer St, Downtown; d incl breakfast from $200; Granville) The high-ceilinged rooms at this well-maintained heritage hotel combine glossy hardwood floors, a sprinkling of antiques, an occasional bay window and plenty of historical charm. The best rooms are in the extension, where raindrop showers, marble bathroom floors and flatscreen TVs add a slice of luxe. Rates include continental breakfast and rooms are provided with fans in summer.

Travellers on a budget should consider the hotel's exposed-brick 'Euro Rooms,' which have their own sinks but share recently upgraded bathrooms with up to three other rooms. The Victorian has famously friendly staff and is brilliantly located just steps from both Gastown and the downtown core.

BURRARD HOTEL HOTEL $$

Map p266 (604-681-2331; www.theburrard.com; 1100 Burrard St, Downtown; d from $240; 2) A groovy makeover a few years back transformed this 1950s downtown motel into a knowingly cool sleepover with a tongue-in-cheek retro feel (neon exterior sign included). Colorful, mostly compact rooms have been spruced up with modern flourishes and contemporary amenities such as refrigerators and flatscreens. But not everything has changed; the hidden interior courtyard's towering palm trees echo yesteryear Vegas.

The hotel's extras include free loaner bikes and access to a nearby gym; there's also a guest laundry if you need to wash your undies. Overnight parking costs $28 but the building's main level includes a coffee shop and a popular Burgoo restaurant, so you might not need to drive anywhere after all.

ST REGIS HOTEL BOUTIQUE HOTEL $$$

Map p266 (604-681-1135; www.stregishotel.com; 602 Dunsmuir St, Downtown; d incl breakfast from $325; Granville) An elegant art-lined boutique sleepover in a 1913 heritage shell. Befitting its age, almost all the rooms seem to be a different size, and they exhibit a loungey élan with deco-esque furniture, earth-toned bedspreads, flatscreen TVs and multimedia hubs. Rates include value-added flourishes such as cooked breakfasts, access to the nearby gym and free long-distance and international phone calls.

The St Regis is well located in the heart of the action, offers top-notch service and has a business center if you've left your device at home. Overnight parking is $30.

L'HERMITAGE HOTEL BOUTIQUE HOTEL **$$$**

Map p266 (☎778-327-4100; www.lhermitagevancouver.com; 788 Richards St, Downtown; d from $420; P ❄ @ 📶 ≋ 🐾; S Vancouver City Centre) This discreet, well-located property is divided between longer-stay suites and guests just dropping in for the night. Either way, you'll find excellent service as well as a contemporary designer feel combined with artsy flourishes in the rooms, some of which offer kitchens. A library-style common lounge has a 'secret' garden terrace; there's also an adjoining Jacuzzi and a lap pool.

There's a well-equipped gym and a steam room here, and you're just steps from a tasty menu of local restaurants. Free loaner bikes are available if you fancy exploring the city's ever-expanding network of urban bicycle lanes. Overnight parking costs $35.

EXCHANGE HOTEL BOUTIQUE HOTEL **$$$**

Map p266 (☎604-563-4693; www.exchangehotelvan.com; 475 Howe St, Downtown; d from $475; P ❄ 📶 🐾; S Waterfront) Vancouver's newest 'it' hotel has transformed the city's former stock-exchange tower into a swank, well-located sleepover. It is studded with stylish, cleverly detailed rooms that are a cut above most city-center properties, so expect floor-to-ceiling windows, herringbone-patterned wooden floors and first-name service from the smiling staffers. Walking distance to an array of restaurants; the hotel's lobby bar is a cocktail-quaffing hotspot.

Overnight parking costs $48.

WEDGEWOOD HOTEL & SPA BOUTIQUE HOTEL **$$$**

Map p266 (☎604-689-7777; www.wedgewoodhotel.com; 845 Hornby St, Downtown; d from $450; P ❄ @ 📶; 🚌5) The last word in old-world European-style luxury, the elegant Wedgewood drips with top-hatted charm. The friendly staff is second to none, rooms are stuffed with reproduction antiques and balconies enable you to smirk at the seemingly grubby plebs shuffling past below. Steam up your monocle with a spa trip, then sip a signature cocktail in the sleek lobby bar.

ROSEWOOD HOTEL GEORGIA HOTEL **$$$**

Map p266 (☎604-682-5566; www.rosewoodhotels.com; 801 W Georgia St, Downtown; d from $650; P ❄ @ 📶 ≋ 🐾; S Vancouver City Centre) A historic downtown property that underwent a spectacular renovation a few years back, bringing it back to its sumptuous 1927 glory days. Despite the abstract modern art lining its public areas, the hotel's rooms take a classic, elegant approach with warming earth and coffee tones, pampering treats such as deep soaker tubs and (in some rooms) sparkling downtown cityscape views.

Save time for the swank lobby-level restaurant. Alongside the hotel's successful resurrection, it's become one of the top places to be seen for the city's social set – and you, if you look the part. Overnight parking is $55.

FAIRMONT HOTEL VANCOUVER HOTEL **$$$**

Map p266 (☎604-684-3131; www.fairmont.com/hotel-vancouver; 900 W Georgia St, Downtown; d from $500; P ❄ @ 📶 ≋ 🐾; S Vancouver City Centre) Opened in 1939 by visiting UK royals, this gargoyle-topped grand dame is a Vancouver historic landmark. Despite its vintage provenance, the hotel carefully balances comfort with elegance; the lobby is bedecked with crystal chandeliers but the rooms have an understated business-hotel feel. If you have the budget, check into the Gold Floor for a raft of pampering extras.

If you're interested in the hotel's storied heritage, nip downstairs to find some untouched art-deco flourishes. And if you're missing your pooch back home, there are two friendly dogs available for guest walkies; you'll find them reclining on their own daybeds near the concierge desk. Overnight parking costs $62.

FAIRMONT PACIFIC RIM HOTEL **$$$**

Map p266 (☎604-695-5300; www.fairmont.com/pacific-rim-vancouver; 1038 Canada Pl, Downtown; d from $600; P ❄ 📶 ≋ 🐾; S Waterfront) Near the convention center, this superbly stylish 367-room property is Vancouver's newest Fairmont. While many rooms have city views, the ones with waterfront vistas will blow you away, especially as you sit in your jetted tub or cube-shaped Japanese bath with a glass of bubbly. Extras include gratis BMW loaner bikes plus an outdoor terrace swimming pool.

ARTSY SLEEPOVERS

The Rosewood Hotel Georgia (p207) has arguably the city's best hotel art collection. Dominated by modern Canadian art, its public spaces have a gallery feel with abstract works by the likes of Alan Wood, Marcel Barbeau and Guido Molinari studding the walls. The highlight, though, is in the lobby and it's the only piece by a non-Canadian artist. Entitled *Internity*, the 3D work by Brit artist Patrick Hughes shifts perspective as you move in front of it and is a real eye-popper.

Over in the West End, Vancouver's self-proclaimed 'art hotel', the Listel Hotel, has a curatorial arrangement with local galleries and museums that means its corridors are lined with display cases of intriguing art; First Nations carvings and contemporary abstract works dominate. There's an even more dedicated indigenous-art approach at Skwachàys Lodge (p210), a newer boutique hotel where every room has been designed in collaboration with a different First Nations artist.

Check out the wrap-around text-art installation on the hotel's glass exterior. And stick around for drinks in the sleek Botanist restaurant, complete with its own cocktail-forward bar. Soothe your hangover away the next day at the Willow Stream Spa, one of the area's most popular pampering options. Overnight parking costs $55.

West End

HI VANCOUVER DOWNTOWN HOSTEL **$**

Map p270 (604-684-4565; www.hihostels.ca/en/destinations/british-columbia/hi-vancouver-downtown; 1114 Burnaby St, West End; dm/r from $62/135; @; 6) It says 'downtown' but this purpose-built hostel is on a quiet residential West End side street a couple of downhill blocks from the beach. It's popular with older hostelers and families, the dorms are all small and rates include continental breakfast. Private rooms with their own sinks are available. There's also bike storage, a full kitchen and a cool rooftop patio.

At this most 'institutional' of Vancouver's three HI hostels, the front-deskers are especially friendly. Book well ahead for private rooms, and ask about their popular Stanley Park (p58) tours.

★**SUNSET INN & SUITES** HOTEL **$$**

Map p270 (604-688-2474; www.sunsetinn.com; 1111 Burnaby St, West End; d incl breakfast $225; P@; 6) A good-value cut above most of Vancouver's self-catering suite hotels, the popular Sunset Inn offers larger-than-average rooms with kitchens. Each has a balcony, and some – particularly those on south-facing higher floors – have partial views of English Bay. Rates include continental breakfast (with make-your-own waffles) and, rare for Vancouver, free parking. The attentive staff is among the best in the city.

Sunset Inn is sitting pretty near a wide array of West End shops and restaurants, as well as Sunset Beach and the bustling Davie St 'gayborhood.' A handy on-site laundry for guests is also available. And if you fancy a night in, the front desk can loan you a free movie or two.

SYLVIA HOTEL HOTEL **$$**

Map p270 (604-681-9321; www.sylviahotel.com; 1154 Gilford St, West End; d from $199; P@; 5) This ivy-covered 1912 charmer enjoys a prime location overlooking English Bay. Generations of guests keep coming back – many requesting the same room every year – for a dollop of old-world ambience, plus a side order of first-name service. The rooms, some with older furnishings, have an array of comfortable configurations; the best are the large suites with kitchens and waterfront views.

If you don't have a room with a view, decamp to the large, lobby-level bar to nurse a cocktail and watch the sun set over the beach. Overnight parking costs $18.

BUCHAN HOTEL HOTEL **$$**

Map p270 (604-685-5354; www.buchanhotel.com; 1906 Haro St, West End; d with/without bath $149/109; P; 5) The 1926-built Buchan, just steps from Stanley Park (p58), has bags of charm. Facilities were being upgraded on our visit and while prices have risen somewhat with the arrival of new owners, sleepovers here are still typically good value, especially off-season. There's a wide array of rooms, including some with shared bathrooms, but all are clean and well maintained. Expect friendly front-deskers.

There's also a comfy guest lounge; other extras include storage facilities for bikes and skis as well as handy laundry machines. If you're driving, there's some free parking around the neighborhood, or you can pay $10 to park overnight at the hotel (spaces limited). There are many midrange dining options nearby, including a charming Italian restaurant at the base of the building.

TIMES SQUARE SUITES HOTEL APARTMENT $$$

Map p270 (604-684-2223; www.timessquaresuites.com; 1821 Robson St, West End; d from $300; P; 5) Superbly located a short walk from Stanley Park (p58), this West End hidden gem (even the entrance can be hard to spot) is a comfy apartment-style Vancouver sleepover. Rooms are mostly spacious one-bedroom suites with tubs, laundry facilities, full kitchens and well-maintained (if slightly 1980s) decor. There's a supermarket across the street plus a wide array of restaurants just steps away.

Choose a back suite if you want to be away from the busy road. Up to three adults can be accommodated in each suite (all are equipped with sofa beds). Make sure you visit the shared rooftop patio: the ideal place to while away an evening with a glass of wine, and it has a communal barbecue.

LISTEL HOTEL BOUTIQUE HOTEL $$$

Map p270 (604-684-8461; www.thelistelhotel.com; 1300 Robson St, West End; d from $340; P@; 5) A lounge-cool sleepover with famously friendly front-deskers. Rooms at the Listel have a relaxed West Coast feel and typically feature striking original artworks. But it's not all about looks; cool features include glass water bottles in the rooms, a daily wine reception (from 5pm) and the free use of loaner e-bikes if you want to explore nearby Stanley Park (p58).

Steps from Robson St's shopping and dining hot spots, the hotel's on-site Forage (p69) restaurant and Canadiana-themed Timber (p70) bar mean you might just remain here for the duration of your stay in the city. Overnight parking is $31.

LODEN HOTEL BOUTIQUE HOTEL $$$

Map p270 (604-669-5060; www.theloden.com; 1177 Melville St, West End; d from $500; P@; S Burrard) This deeply stylish 77-room hotel is the real designer deal. Its chic, mocha-hued rooms have an original, contemporary feel, with luxe accoutrements including marble-lined bathrooms and oh-so-civilized heated floors. Service is top notch; try the lobby's Tableau resto-bar as well as the complimentary London taxi-cab limo service. Free loaner cruiser bikes are available; they're perfect for exploring the Stanley Park Seawall (p52).

Overnight parking costs $45.

ENGLISH BAY INN B&B $$$

Map p270 (604-683-8002; www.englishbayinn.com; 1968 Comox St, West End; d from $310; P; 6) Each of the antique-lined rooms in this Tudor-esque B&B near Stanley Park (p58) has a private bathroom, and some have sumptuous four-poster beds. Five of the six rooms are for adults only, while the sixth is a family-friendly self-contained basement apartment for up to four occupants. Rates include a multicourse breakfast, except for the family room, which has its own full kitchen.

This property has been a charmer for years, with many loyal guests coming back. Free parking is available, although there are only three spots so you need to reserve ahead.

SHANGRI-LA HOTEL HOTEL $$$

Map p270 (604-689-1120; www.shangri-la.com/vancouver; 1128 W Georgia St, West End; d from $540; P@; S Burrard) Occupying the lower floors of one of the city's tallest glass towers, the Shangri-La redefined opulent Vancouver sleepovers when it opened. Many of the sleek, contemporary-classic rooms are bright and chic, often with subtle Asian flourishes, while detailing extras

HOTELS WITH HISTORY

- Fairmont Hotel Vancouver (p207) The city's lovely, gargoyle-topped grand hotel has had several royal guests over the years.
- Rosewood Hotel Georgia (p207) Restored to its 1920s golden-age glory; glam former guests include Sinatra, Dietrich and Presley (not on the same night).
- Sylvia Hotel (p208) Ivy-covered West End landmark where Errol Flynn is said to have had more than a drink or two.

TASTY HOTEL BARS

- Fairmont Pacific Rim (p207) Swish bar ideal for cocktails and schmoozing.
- Sylvia Hotel (p208) Lovely bar with views across English Bay.
- Loden Hotel (p209) Slick spot for pre-dinner cocktails.
- Opus Hotel (p210) Dress to hang with the Yaletown glitterati.
- Listel Hotel (p209) Home of a Canadiana-themed bar with a craft-beer bent.

include automatic bathroom blinds so you can shower behind the floor-to-ceiling windows without startling passers-by outside.

Service is of the highly attentive, first-name variety and there's also an excellent full-service spa. If you have any money left after splurging on your room, check out the luxury boutiques on adjacent Alberni St, including Prada and Tiffany. Overnight parking is $48.

Gastown & Chinatown

★SKWACHÀYS LODGE BOUTIQUE HOTEL **$$**

Map p273 (☎604-687-3589; www.skwachays.com; 29 W Pender St, Chinatown; d from $300; ❄📶; Ⓢ Stadium-Chinatown) The 18 small but elegantly designed rooms at this sparkling First Nations art hotel include the captivating Forest Spirits Suite, with floor-to-ceiling birch branches, and the sleek Longhouse Suite, with its illuminated metalwork frieze. Deluxe trappings, from plasma TVs to eco-friendly toiletries, are standard and there's an on-site gallery for purchasing one-of-a-kind artworks. The main streets of Gastown and Chinatown are just steps away.

An inviting and immersive cultural sleepover, the property is owned by the Vancouver Native Housing Society and, separate from the hotel, there are live-work artist studios here, each subsidized by profits from the hotel and its fair-trade gallery.

Yaletown & Granville Island

YWCA HOTEL HOTEL **$**

Map p274 (☎604-895-5830; www.ywcahotel.com; 733 Beatty St, Yaletown; s/d/tr without bath $106/118/173; P ⊖ ❄ @ 📶; Ⓢ Stadium-Chinatown) A good-value, well-located option with nicely maintained (if spartan) rooms of the student-accommodations variety. There's a range of configurations, from singles to five-bed rooms, plus shared, semi-private or private bathrooms. Each room has a TV and mini-refrigerator and there are TV lounges and communal kitchens too. Rates include access to the YWCA Health & Fitness Centre, a 15-minute walk away.

This is a great option for budget-conscious families; kids get a toy upon check-in. Despite the slightly institutionalized feel, the staff are friendly and helpful. And if you stay here off-season, room rates are considerably lower, including good rates for weekly stays. Expansion of the hotel was underway during our last visit, with 65 rooms being added in a new tower.

OPUS HOTEL BOUTIQUE HOTEL **$$$**

Map p274 (☎604-642-6787; www.opushotel.com; 322 Davie St, Yaletown; d $500; P ❄ 📶 🐾; Ⓢ Yaletown-Roundhouse) The 96-room Opus kick-started Vancouver's boutique-hotel scene and, with regular revamps, it's remained one of the city's top sleepover options. The designer rooms have contemporary-chic interiors with bold colors, mod furnishings and feng-shui bed placements, while many of the luxe bathrooms have clear windows overlooking the streets (visiting exhibitionists take note).

A model of excellent service, the Opus has a slick on-site bar and a quality Italian restaurant, while all rooms come with loaner iPads. And if you need to get around town, you can borrow a gratis bike – an excellent incentive not to bring your car since parking here costs $45 per night.

GEORGIAN COURT HOTEL HOTEL **$$$**

Map p274 (☎604-682-5555; www.georgiancourt.com; 773 Beatty St, Yaletown; d $400; P ❄ 📶 🐾; Ⓢ Stadium-Chinatown) This under-the-radar, European-style property has never changed its old-school approach to good service and solid, dependable amenities. Rooms have an elegant, business-hotel feel but the spacious apartment-style executive corner suites – with their quiet, recessed bedrooms – are best. There's a small on-site fitness room (plus free loaner bicycles) and the hotel runs a shuttle bus around the city for guests.

A good location near the city center adds to the appeal here, and if you're planning to catch a hockey, football or soccer game, the city's two main stadiums are just steps away. Overnight parking costs $30.

GRANVILLE ISLAND HOTEL BOUTIQUE HOTEL **$$$**

Map p275 (☎604-683-7373; www.granvilleisland hotel.com; 1253 Johnston St, Granville Island; d $400; P ❄ @ ☎ 🐾; 🚌50) This gracious boutique property hugs Granville Island's quiet southeastern tip, enjoying tranquil views across False Creek to Yaletown's mirrored towers. You'll be a stroll from the Public Market, with shopping and theater options on your doorstep. Rooms have a West Coast feel with some exposed-wood flourishes. There's also a rooftop Jacuzzi, while the on-site brewpub-restaurant has one of the city's best patios.

You're close to the seawall bike trail here (the hotel can rent you a bike) if you fancy pedaling to UBC or, in the opposite direction, Stanley Park. Car parking is outside the hotel and costs $15 per day.

HOTEL BLU HOTEL **$$$**

Map p274 (☎604-620-6200; www.hotelblu vancouver.com; 177 Robson St, Yaletown; d $400; @ ☎ 🏊 🐾; S Stadium-Chinatown) Brilliantly located near the center of downtown (and also major sports stadiums), this newer, condo-style tower hotel offers a range of comfortably mod rooms, including swanky two-level suites that you might like to move into permanently. Rates often include breakfast; check the website for the latest deals.

There's a free shuttle-bus service for hotel guests plus gratis loaner bikes if you fancy getting around under your own steam. Valet parking is $30 per day.

Fairview & South Granville

DOUGLAS GUEST HOUSE GUESTHOUSE **$$**

Map p280 (☎604-872-3060; www.douglas. beautifulguesthouse.ca; 456 W 13th Ave, Fairview; d from $115; P ☎; 🚌15) A tomato-soup-hued Edwardian house in a side street near City Hall, the Douglas offers good rates (especially in winter) and a laid-back feel that means you don't have to worry about creaky floorboards. Its rooms – comfortable rather than antique-lined – include smaller units with shared bathrooms, larger doubles with private bathrooms and kitchen-equipped garden suites. Off-street parking and a vegetarian cooked breakfast is included.

WINDSOR GUEST HOUSE B&B **$$**

Map p280 (☎604-872-3060; www.windsor. beautifulguesthouse.ca; 325 W 11th Ave, Fairview; d from $155; P 🚭 ☎; S Broadway-City Hall) This 1895 wood-built mansion has a homely, lived-in feel, complete with a yesteryear veranda and stained-glass windows. The good-value rooms vary greatly in size and some have shared bathrooms. The recommended top floor 'Charles Room' is quaint, quiet and small with a patio overlooking downtown that's shared with the neighboring room. A cooked vegetarian breakfast is included, along with free off-street parking.

Kitsilano & University of British Columbia

HI VANCOUVER JERICHO BEACH HOSTEL **$**

(☎604-224-3208; www.hihostels.com; 1515 Discovery St, Kitsilano; dm/d $43/86; ⊙May-Sep; P @ ☎; 🚌4) One of Canada's largest hostels looks like a Victorian hospital but has a scenic near-the-beach location. Basic rooms make this the least palatial Vancouver HI hostel, but it has a large kitchen, bike rentals and a popular licenced cafe. Dorms are also larger here. Book ahead for the popular

APARTMENT RENTALS

Private vacation rentals surged in Vancouver a few years back but the city's recently introduced regulations on short-term lettings have since reduced the number of available listings. If you're staying in a property for under 30 days, it must hold a valid short-term rental business license in order to comply with local rules. There's still a good range of options to choose from but early booking is advised, especially for summer stays. Rental services such as Airbnb (www.airbnb.com) and VRBO (www.vrbo.com) operate here, and you'll find a good concentration of listings downtown as well as in quieter neighborhoods including Kitsilano, Strathcona and Shaughnessy.

budget-hotel-style private rooms (with shared and private bathroom options).

For many, this hostel delivers more of a vacation than its downtown siblings due to its retreat-like beach proximity. Take bus 4 west along 4th Ave and disembark at the intersection with NW Marine Dr. The hostel is a short stroll downhill from there. It's also a 10-minute bus hop to the University of BC if you want to avail yourself of the museums and restaurants there – or just pretend you're still a student.

UNIVERSITY OF BRITISH COLUMBIA ACCOMMODATION ACCOMMODATION SERVICES $$

Map p286 (☎604-822-1000; www.suitesatubc.com; 5961 Student Union Blvd, UBC; r $49-165; ; 99B-Line) Pretend you're still a student with a UBC campus sleepover. Well-maintained options include great-value student-style single rooms as well as suites with private rooms and shared kitchens. Superior rooms with private kitchen facilities are also available, including the top-of-the-range West Coast Suites with their comfortable, hotel-style feel.

Ideal for groups or budget travelers who want to be close to UBC's array of museum, garden and gallery attractions. Downtown is 45 minutes away via transit.

North Shore

THISTLEDOWN HOUSE B&B $$

Map p284 (☎604-986-7173; www.thistle-down.com; 3910 Capilano Rd, North Vancouver; d incl breakfast from $215; ; 236) Located on the road between Capilano Suspension Bridge and Grouse Mountain (p182), this adult-oriented 1920s arts-and-crafts-style house is superior to most B&Bs; gourmet breakfast is included. Among its six elegantly decorated rooms, the most palatial suite ('Under the Apple Tree') is surprisingly secluded and has a beautiful fireplace, sunken sitting room, jetted bathtub and large windows opening onto a private patio.

The owners are friendly and helpful, and have plenty of suggestions for what to do in the area during your stay.

PINNACLE HOTEL AT THE PIER HOTEL $$$

Map p284 (☎604-986-7437; www.pinnaclehotelatthepier.com; 138 Victory Ship Way, North Vancouver; d $340; P; Seabus Lonsdale Quay) North Van's best hotel is an excellent option if you want to stay on this side of the water and hop to Vancouver's city center on the nearby SeaBus. Rooms are furnished with contemporary elegance, calming hues favored over bold colors. Harbor views are recommended and there are free loaner bikes if you want to explore the area.

Fitness buffs will enjoy the property's large gym and pool. Lonsdale Quay Public Market (p186) is just steps away, while you'll also be in the heart of the up-and-coming Shipyards neighborhood where restaurants and bars await.

LONSDALE QUAY HOTEL BOUTIQUE HOTEL $$$

Map p284 (☎604-986-6111; www.lonsdalequayhotel.com; 123 Carrie Cates Ct, North Vancouver; d $300; P; SeaBus to Lonsdale Quay) This waterfront North Van sleepover has upgraded its rooms to include hardwood floors, some rustic-chic furnishings and new modern art flourishes. It's attached to the public market building a short walk from the SeaBus terminal. There are numerous good restaurants nearby, and you can work off any vacation excesses in the gym.

If you really want to indulge, the splendid top-tier suites have curved-window views of the downtown towers twinkling across Burrard Inlet.

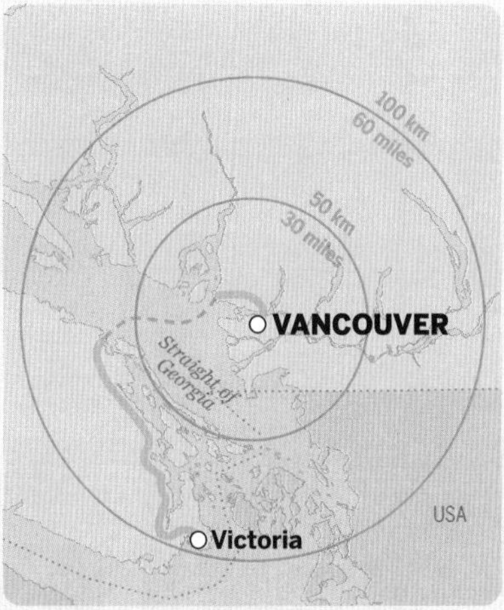

Victoria

Victoria's Top Five

❶ Going full pelt or ambling slowly on a bike through leafy woodland on **Galloping Goose Trail** (p224), running to and from Victoria's urban core.

❷ Paying homage to Canada's westernmost province and enjoying world-class temporary exhibitions in BC's most prestigious museum, the **Royal BC Museum** (p214).

❸ Reevaluating the decadent, sometimes squabbling lifestyles of Victoria's Victorian pioneers at **Craigdarroch Castle** (p215).

❹ Splurging on a full-blown afternoon tea on a three-tier tray in the regal lobby-lounge of **Fairmont Empress Hotel** (p225), a historic-monument hotel.

❺ Lining your stomach for a potential pub crawl with fish-and-chips at **Fisherman's Wharf** (p217), a merry assemblage of homes and snack shacks aside the Inner Harbour.

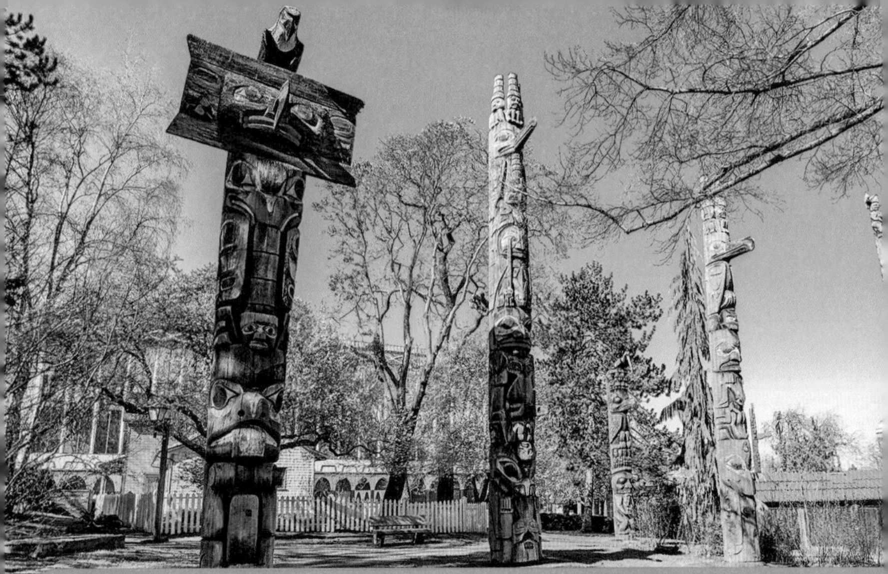

POEMNIST/SHUTTERSTOCK ©

TOP EXPERIENCE

EXPLORE HISTORY AT THE ROYAL BC MUSEUM

BC's most illustrious museum provides a definitive overview of the province's natural and human history, including an exhaustive section on the region's nearly 200 First Nations. Propping it up are famously well-curated temporary exhibitions, often of an anthropological bent. Make a day of it by taking in a show at the onsite IMAX Theatre (p223) and browsing several outdoor exhibits in an adjacent park.

The museum's permanent collection is known for its recreations of various Pacific Northwest ecosystems both prehistoric and contemporary. The biggest head-turner is a life-size model of a woolly mammoth complete with meter-long fur, but you'll also spy bears, cougars and marine life. As the human history section unfolds, you'e taken down a diorama of a Victoria street from the early 20th century complete with cinema, hotel and mini-Chinatown. There's also a full-scale replica of George Vancouver's 1789 ship, HMS *Discovery*.

The First Nations collection is extensive with room for only a fraction of it to be displayed. Look out for a recreated Kwakwaka'wakw clanhouse and a sonic exhibit that greets you in 34 different indigenous languages.

The outside exhibits are clustered in **Thunderbird Park** (pictured) and include totem poles and a small log-cabin schoolhouse dating from 1844.

DON'T MISS

- Natural history section
- First Nations exhibits
- IMAX Theatre

PRACTICALITIES

- Map p220, D4
- 250-356-7226
- www.royalbcmuseum.bc.ca
- 675 Belleville St
- adult/child $17/11, incl IMAX $26.95/21.25
- 10am-5pm daily, to 10pm Fri & Sat mid-May–Sep
- 70

GAGLIARDIPHOTOGRAPHY/SHUTTERSTOCK ©

TOP EXPERIENCE
GET MEDIEVAL AT CRAIGDARROCH CASTLE

Medieval knights might never have roamed the evergreen forests of Vancouver Island, but its historic capital, Victoria, has an impressive castle nonetheless. With its grey stone walls, cylindrical turrets and regal interior, Craigdarroch looks like a miniature version of Balmoral, the royal residence of the Queen in Scotland. Not coincidentally, it was built in medieval Gothic style in the 1880s by a Scottish coal-mining baron named Robert Dunsmuir.

Dunsmuir died in 1889 before the house was finished, but his family quickly moved in and engaged in a lengthy squabble over his inheritance (their story is related in one of the rooms inside). On the death of Dunsmuir's widow, the land was sold off and the house was bizarrely given away in a raffle. In the ensuing years it has served as a military hospital, a college and a music conservatory but, since 1975, has been lovingly preserved by a local historical society that has returned its splendid interior to its late-19th-century high-water mark.

The self-guided tour inside takes you up a spectacular wood-paneled staircase to four floors of time-stood-still rooms, from a lavish dining room laid out for dinner to a diminutive smoking room filled with wonderful Victorian clutter.

DON'T MISS

- Staircase
- Tower lookout
- Dining room
- Dance hall

PRACTICALITIES

- Map p220, H3
- 250-592-5323
- www.thecastle.ca
- 1050 Joan Cres
- adult/child $14.60/5.10
- 9am-7pm mid-Jun–early Sep, 10am-4:30pm early Sep–mid-Jun
- P
- 14

Explore

Double-decker buses, afternoon tea, homes that look like castles, and pubs with names like the Sticky Wicket and the Penny Farthing... Victoria has long traded on its British affiliations. But while the fish-and-chips remain first class and summer cricket games still enliven Beacon Hill Park, the days when Victoria was more British than Britain are long gone. In Victoria 2.0, the food culture embraces fusion, the beer leans toward craft brews and the abundance of bicycles seems to have more in common with Holland than England.

Compared to the glassy skyscrapers of Vancouver, Victoria is more laid back and low rise. On balmy summer days, a distinct holiday atmosphere takes over as people pile off the ferries to escape the mayhem of the mainland and forget work. Sure, Victoria might have become trendier and more sophisticated in recent years but, in pace and essence, it remains comfortingly old fashioned.

The Best...

- **Place to Eat** Brasserie L'École (p222)
- **Place to Drink** Drake (p231)
- **Place to Sleep** Abigail's Hotel (p225)

Top Tip

Leave your car on the mainland. You can walk straight off the ferry and onto a half-hourly double-decker bus that'll take you into downtown Victoria for only $2.50.

Getting There & Away

- **Air** The delightfully scenic downtown-to-downtown floatplane services operated from Vancouver by Harbour Air (www.harbourair.com) take around 30 minutes.
- **Boat** BC Ferries (www.bcferries.com) services from mainland Tsawwassen arrive at Swartz Bay, a transit-bus ride from Victoria (bus 70).
- **Bus** BC Ferries Connector (www.bcfconnector.com) buses take passengers from downtown Vancouver to downtown Victoria via the ferry.
- **Car** Drive to BC Ferries' Tsawwassen terminal, trundle onto the Victoria-bound ferry, then hit the island's Hwy 17 into Victoria (32km).

Getting Around

- **Bicycle** Victoria is a great cycling city. Check the website of the Greater Victoria Cycling Coalition (www.gvcc.bc.ca) for local resources. Bike rentals are offered by Cycle BC Rentals (victoria.cyclebc.ca) or Pedaler (www.thepedaler.ca).
- **Boat** Victoria Harbour Ferry (www.victoriaharbourferry.com) calls in at over a dozen docks around the Inner Harbour and beyond with its colorful armada of little boats.
- **Bus** Victoria Regional Transit (www.bctransit.com/victoria) buses (single fare/day pass $2.50/5) cover a wide area from Sidney to Sooke, with some routes served by modern-day double-deckers.
- **Taxi** Main operators include Yellow Cab (www.yellowcabvictoria.com) and Bluebird Cabs (www.taxicab.com).

Need to Know

- **Location** 112km southwest of Vancouver
- **Tourist Office Tourism Victoria Visitor Centre** (Map p220; ☎250-953-2033; www.tourismvictoria.com; 812 Wharf St; ⏰8:30am-8:30pm mid-May–Aug, 9am-5pm Sep–mid-May; 🚌70)
- **Area Code** ☎250

SIGHTS

ROYAL BC MUSEUM MUSEUM

See p214.

CRAIGDARROCH CASTLE MUSEUM

See p215.

PARLIAMENT BUILDINGS HISTORIC BUILDING

Map p220 (☎250-387-3046; www.leg.bc.ca; 501 Belleville St; ⏰tours 9am-5pm mid-May–Aug, from 8:30am Mon-Fri Sep–mid-May; 🚌70) FREE

This dramatically handsome confection of turrets, domes and stained glass is British Columbia's working legislature and is also open to visitors. You can go behind the facade on a free 45-minute guided tour then stop for lunch at the 'secret' politicians' restaurant (p219) inside. Return in the evening when the elegant exterior is illuminated like a Christmas tree.

The buildings were constructed in the 1890s in a mix of renaissance, Romanesque and classical styles after the government

WORTH A DETOUR

CUMBERLAND

Mixing dusty coal-mining history with contemporary hipness, the village of Cumberland in the Comox Valley is well worth a visit. Its only notable street (named 'Dunsmuir' after the settlement's founder) is lined with frontier-style buildings constructed on the back of a 19th-century coal boom, while the quirky town **museum** (☎250-336-2445; www.cumberlandmuseum.ca; 2680 Dunsmuir Ave; adult/child $5/4; ⏰10am-5pm Jun-Aug, closed Mon Sep-May) relates tales of erstwhile labor strife. But Cumberland's modern reincarnation is decidedly less industrial, courtesy of a world-class network of interconnecting mountain-bike trails that sit (literally) one pedal-turn from the village center.

Center of operations is the village's supremely friendly **Dodge City Cycles** (☎250-336-2200; www.dodgecitycycles.com; 2705 Dunsmuir Ave; bike rentals 2/24 hours $50/120; ⏰9am-6pm Mon-Sat, 10am-2:30pm Sun) which can kit you out with everything you need bike-wise and provide maps and insider chat on the best trails for your ability. Nearby, a cluster of trendy cafes and restaurants on Dunsmuir fuel the summer influx of two-wheeled visitors.

Cumberland is a 2¾-hour drive northwest of Victoria and thus a long day trip. For full village immersion, stay overnight at **Riding Fool Hostel** (☎250-336-8250; www.ridingfool.com; 2705 Dunsmuir Ave; dm/r $32/68; @📶) affiliated with the bike shop.

had outgrown the original legislature, the less illustriously named 'Birdcages.' The current ceremonial entrance has a mosaic floor and is embellished with Italian marble, while the graceful dome is topped on the outside by a gold-encrusted statue of George Vancouver (an early explorer of BC's coastal regions).

BEACON HILL PARK PARK

Map p220 (www.victoria.ca/EN/main/residents/parks/beacon-hill.html; Douglas St; P 👪; 🚌3) Fringed by crashing ocean, this waterfront park is ideal for feeling the breeze in your hair – check out the windswept trees along the cliff top. You'll also find a gigantic totem pole, Victorian cricket pitch and a marker for Mile 0 of Hwy 1, alongside a statue of the Canadian legend Terry Fox, who ran across the country in 1980 for cancer research. If you're here with kids, consider the popular children's farm (www.beaconhillchildrensfarm.ca) as well.

MINIATURE WORLD MUSEUM

Map p220 (☎250-385-9731; www.miniatureworld.com; 649 Humboldt St; adult/child $16/8; ⏰9am-9pm mid-May–mid-Sep, to 5pm mid-Sep–mid-May; 👪; 🚌70) Tucked along the side of the Fairmont Empress Hotel, this huge collection of skillfully crafted models depicting important battles, historic towns and popular stories is far more fascinating than it sounds. Lined with dozens of diminutive diorama scenes, divided into themes ranging from Camelot to space and from fairyland to Olde England, it has plenty of push-button action, several trundling trains and the chance to see yourself on a miniature movie-theater screen. An immaculately maintained reminder of innocent yesteryear attractions.

VICTORIA BUG ZOO ZOO

Map p220 (☎250-384-2847; www.victoriabugzoo.com; 631 Courtney St; adult/child $12/8; ⏰10am-5pm Mon-Fri, to 6pm Sat & Sun, reduced hours Sep-May; 👪; 🚌70) It's not big, nor are its resident critters (although some of them are alarmingly colossal by insect standards); however, this diminutive indoor 'zoo' is a small marvel thanks to the enthusiasm and knowledge of its guides. Atlas beetles, dragon-headed crickets and thorny devils are all explained, admired and – on occasion – lifted out of their tanks to be handed around for closer inspection. Children are the main audience, but this is a hugely entertaining and educational experience on any level.

FISHERMAN'S WHARF LANDMARK

Map p220 (www.fishermanswharfvictoria.com; just off Fisherman's Wharf Park; P; 🚌30) A waterfront walk from the Inner Harbour (or, better yet, a short hop by mini-ferry) delivers you to this floating, boardwalk-linked clutch of houseboats, shops and food shacks (including ones serving up fish-and-chips). A fun and easy excursion for an hour or so.

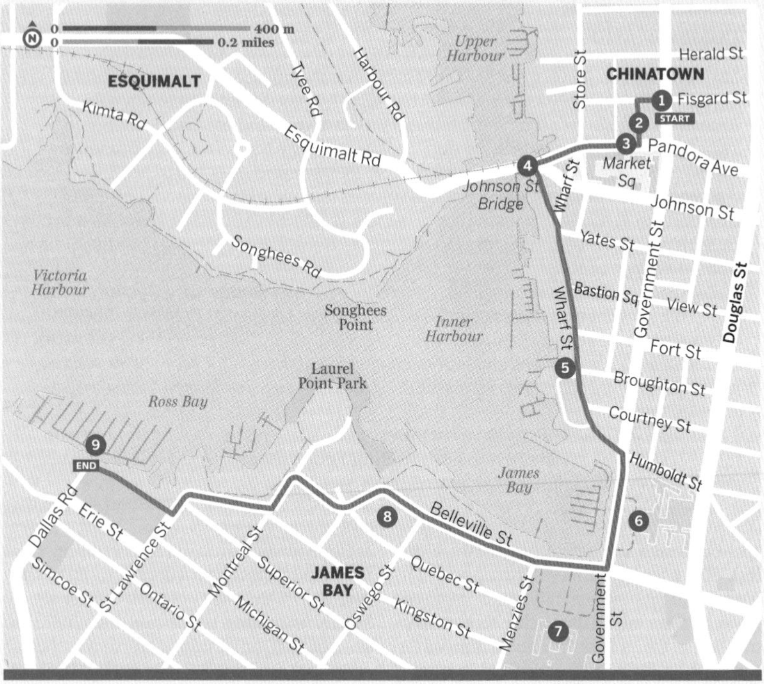

Neighborhood Walk
Chinatown & the Inner Harbor

START CHINATOWN GATE
END FISHERMAN'S WHARF
LENGTH 2KM; 1½ HOURS

Victoria's Chinatown is small, but it's North America's second-oldest after San Francisco.

A handsome **1 gate** near the corner of Government and Fisgard Sts marks its entrance. Beyond lies Fisgard, the most ostensibly Chinese of the quarter's compact streets, studded with neon signs and traditional grocery stores.

On the south side is **2 Fan Tan Alley**, a narrow passageway connecting with Pandora Ave. Once a muddle of opium dens and gambling clubs, it's now a bastion of used record stores and trinket shops.

Watch out while crossing **3 Pandora Ave**, Victoria's first street with a separated bike lane, then turn right and stroll past vintage clothes shops and pubs.

Ahead is **4 Johnson St Bridge** (p219), a bascule (lifting) bridge completely remodeled in 2018. From here, turn left into Wharf St and look for a small **5 monument** near the Broughton St junction. It's where 1843-built Fort Victoria once stood: a fur-trading post that preempted the city. Nothing remains except for old mooring rings.

Curve round to the Inner Harbour, dominated by the palatial **6 Fairmont Empress Hotel** (p225). If you're feeling thirsty (and rich), pop inside for afternoon tea.

At right angles to the Empress and equally regal is BC's **7 Parliament building** (p215). Follow Belleville St west past accommodations including the heritage, Queen Anne–style **8 Huntingdon Manor Hotel**.

The main road kinks inland into the quiet James Bay neighborhood, an affluent mix of apartment blocks and historic houses, before emerging at **9 Fisherman's Wharf** (p216) where floating homes and fish-and-chips are de rigueur.

EMILY CARR HOUSE MUSEUM

Map p220 (☎250-383-5843; www.emilycarr.com; 207 Government St; adult/child $6.75/4.50; ⊙11am-4pm Tue-Sat May-Sep; P; 🚌3) The birthplace of BC's best-known painter, this bright-yellow gingerbread-style house has plenty of period rooms, plus displays on the artist's life and career. There are changing displays of local contemporary works, but head to the **Art Gallery of Greater Victoria** (Map p220; ☎250-384-4171; www.aggv.ca; 1040 Moss St; adult/child $13/2.50; ⊙10am-5pm Tue, Wed, Fri & Sat, to 9pm Thu, noon-5pm Sun; 🚌14) if you want to see more of Carr's paintings.

ROBERT BATEMAN CENTRE GALLERY

Map p220 (☎250-940-3630; www.batemancentre.org; 470 Belleville St; adult/child $10/6; ⊙10am-5pm daily, to 9pm Fri & Sat Jun-Aug; 🚌70) Colonizing part of the Inner Harbour's landmark Steamship Terminal building, this gallery showcases the photo-realistic work of Canada's most celebrated nature painter, the eponymous Bateman, along with a revolving roster of works by other artists. Start with the five-minute intro movie, then check out the dozens of achingly beautiful paintings showing animals in their natural surroundings in BC and beyond.

JOHNSON ST BRIDGE BRIDGE

Map p220 (🚌24) Victoria's much-loved bascule bridge across the Inner Harbour reopened in March 2018 with a handsome new streamlined structure replacing the steel-and-concrete construction of old. As well as swinging skywards to let boat traffic pass underneath, the bridge shines a luminous blue at night. There are separate lanes for bikes and pedestrians to cross.

EATING

Victoria's dining scene has been radically upgraded in recent years. Pick up the free *Eat Magazine* to check out the latest foodie happenings. Looking for browsable options? Check out downtown's Fort St, the city's de facto dining row.

RED FISH BLUE FISH SEAFOOD $

Map p220 (☎250-298-6877; www.redfish-bluefish.com; 1006 Wharf St; mains $6-18; ⊙11am-7pm Mar-Oct; 🚌70) On the waterfront boardwalk at the foot of Broughton St, this freight-container takeout shack serves fresh-made, finger-licking sustainable seafood. Highlights include jerk fish poutine, amazing chowder and tempura-battered oysters (you can also get traditional fish-and-chips, of course). Expanded new seating has added to the appeal but watch out for hovering gull mobsters as you try to eat.

CRUST BAKERY BAKERY $

Map p220 (☎250-978-2253; www.crustbakery.ca; 730 Fort St; baked goods $3-6; ⊙8am-5:30pm; 🚌14) There are several bakeries on this stretch of Fort St, but the Crust jumps out at you first. Maybe it's the deliciousness of the aromas, or the delicate presentation, or the rich buttery-ness of the croissants, savory pastries and sweet tartlets with flavors like chocolate mousse and crème brûlée.

★JAM CAFE BREAKFAST $$

Map p220 (☎778-440-4489; http://jamcafes.com; 542 Herald St; breakfast $13-17; ⊙8am-3pm; 🚌70) No need to conduct an opinion poll: the perennial lines in the street outside Jam suggest that this is the best breakfast spot in Victoria. The reasons? Tasteful vintage decor (if you'll excuse them the moose's head); fast, discreet service; and the kind of creative breakfast dishes that you'd never have the energy or ingenuity to cook yourself.

FISHHOOK SEAFOOD $$

Map p220 (☎250-477-0470; www.fishhookvic.com; 805 Fort St; mains $13-24; ⊙11am-9pm; 🚌14) Don't miss the smoky, coconutty chowder at this tiny Indian- and French-influenced seafood restaurant, but make sure you add a tartine open-faced sandwich: it's the house specialty. If you still have room (and you're reluctant to give up your place at the communal table), split a seafood biryani platter with your dining partner. Focused on local and sustainable fish.

LEGISLATIVE DINING ROOM CANADIAN $$

Map p220 (☎250-387-3959; www.leg.bc.ca; 501 Belleville St, Parliament Buildings; mains $9-18; ⊙8am-3pm Mon-Thu, to 2pm Fri; 🚌70) One of Victoria's best-kept dining secrets, the Parliament Buildings (p216) have its own subsidized, old-school restaurant where both MLAs and the public can drop by for a silver-service menu of regional dishes, ranging from salmon salads to velvety steaks and a BC-only wine list. Entry is via the security desk just inside the building's main entrance; photo ID is required.

Victoria

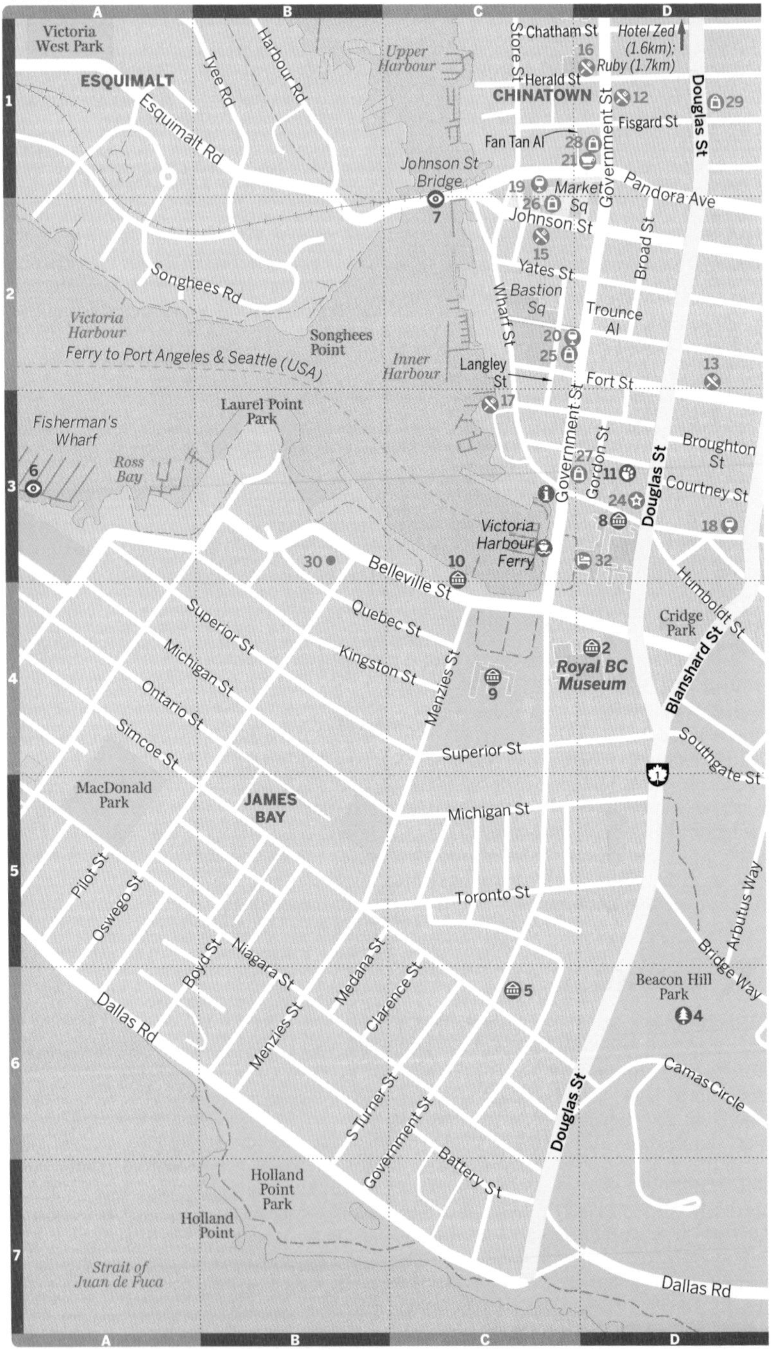
A
B
C
D
1
2
3
4
5
6
7
Victoria West Park
ESQUIMALT
Tyee Rd
Harbour Rd
Upper Harbour
Esquimalt Rd
Store St
Chatham St
Herald St
CHINATOWN
Hotel Zed (1.6km); Ruby (1.7km)
16
12
29
Douglas St
Government St
Fisgard St
Fan Tan Al
28
21
Johnson St Bridge
7
19
Market Sq
26
Pandora Ave
Johnson St
15
Broad St
Yates St
Songhees Rd
Bastion Sq
Wharf St
Trounce Al
Victoria Harbour
Songhees Point
Ferry to Port Angeles & Seattle (USA)
Inner Harbour
Langley St
20
25
Fort St
13
17
Laurel Point Park
Fisherman's Wharf
Ross Bay
6
Gordon St
27
11
Broughton St
Courtney St
24
8
18
Victoria Harbour Ferry
10
30
32
Belleville St
Humboldt St
Cridge Park
Superior St
Quebec St
Michigan St
Kingston St
Menzies St
2
Royal BC Museum
9
Blanshard St
Ontario St
Simcoe St
Southgate St
MacDonald Park
JAMES BAY
Michigan St
Pilot St
Oswego St
Toronto St
Arbutus Way
Boyd St
Niagara St
Medana St
Clarence St
Bridge Way
Beacon Hill Park
4
5
Dallas Rd
Menzies St
Camas Circle
S Turner St
Government St
Battery St
Holland Point Park
Holland Point
Strait of Juan de Fuca
Dallas Rd

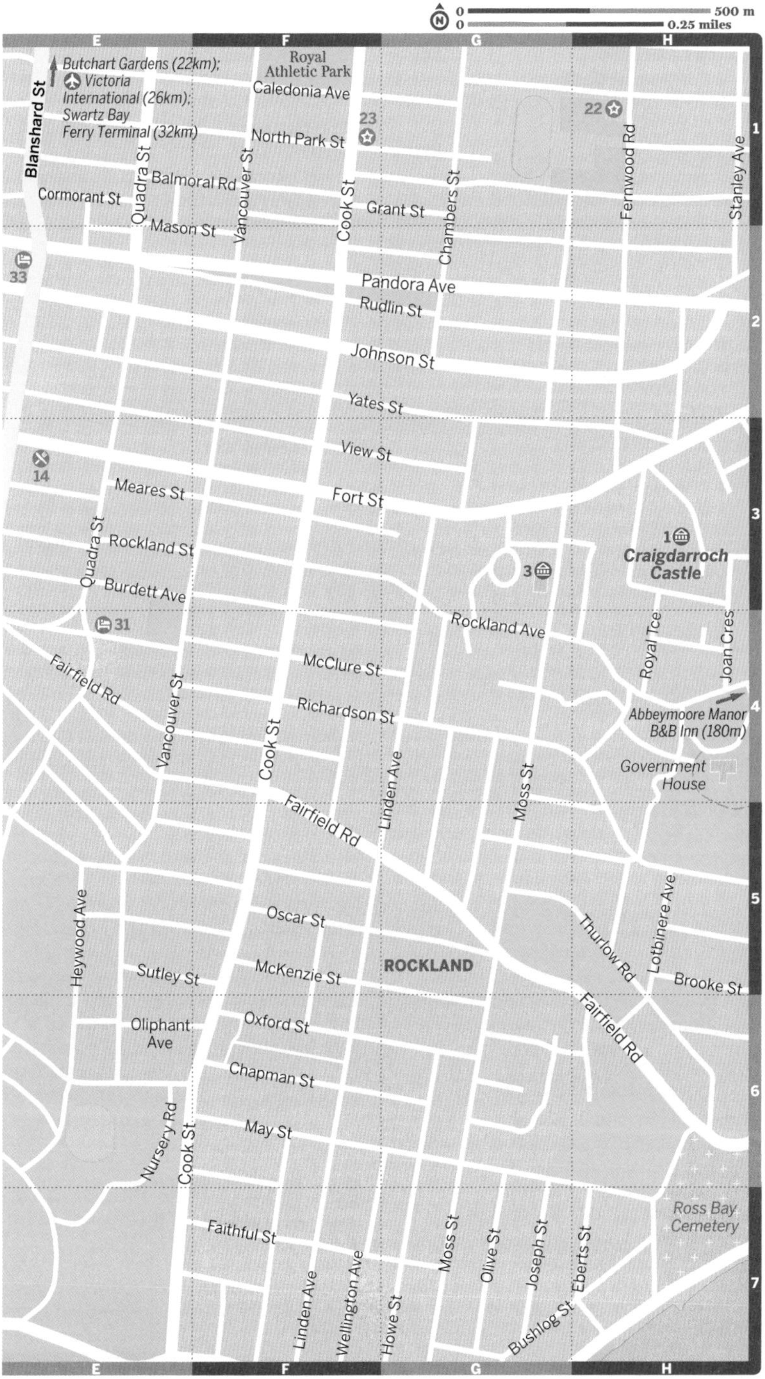

0 500 m
0 0.25 miles
Butchart Gardens (22km); Victoria International (26km); Swartz Bay Ferry Terminal (32km)
Royal Athletic Park
Caledonia Ave
North Park St
Balmoral Rd
Cormorant St
Mason St
Grant St
Pandora Ave
Rudlin St
Johnson St
Yates St
View St
Fort St
Meares St
Rockland St
Burdett Ave
Rockland Ave
McClure St
Richardson St
Fairfield Rd
Oscar St
McKenzie St
Sutley St
Oliphant Ave
Oxford St
Chapman St
May St
Faithful St
Blanshard St
Quadra St
Vancouver St
Cook St
Chambers St
Fernwood Rd
Stanley Ave
Linden Ave
Moss St
Royal Tce
Joan Cres
Abbeymoore Manor B&B Inn (180m)
Government House
Craigdarroch Castle
Heywood Ave
Thurlow Rd
Lotbinere Ave
Brooke St
ROCKLAND
Nursery Rd
Wellington Ave
Howe St
Olive St
Joseph St
Eberts St
Bushlog St
Ross Bay Cemetery
1
3
14
22
23
31
33
E
F
G
H
1
2
3
4
5
6
7

Victoria

VENUS SOPHIA VEGETARIAN **$$**

Map p220 (☎250-590-3953; www.venussophia.com; 540 Fisgard St; afternoon tea $14-30; ⏰10am-6pm Jul & Aug, from 11am Wed-Sun Sep-Jun; ; 🚌70) A delightful cream-walled tearoom combining traditional tea service (including a very reasonable $14 cream tea) with beautifully presented vegetarian lunches, this is a uniquely tranquil respite from Chinatown's sometimes busy streets. Try the artichoke and ricotta quiche with organic tea (served in mismatched vintage cups) from the wide selection.

★**BRASSERIE L'ÉCOLE** FRENCH **$$$**

Map p220 (☎250-475-6260; www.lecole.ca; 1715 Government St; mains $20-50; ⏰5:30-10pm Tue-Thu, to 11pm Fri & Sat; 🚌70) *Bonsoir!* You may have just arrived at the best restaurant in Victoria, a small but wonderfully elegant bistro discreetly furnished in *la mode français*, but without any of the infamous Parisian pretension. Service is warm and impeccable, and the renditions of classic French dishes are exquisitely executed. *Moules-frites*, duck confit and superb Bordeaux wines all hit the spot.

The restaurant operates on a first-come, first-served basis and there's often a line when it opens at 5:30pm. Join it!

★**IL TERRAZZO** ITALIAN **$$$**

Map p220 (☎250-361-0028; www.ilterrazzo.com; 555 Johnson St; mains $21-44; ⏰11:30am-3pm & 5pm-late Mon-Fri, 5pm-late Sat & Sun; 🚌24) Authentic Italian flavors melded with a laid-back Victoria spirit make a devastatingly good combo. If you don't believe us, come to Il Terrazzo, a restaurant that's as much about its atmosphere and service as it is about its Italian-inspired, locally nurtured food. Aside from the usual suspects (seafood linguine, Margherita pizza), there are a handful of more unusual renditions.

DRINKING & NIGHTLIFE

Victoria is one of BC's best beer towns; look out for local-made craft brews at pubs around the city. There is also a good smattering of traditional pubs, some of which wouldn't look out of place in England.

★DRAKE
BAR

Map p220 (☎250-590-9075; www.drakeeatery.com; 517 Pandora Ave; ⏰11:30am-midnight; 📶; 🚌70) Victoria's best tap house, this red-brick hangout has more than 30 amazing craft drafts, typically including revered BC producers Townsite, Driftwood and Four Winds. Arrive on a rainy afternoon and you'll find yourself still here several hours later. Food-wise, the smoked tuna club is a top-seller but the cheese and meat boards are ideal for grazing.

★GARRICK'S HEAD PUB
PUB

Map p220 (☎250-384-6835; www.garrickshead.com; 66 Bastion Sq; ⏰11am-late; 🚌70) A great spot to dive into BC's brilliant craft-beer scene. Pull up a seat at the long bar with its 55-plus taps – a comprehensive menu of beers from Driftwood, Phillips, Hoyne and beyond. There are always 10 rotating lines with intriguing tipples (ask for samples) plus a comfort-grub menu of burgers and such to line your boozy stomach.

CLIVE'S CLASSIC LOUNGE
LOUNGE

Map p220 (☎250-361-5684; www.clivesclassiclounge.com; 740 Burdett Ave; ⏰5pm-midnight Sun-Thu, to 1am Fri & Sat; 🚌70) Tucked into the lobby level of the Chateau Victoria Hotel, this is the best spot in town for perfectly prepared cocktails. Completely lacking the snobbishness of most big-city cocktail haunts, this ever-cozy spot is totally dedicated to its mixed-drinks menu, which means timeless classic cocktails, as well as cool fusion tipples that are a revelation.

HABIT COFFEE
COFFEE

Map p220 (☎250-294-1127; www.habitcoffee.com; 552 Pandora Ave; ⏰7am-6pm Mon-Fri, from 8am Sat & Sun; 📶; 🚌70) 🌿 If you like your coffee ethically sourced and sustainably produced, hit Habit, where the potent brews and simple snacks are made with practically zero waste and the staff use bicycles to transport goods between two Victoria locations.

☆ ENTERTAINMENT

Check the weekly freebie *Monday Magazine* for the lowdown on local happenings. Entertainment resources online include **Live Victoria** (www.livevictoria.com) and **Play in Victoria** (www.playinvictoria.net).

BELFRY THEATRE
THEATER

Map p220 (☎250-385-6815; www.belfry.bc.ca; 1291 Gladstone Ave; 🚌22) The celebrated Belfry Theatre showcases contemporary plays in its lovely former-church-building venue, a 20-minute stroll from downtown.

VIC THEATRE
CINEMA

Map p220 (☎250-389-0440; www.thevic.ca; 808 Douglas St; 🚌70) Screening arthouse and festival movies in the heart of downtown, the Vic charges a $2 membership alongside your ticket admission.

LOGAN'S PUB
LIVE MUSIC

Map p220 (☎250-360-2711; www.loganspub.com; 1821 Cook St; ⏰3pm-1am Mon-Fri, from 10am Sat, 10am-midnight Sun; 🚌6) This no-nonsense pub looks like nothing special from the outside, but since 1997 the Logan has been the hotbed of Victoria's alt-rock scene. Come here to see bands with names like Alcoholic White Trash and Acid Mothers Temple. Fridays and Saturdays are best. Check the online calendar to see what's coming up. It's a 10-minute walk from downtown.

IMAX THEATRE
CINEMA

Map p220 (☎250-480-4887; www.imaxvictoria.com; 675 Belleville St, Royal BC Museum; tickets $11.95; 🚌70) The IMAX Theatre at the Royal BC Museum (p214) shows larger-than-life documentaries and Hollywood blockbusters. The theater opens at 10am and closes after the last film (see website for details).

SHOPPING

While Government Street is a souvenir-shopping magnet, those looking for more original purchases should head to the Johnson St stretch between Store and Government Sts, which is lined with cool independent stores.

★MUNRO'S BOOKS
BOOKS

Map p220 (☎250-382-2464; www.munrobooks.com; 1108 Government St; ⏰9am-6pm Mon-Wed, to 9pm Thu-Sat, 9:30am-6pm Sun; 🚌70) The name is no coincidence. Victoria's cathedral to reading was established in 1963 by Nobel-prize-winning Canadian author Alice Munro and her husband Jim. Encased in a heritage building on the city's famous Government St, it's an obligatory pilgrimage for bibliophiles with its high ceilings, wide array of local-interest tomes and well-read staff, some of whom have worked here for decades.

REGIONAL ASSEMBLY OF TEXT STATIONERY

Map p220 (☎778-265-6067; www.assemblyoftext.com; 560 Johnson St; ⊙11am-6pm Mon-Sat, noon-5pm Sun; 🚌70) This branch of Vancouver's charming hipster stationery store is socked into a quirky space resembling a hotel lobby from 1968. You'll find the same clever greeting cards and cool journals, plus the best Victoria postcards ever. Add the button-making table, typewriter stations and a *Mister Mitten* chapbook purchase and you'll be beaming brighter than a shiny new paper clip.

SILK ROAD TEA

Map p220 (☎250-704-2688; https://silkroadteastore.com; 1624 Government St; ⊙10am-5:30pm Mon-Sat, 11am-5pm Sun; 🚌70) A pilgrimage spot for fans of regular and exotic teas, where you can pick up all manner of leafy paraphernalia. Alternatively, sidle up to the tasting bar to quaff some adventurous brews. There's also a small on-site spa, where you can indulge in oil treatments and aromatherapy.

ROGERS' CHOCOLATES FOOD

Map p220 (☎250-881-8771; www.rogerschocolates.com; 913 Government St; ⊙9:30am-7pm; 🚌70) This charming, museum-like confectioner serves the best ice-cream bars, but repeat offenders usually spend their time hitting the 20-flavor-strong menu of rich Victoria Creams (soft-centered chocolates), one of which is usually enough to substitute for lunch. Varieties range from peppermint to seasonal specialties and they're good souvenirs, if you don't eat them all before you get home (which you will).

VICTORIA PUBLIC MARKET MARKET

Map p220 (☎778-433-2787; www.victoriapublicmarket.com; 1701 Douglas St; ⊙10am-6pm Mon-Sat, 11am-5pm Sun; 🚌4) At this indoor market lined with artisan food businesses, tempting deli counters and food-court dining, you'll find everything from chocolate to cheese to challenge your diet. Check the website for upcoming events, too.

SPORTS & ACTIVITIES

If you could single out two headline Victoria activities they would be cycling and whale-watching.

★GALLOPING GOOSE TRAIL CYCLING

Victoria's best-loved trail follows the grade of an old railway line and is named for an erstwhile train carriage that rattled through these parts in the early 20th century. As a result, the trail is flat, passable on a hybrid bike, and flecked with remnants of Vancouver Island's pioneering railroad history, including several trestles and a smattering of explanatory boards.

The first 13km is on concrete and relatively urban. Further west, the trail becomes increasingly rural, with pastoral sections interspersing with woodland and regular glimpses of water (both bays and lakes).

★PEDALER CYCLING

Map p220 (☎778-265-7433; www.thepedaler.ca; 321 Belleville St; tours from $50, rentals per day $30; ⊙9am-6pm, reduced hours Nov–mid-Mar) Pedaler offers bike rentals and several guided two-wheeled tours around the city, including the 'Hoppy Hour Ride' with its craft-beer-sampling focus. Get kitted out with a sturdy hybrid at the office in the 'olde' Huntingdon Manor building and go explore the Galloping Goose Trail. Helmets, locks and rain ponchos are thrown in.

TOP FESTIVALS

Victoria has a wide array of events for locals and visitors throughout the year with a strong bias toward music and the performing arts. Specific Canadian celebrations such as **Victoria Day** (the second-to-last Monday in May) and **Canada Day** (July 1) are always good, if busy, times to visit. Among our other favorites are **Rifflandia** (www.rifflandia.com), **Victoria Fringe Theatre Festival** (www.victoriafringe.com) and **Victoria International JazzFest** (www.jazzvictoria.ca).

CYCLING AROUND VICTORIA

Victoria is a progressive city when it comes to cycling and its biking infrastructure has improved by leaps and bounds in recent years. In 2017, the first proper downtown bike lane (with its own traffic lights and signage) was laid on Pandora St. The plan is to have another 32km of separated bike lanes in place by 2022.

The bike-friendliness dates from the 1990s when two regional hiking-biking trails were developed to connect Victoria with the surrounding countryside. The 55km Galloping Goose Trail runs along an old railway line to Sooke and beyond, while the 33km Lochside Regional Trail connects downtown Victoria with the Swartz Bay Ferry Terminal. Both trails allow cyclists to pedal unmolested by traffic right into the heart of the city. They share a southern nexus on the downtown side of the Johnson St Bridge, recently equipped with a designated bike lane.

EAGLE WING TOURS WHALE-WATCHING
Map p220 (☎250-384 8008; www.eaglewingtours.ca; 12 Erie St, Fisherman's Wharf; adult/child from $115/75; ⏲Mar-Oct) Popular and long-established operator of whale-watching boat tours.

SLEEPING

From heritage B&Bs to cool boutiques and swanky high-end options, Victoria is stuffed with accommodations for all budgets. Off-season sees great deals. Tourism Victoria's **room-reservation service** (☎800-663-3883, 250-953-2033; www.tourismvictoria.com/hotels) can show you what's available. Keep in mind that most downtown accommodations also charge for parking.

★**OCEAN ISLAND INN** HOSTEL $
Map p220 (☎250-385-1789; www.oceanisland.com; 791 Pandora Ave; dm/d from $36/56; @📶; 🚌70) The kind of hostel that'll make you want to become a backpacker (again), the Ocean is a fabulous blitz of sharp color accents, global travel memorabilia and more handy extras than a deluxe five-star hotel. Bank on free breakfast (including waffles!), free dinner, a free nightly drink, free bag storage (handy for the West Coast Trail) and free friendly advice.

HOTEL ZED MOTEL $$
(☎250-388-4345; www.hotelzed.com; 3110 Douglas St; d from $209; P📶🏊🐾; 🚌70) If you like an accommodations that – in its own words – likes to 'rebel against the ordinary' then you'll love the Zed, an eccentric motel that has been given a tongue-in-cheek retro makeover, complete with rainbow paintwork and free VW-van rides to downtown (a 20-minute walk away). The rooms are also fun: 1970s phones, bathroom comic books and brightly painted walls.

Loaner bikes and free coffee are provided via the front desk and there's also a great **diner** (☎250-507-1325; www.therubyvictoria.com; mains $14-19; ⏲8am-3pm Mon-Tue, to 8:30pm Wed-Sun) if you're hungry.

ABBEYMOORE MANOR B&B INN B&B $$
(☎250-370-1470; www.abbeymoore.com; 1470 Rockland Ave; d from $239; P@📶; 🚌14) A Victoria B&B worthy of Queen Victoria, the Abbeymoore has a decidedly posh address and was designed in the arts-and-crafts style in 1912. Seven deluxe rooms mix period details with satisfying modern touches in a way that is grand rather than kitschy.

★**ABIGAIL'S HOTEL** B&B $$$
Map p220 (☎250-388-5363; www.abigailshotel.com; 906 McClure St; d from $249; P@📶; 🚌7) A boutique hotel with the ambience of a B&B, the historic, regal and faintly English Abigail's is Victoria's most Victorian accommodations despite the fact it was only built in 1930 with a mock Tudor facade. Near-perfect rooms come with heavy drapes, shapely furniture and marble bathrooms. In the morning, you can swan downstairs for a spectacular breakfast.

FAIRMONT EMPRESS HOTEL HOTEL $$$
Map p220 (☎250-384-8111; www.fairmont.com/empress-victoria; 721 Government St; d from $340; P❄@📶🏊; 🚌70) One of the most famous hotels in Canada, the Empress was built in 1908 in French-chateau-esque style. There have been numerous renovations and a who's-who of famous guests, from movie stars to royalty, prancing through in the years since. Modern-day guests can still expect classic decor and effortlessly solicitous service.

1

Vancouver Island Activities

With only 775,000 people inhabiting an area the size of Belgium, Vancouver Island has plenty of wilderness to admire, utilize and disappear into. Here are our top five activities.

Surfing

Surfing is a Vancouver Island signature activity. The reason? Tofino, a small West Coast town which catches giant Pacific waves and has developed a laid-back surfing scene par excellence.

There are several surfable beaches in and around Tofino, so you'll rarely have to fight over wave space. Ideal for first-timers, there's a full gamut of surf schools and board-rental outlets here. Surfers here don wetsuits year-round, with hoods and gloves also advisable.

Cycling

Victoria is one of Canada's best cycling cities, with a growing network of separated bike lanes. You can also cycle into the city's farm-dotted hinterland within half an hour, via well-maintained interurban trails that avoid major roads. Other towns with good cycling cultures include Tofino and Campbell River.

Vancouver Island also excels in off-road mountain biking. The main nexus is the small town of Cumberland in the Comox Valley, a mountain-biking destination of world renown.

Hiking

The island has a trio of spectacular multiday coastal trails that contour the wave-lashed Pacific in the north and west. The best known is the West Coast Trail,

CHASE CLAUSEN/SHUTTERSTOCK ©

RUSS HEINL/SHUTTERSTOCK ©

1. Surfers at Long Beach, Tofino **2.** Skier on Mt. Washington **3.** Hiker on the Juan de Fuca Trail

EB ADVENTURE PHOTOGRAPHY/SHUTTERSTOCK ©

a 75km jaunt usually spread over five to seven days that tracks an unpopulated section of the Pacific Rim National Park Reserve. Hiking numbers are limited; reservations are required.

There's also the Juan de Fuca Trail (47km), immediately south of the West Coast Trail, and the remote North Coast Trail (59km) on the island's northern tip. Neither requires reservations.

Kayaking

Arguably, the number-one multiday kayaking adventure here is the Broken Group Islands, a nebulous archipelago at the mouth of Barkley Sound that lies within the Pacific Rim National Park Reserve. Trips out of Ucluelet and Port Alberni last several days and involve camping.

There are also lots of shorter kayaking options. For safe, family-friendly and/or beginner kayaking, Victoria's sheltered Inner Harbour and Tofino's Clayoquot Sound are ideal. Incorporating kayaking with whale-watching is a specialty in Telegraph Cove in the northeast.

Skiing

Little-visited by off-islanders, despite being only 90 minutes north of Nanaimo. Mt Washington has a couple of lodges and a handful of chalets. But alongside its unhurried vibe, it has one of the highest annual snow dumps in North America.

The island's only other ski area, Mt Cain Alpine Park, is a community-run nonprofit two hours north of Campbell River. It's open weekends only.

4

5

4. Kayaking in the Broken Group Islands

5. Mountain biking in Cumberland (p217), Comox Valley

Understand Vancouver

History

Vancouverites routinely say there's no history here, usually in jealous reference to 'all those lovely heritage buildings in Europe.' But the fact is Vancouver has a rich and tumultuous past stretching back many thousands of years. Stand by for tales of thriving old First Nations communities; Spanish and English explorers who poked around the region for the first time; and an Englishman who kick-started the modern-day city with a barrel of whiskey and a pub-building project.

Living off the Land

The ancestors of Vancouver's First Nations people were in British Columbia (BC) at least 10,000 years ago, with many setting up camp along the coastline in areas still regarded as important First Nations lands to this day.

These first people lived in villages comprising wood-plank houses arranged in rows, often surrounded by a stockade. Totem poles were set up as an emblem of family or clan. It's not surprising that these groups settled this area: the local beaches and rivers teemed with seafood; the forests bristled with tasty wildlife, including deer and elk; and fat silvery salmon were abundantly available to anyone who fancied outsmarting the odd bear for the privilege.

Best History Books

The Chuck Davis History of Metropolitan Vancouver (Chuck Davis)

Vanishing Vancouver: The Last 25 Years (Michael Kluckner)

Vancouver in the Seventies: Photos from a Decade that Changed the City (Kate Bird)

Several distinct communities formed. The Musqueam populated Burrard Inlet, English Bay and the mouth of the Fraser River. They shared some of this area with the Squamish, who were largely based at the head of Howe Sound, but also had villages in North and West Vancouver, Kitsilano Point, Stanley Park and Jericho Beach. The Kwantlen controlled the area around New Westminster, while Delta and Richmond were home to the Tsawwassen. The Tsleil-Waututh occupied much of North Vancouver, while Coast Salish tribes, such as the Cowichan, Nanaimo and Saanich, set up seasonal camps along the Fraser River when the salmon were running.

Scant evidence exists about this intriguing period in Vancouver's history: most settlements have crumbled to dust and few have been rediscovered by archaeologists. In addition, these early settlers generally

TIMELINE

8000 BC

Evidence of the region's first inhabitants dates from this time; whether they arrived from Asia across the Bering Strait or were here already is a point of contention among historians.

1774

The Spanish arrive in the area in search of the fabled Northwest Passage. They don't venture any further than Vancouver Island's Nootka Sound.

1792

The Brits join the party when Royal Navy Captain George Vancouver sails into Burrard Inlet. He stays just 24 hours before setting sail again.

maintained oral records – they told each other (often in song) the stories of their ancestors, rather than writing things down for posterity. This method would have been highly successful until the arrival of the Europeans.

Captain Van Hits Town

After centuries of unhindered First Nations occupation, Europeans began arriving in the late 18th century. The Spanish sent three expeditions between 1774 and 1779 in search of the fabled Northwest Passage. British explorer Captain James Cook elbowed into the area from the South Pacific in 1779. He had a similar Northwest Passage motive but when he hit the west coast of Vancouver Island he believed it to be the mainland. It wasn't until 1791 that the Strait of Georgia near what we now call Vancouver was properly explored. Spanish navigator José María Narváez did the honors, sailing all the way into Burrard Inlet.

Next up was Captain George Vancouver, a British navigator. In 1792 he glided into the inner harbor and spent one day here – an auspicious day, as it turned out. When he arrived, he discovered that the Spanish, in ships under the command of captains Valdez and Galiano, had already claimed the area. Meeting at what is today known as Spanish Banks, the men shared area navigational information. Vancouver made a note of the deep natural port, which he named Burrard after one of his crew. Then he sailed away, not thinking twice about the place that would eventually be named after him.

The Spanish landed here before the Brits. Captain José María Narváez named the shoreline stretch where he set foot Islas de Langara, now Spanish Banks. This early influence is reflected around the BC coastline, where islands are called Saturna, Galiano and Texada.

As Spanish influence in the area waned over the next few years in favor of the more persistent British, explorers such as Simon Fraser and Alexander Mackenzie began mapping the region's interior, opening it up for overland travelers, the arrival of the legendary Hudson's Bay Company, and the eventual full entry of the region into the British Empire.

Gold & Timber

In 1858, gold was discovered on the banks of the Fraser River, and more than 25,000 shiny-eyed prospectors rapidly swept in. To maintain order and control, the mainland officially became part of the British Empire at this time. James Douglas was sworn in as the governor of the region, which included Vancouver Island. In a proclamation at Fort Langley on November 19, 1858, British Columbia officially came into being.

The first lumber mills were set up along the Fraser River in 1860, and their logging operations cleared the land for farms across the region. It wasn't long before operators began chewing northward through the trees toward Burrard Inlet. In 1867 Edward Stamp's British-financed

1827

The Hudson's Bay Company builds Fort Langley, the first European settlement to spring up in the region.

1858

Gold is discovered on the banks of the Fraser River, prompting more than 25,000 prospectors to arrive with picks and pans. Most leave empty-handed.

1867

John 'Gassy Jack' Deighton rows in with a barrel of whiskey and some big ideas. He opens a saloon, and a small, thirsty settlement – called Gastown – springs up near the entrance.

1871

With the promise of access to a new national railway network, BC joins the Canadian Confederation. Sixteen years later, the railway rolls into the region.

Hastings Mill, on the south shore of the inlet, established the starting point of a town that would eventually become Vancouver.

With the promise of access to a new national railway network, BC joined the Canadian Confederation in 1871. It would be another 16 years before the railway actually rolled into the region.

The City's Boozy Start

In 1867, Englishman John 'Gassy Jack' Deighton rowed into Burrard Inlet with his First Nations wife, a small dog and a barrel of whiskey. He knew the nearest drink for thirsty mill workers was 20km away so he asked them to help him build a tavern. Within 24 hours the Globe Saloon was in business. And when a village sprang up around the establishment it was quickly dubbed 'Gastown.' In 1870, in an attempt to formalize the ramshackle township, the colonial administration renamed it 'Granville,' although almost everyone still called it Gastown.

Among the reminders of early Vancouver are Kitsilano's Old Hastings Mill Store Museum and Gassy Jack's statue in Maple Tree Sq. Next to the statue, the Byrnes Block is the oldest Vancouver building still in its original location. It was built just after the 1886 Great Fire.

Selected over Port Moody, a rival mill town, as the new western railway terminus for the Canadian Pacific Railway (CPR), the town of Granville was incorporated as the City of Vancouver in April 1886. According to legend, this name was chosen by CPR manager William Van Horne, who reasoned the new city needed a grand moniker to live up to its future as a great metropolis. He is said to have selected the name 'Vancouver' to recall the historic seafarer who literally put the area on the map.

The first piece of business for Vancouver's new council was to establish the city's first park – and so Stanley Park was born. But the city faced a less enjoyable task at the tender age of two months: on June 13, 1886, a fire lit by CPR workers to clear brush rapidly spread out of control. The 'Great Fire,' as it came to be known, took 45 minutes to destroy Vancouver's 1000 wooden structures, killing as many as 28 people (the number remains disputed) and leaving 3000 homeless.

Reconstruction was under way within a few hours, but this time the buildings were fashioned from stone and brick. A few months later, on May 23, 1887, Locomotive 374 pulled the first transcontinental passenger train into the city and Vancouver was back in business. Within four years, it grew to a population of 13,000, and between 1891 and 1901 the population skyrocketed to more than double that.

Growing Pains

The railway was responsible for shaping much of the city as it exists today, with the CPR developing several key neighborhoods for new residential developments. During the first 30 years of the 20th century, the suburbs around the city also grew substantially. When Point Grey and

1886

The fledgling town is incorporated as the City of Vancouver. Within weeks, the new city burns to the ground in just 45 minutes.

1887

Locomotive 374 pulls the first transcontinental passenger train into a rebuilt Vancouver, and the town is back in business.

1901

First Nations communities, who have lived here for thousands of years, are displaced from their settlements in the Vanier Park area, as colonials fell forests.

1949

The region's Chinese, Japanese and First Nations peoples finally gain the right to vote in provincial elections.

South Vancouver amalgamated with the city in 1929, Vancouver became Canada's third-largest city – a ranking it retains today.

While the 1930s Great Depression saw the construction of several public works – the Marine Building, Vancouver City Hall, the third and present Hotel Vancouver and the Lions Gate Bridge, to name a few – many people were unemployed, as was the case throughout Canada. This marked a time of large demonstrations, violent riots and public discontent.

WWII helped to pull Vancouver out of the Depression by creating instant jobs at shipyards, aircraft-parts factories and canneries, and in construction with the building of rental units for the increased workforce. Japanese Canadians didn't fare so well. In 1942, following the bombing of Pearl Harbor, they were shipped to internment camps and had to endure the confiscation of their land and property, much of which was never returned.

Chinese, Japanese and First Nations people were finally given the provincial vote in 1949.

Expo-Sing the City

By the start of the 1950s Vancouver's population was 345,000 and the area was thriving. In the 1960s and '70s, the city was known for its counterculture edge centered on Kitsilano. Canada's gay-rights movement began here in 1964 when a group of feminists and academics started the Association for Social Knowledge, the country's first gay-and-lesbian discussion group. In 1969 the Don't Make a Wave Committee formed to protest US nuclear testing in Alaska. A few years later, it morphed into the environmental organization Greenpeace.

Vancouver's revolutionary fervor eventually cooled and economic development became the region's main pastime. Nothing was more important to Vancouver in the 1980s than Expo '86, the world fair, regarded by many as the city's coming of age. The six-month event, coinciding with Vancouver's 100th birthday, brought millions of visitors in and kick-started regeneration in several old neighborhoods. Facilities built for Expo included the landmark 60,000-seat BC Place Stadium.

Locomotive 374 pulled the first transcontinental passenger train into Vancouver in 1887, but was left to rot on a local beach for decades after its retirement. A long-overdue campaign to restore it culminated in its unveiling in a purpose-built Yaletown home in the mid-1980s.

Multicultural Milestones

The brewing issue of First Nations land rights spilled over in the late 1980s, with a growing number of rallies, road blockades and court actions in the region. Until 1990 the provincial government refused to participate in treaty negotiations. That changed in December of that year when the BC Claims Task Force was formed among the Canadian and

1956

The West End is rezoned for greater population density. Hundreds of wooden homes are bulldozed for apartment blocks.

1964

Canada's gay-rights movement begins when feminists and academics create the Association for Social Knowledge, the country's first gay-and-lesbian discussion group.

1979

Granville Island is developed from an industrial wasteland into one of Vancouver's most popular hangouts. A cement factory remains, to keep the faith.

1983

BC Place Stadium polishes its roof and opens for business, and the old courthouse building is transformed into the Vancouver Art Gallery.

BC governments and the First Nations Summit, with a mission to figure out how the three parties could resolve land-rights matters. It has been a slow-moving, ongoing process.

The 1990s also saw the region becoming increasingly multicultural. Prior to the British handover of Hong Kong to China in 1997, wealthy Hong Kong Chinese migrated to BC's Lower Mainland area, boosting the area's permanent Asian population by about 85%. Real-estate prices rose, with Vancouver's cost-of-living figures suddenly rivaling those of London, Paris and Tokyo. By 1998 immigration had tapered off but the city's transformation into a modern, multicultural mecca was complete. By then, about 40% of Vancouver residents were foreign born, and an ethnic smorgasbord of restaurants, stores and cultural activities had emerged.

A few steps from Chinatown's Millennium Gate, Shanghai Alley was once home to hundreds of immigrant Chinese men, domiciled in cheap lodgings. With its own shops, restaurants and 500-seat theater, it was designed as a one-way street that could be defended in the event of attack from locals.

Going for Gold

In the opening decade of the new millennium, Vancouver became a regular on those global surveys that designate the best places in the world to live. Seizing the initiative and recalling the success of Expo '86, the region again looked to the future, winning the bid to host the 2010 Olympic and Paralympic Winter Games.

With events staged in and around the city, and also at Whistler, a global TV audience of more than two billion gazed admiringly at picture-perfect snow-and-blue-sky vistas. And while many locals grumbled about the cost of the Games, the city exploded into a 17-day mardi gras of support that surprised even the organizers.

This all-enveloping Canadian pride hit fever pitch during the men's gold-medal hockey game, when the host nation beat the US with a dreamlike last-gasp goal. For many Vancouverites, this moment was the best thing that's ever happened in the city's short modern history.

For decades a neon-lit 'W' stood atop the old Woodward's department store. But when the building was redeveloped it was found to be severely corroded. A new one was created in its place, and the old one is preserved in a glass case at ground level.

Gentrification

After the Olympics, a new wave of development took hold in the city, especially in those areas that had traditionally seen little change in decades past. One such controversial neighborhood was suddenly part of the new plans.

Long blighted by drugs, prostitution and crime, the Downtown Eastside – centered on Main and Hastings Sts – had been a no-go skid row for years. Politicians have made regular pronouncements about solving the area's problems, but progress has been halting. The opening of a large new housing, shops and university-campus complex on the old Wood-

1985

The first SkyTrain line opens, creating a link between the communities of New Westminster and Vancouver.

1986

The international spotlight shines on Vancouver as the Expo '86 world fair dominates the summer, bringing Sheena Easton and Depeche Mode to local stages.

1996

With the Hong Kong handover to China imminent, Vancouver sees a massive influx of Asian immigrants into the city. Richmond transforms into the region's new Chinatown.

2003

BC and Ontario lead North America by making same-sex marriage legal. Vancouver becomes a hot spot for elopements.

ward's department-store site in 2010 seemed to be a catalyst for change, with new businesses recolonizing the area's paint-peeled storefronts for the first time in decades.

This gentrification drive is not without controversy, though. While city hipsters move into pricey loft apartments and quaff flat whites in exposed-brick coffee shops, the residents who have called this area home for decades are feeling increasingly marginalized. In 2013, antigentrification protesters picketed new restaurants in the area and appealed for more social housing to be part of the city's future plans. By 2019, the phrase 'renoviction' had entered the local lexicon, describing the removal of long-term residents from their homes by landlords planning to upgrade and charge far higher rents to new tenants. Finding the right balance between new development and support for the people who already live here is now one of Vancouver's biggest challenges.

Vancouver's history has always been about gentrification, with large tracts of forested land torn up for housing from day one. In the early 1900s, the Shaughnessy Heights neighborhood was created as a swank enclave of turreted mansions for the city's rich. Fans of heritage architecture love visiting this area today.

Real Estate Rumble

Rising housing costs haven't just been a challenge for poorer Vancouverites in recent years. Expo '86 and the 2010 Winter Olympics were almost 25 years apart, but they affected the city in similar ways. They brought Vancouver to the attention of many more people around the world; specifically, people with money to purchase real estate. Strike up a conversation with many locals here and it's usually just a matter of minutes before they mention Vancouver housing prices that have made the city the most expensive metropolis in Canada. There are several contributing factors but the result is that younger locals who are not able to splash out up to $2 million on purchasing a family home talk more than ever about leaving the city. Current mayor Kennedy Stewart made affordable housing a key issue of his 2018 election campaign, while a new left-leaning provincial government has also introduced rules against vacant properties and speculation by overseas investors. It remains to be seen just how 'affordable' latter-day Vancouver housing can become, though.

Pandemic Challenges

COVID-19's spring 2020 arrival produced a rollercoaster of new regulations, business closures and personal challenges for Vancouverites. Directed by BC's Public Health Officer, Bonnie Henry, locals signed-up for vaccines in impressive numbers. But the pandemic also triggered widespread introspection, with many re-assessing careers, rediscovering local nature and re-prioritizing their lives.

2010

Locals party as Vancouver hosts the Olympic and Paralympic Winter Games. Flags are waved, national anthems sung and Canada wins gold in men's hockey.

2011

Vancouver celebrates its 125th birthday, but the party doesn't quite match that of the Olympics.

2018

New mayor Kennedy Stewart promises to tackle the city's challenging affordable housing issue.

2020-1

COVID-19 triggers lockdowns and other BC-wide health orders but the number of fully vaccinated locals soon climbs above 80 percent.

Green Vancouver

It's hard to see Vancouver as anything but a green city: its dense forests and verdant, rain-fed plant life make nature an ever-present fact of life here. But beyond the breathtaking visuals, how does the city measure up to its environmental responsibilities? And – just as importantly – what can Vancouver-bound visitors do to reduce their own environmental footprint in the region without turning their vacation into a monastic, fun-free zone?

Painting the Town Green

Vancouver has an international reputation for being a green city, but that doesn't mean everyone here wears biodegradable shoes and eats only elderly vegetables that have died of natural causes. In fact, if you stroll the Robson St boutiques or dip into a take-out coffee shop, it's easy to think that 'green Vancouver' doesn't exist at all. As with many of the city's best features, you have to do a little digging.

Given the city's breathtaking natural surroundings, it was just a matter of time before Vancouver's residents were inspired to protect the planet, which explains why a few of them began gathering in a Kitsilano basement in 1969 to plan the fledgling Don't Make a Wave Committee's first protest against nuclear testing in Alaska. By the time their campaign boat entered the Gulf of Alaska in 1971, they had renamed themselves Greenpeace and sailed into environmental history. Greenpeace set the tone and the city has since become a headquarters for environmental groups, from the Wilderness Committee to the David Suzuki Foundation.

There are more than 175 plug-in recharging points for electric vehicles in Vancouver, many of them operated by the City, which charges up to $2 per hour.

Actions speak louder than words, however, and Vancouver's green scene is not just about protest and discussion. The city is home to dozens of large and small eco-initiatives, enabling many locals to color their lives as green as they choose. Vancouver has one of the largest hybrid-vehicle taxi fleets in North America and has a commitment to mass public transportation, including electric trolley buses and a light-rail train system. Carpooling and rideshare alternatives to traditional car hire are also big here, with Evo and Car2Go ubiquitous on city streets.

And while developers tout their green credentials as if they're saving the planet single-handedly, few of the city's new towers are built

VANCOUVER'S HIGH LINE

The City of Vancouver suddenly created a new public park in 2016 after purchasing 9km of disused railway-line land that runs south from Kitsilano to Marpole and the Fraser River. The **Arbutus Greenway** (p166) has been wildly popular since it opened and new features will be added over the coming years. Currently, the 17-hectare ribbon-like space is a tree-fringed cycling and walking route that acts as a promenade for laid-back locals on sunny days. It's a great way to explore the city's urban nature, from butterflies and wildflowers to birdlife that often includes hummingbirds and northern flicker woodpeckers.

without key environmental considerations. Vancouver is also a leader in 'green roofs' – planted rooftops that curb wasted energy through natural evaporation in summer and natural insulation in winter. Check out the convention center West Building's shaggy grass rooftop plus the newly opened public garden on top of the Colosseum-like Public Library building.

On the Ground

Several Vancouver accommodation options have introduced dedicated environmental programs. Opus Hotel (p210), for example, has a water- and energy-conservation scheme; the Fairmont Hotel Vancouver (p207) deploys energy-efficient lighting; and the Listel Hotel (p209) has installed its own power-generating solar panels.

Dining is also firmly on the green agenda here. Spearheaded by the Vancouver Aquarium and a growing menu of city restaurants, **Ocean Wise** (seafood.ocean.org) encourages sustainable fish and shellfish supplies that minimize environmental impact. The website lists participating restaurants; check local menus for symbols indicating Ocean Wise dishes. A similar, smaller movement called the **Green Table Network** (www.greentable.net) can help you identify considerate area restaurants that try to source all their supplies – not just seafood – from sustainable, mostly local, sources. Many new vegetarian restaurants have also opened in the city in recent years, with locals embracing plant-based diets in ever-increasing numbers.

Sustainability has a social side in **Vancouver with Green Drinks** (www.greendrinks.org), a monthly drop-in gathering for anyone interested in environmental issues. The meetings usually attract more than 100 regulars for engaging discussions on alternative energy, global warming and the sky-high price of organic groceries. Speaking of groceries, there are lots of sustainable food-shopping options around the city, but the area's farmers markets are the ideal way to eat well and do your bit for the world. See www.eatlocal.org for listings of several area markets.

Consider hopping onto two wheels to get around the city. Vancouver has more than 300km of designated bike lanes, so you can see the sights without burning up the planet. Bike rentals are easy to come by and many operators can get you out for a citywide pedal. The city also has a popular public bike share scheme called Mobi; see www.mobibikes.ca for information.

Every June or July, several Vancouver neighborhoods banish their cars and turn themselves into pedestrian-only zones. Over the years, Car Free Day Vancouver (p121) has grown to become one of the city's most popular, family-friendly street parties, with thousands of locals rolling in for food stands, live music, craft stalls and a large serving of exhaust-free fun.

Tree Hugging

It's hard not to be impressed by the towering Douglas firs in Stanley Park or the cherry-blossom trees that flower around the city in spring. But for many, fall is the best time to hang out with the trees. Burnished copper, pumpkin-orange, deep candy-apple red: the seemingly infinite colors of autumn under cloudless blue skies make this the favorite season for many Vancouverites, and it's one of the rare times you'll see locals reaching for their cameras. If you're here in October, charge up your camera, slip into comfortable walking shoes and hunt down the following pigment-popping locations.

Make a beeline for Stanley Park. Hit the seawall – by bike or on foot – to find rusty amber hues and Japanese-maple reds studding the evergreen Douglas firs. If you don't have time for a full-on Stanley Park jaunt, weave towards nearby English Bay. The beach at the end of Denman St will require your camera's panorama setting. You'll find a glittering, gently rippling waterfront, backed by a stand of achingly beautiful

Vancouver's Greenest Attractions

Stanley Park (p52)

Stanley Park Nature House (p61)

UBC Botanical Garden (p167)

Arbutus Greenway (p166)

VanDusen Botanical Garden (p150)

FIRST NATIONS NATURE TOUR

For a fascinating introduction to the rich First Nations understanding of local plants, book ahead for a Talking Trees Tour of Stanley Park with Talaysay Tours (p248). Your guided wander will tell you all about the food and medicinal uses of many of the region's plants and trees, offering stories of sustainability that have been around for thousands of years.

mature trees, each seemingly a different color. Not surprisingly, this is also a great location for sunset shots. If it's raining, nip into the lounge bar of the nearby ivy-shrouded Sylvia Hotel: it faces the water, so you'll still have a great view.

If you're wondering what trees you're passing as you wander around the city, pick up a copy of the *Vancouver Tree Book* (David Tracey; 2016). This handy pocket guide will help you identify everything from Pacific yews to paperback maples, and it also includes some recommended tree tour routes.

Across town at Queen Elizabeth Park, weave uphill among the trees from the Cambie St entrance. Aim towards the Bloedel Conservatory dome at the summit for a spectacular squirrel's-eye view across the foliage. On a fine day, you'll also have one of the best wide-angled vistas over the glass-towered city, framed by ice-frosted mountains. And if it's time to warm up, nip inside the Conservatory where the tropical plants and neon-bright birds are guaranteed to give your day a splash of extra color.

It's not all parks, of course. Many of Vancouver's older residential neighborhoods resemble spilled paintboxes of color every fall. The West End neighborhood is striped with residential streets where fall-flavored trees mix with bright-painted heritage houses: on a honey-lit, sunshine-steeped day, you can hear the photographers clicking madly here. One of the best spots is Mt Pleasant's 10th Ave, especially in the section running east from City Hall. Like a walk-through kaleidoscope, the dozens of century-old chestnut trees here create a tunnel of rich orange and yellow – above a dense carpet of fallen chestnuts that's like walking on shiny cobbles.

Green Shoots

Many Vancouver green initiatives are at the grassroots community level and one of our favorites is the city's Pop-up Library phenomenon. Several neighborhoods across Vancouver have built their own pop-up mini-libraries for all to use. These free-to-use book exchanges sit outside on residential streets – covered, of course, to stop the dog-eared tomes suffering on Vancouver's frequent rainy days. There are at least five dotted around local communities. One of the largest is the St George Sharing Library, a double-shelved covered table a few steps from the intersection of East 10th Ave and St George St. It's always bulging with well-used paperbacks, from pulp fiction to self-published screeds on communism and the occasional Lonely Planet guidebook.

Vancouver's **Fruit Tree Project Society** (www.vancouverfruittree.com) deploys a green army of volunteers to harvest treats that would otherwise rot on trees around the city. Hundreds of pounds of fruit are collected every year and the goodies – typically plums, apples, pears and grapes – are redistributed to those in need around the city.

Arts & Culture

It's more than easy to believe that Vancouver's calf-busting outdoorsy locals must be philistines when it comes to arty pursuits – how can mountain bikers be interested in galleries, dance and literature, you might ask? But in reality, this city by the sea is a major Canadian cultural capital. With a little digging, visitors will be able to tap into this primarily grassroots scene. Ask the locals for tips and pick up a copy of the free weekly *Georgia Straight*.

Visual Arts

British Columbia (BC) strongly identifies with three main forms of visual arts, and each is well represented in galleries and public spaces throughout Vancouver. Historic and contemporary indigenous works are displayed at unique institutions such as the University of British Columbia's spectacular Museum of Anthropology (p164) and downtown's newer Bill Reid Gallery of Northwest Coast Art (p57). Latter-day painting and photoconceptualism (often called the 'Vancouver School' of photography) are exhibited at the Vancouver Art Gallery (p55), Contemporary Art Gallery (p60) and a multitude of private galleries. For further information on the local art scene, visit www.art-bc.com.

Vancouver provides plenty of opportunities to meet the region's creative types face to face, including one annual event that has never been more popular. November's partylike Eastside Culture Crawl (p91) sees hundreds of East Vancouver artists opening their studios for visitors to wander around. It's the best art event in the city, and a firm local favorite. An even bigger celebration will likely take place when the Vancouver Art Gallery (p55) makes its long-anticipated move to a grand new downtown venue sometime over the next few years; check the website for the latest updates.

Public Art

Vancouver has a vigorous public-art program and you'll likely spot challenging installations, decorative apartment-building adornments and sometimes puzzling sculptures dotted throughout the city. Check www.vancouver.ca/publicart for an online registry of works and some handy maps, or pick up the excellent book *Public Art in Vancouver: Angels Among Lions,* by John Steil and Aileen Stalker. It has photos of and information on more than 500 works around the city, divided into neighborhoods. Also, check the website of the Vancouver Biennale (p75), a massive public-art showcase, staged in two-year chunks, that brings monumental, often challenging, installations to the city's streets from artists around the world. The website shows where to find these works and plot your own walking tour.

Among the public artworks to look out for in Vancouver are the 14 smiling, oversized bronze figures near the shoreline of English Bay, which form one of Canada's most photographed art installations; the five wrecked cars piled on top of a cedar tree trunk near Science World; the pixelated-looking orca alongside downtown's Convention Centre

Shopping for Arts & Crafts

Pacific Arts Market (p159)

Circle Craft (p112)

Bird on a Wire Creations (p143)

Crafthouse (p114)

Eastside Culture Crawl (p91)

extension; the towering neon cross at Clark Dr and E 6th Ave; the silver replica of a freight shed on piles by Liz Magor, on the Coal Harbour seawall; and, of course, the quirky white-painted poodle on Main St that locals either love or loathe.

There's also been a big push to encourage giant murals around the city in recent years; you'll find dozens of these huge, eye-catching works on and around Main St. Vancouver International Airport is also worthy of a photographic snap or two: between the international and US check-in desks, the magnificent bronze *Spirit of Haida Gwaii* by Bill Reid is the terminal's focal point, while other handsome indigenous pieces dot the terminal buildings.

First Nations Art

First Nations artists have contributed mightily to Vancouver's historic and contemporary visual-arts scene, particularly through carving. Two carvers who preserved the past while fostering a new generation of First Nations artists were Charles Edenshaw, the first professional Haida artist, who worked in argillite, gold and silver; and Mungo Martin, a Kwakiutl master carver of totem poles. Martin passed on his skills to Bill Reid, the outstanding Haida artist of his generation and the first Haida artist to have a retrospective exhibition at the Vancouver Art Gallery. His work is permanently displayed at the Museum of Anthropology (p164) and also at downtown's Bill Reid Gallery of Northwest Coast Art (p57), where exquisite works from other First Nations artists are also on display. Vancouver is also well stocked with private galleries where you can buy authentic First Nations art from this region, including the long-established Hill's Native Art (p144) on Broadway.

One of the world's hottest First Nations artists, Brian Jungen disassembles well-known objects and recreates them in challenging new forms, usually fusing them with traditional arts-and-crafts visuals. His most famous works are the masks made from resewn sections of Nike running shoes, and his detailed whalebone sculptures created from humdrum plastic chairs.

Vancouver Indie Flicks

On the Corner *(2003) Fictional account of life on the Downtown Eastside.*

Carts of Darkness *(2008) Documentary exploring the 'extreme sport' of shopping-cart racing among local bottle pickers.*

Double Happiness *(1994) Generational differences in a colorful Chinese-Canadian family in Vancouver.*

The Delicate Art of Parking *(2003) Documentary-style comedy about Vancouver parking enforcers.*

Performance Arts

Vancouver has a strong reputation for stage performance and is especially well represented in dance and live theater.

Second only to Montréal as a hotbed of contemporary Canadian dance, Vancouver is home to dozens of professional companies. The Dance Centre (p75) is the main twinkle-toes resource in the province. Its range of activities is unparalleled in Canada, including support for professional artists, operation of Western Canada's flagship dance facility, and presentation of a huge number of programs and events for the public. Dance events are scheduled throughout the city, including the three-week-long Vancouver International Dance Festival in spring and the 10-day Dancing on the Edge event in July.

Vancouver is also home to a vibrant theater scene. But rather than one or two major theaters, you'll find many smaller stages dotted around the city. The **Arts Club Theatre Company** (☎604-687-1644; www.artsclub.com; tickets from $29; ⏲Sep-Jun) is the city's largest theatrical troupe, and the host of fringelike smaller venues and companies include the Cultch (p128) and Firehall Arts Centre (p93). Events-wise, plan your visit for the Bard on the Beach Shakespeare festival (p173), the Vancouver Fringe Festival (p110) or the PuSh Festival (p37). And, if you're a fan of alfresco shows, the outdoor Malkin Bowl in Stanley Park is home to the summer season Theatre Under the Stars (p74) troupe.

Vancouver International Jazz Festival

Music

Vancouver has a strong and diverse music tradition founded on decades of homegrown talent. D.O.A., Dan Mangan, Sarah McLachlan, Brasstronaut, Bear Mountain, New Pornographers, Michael Bublé and many others have all emerged through the diverse local scene. The city's music scene is liveliest at the grassroots level, where local indie acts hit stages small, and slightly larger, every night of the week. There are a number of top venues worth catching shows in, including the Commodore Ballroom (p74), Biltmore Cabaret (p141) and Rickshaw Theatre (p93), while favorite local stores such as Neptoon Records (p143) and Red Cat Records (p142) are great for recommendations, as is the free local-music magazine *Discorder*.

Vancouver also has one of Canada's most vital classical-music scenes, with chamber and choral groups particularly well represented. Favorites include the Vancouver Bach Choir, whose Messiah sing-along is a Christmastime legend; the internationally renowned Vancouver Chamber Choir, which covers everything from jazz to avant-garde; and the **Vancouver Symphony Orchestra** (☎604-876-3434; www.vancouversymphony.ca), which effortlessly draws serious music fans and first timers with a stirring mix of classics and 'pops'.

Vancouver hosts live music events throughout the year, with summer the best time for some outdoor tunes. Among the most popular events are the **Vancouver International Jazz Festival** (www.coastaljazz.ca; ⌚Jun) and the **Vancouver Folk Music Festival** (www.thefestival.bc.ca; Jericho Beach Park, Kitsilano; tickets from $55; ⌚mid-Jul; 🚌4). For dozens of local live acts, schedule your visit for the annual alfresco Khatsahlano Street Party (p168) in Kitsilano.

Blog It

Before you hit town, jump into the indie scene via these eclectic local-music blogs:

Backstage Rider *(www.backstagerider.com)*

Vancity Music Scene *(www.vancitymusicscene.blogspot.ca)*

Groundwerk Vancouver *(www.groundwerkvancouver.com)*

Cinema & Television

The movie industry has a starring role in Vancouver's 'Hollywood North' economy. True, not many stories are set in the city – few know that *Rise of the Planet of the Apes* and the *Deadpool* films were made here – but the industry is home to a couple hundred productions every year. The influential Vancouver Film School counts director/actor/screenwriter Kevin Smith (of *Clerks* fame) among its most famed grads, while actors who have moved on to global acclaim from the city include Seth Rogen, Ryan Reynolds and Michael J Fox.

Alongside a full range of local movie theaters, Vancouver is home to many niche film festivals staged in the city throughout the year, and the giant Vancouver International Film Festival is one of the city's most popular annual cultural events. Second only to Toronto's film fest in size, it's a 17-day showcase of great flicks from Canada and around the world. The city also nurtures budding filmmakers through the likes of the Celluloid Social Club; held monthly at the Anza Club near Main St, it's a hangout for aspiring movie creatives and is open to all comers.

Best of Vancouver Authors

City of Glass *(Douglas Coupland; 2000) Affectionate homage to the city by one of its leading authors.*

Vancouver Special *(Charles Demers; 2009) Black-and-white images and warts-and-all reflections on the city.*

Runaway: Diary of a Street Kid *(Evelyn Lau; 2001) Deeply personal memoir about life on the streets in Vancouver.*

The Jade Peony *(Wayson Choy; 1995) Immersive memoir of growing up in a Chinese immigrant family in Vancouver in the 1930s.*

Literature

Vancouver is a highly bookish city, home to a healthy round of bookstores and a large volume of literary events to keep local and visiting bookworms fully enthralled. Among the city's favorite bookshop hangouts are Macleod's Books (p76), Paper Hound (p76) and Pulpfiction Books (p144), where stacks of used tomes invite cozy browsing on rainy days. If you really want to see how serious the city is about books, visit the landmark Vancouver Public Library (p60), shaped like the Colosseum. There are plenty of ways to rub bookish shoulders with the locals at events that include poetry slams, the Word on the Street book and magazine festival (www.wordvancouver.ca), and the **Vancouver Writers Fest** (www.writersfest.bc.ca; Granville Island; tickets from $15; ⏲late Oct; 🚌50), where you're likely to run into every book lover in town.

Local authors past and present who have garnered international reputations include Douglas Coupland, William Gibson and Malcolm Lowry. Coupland is the city's most famous living author, with celebrated works including *Generation X* and *J-Pod*.

A strong nonfiction bent also exists within the local literary scene, with two Vancouver authors producing back-to-back wins in Canada's prestigious Charles Taylor Prize for Literary Nonfiction. Charles Montgomery's *The Last Heathen: Encounters with Ghosts and Ancestors in Melanesia* (later published around the world as *The Shark God*) led the way, followed by his colleague James Mackinnon who won for *Dead Man in Paradise*. Mackinnon also produced the excellent *Once and Future World: Nature As It Was, As It Is, As It Could Be*.

TOTORORO/GETTY IMAGES ©

Survival Guide

Transportation

ARRIVING IN VANCOUVER

Most visitors will arrive by air at Vancouver International Airport, south of the city in Richmond. Alternatively, US trains trundle in from Seattle to Pacific Central Station, located on the southern edge of Vancouver's Chinatown district. Cross-border inter-city bus services also arrive at this terminal. Vancouver is only an hour or so from several US border crossings, so driving is a popular way to access the city from the US. Public and private ferry operators also service the region from around BC, while cross-Canada rail, bus and flight operations also terminate in Vancouver, which is the main gateway for accessing destinations throughout British Columbia (BC).

Flights, cars and tours can be booked online at lonelyplanet.com/bookings.

Vancouver International Airport

Canada's second-busiest airport, **Vancouver International Airport** (YVR; Map p198; ☎604-207-7077; www.yvr.ca; 3211 Grant McConachie Way, Richmond; 📶) is 13km south of downtown in the city of Richmond. There are two main terminals – international (including flights to the US) and domestic – just a short indoor stroll apart. A third (and much smaller) South Terminal is located a quick drive away; free shuttle-bus links are provided. This terminal services floatplanes, helicopters and smaller aircraft traveling to small communities in BC and beyond. In addition, short-hop floatplane and helicopter services (p245) to and from Vancouver Island and beyond also depart from the city's downtown waterfront, near Canada Place.

The main airport has shops, food courts, currency-exchange booths and a tourist information desk. It's also dotted with handsome aboriginal artworks. Baggage carts are free (no deposit required) and there is also free wi-fi.

Train

SkyTrain's 16-station **Canada Line** (see the route maps at www.translink.ca) operates a rapid-transit train service from the airport to downtown. Trains run every few minutes from early morning until after midnight and take around 25 minutes to reach downtown's Waterfront Station. The airport station is located just outside, between the domestic and international terminals. Follow the signs from inside either terminal and buy your ticket from the platform vending machines. These accept cash and credit cards – look for green-jacketed

CLIMATE CHANGE & TRAVEL

Every form of transport that relies on carbon-based fuel generates CO_2, the main cause of human-induced climate change. Modern travel is dependent on aeroplanes, which might use less fuel per kilometre per person than most cars but travel much greater distances. The altitude at which aircraft emit gases (including CO_2) and particles also contributes to their climate change impact. Many websites offer 'carbon calculators' that allow people to estimate the carbon emissions generated by their journey and, for those who wish to do so, to offset the impact of the greenhouse gases emitted with contributions to portfolios of climate-friendly initiatives throughout the world. Lonely Planet offsets the carbon footprint of all staff and author travel.

Canada Line staff if you're bleary-eyed and need assistance after your long-haul flight. Fares from the airport cost between $8 and $10.75, depending on your destination and the time of day.

Taxi

➡ Follow the signs from inside the airport terminal to the cab stand just outside. A system of zone fares operates from YVR; your fare will typically be between $20 and $45 (most downtown Vancouver destinations cost $35). Confirm your fare with the driver before you set off.

➡ Rates do not include tips; 15% is the norm.

➡ Limo-car services are also available close to the main taxi stand. Expect to pay around $20 more for your ride to the city if you want to arrive in style.

Car

Most major car-rental agencies have desks at the airport, as well as multiple offices around the city. Once you're strapped in – seat belts are compulsory here – proceed east after leaving the airport on Grant McConachie Way, and follow the Vancouver signs over the Arthur Laing Bridge. Take the Granville St exit and travel north along Granville St with the mountain ahead of you. Depending on traffic, you'll be in the downtown core in around 30 minutes.

Pacific Central Station

Train

➡ **Pacific Central Station** (1150 Station St, Chinatown; Ⓢ Main St-Science World) is the city's main terminus for long-distance trains from across Canada on **VIA Rail** (www.viarail.com), and from Seattle (just south of the border) and beyond on **Amtrak** (www.amtrak.com).

➡ The Main St-Science World SkyTrain station is just across the street for connections to downtown and beyond.

➡ There are car-rental desks in the station and cabs are also available just outside the building.

Bus

➡ Intercity nontransit buses trundle into Vancouver's neon-signed **Pacific Central Station** (1150 Station St, Chinatown; Ⓢ Main St-Science World). Almost all Greyhound bus services (www.greyhound.com) into Vancouver have been cancelled in recent years; the only remaining route is from Seattle (from $20; four hours). **BC Connector** (www.bcconnector.com) operates bus services from Kelowna, Kamloops and Whistler as well as Victoria (via BC Ferries). Cross-border services from **Bolt Bus** (www.boltbus.com) and **Quick Shuttle** (www.quickcoach.com) also arrive here.

➡ The Main St-Science World SkyTrain station is just across the street for connections to downtown and the suburbs.

➡ There are car-rental desks in the station and cabs are available just outside.

Tsawwassen & Horseshoe Bay Ferry Terminals

BC Ferries (☎250-386-3431; www.bcferries.com) services arrive at Tsawwassen, an hour south of Vancouver, and at Horseshoe Bay, 30 minutes from downtown in West Vancouver. The company operates one of the world's largest ferry networks, including some spectacular routes throughout the province.

Main services to Tsawwassen arrive from Vancouver Island's Swartz Bay, near Victoria, and Duke Point, near Nanaimo. Services also arrive from the Southern Gulf Islands.

Services to Horseshoe Bay arrive from Nanaimo's Departure Bay. Services also arrive here from Bowen Island and from Langdale on the Sunshine Coast.

To depart Tsawwassen via transit, take bus 620 (adult/child $5.70/3.90) to Bridgeport Station in Richmond and transfer to the Canada Line. It takes about an hour to reach downtown.

From Horseshoe Bay to downtown, take bus 257 (adult/child $4.20/2.90), which is faster than bus 250. It takes about 40 minutes.

V2V Vacations (Map p270; ☎855-554-4679; www.v2vvacations.com; Vancouver Harbour Flight Centre, 1055 Canada Pl; one-way from $110; ⏲Mar-Oct) also operates upmarket walk-on boat services to Vancouver's downtown waterfront from Victoria's harborfront (adult/child from $220/110, March to October). Travel time is three to four hours.

Downtown Waterfront

➡ Handy floatplane services swoop directly into the downtown waterfront area from Vancouver Island and points around BC. These include frequent **Harbour Air Seaplanes** (☎604-274-1277; www.harbourair.com) services from Victoria's Inner Harbour and beyond.

➡ For a different type of ride, **Helijet** (☎604-273-4688; www.helijet.com) helicopter services arrive on the downtown waterfront, just east of Canada Place, from Victoria and beyond.

GETTING AROUND VANCOUVER

Bicycle

➡ Vancouver is a relatively good cycling city, with more than 300km of designated routes crisscrossing the region.

➡ Cyclists can take their bikes for free on SkyTrains, SeaBuses and transit buses, which are all now fitted with bike racks. Cyclists are required by law to wear helmets.

➡ There are dedicated bike lanes in the city, and locals and visitors alike can use **Mobi** (☎778-655-1800; www.mobibikes.ca), a public bike-share scheme.

➡ Download free cycle route maps from the TransLink website (www.translink.ca) or plan your route using https://vancouver.bikerouteplanner.com.

➡ If you're traveling sans bike, you can also rent wheels from businesses around the city, especially on Denman St near Stanley Park – home of Vancouver's most popular scenic cycling route.

ONLINE CYCLING RESOURCES

City of Vancouver (www.vancouver.ca/cycling) Route maps and bike-friendly info.

BC Cycling Coalition (www.bccc.bc.ca) Local resources for cyclists.

HUB (www.bikehub.ca) The locals' main bike-based resource.

Let's Go Biking (www.letsgobiking.net) Showcasing recommended routes around the region.

Bus

➡ Vancouver's **TransLink** (www.translink.ca) bus network is extensive. All vehicles are equipped with bike racks and all are wheelchair accessible. Exact change (or more) is required; buses use fare machines and change is not given. Fares cost adult/child $3/1.95 and are valid for up to 90 minutes of transfer travel. While Vancouver's transit system covers three geographic fare zones, all bus trips are regarded as one-zone fares.

➡ Bus services operate from early morning to after midnight in central areas. There is also an additional 12-route NightBus system that runs from 2am. Look for NightBus signs at designated stops.

Boat

Waterfront Vancouver makes use of its waterways for local travel, via transit services and private providers.

Ferry

➡ The iconic SeaBus shuttle is part of the TransLink transit system (regular transit fares apply) and it operates throughout the day, taking around 15 minutes to cross Burrard Inlet between Waterfront Station and North Vancouver's Lonsdale Quay. At Lonsdale you can then connect to buses servicing North Vancouver and West Vancouver; this is where you pick up bus 236 to both Capilano Suspension Bridge and Grouse Mountain.

➡ SeaBus services leave from Waterfront Station between 6:16am and 1:22am, Monday to Saturday (8:16am to 11:16pm on Sunday). Vessels are wheelchair accessible and bike-friendly.

➡ Tickets must be purchased from vending machines on either side of the route before boarding. The machines take credit and debit cards, and also give change up to $20 for cash transactions.

Miniferry

Operators offer day passes (adult $16) as well as discounted books of tickets for those making multiple water hops. Single trips cost from $3.50.

Aquabus Ferries (☎604-689-5858; www.theaquabus.com; adult/child from $3.50/1.75) Runs frequent minivessels (some big enough to carry bikes) between the foot of Hornby St and Granville Island. It also services several additional spots along the False Creek waterfront, as far as Science World.

False Creek Ferries (Map p266; ☎604-684-7781; www.granvilleislandferries.bc.ca; adult/child from $3.50/2.25) Operates a similar Granville Island service from Sunset Beach, and has additional ports of call around False Creek.

Car & Motorcycle

For sightseeing in the city, you'll be fine without a car (the city center is especially easy to explore on foot and transit routes are extensive). For visits that incorporate the wider region's mountains and communities, however, a vehicle makes life much simpler: the further you travel from downtown, the more limited your transit options become.

Driving

➡ Seat belts are mandatory here, and there is also a ban on using handheld electronic devices while driving.

➡ Vancouver doesn't have any expressways going through its

TRANSIT TICKETS & PASSES

➡ Along with trip-planning resources, the TransLink website (www.translink.ca) has a comprehensive section on fares and passes covering its combined bus, SeaBus and SkyTrain services.

➡ The transit system is divided into three geographic zones. One-zone trips cost adult/child $3/1.95, two zones $4.25/2.95 and three zones $5.75/3.95. All bus trips are one-zone fares. If you buy a stored-value plastic Compass Card, fares are charged at a lower rate.

➡ You can buy single-use paper tickets and all-access paper DayPasses (adult/child $10.50/8.25) from vending machines at SeaBus and SkyTrain stations. You can also buy stored-value Compass Cards ($6 deposit) from these machines or at designated Compass retailers around the city, including London Drugs branches.

➡ After 6:30pm, and on weekends or holidays, all transit trips are classed as one-zone fares. Children under five travel for free on all transit services at all times.

core, which can lead to some major congestion issues. Evening rush-hour traffic can be a nightmare, with enormous lines of cars snaking along W Georgia St waiting to cross the Lions Gate Bridge. Try the Second Narrows Ironworkers Memorial Bridge (known simply as the Second Narrows Bridge to most locals) if you need to access the North Shore in a hurry. Other peak-time hot spots to avoid are the George Massey Tunnel and Hwy 1 to Surrey.

➡ For route planning and driving conditions throughout the region, visit www.drivebc.ca.

Parking

Parking is at a premium in downtown Vancouver: there are some free spots on residential side streets but many require permits, and traffic wardens are predictably predatory. Many streets also have metered parking (up to $6 per hour). Pay-parking lots (typically from $6 per hour) are a better proposition – arrive before 9am at some for early-bird, day-rate discounts. For an interactive map of parking-lot locations, check EasyPark (www.easypark.ca).

Rental

Major car-rental agencies with offices around the city and at Vancouver International Airport:

Avis (☎604-606-2847; www.avis.ca)

Budget (☎604-668-7000; www.budgetbc.com)

Enterprise (☎604-688-5500; www.enterprisecar.ca)

Hertz (☎604-606-4711; www.hertz.ca)

Thrifty (☎800-334-1705; www.thriftycanada.ca)

Train

➡ TransLink's SkyTrain rapid-transit network is a great way to move around the region, especially beyond the city center. A new route to the University of BC campus is expected to open in the coming years.

➡ Compass tickets for SkyTrain trips can be purchased from station vending machines (change is given; machines also accept debit and credit cards) prior to boarding.

➡ SkyTrain journeys cost $3 to $5.75 (plus $5 more if you're traveling from the airport), depending on how far you are journeying.

Canada Line

➡ Links the city to the airport and Richmond.

➡ Trains run every few minutes throughout the day.

➡ If you're heading for the airport from the city, make sure you board a YVR-bound train – some head to Richmond but not to the airport.

Expo Line

➡ Operates two routes: one between downtown Vancouver's Waterfront and Surrey's King George; and the other between Waterfront and Burnaby's Production Way-University.

➡ Trains run every few minutes throughout the day.

Millennium Line

➡ Links Vancouver's VCC-Clark to suburban Burnaby, Port Moody and Coquitlam.

➡ Trains run every few minutes throughout the day.

Taxi

At the time of research, Vancouver was in the process of paving the way for ride-hailing schemes such as Uber and Lyft. Until then, try the following long-established taxi companies:

Black Top & Checker Cabs (☎604-731-1111; www.btccabs.ca; 📶)

Vancouver Taxi (☎604-871-1111; www.vancouvertaxi.cab)

Yellow Cab (☎604-681-1111; www.yellowcabonline.com; 📶)

TOURS

Bus & Boat Tours

Westcoast Sightseeing (☎604-451-1600; www.westcoastsightseeing.com; adult/child from $39/20) Offering two looped hop-on hop-off bus routes and duration packages of 24 hours or 48 hours, with departures every 20 minutes during peak season. There's also a wide range of additional services, including popular Christmas-season karaoke tours and excursions beyond the city.

Landsea Tours (☎604-255-7272; www.vancouvertours.com; adult/child from $65/35) Landsea's comfortable hop-on hop-off coach tours include 15 stops around the city, with tickets valid for 24 hours of travel.

Harbour Cruises (Map p287; ☎604-688-7246; www.boatcruises.com; 501 Denman St, West End; adult/child from $39/12; ⊙May–mid-Oct; 🚌19) View Vancouver – and some unexpected wildlife – from the water on a one-hour narrated harbor tour, weaving past Stanley Park, Lions Gate Bridge and the North Shore mountains. There's also a popular 2½-hour sunset dinner cruise (adult/child $87/73) plus a long, languid lunch trek to lovely Indian Arm ($76) that makes you feel like you're a million miles from the city.

Specialty Tours

Vancouver Foodie Tours (☎604-295-8844; www.foodietours.ca; tours from $65) A popular culinary-themed city stroll operator running three taste-tripping tours in Vancouver; choose between Best of Downtown, Gastronomic Gastown and Granville Island tours. Friendly red-coated guides lead you through belly-pleasing wanders with plenty to eat and drink; the trick is not to dine before you arrive.

Talaysay Tours (☎604-628-8555; www.talaysay.com; tours adult/child from $40/32) Providing a range of authentic First Nations–led tours, including a signature Stanley Park walking option, this operator also hosts additional tours around the region.

Cycle City Tours (Map p266; ☎604-618-8626; www.cyclevancouver.com; 648 Hornby St, Downtown; tours from $65, bicycle rentals per hour/day $9.50/38; ⊙9am-6pm, reduced hours in winter; Ⓢ Burrard) Striped with bike lanes, Vancouver is a good city for two-wheeled exploring. But if you're not great at navigating, consider a guided tour with this popular operator. Their Grand Tour ($90) is a great city intro, while their Craft Beer Tour ($90) includes brunch and three breweries. Alternatively, go solo with a rental; there's a bike lane outside the store. If you've ever fancied trying an electric bike, they offer that option on one of their guided tours. They also have a rentals-only store at 1344 Burrard St.

Harbour Air (Map p270; ☎604-274-1277; www.harbourair.com; 1055 Canada Pl, Downtown; tours from $99; Ⓜ Waterfront) A thrilling way to explore Vancouver's breathtaking natural setting, these panoramic floatplane flights will have you soaring over mountains, forests and coastlines – before a dramatic downtown water landing brings you back down to earth.

Vancouver Brewery Tours (☎604-318-2280; www.vancouverbrewerytours.com; tours from $70) If you're worried about over-imbibing at Vancouver's amazing microbreweries and forgetting where you hotel is, take a tour with these friendly folks. Their van will take you to three choice beermakers, samples included. Additional beery tours, including Gastown and Brewery Creek, are also available.

Walking Tours

Architectural Institute of British Columbia (☎604-683-8588; www.aibc.ca; tours $10; ⊙Tue-Sun Jul & Aug) Local architecture students conduct these excellent two-hour wanders, focusing on the buildings, history and heritage of several key Vancouver neighborhoods. There are six tours in all, covering areas including Gastown, Strathcona, Yaletown, Chinatown, downtown and the West End. If you're visiting Victoria, tours operate there as well.

Forbidden Vancouver (☎604-227-7570; www.forbiddenvancouver.ca; tours from $25) This quirky company offers highly entertaining tours, including a delve into Prohibition-era Vancouver, a Stanley Park 'secrets' tour and a combination chocolate-tasting and art-deco architecture walk. They also host regular behind-the-scenes tours of the infamous Penthouse nightclub as well as a recently added walk-and-talk around the city's LGBT+ history.

Historical Chinatown Tours (www.chinatowngirl.ca; tours from $65) Get the lowdown on Vancouver's historic Chinatown via an in-depth guided tour with local Judy Lam Maxwell.

Tour Guys (☎778-995-5484; www.tourguys.ca; free-$10) Free neighborhood tours around Vancouver (gratuities of $5 to $10 are expected). Paid private tours are also available. The free tours are very popular during the peak summer period so book ahead via the website.

Directory A–Z

Accessible Travel

Vancouver is an accessible city. On your arrival at the airport, vehicle-rental agencies can provide prearranged cars with hand controls. Accessible cabs are also widely available at the airport and throughout the city, on request.

All TransLink SkyTrain, SeaBus and transit bus services are wheelchair accessible. Check the TransLink website (www.translink.ca) for a wide range of information on accessible transport around the region. Head to www.accesstotravel.gc.ca for information and resources on accessible travel across Canada. In addition, download Lonely Planet's free Accessible Travel guides from http://lptravel.to/AccessibleTravel.

Service dogs may legally be brought into restaurants, hotels and other businesses in Vancouver. Almost all downtown sidewalks have sloping ramps, and most public buildings and attractions are wheelchair accessible. Check the City of Vancouver's dedicated website (www.vancouver.ca/accessibility) for additional information and resources.

Other helpful resources:

Disability Alliance BC (☎604-875-0188; www.disabilityalliancebc.org) Programs and support for people with disabilities.

CNIB (☎604-431-2121; www.cnib.ca) Support and services for the visually impaired.

Western Institute for the Deaf & Hard of Hearing (☎604-736-7391; www.widhh.com) Interpreter services and resources for the hearing impaired.

Discount Cards

Vancouver City Passport (www.citypassports.com; $29.95) Discounts at attractions, restaurants and activities across the city for up to two adults and two children.

Vanier Park ExplorePass (www.spacecentre.ca/explore-pass; adult/child $42.50/36.50) Combined entry to the Museum of Vancouver (MOV), Vancouver Maritime Museum and HR MacMillan Space Centre. Includes one entry to each attraction and is available at any of the three sites. There is also a separate **Dual Pass** (adult/child $31.50/18.50) covering the MOV and the Space Centre only.

UBC Museums Pass (adult/child/family $25/20/60) Combined entry to the Museum of Anthropology (MOA) and Beaty Biodiversity Museum plus 10% discount in their gift shops.

UBC Gardens & MOA Pass (adult/child/family $27/23/65) Combined entry to the Museum of Anthropology (MOA), UBC Botanical Garden and Nitobe Memorial Garden plus 10% discount in their gift shops.

Vancouver Attractions Group (www.vancouverattractions.com) Coupons and discounted entry tickets for multiple Vancouver-area attractions.

Electricity

Type A
120V/60Hz

Type B
120V/60Hz

Emergency

Police, Fire & Ambulance	☎911
Police (non-emergency number)	☎604-717-3321

Internet Access

Vancouver hotels routinely provide in-room wi-fi or (less often) high-speed cable internet services. It's usually free but check with your hotel when booking. The wi-fi icon used throughout the listings in this book indicates where free wi-fi is available. The computer icon shows where computers are offered for guests to use.

Almost all cafes and coffee shops offer free wi-fi; ask at the counter if a password is required. The **Vancouver Public Library** (☎604-331-3603; www.vpl.ca; 350 W Georgia St, Downtown; ⏰10am-9pm Mon-Thu, to 6pm Fri & Sat, 11am-6pm Sun; 📶; Ⓢ Stadium-Chinatown) also offers free wi-fi and internet-enabled computers. In addition, there are more than 500 free public access wi-fi locations around the city; for information on this network, visit www.vancouver.ca/your-government/vanwifi.

If you don't have your device with you, check your email for free in the Apple Store in downtown's Pacific Centre mall.

Medical Services

There are no reciprocal healthcare arrangements between Canada and other countries. Non-Canadians usually pay cash up front for treatment, so taking out travel insurance with a medical-cover component is strongly advised. Medical treatment in Canada is expensive: hospital beds can cost up to $2500 a day for nonresidents.

Clinics

The following walk-in services cater to visitors:

Care Point Medical & Wellness Clinics (☎604-254-5554; www.carepoint.ca; 1623 Commercial Dr; ⏰9am-4pm Mon-Fri, 9am-2pm Sat & Sun; 🚌20) Appointments not necessary but can be booked online. See www.carepoint.ca for locations.

Stein International Medical Clinic (☎778-995-7834; www.steinmedical.com; 550 Burrard St; ⏰11am-5pm Mon-Fri, 9am-1pm Sat; Ⓢ Burrard) Appointments not necessary.

Travel Medicine & Vaccination Centre (☎604-681-5656; www.tmvc.com; 666 Burrard St, Downtown; Ⓢ Burrard) Specializing in travel shots; appointments required.

Ultima Medicentre (☎604-683-8138; 1055 Dunsmuir St, Downtown; ⏰8am-5pm Mon-Fri; Ⓢ Burrard) Appointments not necessary.

Emergency Rooms

Vancouver's emergency rooms include:

BC Children's Hospital (☎604-875-2345; www.bcchildrens.ca; 4480 Oak St, Cambie; 🚌17)

St Paul's Hospital (☎604-682-2344; 1081 Burrard St, Downtown; 🚌22)

Vancouver General Hospital (☎604-875-4111; www.vch.ca; 855 W 12th Ave, Fairview; Ⓜ Broadway-City Hall)

Pharmacies

Vancouver is well stocked with pharmacies.

Shoppers Drug Mart (☎604-669-2424; 1125 Davie St, West End; ⏰24hr; 🚌6)

Money

Canadian dollars come in $5 (blue), $10 (purple), $20 (green), $50 (red) and $100 (brown) denominations, and bills are now plasticized rather than paper as originally. Coins come in nickel (5¢), dime (10¢), quarter (25¢), 'loonie' ($1) and 'toonie' ($2) coins. The penny (1¢) has been phased out, although cash registers in most stores and businesses still include penny amounts; the price you actually pay will be rounded up or down to the nearest 0 or 5.

ATMs

Interbank ATM exchange rates usually beat the rates offered for traveler's checks or foreign currency. Canadian ATM fees are generally low, but your home bank may charge another fee on top of that. Some ATM machines also dispense US currency; ideal if you're planning a trip across the border. ATMs abound in Vancouver, with bank branches congregating around the business district bordered by Burrard, Georgia, Pender and Granville Sts.

LISTEN LOCAL

Around Vancouver, flip the dial to these stations or listen in online before you arrive:

CBC Radio One (690AM, 88.1FM; www.cbc.ca/bc) Canadian Broadcasting Corporation's commercial-free news, talk and music station.

CFOX (99.3FM; www.cfox.com) Rock and chatter.

News 1130 (1130AM; www.citynews1130.com) News 24/7.

News Talk 980 CKNW (980AM; www.globalnews.ca/radio/cknw) News, traffic, sports and talk.

Peak (102.7FM; www.thepeak.fm) Popular alternative, indie & new-rock station.

Drugstores also frequently have ATMs.

Changing Money

You can exchange currency at most main bank branches, which often charge less than the *bureaux de change* dotted around the city. In addition to the banks, try **Vancouver Bullion & Currency Exchange** (☎604-685-1008; www.vbce.ca; 800 W Pender St, Downtown; ⌚8:30am-5pm Mon-Fri; Ⓢ Granville), which often offers a wider range of currencies and competitive rates.

Credit Cards

Visa, MasterCard and American Express are widely accepted in Canada. Credit cards can get you cash advances at bank ATMs, usually for an additional surcharge. Be aware that many US-based credit cards often convert foreign charges using unfavorable exchange rates and fees.

Tipping

Restaurant wait staff 15% to 18%

Bar servers $1 per drink

Hotel bellhops $2 per bag

Taxis 10% to 15%

Opening Hours

Most business hours are consistent throughout the year, with the exception of attractions, which often reduce their hours slightly outside the summer.

Banks 9am to 5pm weekdays, with some opening Saturday mornings.

Shops 10am to 6pm Monday to Saturday; noon to 5pm Sunday.

Restaurants 11:30am to 3pm and 5 to 10pm.

Coffee shops & cafes From 8am, some earlier.

Pubs & bars Pubs open from 11:30am; bars often open from 5pm. Closing midnight or later.

Post

Canada Post (www.canadapost.ca) may not be remarkably quick, but it is reliable. The standard (up to 30g) letter and postcard rate to destinations within Canada is $1.05. Postcards and standard letters to the US cost $1.27. International airmail for postcards costs $2.65.

Postal outlets are dotted around the city, many of them at the back of drugstores – look for the red Canada Post window signs or head to the handy **Howe St Postal Outlet** (Map p266; ☎604-688-2068; www.canadapost.ca; 732 Davie St, West End; ⌚9am-7pm Mon-Fri, 10am-5pm Sat; 🚌6). There is also a large **Canada Post** (Map p266; www.canadapost.ca; 495 W Georgia St, Downtown; ⌚9am-6pm Mon-Fri; Ⓢ Vancouver City Centre) branch downtown.

Public Holidays

During national public holidays, banks, schools and government offices (including post offices) are closed, and transportation, museums and other services often operate on Sunday schedules. Holidays falling on weekends are usually observed the following Monday.

Major public holidays in Vancouver:

New Year's Day January 1

Family Day Third Monday in February

Good Friday & Easter Monday Late March to mid-April

Victoria Day Third Monday in May

Canada Day July 1

BC Day First Monday in August

Labour Day First Monday in September

Thanksgiving Second Monday in October

Remembrance Day November 11

Christmas Day December 25

Boxing Day December 26

Responsible Travel

➡ Sidestepping the crowds in Vancouver is easy. Escape from downtown to areas such as beachside Kitsilano or the University of British Columbia campus – home to several top-notch attractions and a huge public park.

➡ A car is not strictly required here. Several neighborhoods – Gastown, Yaletown, the West

PRACTICALITIES

Maps

Tourism Vancouver Visitor Centre provides free downtown maps. Alternatively, the laminated *Streetwise Vancouver Map* ($13.50) is sold at some convenience stores. For free online maps, check out the VanMap (www.vancouver.ca/vanmap) system.

Newspapers

Sit down with the *Georgia Straight* (www.straight.com; free every Thursday), an alternative weekly providing Vancouver's best entertainment listings; the *Province* (www.theprovince.com), Vancouver's 'tabloid' daily newspaper; the *Tyee* (www.thetyee.ca), an award-winning online local news source; or the *Vancouver Sun* (www.vancouversun.com), the main city daily.

Radio

Around Vancouver, flip the dial to these stations or listen in online before you arrive: CBC Radio One (690AM, 88.1FM; www.cbc.ca/bc), the Canadian Broadcasting Corporation's commercial-free news, talk and music station; CFOX (99.3FM; www.cfox.com), for rock and chatter; News 1130 (1130AM; www.citynews1130.com), for news 24/7; News Talk 980 CKNW (980AM; www.globalnews.ca/radio/cknw), for news, traffic, sports and talk; or Peak (102.7FM; www.thepeak.fm), the popular alternative, indie and new-rock station.

End and more – are a short walk from downtown and are best-explored on foot. The efficient and user-friendly public transit system also includes SkyTrain, bus and SeaBus services to Granville Island, Commercial Drive, North Vancouver and beyond.

➡ Supporting local businesses with smaller footprints is easy in Vancouver. Drop by farmers' markets and peruse the independent stores and eateries on Main Street, Commercial Drive and more.

➡ Plastic shopping bags, styrofoam food containers and plastic drinking straws are now banned here. And businesses must now charge extra for disposable beverage cups. Plan ahead and bring your own reusable accoutrements.

Safe Travel

Vancouver is relatively safe for visitors.

➡ Purse-snatching and pickpocketing do occur; be vigilant with your personal possessions.

➡ Theft from unattended cars is not uncommon; never leave valuables in vehicles where they can be seen.

➡ Persistent street begging is an issue for some visitors; just say 'Sorry' and pass on if you're not interested and want to be polite.

➡ A small group of hardcore scam artists also works the downtown core, singling out tourists and asking for 'help to get back home.' Do not let them engage you in conversation.

➡ BC's COVID-19 regulations are continually evolving. At the time of writing, public transit and businesses operating indoors required masks, with social distancing and capacity limits also typically in place. Additionally, restaurants, bars, theaters and more need to see proof of vaccination credentials plus ID. For international visitors, show the proof of vaccination you used to enter Canada as well as your passport. For current COVID-19 information for visitors, see hellobc.com/know-before-you-go

Taxes & Refunds

A 5% Goods and Services Tax (GST) plus 7% Provincial Sales Tax (PST) is levied on many purchases, with some exceptions. These are not included in advertised prices, but are added at the checkout.

There is also a 3% hotel tax, called the Municipal and Regional District Tax.

Visitor tax rebates have mostly been discontinued. Check with the **Canada Revenue Agency** (www.canada.ca/en/revenue-agency) for details.

Telephone

Most Vancouver-area phone numbers have the area code ☎604; you can also expect to see ☎778. Dial all 10 digits of a given phone number, including the three-digit area code and seven-digit number, even for local calls. In some instances (eg between Vancouver and Whistler), numbers will have the same area code but will be long-distance; at such times you need to dial ☎1 before the area code.

Always dial ☎1 before other domestic long-distance and toll-free numbers. Some toll-free numbers are good anywhere in North America, others within Canada only. International rates apply for calls to the US, even though the dialing code (+1) is the same as for Canadian long-distance calls. Dial ☎011 followed by the country code for all other overseas direct-dial calls.

Cell Phones

Cell phones use the GSM and CDMA systems, depending on your carrier. Check with your cellular service provider before you leave about using your phone in Canada. Calls may be routed internationally, and US travelers should beware roaming surcharges (it can become very expensive for a 'local' call).

Phonecards

Prepaid phonecards for long-distance and international calls can be purchased at convenience stores, gas stations and some post offices. Beware some phonecards that advertise the cheapest per-minute rates, as they may also charge hefty connection fees for each call. Leading local phone company Telus (www.telus.com) offers a range of reliable phonecards available in retail outlets around the city.

Time

Vancouver is in the Pacific time zone (PST/PDT), the same as the US West Coast. At noon in Vancouver it's:

- 11am in Anchorage
- 3pm in Toronto
- 3pm in New York
- 8pm in London
- 9pm in Paris
- 6am (the next day) in Sydney
- 8am (the next day) in Auckland

During Daylight Saving Time (from the second Sunday in March to the first Sunday in November), the clock moves ahead one hour.

Toilets

City-run public toilets are not common in Vancouver but there are many places to access the facilities around the city. Public libraries, department stores, shopping malls and larger public parks all have washrooms. There are no fees to use washrooms in Vancouver.

Tourist Information

Tourism Vancouver Visitor Centre (Map p266; ☎604-683-2000; www.tourismvancouver.com; 200 Burrard St, Downtown; ⏰9am-5pm; Ⓢ Waterfront) provides free maps, visitor guides, accommodations and tour bookings, plus brochures on the city and the wider BC region.

Visas

Not required for visitors from the US, the Commonwealth and most of Western Europe for stays up to 180 days. Required by those from more than 130 other countries. However, most visa-exempt foreign nationals flying to Canada still require a $7 Electronic Travel Authorization (eTA). For more information on the eTA, see www.canada.ca/eta. For visa information, visit the **Canada Border Services Agency** (☎204-983-3500; www.cbsa.gc.ca) website.

Women Travelers

Vancouver is generally safe for women traveling solo, although jogging alone after dark in parks and hanging out late at night in the Downtown Eastside without company is best avoided. Note it is illegal to carry pepper spray or mace in Canada. The **Vancouver Women's Health Collective** (☎604-736-5262; www.womenshealthcollective.ca; 29 W Hastings St, Gastown; ⏰9am-5pm Mon, noon-5pm Tue-Thu, 9am-2pm Fri; Ⓢ Stadium-Chinatown) provides advice and referrals for health issues.

Behind the Scenes

SEND US YOUR FEEDBACK

We love to hear from travellers – your comments keep us on our toes and help make our books better. Our well-travelled team reads every word on what you loved or loathed about this book. Although we cannot reply individually to your submissions, we always guarantee that your feedback goes straight to the appropriate authors, in time for the next edition. Each person who sends us information is thanked in the next edition.

Visit **lonelyplanet.com/contact** to submit your updates and suggestions or to ask for help. Our award-winning website also features inspirational travel stories and news.

Note: We may edit, reproduce and incorporate your comments in Lonely Planet products such as guidebooks, websites and digital products, so let us know if you are happy to have your name acknowledged. For a copy of our privacy policy visit lonelyplanet.com/legal.

WRITER THANKS

John Lee

Heartfelt thanks to Maggie for joining me at all those restaurants and for keeping me calm during the brain-throbbing final write-up of this project. Thanks also to Max, our cat, for sticking by my desk and reminding me to chase him around the house. Cheers also to my brother Michael for visiting from England and checking out some local breweries with me: you really know how to go the extra mile.

Brendan Sainsbury

Many thanks to all the skilled bus drivers, helpful tourist information staff, generous hotel owners, expert burger flippers, unobtrusive bears and numerous passers-by who helped me, unwittingly or otherwise, during my research trip. Special thanks to my wife, Liz, my son, Kieran, and my mother-in-law, Ammy, for their company (and patience) on the road.

ACKNOWLEDGEMENTS

Cover photograph: Beautiful view of downtown Vancouver skyline, British Columbia, Canada at sunset; f11photo/Shutterstock ©

Illustrations pp58-9 by Michael Weldon.

Climate map data adapted from Peel MC, Finlayson BL & McMahon TA (2007) 'Updated World Map of the Köppen-Geiger Climate Classification'; Hydrology and Earth System Sciences, 11, 1633–44.

THIS BOOK

This 9th edition of Lonely Planet's *Vancouver & Victoria* guidebook was researched and written by John Lee and Brendan Sainsbury. The previous two editions were also written by John Lee. This guidebook was produced by the following:

Destination Editor Ben Buckner

Senior Product Editors Kate Chapman, Saralinda Turner, Martine Power

Cartographers Rachel Imeson, Corey Hutchison

Product Editors Alex Conroy, Jenna Myers

Book Designers Catalina Aragón, Clara Monitto

Assisting Editors James Appleton, Janet Austin, Andrew Bain, Judith Bamber, Michelle Bennett, Lucy Cowie, Emma Gibbs, Jennifer Hattam, Jodie Martire, Gabrielle Stefanos, Maja Vatrić

Cover Researcher Kat Marsh

Thanks to Ronan Abayawickrema, Sonia Kapoor, Claire Cruickshank, Sasha Drew, Michael Eyer, Alexander Howard, Andi Jones, Anton Kirczenow, Lauren O'Connell, Charlotte Orr, Claire Rourke, Kevin Schultz, Kirby Simpson, Vicky Smith, Leela Tardis, Angela Tinson

See also separate subindexes for:

- EATING P259
- DRINKING & NIGHTLIFE P260
- ENTERTAINMENT P261
- SHOPPING P262
- SPORTS & ACTIVITIES P262
- SLEEPING P263

Index

Sights 000
Map Pages **000**
Photo Pages **000**

Sights 000
Map Pages **000**
Photo Pages **000**

P

Sights 000
Map Pages **000**
Photo Pages **000**

Q

R

S

T

EATING

DRINKING & NIGHTLIFE

☆ ENTERTAINMENT

SHOPPING

SPORTS & ACTIVITIES

SLEEPING

Vancouver Maps

Sights

- Beach
- Bird Sanctuary
- Buddhist
- Castle/Palace
- Christian
- Confucian
- Hindu
- Islamic
- Jain
- Jewish
- Monument
- Museum/Gallery/Historic Building
- Ruin
- Shinto
- Sikh
- Taoist
- Winery/Vineyard
- Zoo/Wildlife Sanctuary
- Other Sight

Activities, Courses & Tours

- Bodysurfing
- Diving
- Canoeing/Kayaking
- Course/Tour
- Sento Hot Baths/Onsen
- Skiing
- Snorkeling
- Surfing
- Swimming/Pool
- Walking
- Windsurfing
- Other Activity

Sleeping

- Sleeping
- Camping
- Hut/Shelter

Eating

- Eating

Drinking & Nightlife

- Drinking & Nightlife
- Cafe

Entertainment

- Entertainment

Shopping

- Shopping

Information

- Bank
- Embassy/Consulate
- Hospital/Medical
- Internet
- Police
- Post Office
- Telephone
- Toilet
- Tourist Information
- Other Information

Geographic

- Beach
- Gate
- Hut/Shelter
- Lighthouse
- Lookout
- Mountain/Volcano
- Oasis
- Park
- Pass
- Picnic Area
- Waterfall

Population

- Capital (National)
- Capital (State/Province)
- City/Large Town
- Town/Village

Transport

- Airport
- BART station
- Border crossing
- Boston T station
- Bus
- Cable car/Funicular
- Cycling
- Ferry
- Metro/Muni station
- Monorail
- Parking
- Petrol station
- Subway/SkyTrain station
- Taxi
- Train station/Railway
- Tram
- Underground station
- Other Transport

Routes

- Tollway
- Freeway
- Primary
- Secondary
- Tertiary
- Lane
- Unsealed road
- Road under construction
- Plaza/Mall
- Steps
- Tunnel
- Pedestrian overpass
- Walking Tour
- Walking Tour detour
- Path/Walking Trail

Boundaries

- International
- State/Province
- Disputed
- Regional/Suburb
- Marine Park
- Cliff
- Wall

Hydrography

- River, Creek
- Intermittent River
- Canal
- Water
- Dry/Salt/Intermittent Lake
- Reef

Areas

- Airport/Runway
- Beach/Desert
- Cemetery (Christian)
- Cemetery (Other)
- Glacier
- Mudflat
- Park/Forest
- Sight (Building)
- Sportsground
- Swamp/Mangrove

Note: Not all symbols displayed above appear on the maps in this book

MAP INDEX

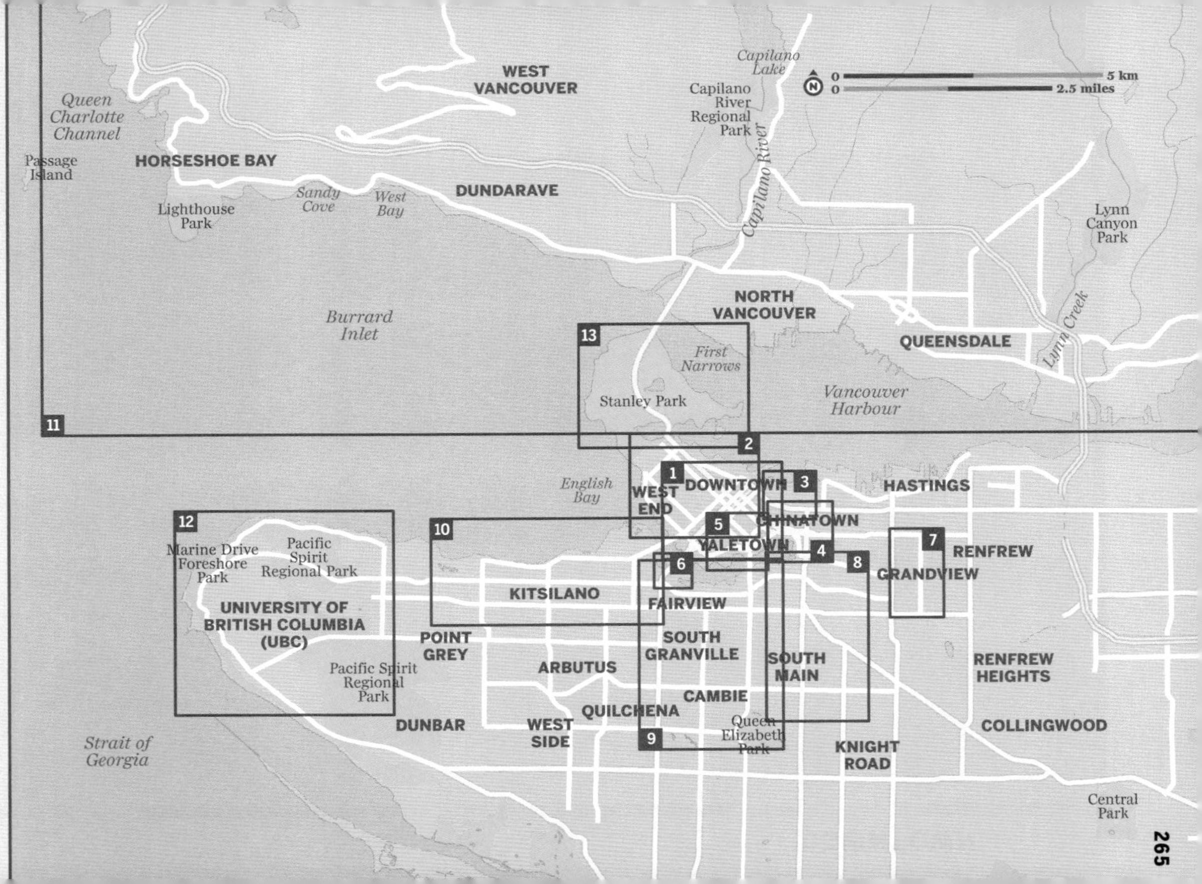

0 5 km
0 2.5 miles
WEST VANCOUVER
Capilano Lake
Capilano River Regional Park
Capilano River
Queen Charlotte Channel
Passage Island
HORSESHOE BAY
DUNDARAVE
Lighthouse Park
Sandy Cove
West Bay
Lynn Canyon Park
Lynn Creek
NORTH VANCOUVER
QUEENSDALE
Burrard Inlet
First Narrows
Stanley Park
Vancouver Harbour
English Bay
WEST END
DOWNTOWN
HASTINGS
CHINATOWN
YALETOWN
RENFREW
GRANDVIEW
KITSILANO
FAIRVIEW
Marine Drive Foreshore Park
Pacific Spirit Regional Park
UNIVERSITY OF BRITISH COLUMBIA (UBC)
POINT GREY
SOUTH GRANVILLE
ARBUTUS
SOUTH MAIN
RENFREW HEIGHTS
CAMBIE
QUILCHENA
DUNBAR
WEST SIDE
Queen Elizabeth Park
KNIGHT ROAD
COLLINGWOOD
Strait of Georgia
Central Park
1
2
3
4
5
6
7
8
9
10
11
12
13

Key on p268

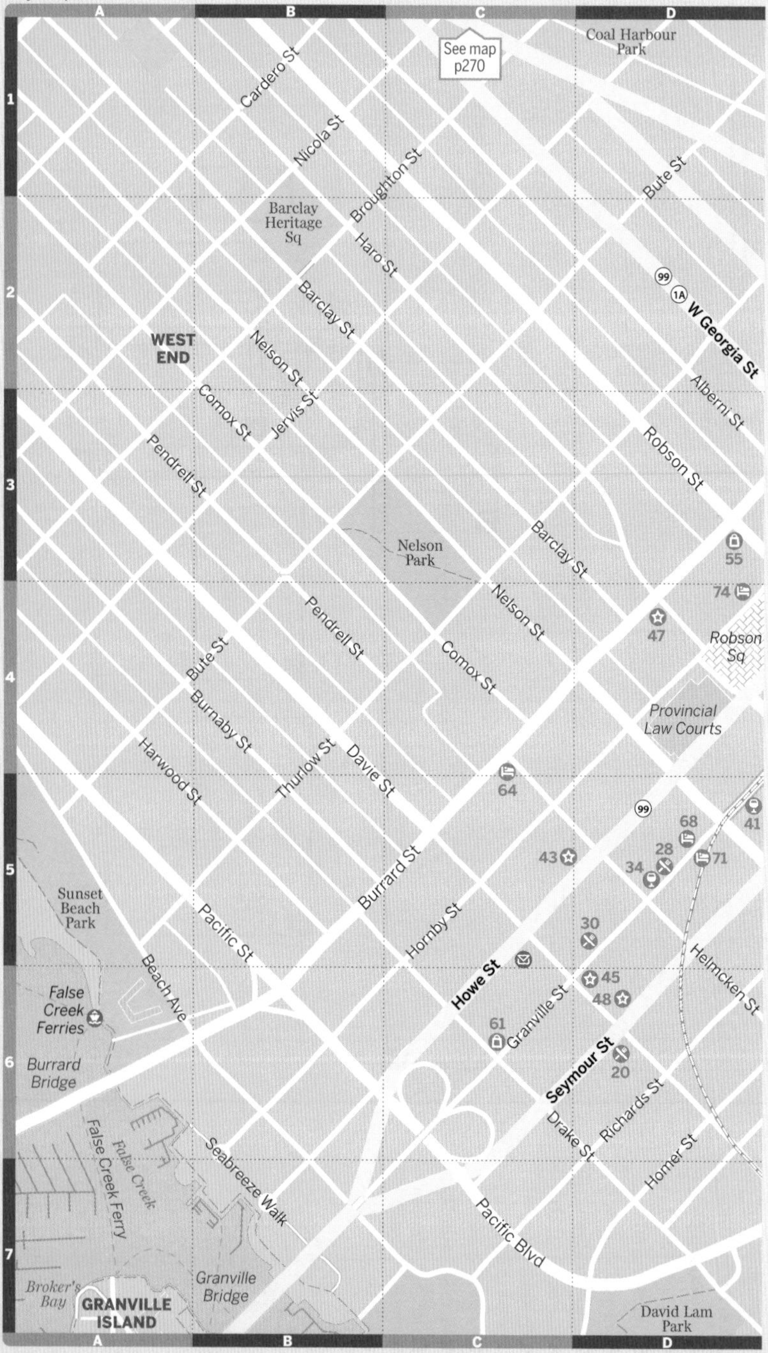

A
B
C
D
1
2
3
4
5
6
7
See map p270
Coal Harbour Park
Cardero St
Nicola St
Broughton St
Bute St
Barclay Heritage Sq
Haro St
Barclay St
W Georgia St
99
1A
WEST END
Nelson St
Comox St
Jervis St
Alberni St
Robson St
Pendrell St
Nelson Park
Barclay St
55
74
Nelson St
47
Robson Sq
Pendrell St
Comox St
Bute St
Burnaby St
Provincial Law Courts
Harwood St
Thurlow St
Davie St
64
99
68
41
28
71
34
43
Burrard St
Sunset Beach Park
Pacific St
30
Hornby St
Helmcken St
Beach Ave
Howe St
45
48
False Creek Ferries
61
Granville St
Burrard Bridge
Seymour St
20
Richards St
Drake St
False Creek Ferry
False Creek
Seabreeze Walk
Homer St
Pacific Blvd
Broker's Bay
Granville Bridge
GRANVILLE ISLAND
David Lam Park

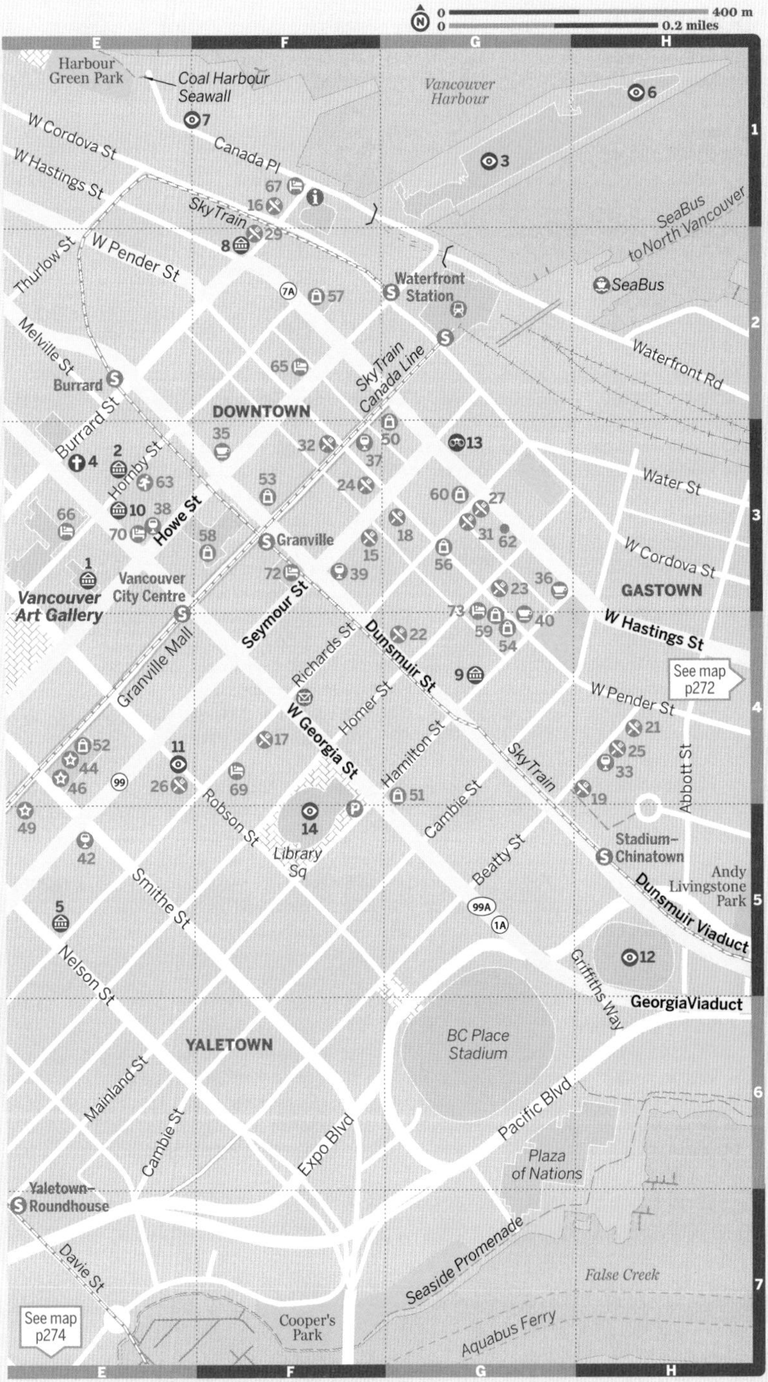

DOWNTOWN
0 400 m
0 0.2 miles
Harbour Green Park
Coal Harbour Seawall
Vancouver Harbour
W Cordova St
Canada Pl
W Hastings St
SkyTrain
SeaBus to North Vancouver
Thurlow St
W Pender St
Waterfront Station
SeaBus
Melville St
SkyTrain Canada Line
Waterfront Rd
Burrard
Burrard St
DOWNTOWN
Hornby St
Water St
Howe St
Granville
W Cordova St
GASTOWN
Vancouver Art Gallery
Vancouver City Centre
Seymour St
W Hastings St
Granville Mall
Richards St
Dunsmuir St
See map p272
W Pender St
W Georgia St
Homer St
Hamilton St
SkyTrain
Abbott St
Robson St
Cambie St
Library Sq
Beatty St
Stadium–Chinatown
Andy Livingstone Park
Smithe St
Dunsmuir Viaduct
Nelson St
Griffiths Way
GeorgiaViaduct
YALETOWN
BC Place Stadium
Mainland St
Pacific Blvd
Cambie St
Expo Blvd
Plaza of Nations
Yaletown–Roundhouse
Seaside Promenade
Davie St
False Creek
Aquabus Ferry
Cooper's Park
See map p274

DOWNTOWN *Map on p266*

WEST END *Map on p270*

Key on p269

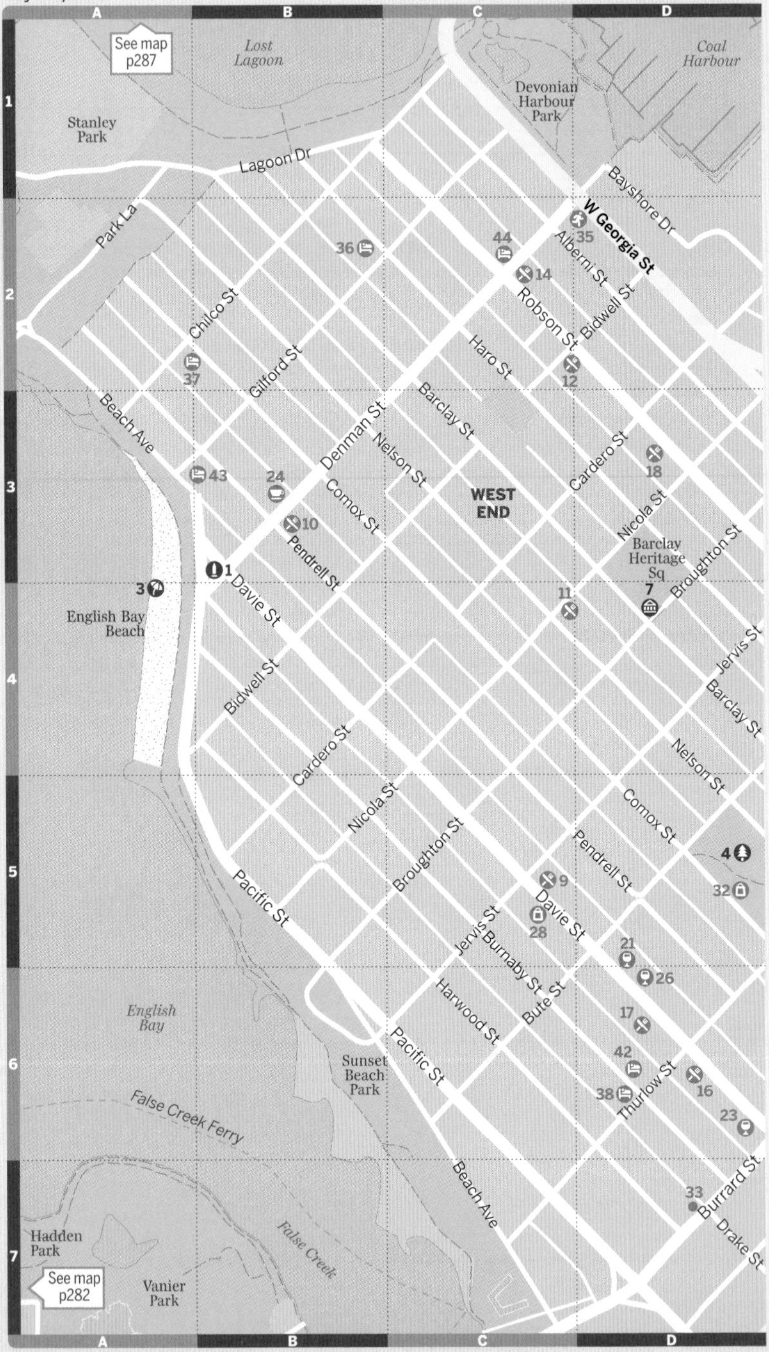
A
B
C
D
1
2
3
4
5
6
7
See map p287
Lost Lagoon
Coal Harbour
Devonian Harbour Park
Stanley Park
Lagoon Dr
Park La
Bayshore Dr
W Georgia St
Alberni St
Bidwell St
Robson St
Haro St
Chilco St
Gilford St
Beach Ave
Denman St
Barclay St
Nelson St
Comox St
Pendrell St
Davie St
Cardero St
Nicola St
Broughton St
WEST END
Barclay Heritage Sq
Jervis St
English Bay Beach
Bidwell St
Cardero St
Nicola St
Broughton St
Barclay St
Nelson St
Comox St
Pendrell St
Pacific St
Jervis St
Burnaby St
Davie St
Bute St
Harwood St
Thurlow St
English Bay
Sunset Beach Park
Pacific St
False Creek Ferry
Beach Ave
Burrard St
Drake St
Hadden Park
False Creek
Vanier Park
See map p282
1
3
4
7
9
10
11
12
14
16
17
18
21
23
24
26
28
32
33
35
36
37
38
42
43
44

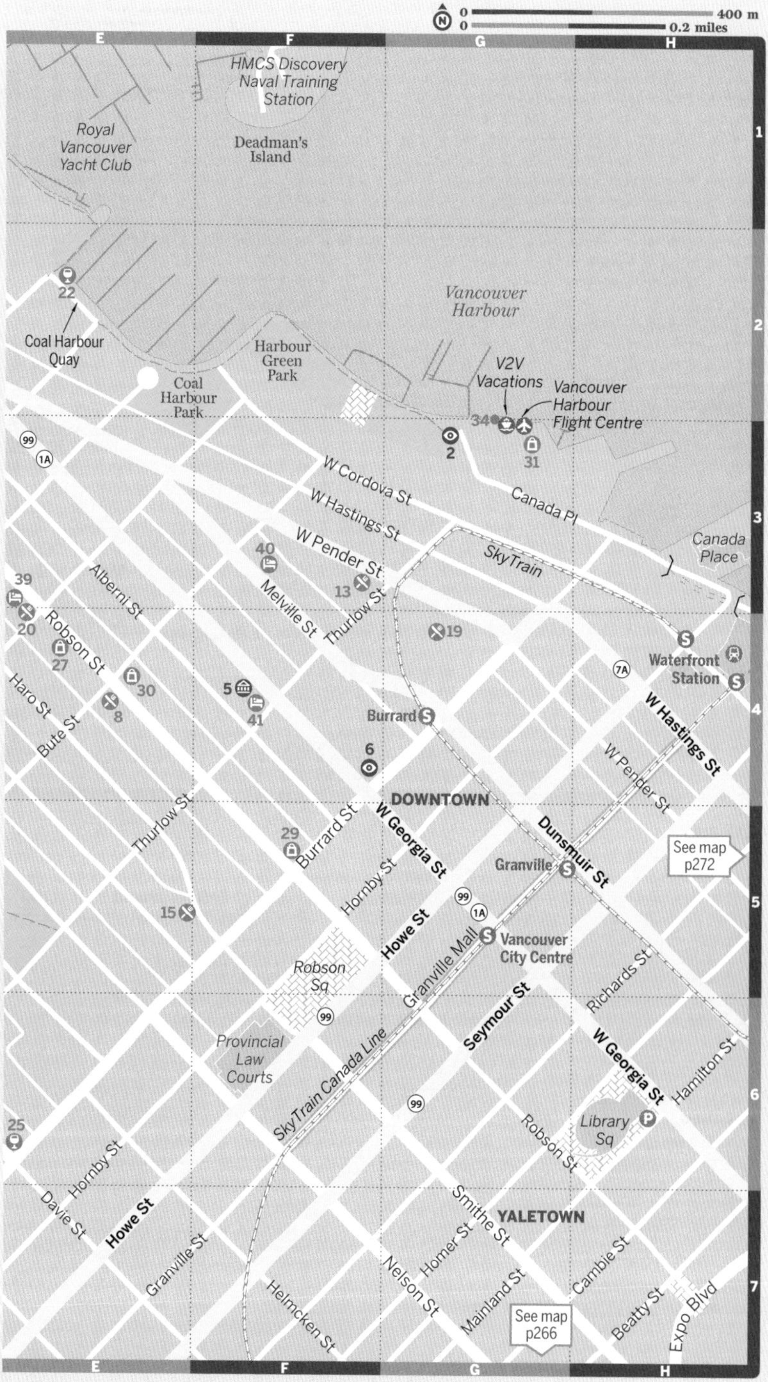
0
400 m
0
0.2 miles
E
F
G
H
1
2
3
4
5
6
7
WEST END
HMCS Discovery
Naval Training
Station
Deadman's
Island
Royal
Vancouver
Yacht Club
Vancouver
Harbour
22
Coal Harbour
Quay
Harbour
Green
Park
Coal
Harbour
Park
V2V
Vacations
Vancouver
Harbour
Flight Centre
34
2
31
W Cordova St
Canada Pl
W Hastings St
W Pender St
SkyTrain
Canada
Place
40
39
20
Alberni St
Melville St
13
Thurlow St
19
Robson St
27
30
Haro St
Bute St
8
5
41
Waterfront
Station
Burrard
6
W Hastings St
W Pender St
DOWNTOWN
Thurlow St
29
Burrard St
W Georgia St
Dunsmuir St
Granville
See map
p272
Hornby St
15
Howe St
Granville Mall
Vancouver
City Centre
Robson
Sq
Richards St
Seymour St
Provincial
Law
Courts
W Georgia St
Hamilton St
SkyTrain Canada Line
25
Library
Sq
Robson St
Hornby St
Davie St
Howe St
Smithe St
YALETOWN
Homer St
Granville St
Cambie St
Helmcken St
Nelson St
Mainland St
See map
p266
Beatty St
Expo Blvd

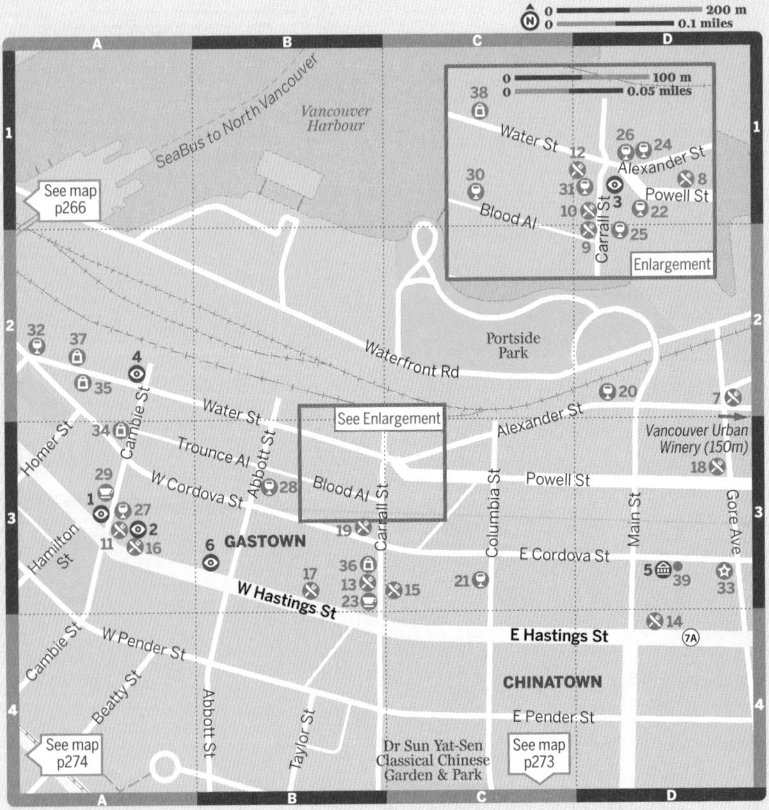

Sights (p82)
1 Dominion Building A3
2 Flack Block A3
Gassy Jack Statue .... (see 3)
3 Maple Tree Square D1
4 Steam Clock A2
5 Vancouver Police Museum & Archives D3
6 Woodward's.................. B3

Eating (p85)
7 Ask for Luigi.................. D2
8 Birds & the Beets........... D1
9 Greek Gastown D2
10 L'Abattoir D1
11 Meat & Bread A3
12 MeeT in Gastown D1
13 Nelson the Seagull........ B3
Nuba .... (see 1)
14 Ovaltine Cafe D4
15 Pidgin............................ C3
16 Purebread....................... A3
17 Save On Meats B3
18 St Lawrence Restaurant D3
19 Tacofino Taco Bar B3

Drinking & Nightlife (p90)
20 Alibi Room..................... D2
21 Back and Forth Bar....... C3
22 Diamond......................... D1
23 East Van Roasters B3
24 Guilt & Co D1
25 Irish Heather.................. D2
26 Local Public Eatery D1
27 Pub 340.......................... A3
28 Revel Room B3
29 Revolver A3
30 Salt Tasting Room C1
31 Six Acres D1
32 Steamworks Brew Pub............................ A2

Entertainment (p93)
33 Firehall Arts Centre D3

Shopping (p95)
34 Basement....................... A3
35 Coastal Peoples Fine Arts Gallery A2
36 Community Thrift & Vintage Frock Shoppe B3
37 Herschel Supply Co A2
38 John Fluevog Shoes C1

Sports & Activities (p97)
39 Sins of the City Walking Tour D3

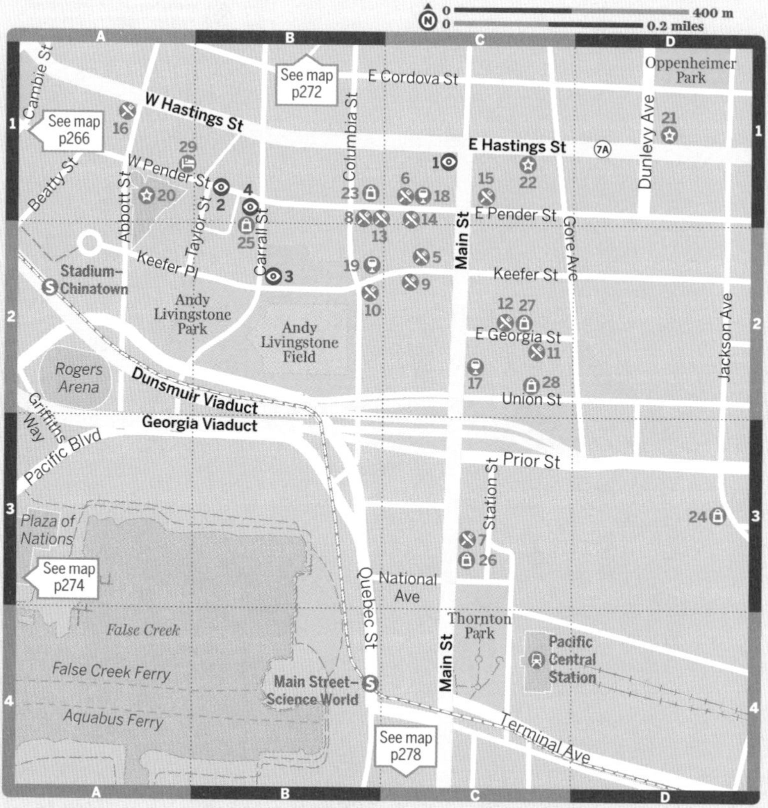

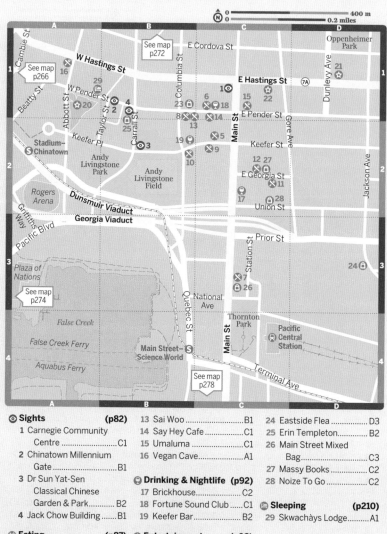

Sights (p82)
1 Carnegie Community Centre ... C1
2 Chinatown Millennium Gate ... B1
3 Dr Sun Yat-Sen Classical Chinese Garden & Park ... B2
4 Jack Chow Building ... B1

Eating (p87)
5 Bao Bei ... C2
6 Bestie ... C1
7 Campagnolo ... C3
8 Chinatown BBQ ... B1
9 Juke Fried Chicken ... C2
10 Pazzo Chow ... B2
11 Phnom Penh ... C2
12 Ramen Butcher ... C2
13 Sai Woo ... B1
14 Say Hey Cafe ... C1
15 Umaluma ... C1
16 Vegan Cave ... A1

Drinking & Nightlife (p92)
17 Brickhouse ... C2
18 Fortune Sound Club ... C1
19 Keefer Bar ... B2

Entertainment (p93)
20 Cineplex Odeon International Village Cinemas ... A1
21 Pat's Pub ... D1
22 Rickshaw Theatre ... C1

Shopping (p95)
23 Blim ... B1
24 Eastside Flea ... D3
25 Erin Templeton ... B2
26 Main Street Mixed Bag ... C3
27 Massy Books ... C2
28 Noize To Go ... C2

Sleeping (p210)
29 Skwachàys Lodge ... A1

YALETOWN

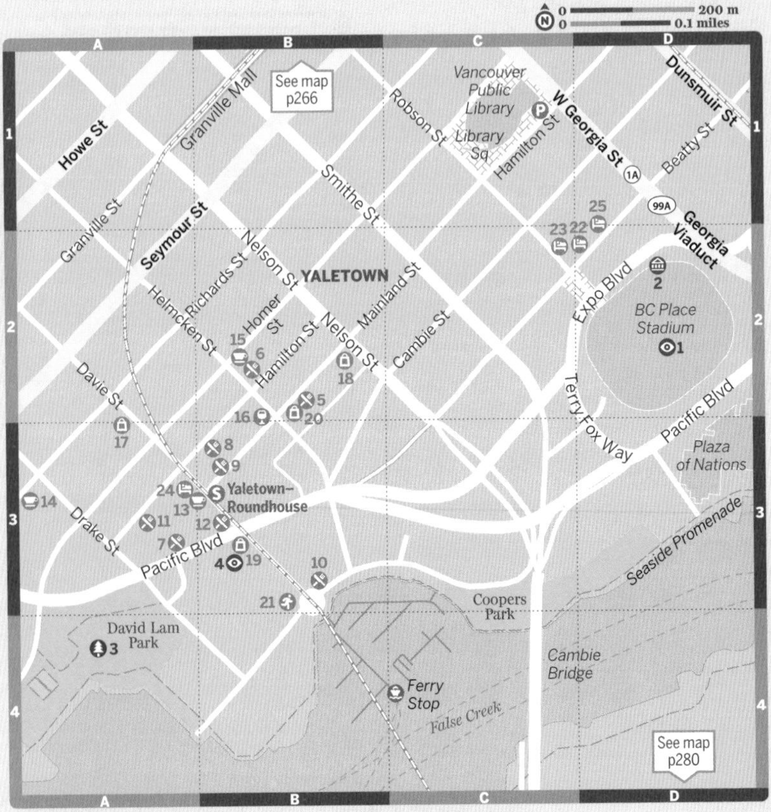

Sights (p102)

1 BC Place Stadium........D2
2 BC Sports Hall of Fame & Museum........D2
3 David Lam Park........A4
Engine 374 Pavilion........(see 4)
4 Roundhouse Community Arts & Recreation Centre........B3

Eating (p103)

5 Bake49........B2
6 Blue Water Cafe........B2
7 DD Mau........A3
8 Flying Pig........B3
9 MeeT........B3
10 Provence Marinaside........B3
11 Rodney's Oyster House........A3
12 Salsa & Agave Mexican Grill........B3

Drinking & Nightlife (p109)

13 Caffe Artigiano........B3
14 Matchstick........A3
15 Small Victory........B2
16 Yaletown Brewing Company........B2

Entertainment (p110)

BC Lions........(see 1)
Vancouver Whitecaps........(see 1)

Shopping (p111)

17 Brooklyn Clothing........A3
18 Karameller Candy Shop........B2
19 Portobello West........B3
20 Woo To See You........B2

Sports & Activities (p114)

21 Reckless Bike Stores........B3

Sleeping (p210)

22 Georgian Court Hotel........D2
23 Hotel BLU........C2
24 Opus Hotel........A3
25 YWCA Hotel........D1

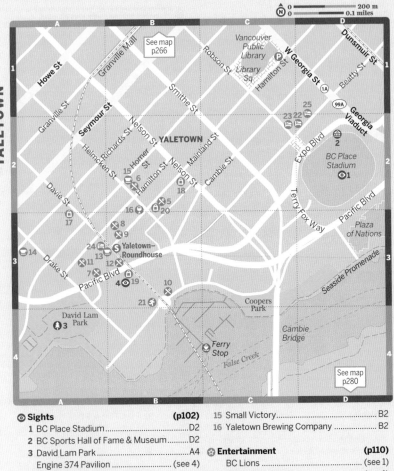

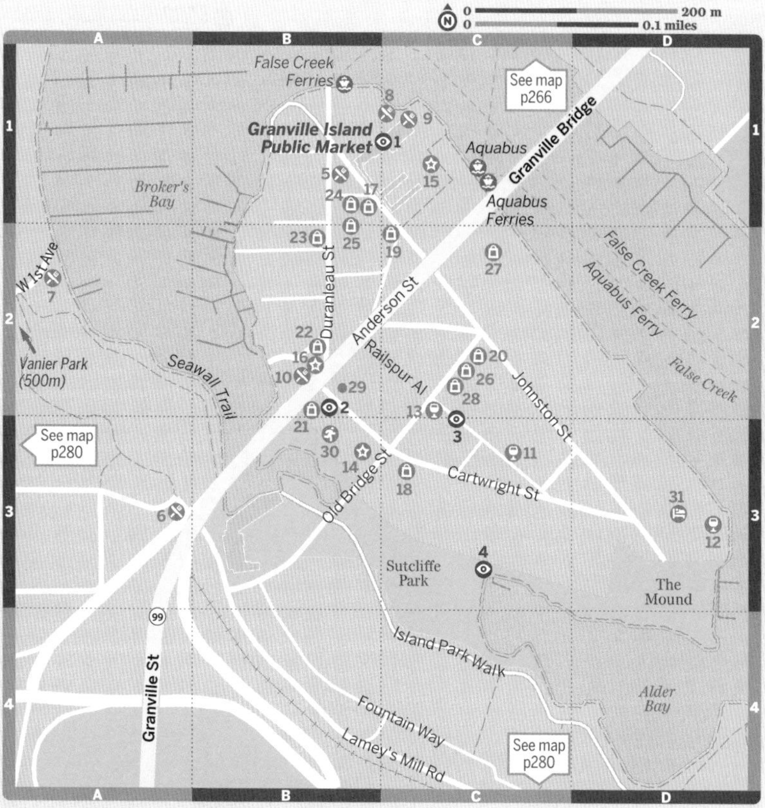

Top Experiences (p100)
1 Granville Island Public Market ... C1

Sights (p103)
2 Kids Market ... B2
3 Railspur Alley ... C3
4 Totem Pole ... C3

Eating (p106)
5 A Bread Affair ... B1
6 Bistro 101 ... A3
7 Go Fish ... A2
8 Popina ... C1
9 Public Market Food Court ... C1
10 Tony's Fish & Oyster Cafe ... B2

Drinking & Nightlife (p109)
11 Artisan Sake Maker ... C3
12 Dockside Brewing Company ... D3
Granville Island Brewing Taproom ... (see 29)
13 Liberty Distillery ... C2

Entertainment (p110)
14 Carousel Theatre ... B3
15 Granville Island Stage ... C1
16 Vancouver Theatresports ... B2

Shopping (p112)
17 Circle Craft ... B1
18 Crafthouse ... C3
19 Gandharva Loka World Music Store ... C2
20 Granville Island Broom Company ... C2
21 Granville Island Licorice Parlour ... B2
22 Karen Cooper Gallery ... B2
23 Make ... B2
24 Net Loft ... B1
25 Paper-Ya ... B2
26 Search & Rescue Denim Company ... C2
27 Silk Weaving Studio ... C2
28 Vancouver Studio Glass ... C2

Sports & Activities (p114)
29 Granville Island Brewing ... B2
30 Granville Island Water Park ... B3

Sleeping (p210)
31 Granville Island Hotel ... D3

Key on p277

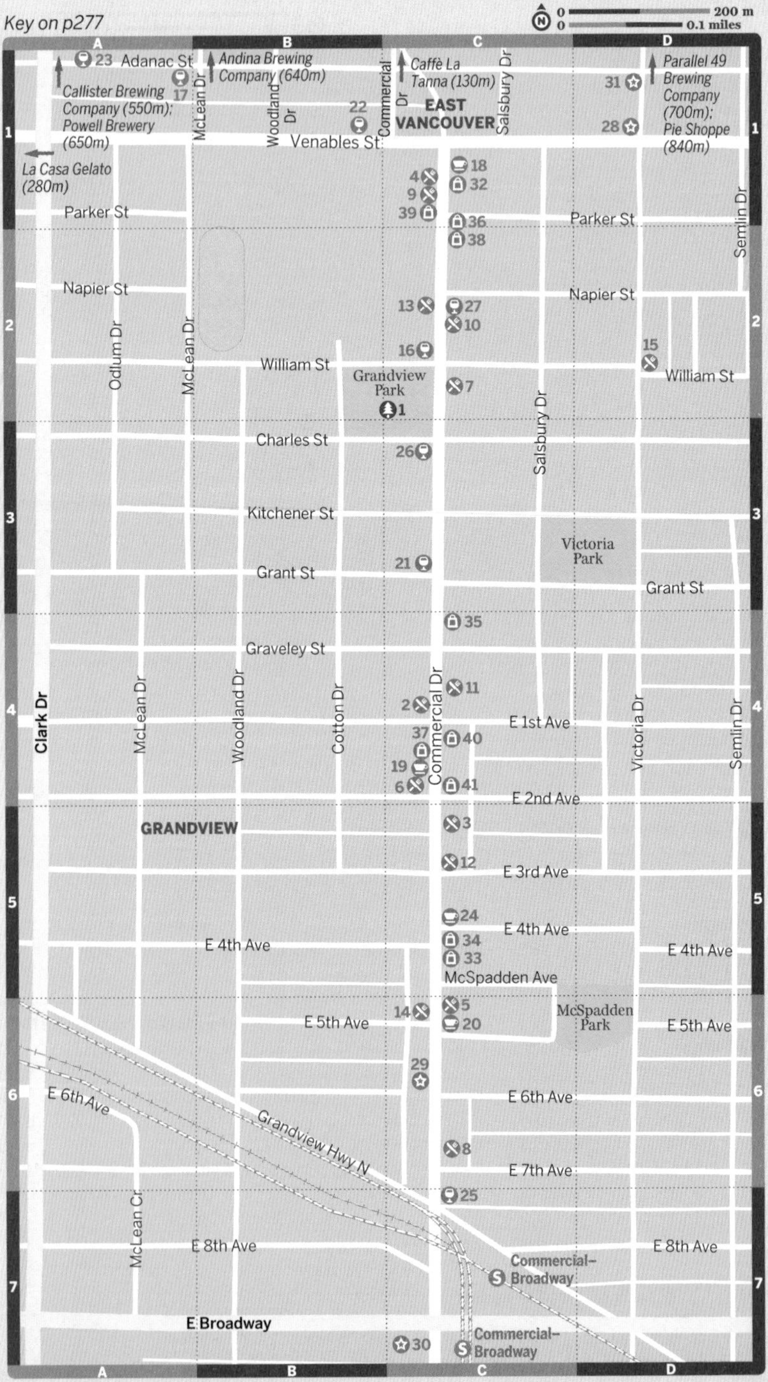
0 200 m
0 0.1 miles
A
B
C
D
1
2
3
4
5
6
7
23
Adanac St
Andina Brewing Company (640m)
Callister Brewing Company (550m); Powell Brewery (650m)
17
McLean Dr
Woodland Dr
22
Commercial Dr
Caffè La Tanna (130m)
EAST VANCOUVER
Salsbury Dr
31
28
Parallel 49 Brewing Company (700m); Pie Shoppe (840m)
Venables St
La Casa Gelato (280m)
18
4
32
9
39
Parker St
36
38
Semlin Dr
Napier St
Odlum Dr
McLean Dr
13
27
10
16
15
William St
Grandview Park
1
7
Salsbury Dr
Charles St
26
Kitchener St
Victoria Park
21
Grant St
35
Graveley St
Clark Dr
McLean Dr
Woodland Dr
Cotton Dr
Commercial Dr
11
2
E 1st Ave
37
40
Victoria Dr
Semlin Dr
19
6
41
E 2nd Ave
GRANDVIEW
3
12
E 3rd Ave
24
E 4th Ave
E 4th Ave
34
33
E 4th Ave
McSpadden Ave
14
5
20
E 5th Ave
McSpadden Park
E 5th Ave
29
E 6th Ave
E 6th Ave
Grandview Hwy N
8
E 7th Ave
25
McLean Cr
E 8th Ave
E 8th Ave
Commercial–Broadway
E Broadway
30
Commercial–Broadway

COMMERCIAL DRIVE *Map on p276*

Sights (p120)

1 Grandview Park C2

Eating (p120)

2 Bench Bakehouse C4
3 Cannibal Cafe C5
4 Downlow Chicken Shack C1
5 Elephant Garden Creamery C6
6 Fratelli Baking C4
7 Havana C2
8 Jamjar C6
9 Kin Kao C1
Kishimoto Japanese Restaurant ..... (see 33)
10 Kulinarya C2
11 La Mezcaleria C4
12 Spade C5
13 Sweet Cherubim C2
14 Tangent Cafe C6
15 Via Tevere D2

Drinking & Nightlife (p125)

16 BierCraft Tap & Tapas C2
17 Bomber Brewing A1
18 Bump n Grind C1
19 Cafe Calabria C4
20 Cafe Deux Soleils C6
21 Charlatan C3
22 East Van Brewing Company B1
23 Off the Rail A1
24 Prado C5
25 St Augustine's C7
26 Storm Crow Tavern C3
27 Wilder Juice C2

Entertainment (p127)

28 Cultch D1
29 Grandview Lanes Bowling Centre C6
30 Rio Theatre C7
Vancouver Poetry Slam ..... (see 20)
31 Wise Hall D1

Shopping (p129)

32 Attic Treasures C1
33 Audiopile C5
34 Canterbury Tales C5
35 Kalena's Shoes C4
36 Kali C1
37 La Grotta del Formaggio C4
38 Licorice Parlour C2
39 Little Miss Vintage C1
40 Mintage C4
41 Pulpfiction Books East C4

Key on p279

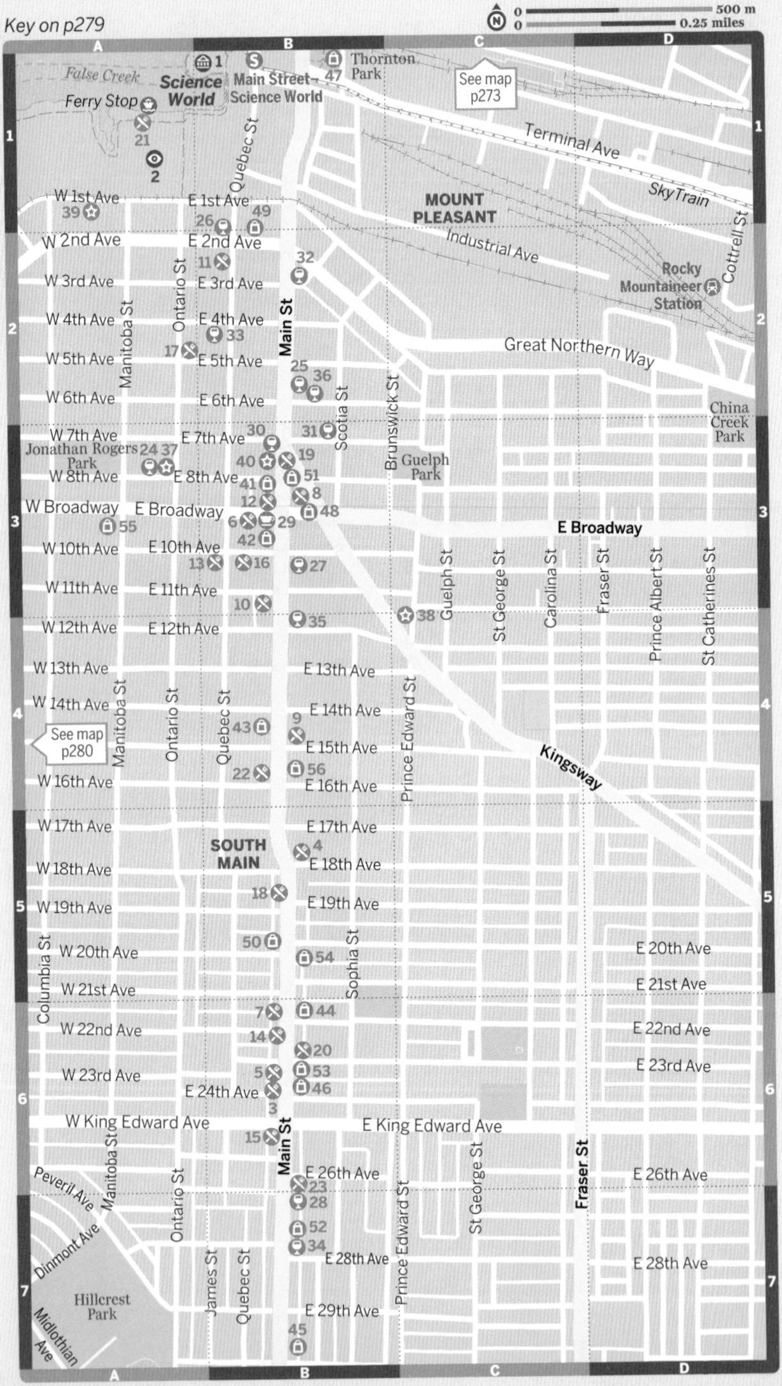
0 500 m
0 0.25 miles
A
B
C
D
1
2
3
4
5
6
7
False Creek
Ferry Stop
Science World
Main Street-Science World
Thornton Park
See map p273
Terminal Ave
SkyTrain
MOUNT PLEASANT
Industrial Ave
Rocky Mountaineer Station
Cottrell St
Great Northern Way
China Creek Park
Quebec St
W 1st Ave
E 1st Ave
W 2nd Ave
E 2nd Ave
W 3rd Ave
E 3rd Ave
W 4th Ave
E 4th Ave
W 5th Ave
E 5th Ave
W 6th Ave
E 6th Ave
W 7th Ave
E 7th Ave
Jonathan Rogers Park
W 8th Ave
E 8th Ave
W Broadway
E Broadway
W 10th Ave
E 10th Ave
W 11th Ave
E 11th Ave
W 12th Ave
E 12th Ave
W 13th Ave
E 13th Ave
W 14th Ave
E 14th Ave
E 15th Ave
See map p280
W 16th Ave
E 16th Ave
W 17th Ave
E 17th Ave
SOUTH MAIN
W 18th Ave
E 18th Ave
W 19th Ave
E 19th Ave
W 20th Ave
E 20th Ave
W 21st Ave
E 21st Ave
W 22nd Ave
E 22nd Ave
W 23rd Ave
E 23rd Ave
E 24th Ave
W King Edward Ave
E King Edward Ave
E 26th Ave
E 28th Ave
E 29th Ave
Manitoba St
Ontario St
Main St
Scotia St
Brunswick St
Guelph Park
Guelph St
St George St
Carolina St
Fraser St
Prince Albert St
St Catherines St
Prince Edward St
Kingsway
Columbia St
Sophia St
James St
Peveril Ave
Dinmont Ave
Hillcrest Park
Midlothian Ave
1
2
21
39
26
49
11
32
33
17
25
36
31
30
24
37
40
19
51
41
8
12
48
55
6
29
42
13
16
27
10
35
38
43
9
22
56
4
18
50
54
7
44
14
20
5
53
46
3
15
23
28
52
34
45
47

MAIN STREET *Map on p278*

FAIRVIEW & SOUTH GRANVILLE

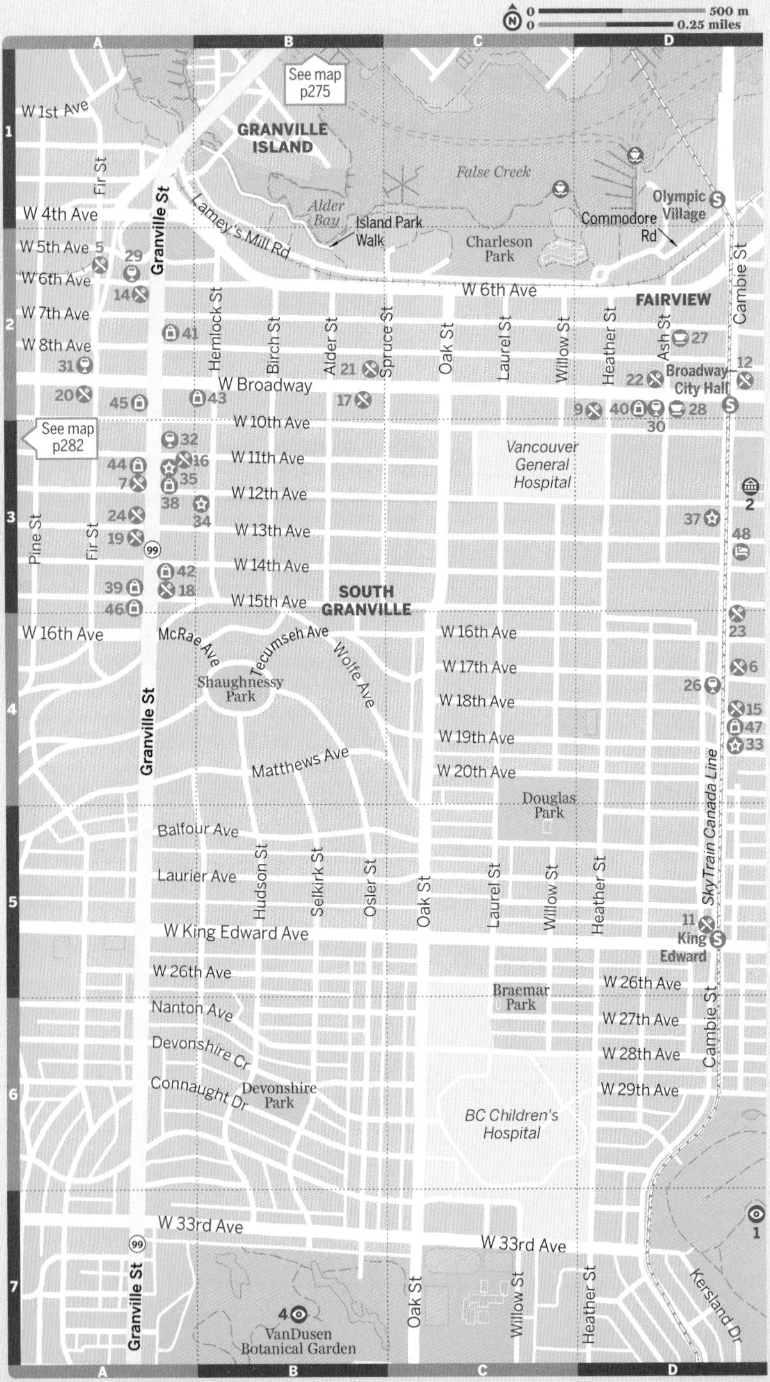

0 500 m
0 0.25 miles
See map p275
See map p282
GRANVILLE ISLAND
False Creek
Alder Bay
Island Park Walk
Lamey's Mill Rd
Charleson Park
Commodore Rd
Olympic Village
FAIRVIEW
SOUTH GRANVILLE
Broadway-City Hall
King Edward
Vancouver General Hospital
BC Children's Hospital
Shaughnessy Park
Douglas Park
Braemar Park
Devonshire Park
VanDusen Botanical Garden
W 1st Ave
W 4th Ave
W 5th Ave
W 6th Ave
W 7th Ave
W 8th Ave
W Broadway
W 10th Ave
W 11th Ave
W 12th Ave
W 13th Ave
W 14th Ave
W 15th Ave
W 16th Ave
W 17th Ave
W 18th Ave
W 19th Ave
W 20th Ave
W King Edward Ave
W 26th Ave
W 27th Ave
W 28th Ave
W 29th Ave
W 33rd Ave
McRae Ave
Tecumseh Ave
Wolfe Ave
Matthews Ave
Balfour Ave
Laurier Ave
Nanton Ave
Devonshire Cr
Connaught Dr
Kersland Dr
Pine St
Fir St
Granville St
Hemlock St
Birch St
Alder St
Spruce St
Oak St
Laurel St
Willow St
Heather St
Ash St
Cambie St
Hudson St
Selkirk St
Osler St
SkyTrain Canada Line

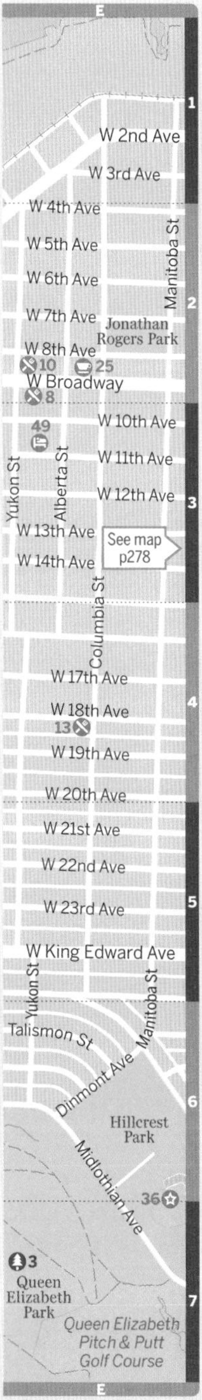

Sights (p150)
1 Bloedel Conservatory D7
2 City Hall D3
3 Queen Elizabeth Park E7
4 VanDusen Botanical Garden B7

Eating (p151)
5 Beaucoup Bakery & Cafe A2
6 Dutch Wooden Shoe Cafe D4
7 Heirloom Vegetarian A3
8 Heritage Asian Eatery E2
9 K Cafe D2
10 La Taquería Pinche Taco Shop E2
11 Landmark Hot Pot House D5
12 Marulilu Cafe D2
13 Mighty Oak E4
14 Paul's Omelettery A2
15 Rain or Shine D4
16 Rangoli A3
17 Salmon n' Bannock B2
18 Small Victory A3
19 Stable House A3
20 Suika A2
21 Tojo's B2
22 Tractor D2
23 Vij's D4
24 West A3

Drinking & Nightlife (p156)
25 Aperture Coffee Bar E2
26 BierCraft Bistro D4
Bump n Grind .... (see 18)
27 Caffè Cittadella D2
28 Elysian Coffee D2
29 Grapes & Soda A2
30 Rogue Kitchen & Wet Bar D2
31 Storm Crow Alehouse A2
32 The Marquis Grill A3
Xing Fu Tang .... (see 33)

Entertainment (p158)
33 Cineplex Park Theatre D4
Kino .... (see 33)
34 Pacific Theatre B3
35 Stanley Theatre A3
36 Vancouver Canadians E6
37 Yuk Yuk's Comedy Club D3

Shopping (p159)
38 Bacci's A3
39 Bau-Xi Gallery A3
40 Book Warehouse D2
41 Ian Tan Gallery A2
42 Meinhardt Fine Foods A3
43 Pacific Arts Market B2
44 Purdy's Chocolates A3
45 Restoration Hardware A2
46 Turnabout A3
47 Walrus D4

Sleeping (p211)
48 Douglas Guest House D3
49 Windsor Guest House E3

Sights **(p166)**

1 Arbutus Greenway H3
HR MacMillan Space Centre .... (see 3)
2 Kitsilano Beach F2
3 Museum of Vancouver H1
4 Old Hastings Mill Store Museum B2
5 Vancouver Maritime Museum G1
6 Vanier Park H1
7 West 4th Avenue F3

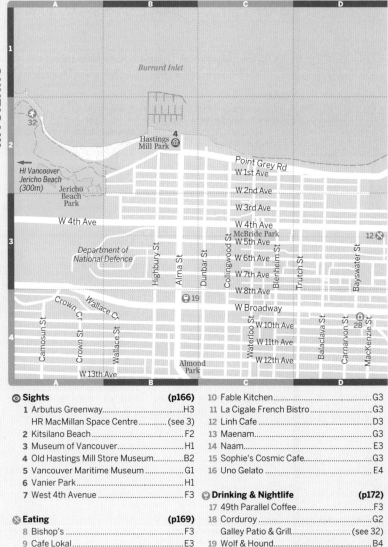

Eating **(p169)**

8 Bishop's F3
9 Cafe Lokal E3
10 Fable Kitchen G3
11 La Cigale French Bistro G3
12 Linh Cafe D3
13 Maenam G3
14 Naam E3
15 Sophie's Cosmic Cafe G3
16 Uno Gelato E4

Drinking & Nightlife **(p172)**

17 49th Parallel Coffee F3
18 Corduroy G2
Galley Patio & Grill .... (see 32)
19 Wolf & Hound B4

Entertainment (p173)

20 Bard on the Beach..H1
21 Cineplex Fifth Avenue Cinemas..................H3
Jericho Folk Club ....(see 32)
22 Kitsilano Showboat F2

Shopping (p175)

23 Arc'teryx G3
24 Gravity Pope..F3
25 Kidsbooks..E4
26 Kitsilano Farmers Market.............................E4
27 Silk Road Tea..G3
28 Stepback..D4
29 Wanderlust..G3
30 Zulu Records...G3

Sports & Activities (p177)

31 Diving Locker E3
32 Jericho Sailing Centre A2
33 Kitsilano Pool..F2
Mac Sailing.......................................(see 32)
Windsure Adventure
Watersports...................................(see 32)

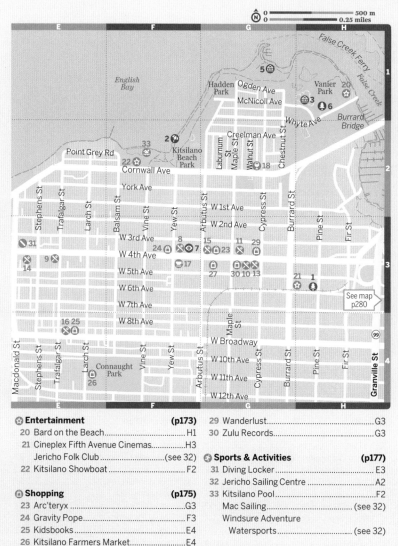

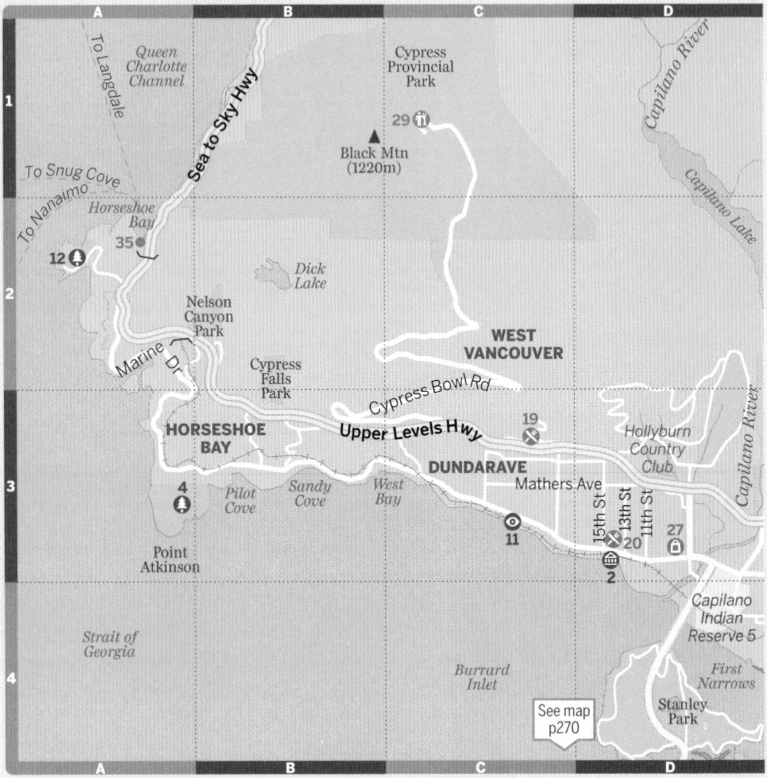

Sights (p182)

1 Capilano Suspension Bridge Park E3
2 Ferry Building Art Gallery D3
3 Grouse Mountain E2
4 Lighthouse Park A3
5 Lynn Canyon Ecology Centre G3
6 Lynn Canyon Park G3
7 Maplewood Farm G4
8 Maplewood Flats Conservation Area G4
9 Mt Seymour Provincial Park H3
10 Polygon Gallery G2
11 West Vancouver Seawall C3
12 Whytecliff Park A2

Eating (p184)

13 Artisan Bake Shoppe G1
14 Burgoo Bistro G2
15 Earnest Ice Cream G1
16 Lift Breakfast Bakery G1
17 Meat at O'Neill's G1
18 Palki Restaurant E4
19 Salmon House on the Hill C3
20 Wooden Fish D3

Drinking & Nightlife (p186)

21 Buddha-Full G1

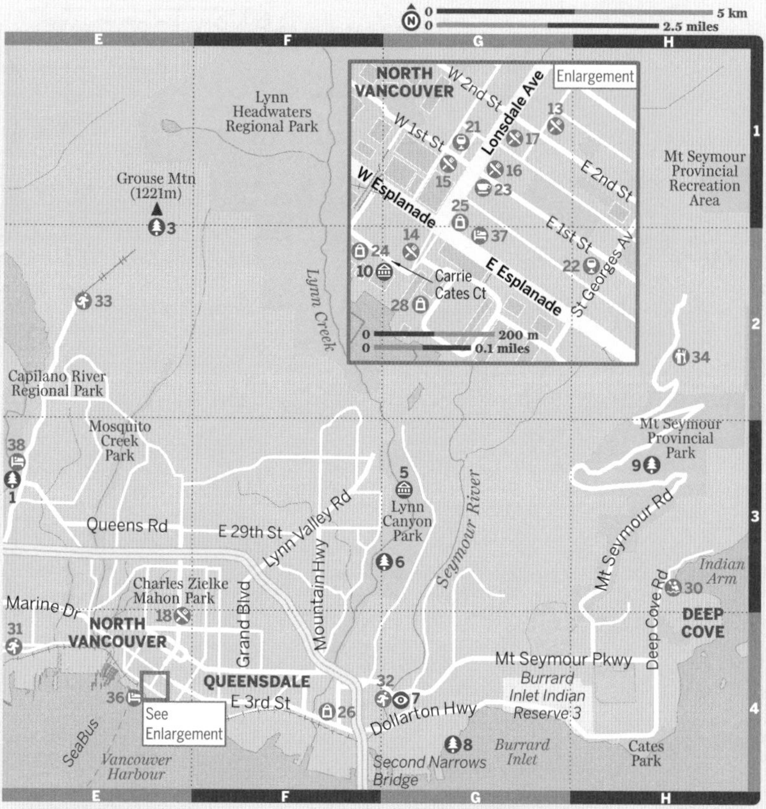

22	Gull Bar & Kitchen	H2
23	West of Java	G1

Shopping (p186)

24	Lonsdale Quay Market	F2
25	Mo's General Store	G1
26	Mountain Equipment Co-op	F4
27	Park Royal	D3
28	Shipyards Night Market	G2

Sports & Activities (p188)

29	Cypress Mountain	C1
	Cypress Provincial Park	(see 29)
30	Deep Cove Kayak Centre	H3
31	Edge Climbing Centre	E4
32	Endless Biking	G4
33	Grouse Grind	E2
	Grouse Mountain	(see 3)
34	Mt Seymour	H2
35	Sewell's Marina	A2

Sleeping (p212)

36	Lonsdale Quay Hotel	E4
37	Pinnacle Hotel at the Pier	G2
38	Thistledown House	E3

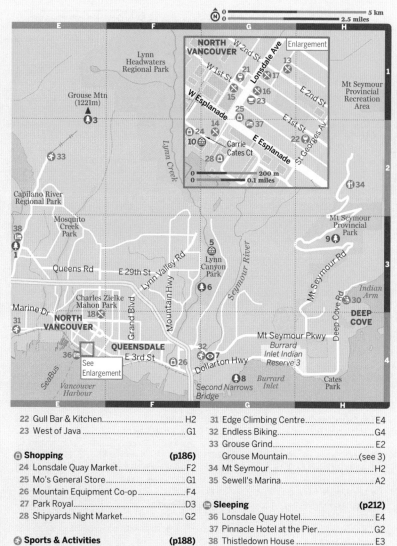

UNIVERSITY OF BRITISH COLUMBIA (UBC)

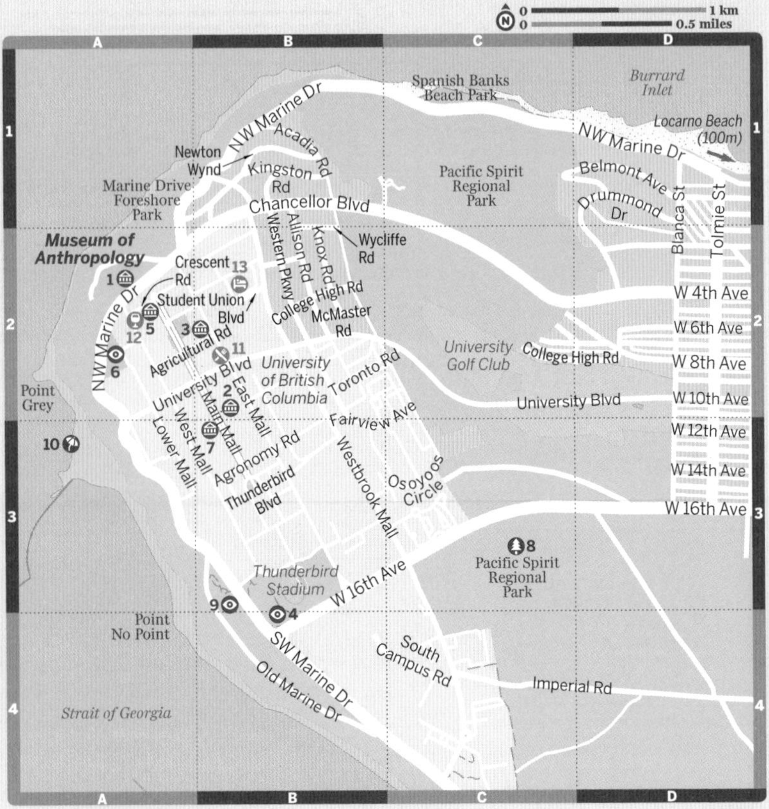

Top Experiences (p164)

1 Museum of Anthropology........A2

Sights (p167)

2 Beaty Biodiversity Museum........B2
3 Chung Collection........B2
4 Greenheart TreeWalk........B4
5 Morris & Helen Belkin Art Gallery........A2
6 Nitobe Memorial Garden........A2
7 Pacific Museum of Earth........B3
8 Pacific Spirit Regional Park........C3
9 UBC Botanical Garden........B3
10 Wreck Beach........A3

Eating (p169)

11 Jamjar Canteen........B2
Rain or Shine........(see 11)

Drinking & Nightlife (p172)

12 Koerner's Pub........A2

Sleeping (p211)

13 University of British Columbia Accommodation........B2

STANLEY PARK

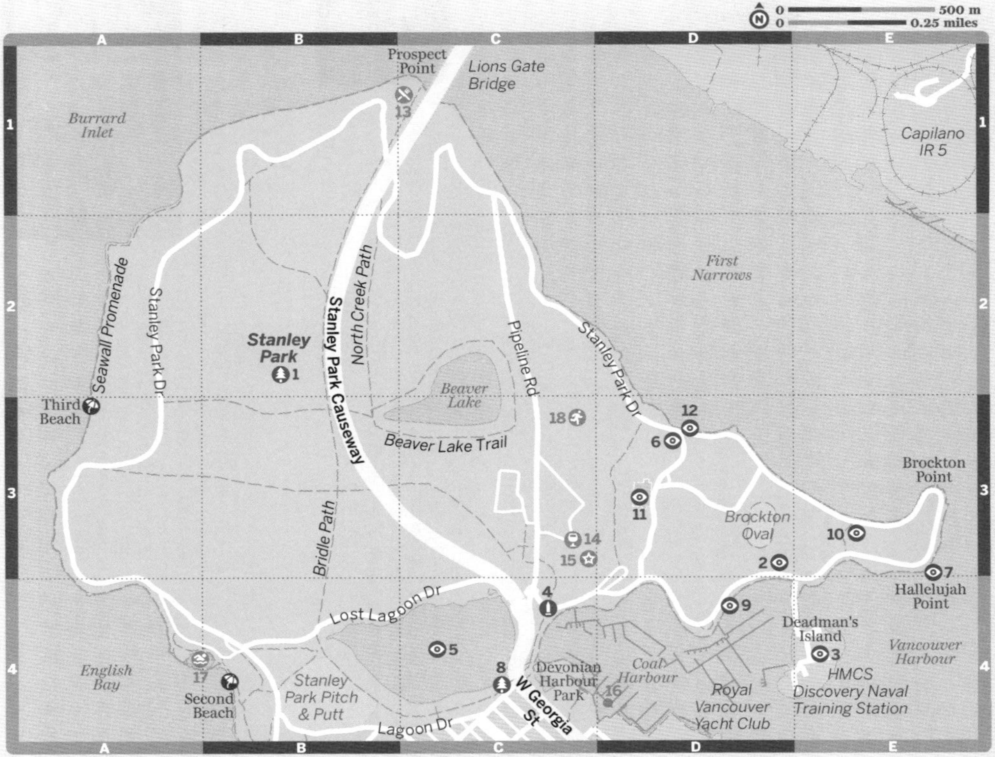

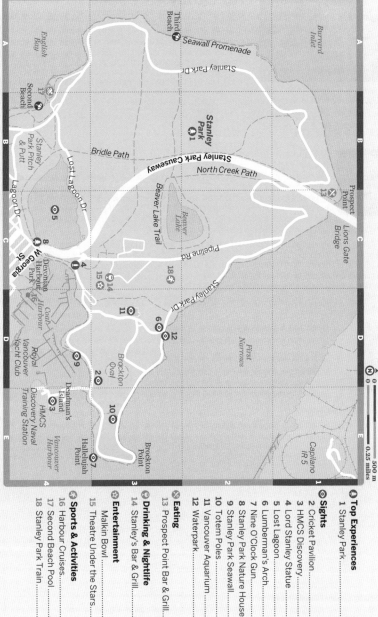

Top Experiences	**(p52)**
1 Stanley Park	B2
Sights	**(p52)**
2 Cricket Pavilion	D3
3 HMCS Discovery	E4
4 Lord Stanley Statue	C4
5 Lost Lagoon	C4
6 Lumberman's Arch	D3
7 Nine O'Clock Gun	E3
8 Stanley Park Nature House	C4
9 Stanley Park Seawall	D4
10 Totem Poles	E3
11 Vancouver Aquarium	D3
12 Waterpark	D3
Eating	**(p70)**
13 Prospect Point Bar & Grill	C1
Drinking & Nightlife	**(p73)**
14 Stanley's Bar & Grill	C3
Entertainment	**(p74)**
Malkin Bowl	(see 15)
15 Theatre Under the Stars	C3
Sports & Activities	**(p78)**
16 Harbour Cruises	D4
17 Second Beach Pool	A4
18 Stanley Park Train	C3

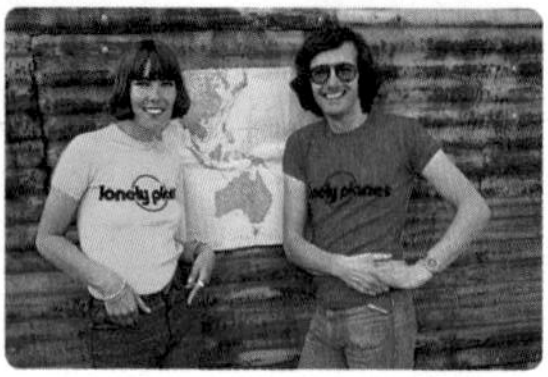

Our Story

A beat-up old car, a few dollars in the pocket and a sense of adventure. In 1972 that's all Tony and Maureen Wheeler needed for the trip of a lifetime – across Europe and Asia overland to Australia. It took several months, and at the end – broke but inspired – they sat at their kitchen table writing and stapling together their first travel guide, *Across Asia on the Cheap*. Within a week they'd sold 1500 copies. Lonely Planet was born.

Today, Lonely Planet has offices in the US, Ireland and China, with a network of over 2000 contributors in every corner of the globe. We share Tony's belief that 'a great guidebook should do three things: inform, educate and amuse'.

Our Writers

John Lee

Born and raised in the historic UK city of St Albans, John grew up in the lengthy shadow of London, finding as many opportunities as possible to gorge on the capital's rich diet of museums and galleries. Slowly succumbing to the lure of overseas exotica, he arrived on Canada's West Coast in 1993 to begin an MA in Political Science at the University of Victoria. Regular trips home to Britain ensued, along with stints living in Tokyo and Montreal, before he returned to British Columbia to become a full-time freelance writer in 1999.

Now living in Vancouver, John specializes in travel writing and has contributed to more than 150 different publications around the world. These include the *Guardian, Independent, Los Angeles Times, Chicago Tribune, Sydney Morning Herald, National Geographic Traveler* and BBC.com. He also has a travel column in Canada's *Globe and Mail* national newspaper. You can read some of his stories (and see some of his videos) online at www.johnleewriter.com. John has worked on around 25 Lonely Planet books, including *Canada, British Columbia, Western Europe, Vancouver* and *Europe on a Shoestring.*

Brendan Sainsbury

Born and raised in the UK in a town that never merits a mention in any guidebook (Andover, Hampshire), Brendan spent the holidays of his youth caravanning in the English Lake District and didn't leave Blighty until he was nineteen. Making up for lost time, he's since squeezed 70 countries into a sometimes precarious existence as a writer and professional vagabond. His rocking chair memories will probably include staging a performance of 'A Comedy of Errors' at a school in war-torn Angola, running 150 miles across the Sahara Desert in the Marathon des Sables, and hitchhiking from Cape Town to Kilimanjaro with an early, dog-eared copy of LP's *Africa on a Shoestring*. In the last eleven years, he has written over 40 books for Lonely Planet from Castro's Cuba to the canyons of Peru. When not scribbling research notes, Brendan likes partaking in ridiculous 'endurance' races, strumming old Clash songs on the guitar, and experiencing the pain and occasional pleasures of following Southampton Football Club.

Published by Lonely Planet Global Ltd
CRN 554153
9th edition – July 2022
ISBN 978 1 78868 452 1

10 9 8 7 6 5 4 3 2 1
Printed in China